The Soul of Cinema

An Appreciation of Film Music

Larry M. Timm
California State University, Fullerton

Prentice Hall

Upper Saddle River, NJ 07458

Library of Congress Cataloging-in-Publication Data

Timm, Larry M.
The soul of cinema : an appreciation of film music / by Larry M. Timm.
p. cm.
Includes index.
ISBN 0-13-030465-4
1. Motion picture music—Analysis, appreciation. I. Title.

MT95.T59 2002
781.5'42—dc21 2001059346

Senior acquisitions editor: Christopher T. Johnson
Production editor: Laura A. Lawrie
Manufacturing and prepress buyer: Benjamin D. Smith
Copy editor: Laura A. Lawrie
Indexer: Robert Swanson/ARC FILMS, INC.
Editorial assistant: Evette Dickerson
Cover image specialist: Karen Sanatar
Image permission coordinator: Michelina Viscusi
Photo researcher: Linda Sykes
Cover design: Bruce Kenselaar
Cover art: Malcolm Arnold conducts the orchestra during the recording of the soundtrack for William Walton's film *The Battle of Britain*. © Hulton-Deutsch Collection/Corbis.

This book was set in 10/12 Palatino by Stratford Publishing Services, Inc., and was printed and bound by Banta Company. The cover was printed by Phoenix Color Corp.

Printed in the United States of America

10 9 8 7 6 5 4 3 2 1

ISBN 0-13-030465-4

Pearson Education Ltd., London
Pearson Education Australia PTY, Limited, Sydney
Pearson Education Singapore, Pte. Ltd
Pearson Education North Asia Ltd, Hong Kong
Pearson Education Canada, Ltd., Toronto
Pearson Educatión de Mexico, S.A. de C.V.
Pearson Education--Japan, Tokyo
Pearson Education Malaysia, Pte. Ltd
Pearson Education, Upper Saddle River, New Jersey

I dedicate this book to my best friend and wonderful wife, Carol, and our sweet daughter, Monique. Also, a special dedication to my fantastic parents, Everett and Jeanne Timm, who were both professional musicians and were the ones who introduced me to the magical world of music. My mother passed away during the time that I was writing the first edition of this book. I'm sure that she is making beautiful music on her flute in heaven.

"Many people seem to assume that because film music serves the visual, it must be something of secondary value. . . . The thing to bear in mind is that film is the youngest of the arts, and that scoring is the youngest of the music arts. We have a great deal of development ahead of us."

—Jerry Goldsmith, film composer

Contents

Preface

My intent in writing this book is to fill a void for a much-needed text on film music appreciation. Although there are other fine books on film music and film composers, at the time of this writing this is the only book designed specifically as a film music appreciation text. Obviously not every person has this enthusiasm for film music that I do, but it is hoped that after traveling through this book, you will come away with an appreciation and understanding of what it takes to make the movies and how their music affects us the way it does. Because this book is meant to be used as a college level "appreciation of film music" text, it has to have limitations both in size and content. After a discussion of the functions of music in film and a general survey of the film music industry, we go back in time and show where it all started. The rest of the text becomes a chronological history of music in film from 1894 to the twenty-first century. Although foreign films and composers are mentioned and/or discussed, *the major thrust of this book is centered on the Hollywood movie industry*. This book also concentrates more on symphonic scores as opposed to jazz, pop, rock, or any other nonsymphonic idiom. Having taught this subject over the years, some of the well-known stories in this book are sometimes paraphrased, because the author hopes to put a fresh new slant on some well-worn tales of yore.

Note to Teachers

Most of the films covered in this book are readily available on video for the convenience of teaching purposes. The author suggests preparing the film clips to be shown prior to the start of each class session.

Acknowledgments

Although much of what is in this book came from years of research and firsthand experience working in the industry, it would not have been possible without the help from interviews or comments of various key people. I would like to thank Dimitrie Leivici, who so graciously arranged some of the interviews for me and provided me with valuable information, and my good friend Fred Karlin, for whom I have the utmost respect. The following people gave of their time and talents: Bill Conti, Sandy De Crescent, Elmer Bernstein, John Corigliano, David Raksin, John Debney, Michael Kamen, Charles Gould, Bruce Broughton, Don Christlieb, Fred Karlin, Alan Silvestri, Irwin Kostal, Elia Cmiral, John Frizzell, Mark Snow, Christian Abbott, Brad Dechter, Robert Elhai, James Newton Howard, John Barry, Mike Tavera, Rolf Kent, David Seubert (Curator of the Bernard Herrmann Collection, UCSB), Jamie Richardson, James Barry, Todd Miller, Adriana Getz, Cynthia Biamon, Pearl Evidente, Dave Bifano, Arnold Lipsman, Ronni Chasen, Maureen O'Conner, Steve at Vangelos Management, Jo Ann Kane, Joanna Beck, John Zifferono, David Arnold, Chris Bleth, Michelle Parker and Monique Ward at Ronni Chasens, Hans Karl, Eric Smith, Jerry Goldsmith, Lois Carruth, John Alexander, Dave and Marlene Stevens, John Shannon, Bob Minor, Basil Poledouris, John Williams, and Jon Burlingame. Many thanks to David Ewart for several photos used in this book, and the Recording Musicians Association. A special thanks to my editor at Simon and Schuster Ms. Janet Wagner (who helped me on my first edition) for her guidance and understanding. I wish to thank my wonderful editor Mr. Chris Johnson and his associate Evette Dickerson at Prentice Hall for their support, patience, and hard work on bringing this second edition to press. Laura Lawrie's watchful eye and professionalism was extremely helpful in editing the text.

We must not forget the studio musicians from around the world, including the men and women of the Recording Musicians Association (RMA) and members of Local 47 (Hollywood). They are the people responsible for bringing the music on the printed page to life. If it weren't for their God-given musical talents, none of us would ever hear any of these magnificent scores.

A very special thanks to my beautiful wife Carol and lovely daughter Monique, who had to endure several months without a husband and a father, as I toiled away back in the library of our old Victorian house preparing and writing this book.

Chapter One

Functions of Film Scoring

Have you ever eaten a fried egg without salt and pepper, or French fries without catsup? Both foods are edible without these extra ingredients; however, most people will agree that both taste a lot better with these "extras." So it is with motion pictures. A movie without music is like a bath without water; something very crucial is missing. *The music is the soul of the movie.* Anyone remotely interested in film knows that music seems to be an indispensable ingredient for filmmakers. Imagine the movie *Jaws* without the driving two-note musical motive to represent the great white shark, or *Star Wars* without the now-famous themes used to enhance the battling of the two opposing forces.

By definition, film music is music that accompanies a film. We will explore this genre of music in more depth and realize that there is a lot more to film music than the preceding short definition.

In filmmaking, there comes a time when the director and actors can convey only so much on screen. Music steps in to say what neither pictures nor words can. Music adds that extra dimension to a given scene that is necessary for the success of conveying the director's intentions. Film music can be a subliminal enhancement that "tops off" the scenes in a movie, making them radiant like a polished jewel. American film composer Don Davis (composer for the popular film *The Matrix*) states that film music must "focus on what the director wants the audience's attention on." Prolific Italian film composer Ennio Morricone stated in an interview with Harlan Kennedy in 1991 that film music "must not add emphasis but must give more body and depth to the story, to the characters, to the language that the director has chosen. It must, therefore, say all that the dialogue, images, and effects cannot say."

For over one hundred years, the general public has never really regarded the music that accompanies films (film music) as highly as the music that accompanies opera or ballet. Why is this so? It's true that music is usually thought of as providing a supporting role to the motion picture. Yet, somehow music for films has not gained the respect it rightfully deserves. During the "silent days" of motion picture history, music was ironically more prominent in its marriage with film than after sound was introduced in the late 1920s. Somehow, sound movies demoted music to a smaller role than it had in the days of silent films. Although film music has been greatly taken for granted by many people, the trend appears to be changing. From 1989 to 1999, the annual sales of movie soundtrack albums has quadrupled, and it is not unusual to see from ten to twenty soundtrack albums perched on *Billboard Magazine*'s weekly album charts.

Over the span of this chapter, we will see just how music is utilized in motion pictures by examining its various functions in motion pictures. The art of composing music for a film is known as *film scoring*.

Before we begin, we must first state that *in most cases, music is part of the postproduction phase of movie making.* The music we hear in movies is usually composed, recorded, and dubbed in *after* the motion picture is filmed. As a result, some people feel that music can step in and save a scene that is poorly directed, poorly acted, or poorly edited. This is a matter of conjecture. Because music is usually added after most of the film has been shot, it would appear that music plays a supporting role that makes it a lesser partner than the other elements within the film. This is simply not so. One thing is for certain: Music is a necessary component that is sorely missed if not present when viewing a completed movie.

If one were to hire one hundred different film composers to score the same scene, there would probably be one hundred different approaches or versions of that particular scene. It would be impossible to cover every possible way in which music is to be used within movies. We are going to look at most of the most often used cases. *The following functions are not in any particular order of occurrence or importance. They are listed at random.*

The **first function** in film scoring is where music can be used **to either intensify or relax the pace of the film.**[1] We could probably all think of instances when we have been on the edge of our seat in a movie theater because of what is happening on the screen. There is probably no better example of how music has helped to create this function than observing the use of music in the 1975 movie *Jaws*. This film, about a giant twenty- to twenty-five-foot great white shark that terrorizes the people of a New England coastal community, was Steven Spielberg's second feature film, made when he was only twenty-six years old. The original fifty-two-day shooting schedule escalated to 155 days, because of foul weather, angry local citizens, and labor disputes, as well as Spielberg's need to constantly rewrite the script. The producers of the film even considered trashing the project. However, through the talents of Spielberg and his crew, not to mention the music of composer John Williams (1932–), the movie turned out to be a $410 million hit. As of 1975, in terms of box office earnings, *Jaws* was the most successful movie of all time. It has been stated that the opening sequence, in which the young girl takes a skinny-dipping excursion and becomes the shark's first victim, is perhaps as celebrated a scene as anything Alfred Hitchcock ever directed. Whether this is true or not, one would have to agree that John Williams's music helps in *intensifying this scene* to the height of frenzy. Williams writes a recurring musical theme first heard at the very beginning of the movie, performed by the low strings of the studio orchestra. *This two-note musical motive has become one of the most recognizable themes in movie history,* and denotes an imminent shark attack to anyone who has ever seen this movie. This idea of characterizing the shark musically with a low, thumping repeated pattern in the bass instruments (a repeated pattern, referred to as an **ostinato** pattern), is perfect for the mindless attack of the shark. According to Williams, "The shark works all on instinct, it's unstoppable, and has a relentless drive. You cannot stop it without destroying it." Williams found a signature for the entire film with this rather simple two-note idea. He also stated, "One could alter this ostinato to very slow to very fast, very soft to very loud. All of these things could be used to manipulate the moment to illustrate that the shark was at the highest pitch of frenzy or something lower. This simple dramatic device seemed to be what we needed." When Williams came to Spielberg back in 1975 after he had written the now-celebrated two-note musical motive, the director was in for quite a surprise. In a 1995 interview, Spielberg stated that, "I expected to hear something kind of weird and melodic, kind of tonal but eerie, of another world . . . almost a bit like outer space inside inner space under the water. . . . But what he played for me on the lower keys of the piano was THUMP-THUMP, THUMP-THUMP, THUMP-THUMP. . . . At first I began to laugh, I thought he was putting me on and John said no . . . THAT'S the theme for *Jaws*!!! After playing it several times it suddenly seemed right, but when I first heard it, it seemed wrong . . . because it just seemed too simple."[2] Although this musical idea was used to signal the

1. Function phrase taken from Mark Evans, *Soundtrack: The Music of the Movies* (New York: Da Capo Press, 1979), p. 212.
2. Above quotes taken from *Jaws* laser disc interview, Copyright 1975, MCA Universal.

Chrissie (played by Susan Backlinie) falls victim to the great white shark as she skinny-dips. Courtesy of Fotos International/Archive Photos.

arrival of the shark, there is one scene in the movie where the shark attacks out of total *silence,* adding further to this movie's suspense. Spielberg said that without Williams's score, the film would have been only half as successful. Not only did this film help to launch Steven Spielberg's career, it also made John Williams a household name to American audiences and this was also the first time Williams won an Academy Award for best Original Score. So, as one views this opening sequence, imagine this without the music and yet realize just how effective this scene is with such a remarkably simple two-note motive. The reader may wish to compare the first shark attack and the accompanying music with that of the second attack in the movie of the young boy. Some of the music is covered up by the cries for help during the first attack. During the attack on the young boy, the pulsating two-note motive is thrust into the forefront of our recognition. The tempo of the music increases as the shark lunges toward Alex. Note that after the attack, the music fades away, leaving us totally numb and in disbelief as to what has just taken place on screen.

Another aspect of the first function in film scoring has the opposite effect on the viewer. This is when music is used to relax the forward pace of the film.

One of the classic horror films of the late twentieth century is Brian DePalma's *Carrie* (1976). The film, based on Stephen King's first novel, is about a high school girl (Carrie White) who is the brunt of her teenage peers' cruelties. She was clumsy in sports, her clothes never fit, and she never really seemed to fit in with the rest of her classmates. One day, she discovered that she could make things move by concentrating on them. At her senior prom she becomes the subject of yet another major prank. She is called up to the stage as their new reigning prom queen. A bucket of pig's blood is dropped from high above the stage down on her in yet another act of humiliation. This time, however, her *telekinetic powers* (her ability to move things with her mind) became a weapon of horror and destruction against those who wronged her. She bolts the doors of the school gymnasium shut with her mind and causes the gym to catch fire, burning and killing those people inside. She escapes, only to perish in her own house as it catches fire and burns to the ground. All of this high-adrenaline action is eased or relaxed in the next scene. In a sequence near the end of the film, we see actress Amy Irving taking a bouquet of flowers to this "grave" site of Carrie White (to pay respects for the vicious things her classmates had done to her earlier in the movie). One can't help but feel *relaxed* to the sound of the beautiful flute solo written by composer Pino Donnagio (1941–). This solo helps to ease the tension of what had just occurred over the last few minutes in the film in which Carrie seeks revenge by killing most of her classmates in the school gymnasium fire caused by her telekinetic powers. However, what follows this relaxing sequence is sure to scare the viewer out of his seat! We have become so *relaxed* by the flute solo that we are *vulnerable for the unexpected surprise* in the next scene of *Carrie*. (The reader is encouraged to view this sequence to get the full meaning of surprise.) Sometimes composers can use their music such as this to make us so relaxed that we are jolted out of our seats when the next tense moment occurs without warning.

Sissy Spacek stars as a tormented high school girl who uses her telekinetic powers in Brian De Palma's classic, Carrie *(1976). Courtesy of United Artists/Archive Photos.*

Next time you watch a movie with high action adventure, you may notice occasional segments in the movie where we are brought back to reality to catch our breath. Many times this type of scene will be accompanied by music that helps to calm us. This method also inversely prepares our reaction for the next fast-paced sequence.

The **second function** of film scoring is to **reflect emotion**.[3] The film composer can prepare us for the emotional impact of a scene by using the appropriate music. This is probably one of the most obvious reasons why music is used in motion pictures. There isn't a moviegoer alive who doesn't remember feeling sad or happy in certain sequences of movies. If one looks back at those particular moments in a film when this happened, chances are these powerful scenes were accompanied by some kind of music. A device often used by composers of film music is to underscore the early parts of a film with a dramatic love theme. The viewer's subconscious will associate these happier moments with this beautiful love theme, although at this point in the drama, the standard moviegoer's mind is probably more engrossed in the dialogue and plot development than the music. Later in the drama, when one of the main characters dies, we are torn apart emotionally as we hear this music restated at the death scene. We wonder why we are so broken up emotionally. It's in strong part because of our association of this love theme in conjunction with the two lovers who are now separated by death. There are many examples of this found in motion pictures.

3. Evans, p. 216.

One very effective example is in the movie *Somewhere in Time* (1980), which contains one of composer John Barry's (1933–) most memorable themes. This is a movie about time travel in which a young man named Richard Collier sees a portrait of an actress from a previous generation whose beauty mesmerizes him into an uncontrollable obsession. Collier begins a laborious process of self-hypnosis to will himself "back in time" from the year 1979 to be with the beautiful actress, Miss Elise McKenna, in the year 1912. Somehow, he is successful. The two eventually meet and fall in love. In this case he is not separated from her by death. Instead, he awakens one morning to find that she has left town with her acting troupe without any word as to where she could be found. We see Collier come out of the hotel lobby crushed emotionally, faced with the prospect that he may never see her again. As he sits down on the porch of the hotel, we see—off in the distance—Elise running up to greet her love, Richard. Yet, at first he still has not realized that she has come back for him. Only we can see her as he has his back turned toward her. Our emotions run wild with anticipation for the two lovers. Meanwhile, underscoring this action is the previously heard love theme, this time at a louder level than ever before. We associate this music with their strong love for one another and we can't help but feel *emotionally* moved by this powerful moment. In this case, the music steals the scene by *reflecting great emotion*.

John Barry has stated that he has received more mail about this score than any other that he has ever written. He continued, "Why the music seemed to magically connect for this film, I don't know. Perhaps it had something to do with the time that I wrote it. My father had died and within sixteen weeks, my mother passed away. I don't usually get that involved with one's personal life. Maybe that had something to do with shaping certain feelings in the score, I don't really know." Perhaps that's why this score has such a universal appeal as a great example of *conveying or reflecting emotion*. Thousands of newlyweds have used this love theme at their weddings and many people confess that the love theme from the movie *Somewhere in Time* is "their love song."

There are times when it is necessary for a composer to step in and provide valuable information to the audience about a character or situation that cannot be conveyed to the filmgoer by the film alone. As an example, when one reads a novel, the author can easily express what a character is thinking by providing several sentences or descriptions of the situation at hand. How does a film director do this if there is no dialogue or narration present? It is accomplished with the appropriate music. He or she would rely on the talents of the film composer to provide the necessary music. A composer can change the way that we look at a character or a situation quite drastically. He or she can make a character appear to be threatening, happy, sad, angry, funny, rejected, overjoyed, confused, or can express just about any other possible human emotion known to the human race. *A composer must have a command of human drama and be able to express or describe that human condition through the use of music. The composer also must be able to describe through music any unseen implication to a given scenario.*

This brings us to the **third function** of film scoring, which is when music is used **to create "unspoken" thoughts of a character or unseen implications of a situation**.[4] Music can be used to transfer *subliminal messages* to the filmgoers where we can feel what the main character is feeling or where the music creates the conditions of the atmosphere on screen so that the members of the audience can almost swear that they were up on the screen with the action. Although one can spot this use more readily in some films than others, one of the most difficult assignments to score was for a film that came out in 1943. The film was called *The Song of Bernadette* and the composer was Alfred Newman (1900–1970). The story involves an incident that took place in 1858, in which a young French girl named Bernadette Soubirorous was visited by a vision of a glorious lady in white. At first, Bernadette was not quite aware of the significance of this vision. All she knew was that the undreamed-of beauty that this lady possessed paralyzed her with unlimited power that will not let her go. We later learn that

4. Function phrase taken from Roy Prendergast, *Film Music: A Neglected Art* (New York: W. W. Norton, 2nd ed., 1992), p. 216.

Richard Collier (Christopher Reeve) is entranced with Elise McKenna (Jane Seymour) as seen in the cult romantic fantasy, Somewhere in Time *(1980). Courtesy of Fotos International/Archive Photos.*

this was a visitation from the Virgin Mary. Since this scene contains no dialogue, it is up to the music to convey the missing information. Newman's score at this point accomplishes the task with great inspiration.

The Wordless Choir

In order to give the ethereal, out-of-this-world implication of the moment, Newman scored the scene with religious-sounding underscoring, complete with the addition of a wordless choir. *A wordless choir has become a favorite technique among Hollywood film composers for moments involving either religious themes or out-of-this-world fantasy-type scenarios*. Basically, a *wordless choir* is a chorus who sings *without* text. They usually sing on the vowel sound of "ah."

The **fourth function** of film scoring is where music is used to literally **parallel or underscore the action.**[5] In essence, if someone runs up the stairs, the music also will ascend and go up a musical scale. Perhaps if a character punches another character in the face, the music may contain an accented musical

5. Evans, p. 225.

Jennifer Jones stars in the inspirational The Song of Bernadette *(1943). Courtesy of Archive Photos.*

chord or loud bass drum beat to *parallel the action*. This technique is known as "Mickey Mousing" the action, because of its obvious similarity to a cartoon that follows or mimics almost every move of its characters. There are certain composers known for their almost overuse of this function in their scores.

A good example of the utilization of this technique may be found in the 1959 film *Ben-Hur*. There are several scenes showing the slaves rowing their oars inside the Roman galleys. Note that as the Roman commander demands the slaves to increase the speed at which they row, the film music of composer Miklos Rozsa (1907–1995) also increases in speed (paralleling the action). This pace finally builds up to a frenzy, and the command is given for the slaves to put down their oars and rest. The music then stops. At this moment the viewer can almost feel the exhaustion of the slaves as we hear them coughing and panting. Not only was the music paralleling the action, it also was acting to intensify the action. *It is not unusual that several functions of film music can overlap one another or coexist within the same scene* as we have seen in this example. As you look at this example from the movie *Ben-Hur,* you might also notice the effectiveness of the editing. As the pace quickens, so, too, the length of scenes becomes more rapid-fire, not too different from today's modern music videos. As each scene becomes shorter and shorter, our pulse quickens with anticipation. The combination of paralleling music and ever-shorter scenes helps to convey the frantic quality of the situation.

There are times when movie directors need to add realism to a given location or authenticity to a given historical period. Perhaps their budget is somewhat limited. Instead of going to Mexico, they might film a sequence on a Hollywood back lot that resembles Mexico. If the film composer supplies some Mexican mariachi music, this will give us the feel that the scene was actually shot in Mexico. Quite often we will watch a film that was actually shot somewhere in America. If music from another country such as Spain, France, or Italy was added to the sequence, we assume that what we are seeing was actually shot on location in that country. By the same token, if a film is about the American Civil War, the film composer can enhance the project with historically accurate music of the period. This brings us to our **fifth function** of music in films. This is when music is used **to create atmosphere of time and place.**[6] In the film *Ben-Hur,* we can see an excellent example of this usage. A moment before the chariot race is to start, the viewer watches the charioteers as they parade around the gigantic Circus Maximus to build the spectators' anticipation of the exciting race that will follow. Miklos Rozsa lends the sound of ancient Rome to the event through his use of brass and Roman percussion. This sound is reminiscent of the grandeur of what we might expect of Caesar's Rome.

Rozsa's music evokes the historic time frame with as much accuracy as possible since there are no known existent examples of music to accompany ancient chariot races.

6. Evans, p. 227.

Rowing scene from Ben-Hur *(1959). Courtesy of Springer/Corbis-Bettmann.*

A favorite category of many moviegoers is comedy. There is a time when music can be used **to create comedy**. This is our **sixth function**.[7] In reality, there are so many examples of this in motion pictures, one could probably write an entire book on the subject. To give you an example of what is meant by this, imagine a serious scene in a detective drama being underscored by music meant for a silly Warner Bros. cartoon. This oxymoronish use of music to the image is sure to solicit a laugh from many in the audience. Elmer Bernstein (1922–) was able to create humor in his score for the film *Airplane!* by approaching each cue as though it was the most important cue in his life. By being "overzealous" as a composer that doesn't have particularly good taste, Bernstein contributed immeasurably to the comical silliness of this picture. We will look at other examples of this later in the book.

As we have already stated in this chapter, the now-famous two-note musical motive that John Williams wrote as the unifying theme in the movie *Jaws* is forevermore associated with sharks. In the world of nineteenth-century operas, composers would write a musical melody or fragment of a melody that would be associated with a given character or situation in the story. Operagoers would gradually link each character with his or her musical motive, known as a *leitmotif*. In the world of film music, this technique also is often utilized. A composer can use this musical theme to convey various intuitive aspects of the story or changes in the characters' thoughts or actions by varying the recognizable musical motive as the story changes.

7. Evans, p. 229.

Charlton Heston in Chariot Race from award-winning Ben-Hur *(1959). Courtesy of Archive Photos.*

If you have seen the *Star Wars* movies, you probably noticed the use of the same opening theme in each of the movies—any fan would recognize Darth Vader's Imperial Force march theme. These musical elements *help to provide unity* to each of these movies in a series just as the James Bond theme or Indiana Jones march theme help to bond each film within the set of films. **To provide unity or coherence to a story**[8] by using a leitmotif is our **seventh function** of film scoring. *It is said that this technique can provide the perfect arc to the story line.* For instance, we might hear a main character's theme (leitmotif) earlier in a movie and not hear it again until that person returns in a very dramatic moment. As that person is seen again, we also hear the theme that we associated with that person at the start of the film. The reiteration of the musical theme, along with that person's return, can "round off" the dramatic "arc" created by such a usage.

There is a time in many motion pictures where a character will reach over and turn on the radio in his car or apartment. This is our **eighth function**: When one can see the source of the music being heard on screen, this is referred to as **source music**.[9] Some scholars refer to source music as *diegetic music.* It also has been called direct music or foreground music. The dramatic underscoring we hear in a

8. Evans, p. 231.
9. Prendergast, p. 217.

movie—that is, the ongoing music soundtrack—is called *nondiegetic music*. This is background music that accompanies the action of the film. It comes from no source within the film and is also what is generally regarded as film music.

What you may not have known is that there are times when the film composer will be required to write the "pop" music in the necessary style that will be emanating as source music. Because of copyright clearance problems, it is sometimes cheaper for the composer to do this than to simply use already existing hit tunes, which may come with a high price tag for "use rights." There are instances in movies when the source of the music is not actually seen on screen. This is known as implied source music.

The **ninth function** of music in films is **when the music plays against the action**. There are many examples of this in films. Generally, this occurs when the composer uses music that opposes what is being seen on screen. For instance, a director may wish to tone down an extremely violent segment of his or her movie by accompanying it with an opera aria or a slow ballad. A good example of this can be seen in the 1997 movie *Face/Off*. There is a sequence in which there is a major shootout between rival forces. Caught in the crossfire is a young boy who is held up in evil-character Dietrich's loft. As this scene begins, we see and hear loud gunfire everywhere. This is accompanied by the energetic underscoring of composer John Powel. Several minutes into this scene, a pair of headphones is placed on the little boy's head so that he can hear the song "Over the Rainbow" from *The Wizard of Oz,* as sung by Olivia Newton-John. This helps the little boy to "escape" what is going on in the room. The violence continues, but this time the full impact is greatly reduced because it is now accompanied by the nonthreatening rendition of "Over the Rainbow." The music here is "playing against the action." It's amazing how effective the use of this song is in toning down the impact of the violence as seen on the screen. Eventually we return to reality as Powel's music returns, along with the loudness of the gun battle. For that brief moment, we were transformed into another dimension as the music "played against the action."

The **tenth function** is when music is used **to speed up scenes that are too slow or slow scenes down that are moving too fast**. There are many examples in films over the years where the action on screen moves at a snail's pace. The composer is brought in to liven the action by using music that plays at a *faster speed* than the action that is seen on the screen. This gives the viewer the impression that what they are seeing is actually moving faster than it actually is. Watch the great Exodus scene from Cecil B. DeMille's *The Ten Commandments* (1956) to see this technique at work. Conversely, if a filmmaker wants to give the illusion that a rapid-paced scene is moving more slowly than it actually is, a film composer can step in and write music that moves along at the speed of a funeral march. This will accomplish the wanted illusion.

Our **eleventh** and final major function of film scoring is when music is **used as a neutral background filler.**[10] This is sometimes referred to as "wall-to-wall" music because of its tendency to be a continuous flow of music running underneath the dialogue without ever letting up. A classic example of this is to watch the movie *Gone With the Wind*. There are many instances in which the music plays throughout the drama with no apparent function. This "wall-to-wall" approach was probably a result of the early filmmakers and composers being accustomed to the continuous flow of music in certain late nineteenth-century operas. It would therefore only seem logical to do the same for movies. Also, people were accustomed to seeing their films of the "silent era" being accompanied by nonstop music as provided by a pianist, theater organist, or pit orchestra.

As we will see later on, there are some action scenes played out without any music at all. In some of today's films, you also might have an action scene underscored by a pop tune from the past. The pop music was not written for the action scene, but somehow it seems to work by adding a quality to the scene that was missing without the addition of the music.

10. Prendergast., p. 219.

The Use of Silence in Motion Pictures

As a filmgoer, you may have never noticed, but one of the greatest ways of accenting a moment in a drama is to precede that moment with a stretch of music that suddenly drops out, leaving silence. The use of silence can be very effective if used correctly. If a score suddenly drops out, the next moment is *accented* by the sudden silence. In some movies, this is abrupt; in others, it can be a gradual fading away of the music. Without silence, the film composer loses his or her most effective weapon. *Music can only make its impact and effect by contrast with silence.* It was said that Mozart himself had remarked that the "most important thing in music was no music at all." For a good example of this, look at the ritual portion of the movie *Rapa Nui* (scored by Stewart Copeland [1952–] in 1994). In this sequence, we see several members of the island compete for the position of tribal leader by swimming across shark-infested waters to bring back a bird's egg, unbroken, in an exciting fight to the finish. In that sequence, about a dozen men vie for the title. After crossing the shark-infested water to retrieve the needed birds' eggs to win the contest, only three men survive that part of the ordeal. As these three men begin their ascent up the steep cliffs toward victory, Stewart Copeland accompanies this with pulse-pounding music, complete with native-sounding drums to set the atmosphere. Whoever reaches the top of the cliff with an unbroken egg will be the winner. The pounding of percussion increases in intensity as the three men struggle for victory. Just when we think one of the men is a few feet from winning, the music stops. The man's footing slips and he crashes to the ground, breaking the egg in the process. This sudden silence amplifies the impact of the scene and the sudden, unexpected outcome of the contest.

In the prom sequence from *Carrie,* we see a good example where the music fades to a near deafening silence after the pig's blood is poured onto Carrie, creating nerve-wracking tension. This is a very effective sequence and should definitely be viewed in its entirety. This movie is easily obtainable on video because of its position as a modern horror classic.

Next time you watch a courtroom drama, listen to see if you hear music sneaking in right before the accused admits their guilt. The music would usually crescendo (get louder) and drop out a second before they burst out with, "Okay, I did it! I killed 'em!" This creates instant drama. Then, in another scenario, as a person is about to stab another person or perhaps shoot them with a gun, this will invariably be preceded with music that suddenly stops at the lunge of the knife or pull of the trigger.

Chris Carter, creator of *The X-Files,* says that a very good composer such as Mark Snow (1946–) knows how to paint the moment and color the contour of the overall story, but—most importantly—"he also knows what to leave out. The empty space is occupied by the tension between the cues. Silence is the key—a composer must appreciate silence."[11]

11. The *Hollywood Reporter,* August 24–30, 1999.

Chapter Two

The Operational Aspects of the Film Music Industry

Producers and Directors

Just look at the end credits of a major motion picture and you will see that an incredible number of people are involved in the making of a film. Several of these people have the greatest influence on the final outcome of the movie and it is therefore necessary to briefly discuss their roles within this creative process. In the most basic of terms, we have a producer and a director who are in charge of seeing that the motion picture is completed. After this we could branch out into many other subcategories such as line producer, assistant producer, first unit director, second unit director, assistant director, and so on. For the purposes of this study, we need to see how the main producer (sometimes referred to as executive producer or in some cases the line producer) and the director of the film relate to the musical aspect of a completed production.

The Producer

The producer *is the person in charge of the ongoing aspects of the production both in terms of organization and finances.* This person is to see the project through its completion from the writing phase to the final editing of the end product seen in the theaters. In many cases, this will be the person who will hire everyone on the project *including* the director and film composer. It is important for the film composer to confer with the producer regarding the amount of money available in the music budget before a single note is written.

The Director

The director *is the person who lends his or her visual interpretation to the shooting script*. This is the person who actually brings the script to life so that what we see up on the screen is full of excitement, drama, and action. He or she will be the person in charge on each day of shooting each scene to make sure every actor and each technician has achieved the best possible results to make the movie a successful venture. The dialogue between a director and a film composer is very crucial to the general impact the musical score will have on each scene in the movie. The director usually has to answer to the producer. At present, it is more popular for directors to produce their own films. This gives them much more creative control and also does away with the need to answer to another voice. Unfortunately, many producers and directors don't have the musical background in order to converse with composers on their level. Because of this, many composers have complained over the years about the great frustrations in dealing with this aspect of their job. Imagine trying to explain to a person from another country whose language you don't know about the elements of chemistry or biology and you can begin to see the parallel problem.

There are many now-famous stories regarding the ignorance, or perhaps the lack of knowledge, of movie executives dealing with film composers. Irving Thalberg (1899–1936) was a genius behind many movies made at MGM. As supervisor of production with a great flair for artistic direction, he helped MGM prosper in the 1930s. His great talents did not include music, however. When an assistant informed him that the reason his most recent film production wasn't going well, he was told that it was because the composer had used *minor chords* in the score. (For those of you reading this who also don't have a musical background, many well-known songs use minor chords.) As stupid as it may now seem, Thalberg sent out a memo within the MGM music department stating that from now on there would be no more minor chords used by MGM composers in their scores!

Another well-known filmmaker was riding down Rodeo Drive in his limousine, hoping to get some culture by listening to a radio station featuring classical music. The radio announcer had just come on and said that the piece of music that had just been played on the radio was Brahms's Fourth Symphony. Hearing this, and liking the music he had just heard, the movie mogul got on his car phone and called his office telling his secretary to call Germany and ask to speak to a Johnny Brahms. He wanted him to be his next film composer! (Of course, Johannes Brahms, the composer that he wanted, had died in 1897.)

A film composer was told by his filmmaker that since the film took place in France, the composer should use a lot of French horns. (French horns have nothing to do with France or sounding "French.")

Film composer Elia Cmiral related the following story:

> While mixing a dramatic orchestral cue, an unsure but very nice and polite director with very vague music understanding asked my engineer, "Can we kind of play less of this deep bum-bum-da-da?" The engineer assumed he must mean basses and drums. All right. Then the director asks, "Can we kind of hear less of this high la-la-la?" The engineer thinks maybe he means first strings and flutes . . . okay. This situation of vague but polite input from the director with the engineer guessing what it might be and faithfully adjusting levels down, basically led to the whole cue falling apart—"Where's the melody, harmony, rhythm?" Frustrated and sweating, the engineer asked the director, "How about if we just pull down the level of the whole orchestra?"

Occasionally a collaborative team of director/composer has been formed with a considerable amount of success, for example, Alfred Hitchcock and Bernard Herrmann, Franklin Schaffner and Jerry Goldsmith, Steven Spielberg and John Williams, Robert Zemeckis and Alan Silvestri, Francois Truffaut and Georges Delerue, and Tim Burton and Danny Elfman.

Five Types of Directors

James Horner (1953–), the composer of the very popular score for the movie *Titanic* (1997), has categorized directors in the following ways:

> (1) There are those who don't want to discuss music and thus rely totally on the know how of the composer; (2) Some directors have a broad musical background and can pull

examples out of existing music to discuss with the composer. [This is probably the best kind of director for which to work]; (3) Unfortunately there are "know-it-all" directors who think they know much more than they actually do know; (4) Then there are those who know a lot more than they let on, yet remain quiet throughout the filmmaking process; (5) Finally, you have the director who can not give up control (the "control freak") and would write the music themselves if they knew how.[1]

The French film composer Maurice Jarre (1924–) (*Doctor Zhivago, Lawrence of Arabia*) said, "The director that knows nothing about music is sometimes the easiest to work with. First of all, he is open. Second, he trusts you a little bit more. The problems come up when a director has a little bit of musical training and thinks of himself as a music professional."[2] Movie director Sidney Lumet knows how to communicate to each film composer in clear helpful ways. He might say, "Can you compose a musical theme that will crack up or deteriorates as the character (represented by that theme) deteriorates?" This is clear and to the point.

During this collaborative process, there is bound to be a certain degree of compromise on the part of the composer. A composer may wish to write a full symphonic score for a specific film. However, the budget may not allow it or the director may have other ideas about his project. With the advent of many new and inexperienced independent directors working today, we are seeing a trend of a reoccurring turnover rate of film composers reaching large proportions. In essence, it is not unusual for one composer to be hired for a specific film only to have his or her score rejected by the director. Another composer will be brought on the project to "salvage" the film. Practically every major film composer working today has had one or more scores rejected by a director or producer. The pressures to perform are immense and the time in which you have as a composer to prove yourself is short. Eventually you are going to lose because the odds are running against you. As the saying goes, "You're only as good as your last film." Some composers are the lucky few who seem to have "legs" in the business. They are the handful who get the majority of the major film assignments. However, even these veteran composers are starting to see some of their scores rejected by some of the new talent coming out of Hollywood.

The executives who are in control today may be gone tomorrow. What's the last thing a movie executive asks his secretary as he leaves for lunch? The answer is, if my boss calls, get his name.

All kidding aside, *this is a tough business and it is a very political business. "It's who you know that counts."* Some people go so far as to say, *"It's not* what *you know, it's who."* Although some enduring human relationships have been formed, many you know in the business will tell you that in Hollywood there is always that underlying feeling in the back of your mind, "What can he do for me or what does he want from me?" It is wise for the composer to associate with as many producers and directors as possible in the hopes that maybe several of these contacts will pan out into future film composing projects. The composer or his agent spend much of their time on the phone making calls to directors and producers. As the film composer Bill Conti (1942–) said, "If you didn't make four calls today to further your career along with all of the other things you must do. . . . That's a failure—but the next day are you back at it."[3] The composer John Debney (1957–) says that he "actively pursues film assignments and actively prods his agents."[4]

1. Paraphrase by author of quote, taken from "James Horner," by Mark Derey, in *Keyboard* magazine, July 1988. Also quoted by Fred Karlin in *Listening to Movies*, p. 13 (New York: Schimer Books).
2. *Getting Started in Film*, American Film Institute (Englewood Cliffs, NJ: Prentice Hall, 1992), p. 313.
3. Phone interview with composer.
4. Interview with author.

Editing the Film

Once the film has been shot, it is time for the film editor (picture editor) to organize all of the scenes shot in the proper order according to the story in the script and splice them together (known as editing). This arrangement of all of the film footage is called the **assembly cut**. Generally, the assembly cut will be quite a bit *longer* than the film's final version released in the theaters. As an example, the assembly cut for the film *Titanic* (1997) was thirty-six hours long—obviously way too long for theatrical distribution. This film was edited down to a running time of about three and one-quarter hours for theatrical release.

The next phase of film editing is when the editor has made a version of the film that might be *within five to fifteen minutes of the film's final length*. This is called the **rough cut**. This version is a result of evaluation of each scene found in the assembly cut by the director, editor, and anyone else closely connected with the film. It is necessary for these people to judge which scenes are most effective. *Once the rough cut is made, this may be shown to preview audiences for an overall feel of the film's strengths and weaknesses*. This version of the film may lack a smooth flow in rhythm at certain edit points and in some cases there may be possible "holes" or placards (stating "scene missing") put up in place of scenes that have not yet been added. With today's computer graphic experts adding special Computer Generated Image (CGI) effects to films at the last minute, this is more common. Scenes that have been edited out of the rough cut will be carefully catalogued in case they are needed later for a complete "director's cut" or "unedited, uncensored version." Whole scenes that are cut out this way are called **outs**. Portions of a longer scene that are trimmed are called **trims**. The rough cut is still not the version of the film that we will see at the major theatrical release or at home on video, laser disc, or DVD. The rough cut is evaluated and edited down to a version that is known as the fine cut. When the director, producer, and others associated with the film decide that there are no more changes needed to be made in the fine cut, the picture is said to be locked. So we say that the **fine or locked cut** is the version of the film that we see in the theaters at the general release. *This is the version of the film with no intention of further editing*. Eventually the music, sound effects, and special effects will all be added to the film and it will be ready for general release. Then an "**answer print**" is delivered to the film laboratory. This is the first combined picture and sound print of the completed film. This version of the film will probably undergo some corrections in terms of light grading, color balance, dissolves, fades, and other printing standards. The answer print (also known as the "approval print" or "first-trial print") will eventually get final approval from the producer. When the filmmakers (producer, director, etc.) accept the quality, the answer print becomes the pristine model of the film to be used for distribution. Hundreds, if not thousands, of duplicate copies of the film will be made from this answer print model or standard for mass distribution in theaters around the country and/or world. It is crucial that a film composer knows which version of the film he or she is viewing when they go in to meet with the director about scoring the film. (This meeting is called the "spotting session.") It would be pointless to write the extra music for an assembly cut when much of this footage may not be used. By the same token, it is important that the composer is viewing the fine or locked cut (if available to the composer) and not the rough cut. If it is a rough cut, it is likely that some of this material also would be deleted. Today, with the popularity of the release of movies on DVD, it is becoming more apparent that many movies are released showing "deleted scenes" that were not used in the theatrical run of the film. In this case, these are scenes that were deleted (yet containing score material from the original score) in postproduction. These last-minute editorial changes were made for reasons such as censorship issues or poor showings at advanced screenings of the film.

The Temp Track

In most cases, previews are shown not with the composer's original score but with *temporary music* dubbed in specifically for this purpose. This temporary musical track is called a **temp track**. It is usually music that comes from previous movie soundtracks. It may even be music from the intended composer's previous film or films. Sometimes it is well-known classical music or perhaps a collection of popular hit songs. This temporary music could be placed in the film by the film editor (picture editor), the music editor, or the director. This procedure has become rather commonplace, because the musical score is usually written *after* the film has been shot. It is necessary for the filmmaker to get a feel for the reaction of the film from various screenings. *Most studios place great emphasis on test screenings.*

Many times, the "temp score" helps the filmmaker with the rhythm and flow of given scenes as well as establishing what kind of music will work best in each sequence. Therefore, we say that *temp scores aid in the editing phase and help to establish a musical concept for the score, as well as illustrating that concept to the film composer*. Many filmmakers realize after seeing a sequence with temp music that the scene needs to be reedited to flow more smoothly. *The ability of the temp score to provide an idea to the composer as to what style of music the director has in mind* as a "communicative device" can be helpful to a composer, but only up to a point. There are some composers who refuse to see a film with a temp score because it interferes with their ability to be original. Other composers will consent to seeing a new film with a temp score but only if it is done with their music from previous films. Then again, there are composers who welcome temp scores, because they feel that this reassures them that they are on the right track with the director's intentions. Temp tracks have been used for several decades for test screening purposes. Its use is now becoming more commonplace for the purpose of communicating the director's intentions than ever before. Because some directors practically fall in love with their temp scores accompanying their films, some composers have found that they need to compose a score that very closely resembles the temp score or they may find themselves being fired or never asked to work again for that particular director. As the composer Christopher Young (1957–) states, "It is almost always impossible to evaluate the success or failure of a score unless you understand the context in which it was written, meaning the score itself."[5]

Here, then, are *four reasons why* we use a *temp track score* in a movie during the editing/preview stages of a film:

1. To help the filmmaker edit the film. Added music will many times expose the need for reediting to make a scene flow more smoothly.
2. To make the movie more marketable during test screenings for sneak preview audiences and studio executives who are potential distributors of the film. It would not only be ineffective to show a new movie without music, it would be nearly insane and could possibly cause the movie to be shelved or scrapped altogether.
3. To determine the musical concept for the score. Basically, temp scores show what works and what doesn't work.
4. To illustrate that musical concept to the composer. Not all composers welcome a temp track during the spotting phase of a film. However, as the composer John Debney says, "If the temp track has been well-crafted, it provides a jumping-off point for discussion with the Director."[6]

Although temp scores are meant to be only temporary, there are instances when the director liked the temp score better than the original score composed for a specific film. As a result, we have movies

5. Quote from *The Score* by Michael Schelle, p. 423.
6. Interview with author.

such as *2001: A Space Odyssey* (1968), *Platoon* (1986), and *The Exorcist* (1973) ending up with temp track material in the final cut of the film instead of the originally intended score. For *2001: A Space Odyssey,* Stanley Kubrick had hired composer Alex North to write the score. Kubrick had temp tracked music of Richard Strauss, Johann Strauss, Jr., and Gyorgy Ligeti in several crucial scenes. Alex North wrote a score for the film, had it recorded by the studio orchestra, and invited his family and friends to attend the world premiere. That night he sat down in the theater with great anticipation only to find to his horror that not a single note of his music was used in the film! It was all the temp track material, which, by the way, is still what we hear on all copies of the film. In the case of *Platoon,* Georges Delerue suffered a similar fate when the American concert hall composer Samuel Barber's *Adagio for Strings* was used as the main recurring theme instead of the powerful string adagio he had written. Barber's work had been written as an arrangement from his first string quartet back in 1936.

The great film composer Bernard Herrmann (1922–1975), who had scored many of Alfred Hitchcock's greatest films, was asked to score *The Exorcist*. The filmmaker William Friedkin said to Herrmann, "I want you to give me a better score than you wrote for *Citizen Kane*." Herrmann replied, "Well, why didn't ya make a better *picture* than *Citizen Kane*?"[7] Herrmann hated the picture and never really wanted to do it. He walked out of the screening room and said, "Why do you show me such rubbish?!" The composer Lalo Schifrin (1932–) was then approached to write a score for this frightening movie. Instead of a score intended for Herrmann or Schifrin, the filmmakers used some twentieth-century avant-garde music written for the concert hall instead of the movies.

Spotting the Film

After the film has been prepared, a film composer is called in to view the completed film with the director, who will discuss the texture of music to be used and where it should be placed. This meeting of the director, film composer, and music editor (and sometimes the producer) to discuss the role and placement of music in the film is called the **spotting session**. Since the film editor also knows the film perhaps as intimately as the director, it is not unusual for them also to be present at the spotting session.

The two most obvious decisions made at a spotting session are (1) to determine which scenes will have music and (2) where the music will start and stop. This might seem easy to a beginner, yet it is a developed skill. Max Steiner (1888–1971), the composer of scores for movies such as *King Kong* (1933) and *Gone With the Wind* (1939) stated that for him the hardest thing about composing for films was not the actual writing of the notes, it was knowing where to start and where to stop the music. *Knowing where to put music and where not to put music is a major factor to successful film scoring*. The composer John Barry feels strongly about this, stating that "the choices about where to put music are the most important decisions you can make." He loves to wait for that special moment when music can enter to "put the scene over the top." Barry firmly believes that the choices made at the spotting session and the relevance that a composer attaches to his or her music and how they explain that relevance to the director is crucial to the success of the score and the movie.

Skilled composers such as John Barry know to take into account all kinds of subtle challenges, for example, the dialogue of the actors. Barry explains that you have actors and actresses who present different challenges. Some actors have high-pitched voices, some possess low, deep voices. Some deliver their sentences very slowly, others at a rapid-fire speed. The film composer must take into account which kind of musical accompaniment will best satisfy each voice pattern. For instance, an actor with a very active speech pattern would best be served with more sustained musical notes. An actor who has a baritone voice should not be accompanied by music played by lower-pitched instruments such as the

7. Steven Smith, *A Heart At Fire's Center* (Berkeley: University of California Press, 1991), p. 331.

cello or bassoon, because they would tend to rob the resonant quality of that actor's voice. In today's theaters or in homes with state-of-the-art sound systems, you have probably noticed that sometimes the actors' voices are coming from the center of the screen; other times you may hear the voices coming from the left or right side of your screen. A composer must know how to handle this. Barry says that his music can create a cushion behind the dialogue. Music can move the actors around up on screen if cleverly done. The composer must know when to use a small ensemble or full orchestra to accompany the dialogue. If done correctly, the composer's music can create weight and depth in the scene.

Each portion of the film that requires music is called a **music cue**. These cues are given a number and location within that reel of film so that they may be easily identified and located. Each music cue also will be given a title for identification and copyright purposes. During the spotting session, the music editor will take detailed notes called **spotting notes**. These spotting notes will be comprised of exact timings of the music cue from the time the music is to start to the time the cue stops. In addition to this, the spotting notes will have scene descriptions. From these notes, the composer can determine the number of minutes of music that will need to be written and recorded so he or she can plan accordingly. Also in the spotting notes may be comments made by the director or producer regarding the shadings and nuances that they hope the composer's music will enhance within the given scene. The music editor also will mark every potential accent point found in each music cue. The composer can elect which of these high points to emphasize in his or her score. Next, the music editor will create from a copy of the film a more detailed breakdown of each scene requiring music. The music editor will obtain a copy of the film to make exact timings. This is often a video copy of the film with a film footage counter and timecode numbers superimposed at the top or bottom of the screen, each in its own window. If the film editor (the person who splices the film scenes together) cuts the finished music on film, these film footages will be helpful. In addition to this, the descriptions will be more detailed now than in the original spotting notes. These descriptions might contain specific actions and any other helpful comments to describe what is necessary for the composer to achieve the best possible results. These more detailed notes are called **breakdown notes** or **timing notes**. *Please note: Some composers refer to timing notes as* **cue sheets**. ("Cue sheet" has several different meanings depending on the period of film history. Before the days of synchronized sound, when the images up on screen were still "silent," a cue sheet was something that listed *suggested music* to be performed in the theaters by the keyboard player or pit orchestra. Later, in the age of sound, "cue sheets" became synonymous with "timing notes.") It is from these timing notes that a composer can work knowing confidently that he or she has all the information necessary to deliver a product worthy of the director's intentions. These timing notes also will contain all of the actors' dialogue so that the composer's music does not conflict with the dialogue. *The dialogue must always reign supreme*. The composer will take home a copy of the film to be scored so that he or she may refer to it as necessary. Although some composers still wish to work from an actual copy of the movie on film, it has become much more convenient for the composer to work with the film copied onto videotape. In recent years, more composers work from a copy of the film on the hard drive of a computer. This enables them to work directly with the computer setup in their studio.

Budgets

After the film has been spotted and the composer is aware of how much music he or she will have to compose, it is necessary for the composer to meet with the producer to see how much money is left in the budget for music. *Music is part of the postproduction phase of movie making*. Therefore, some of the money allocated in the original budget for music may have already been spent for something else.

The film composer Miklos Rozsa once said that, "In a new life, if I ever enter the film business again, I want to be an art director. They are at the beginning of a film's production cycle and they get all the money."[8] *The amount of money must be agreed on before the composer can go on with his project.* Perhaps the director wants a full symphonic score with a 110-piece orchestra. If there were only $50,000 left in the music budget, this would not be possible. It would therefore be necessary for the composer to inform the director that for that kind of money all he will get will probably be a synthesizer score done electronically by the composer himself. It is primarily in Hollywood that music is budgeted as a post-production item.

In France, the whole concept of music in film is different. With a few exceptions, many of the French filmmakers don't place much emphasis on music. Music is not something that comes after the picture has been completed, so therefore is less important. Here is a list of several items that can add to the overall music budget on a major motion picture:

1. **The style of music and its degree of difficulty.** Is it a jazz score? If so, it will probably cost less than a full symphonic score, which uses a 110-piece studio orchestra. Also, if the music is difficult to play at sight the first time, the extra rehearsal time needed to straighten out the difficulties can add to the overall cost.
2. **The number of studio musicians needed to perform the music.** Obviously, the more players needed for a score, the more it will cost to pay for the extra personnel. A composer must determine, with the director and producer, what the music budget will allow in terms of personnel needed for the music. The music contractor can help determine the costs of particular instrumentalists needed.
3. **The amount of music.** The more music there is to record, the more costly the score will be.
4. **If there is any source music needed for the film, usually the music editor or music supervisor will check on the cost of using copyrighted songs.** The music supervisor will help secure the necessary rights and licenses for scripted songs or music, determine master use and sync licensing fees, and negotiate with the company that published or recorded the music for use of the songs within the film. Just to use a song from a pop artist can swell the music budget into an unaffordable category.
5. **The recording time on the scoring stage.** Rental of a scoring stage can become very costly and can add a considerable amount to the budget.
6. **Prerecording.** There are times when a film may contain dance numbers, or perhaps one of the leading characters will appear to sing or play a musical instrument on screen. Music has to be recorded *before* the scene is to be shot so that the dancers will have music to dance to or so that the main character will have music to practice "lip-synching" to if they are to appear to be singing within a given scene.
7. **Mixing also adds to the budget.** This is when the music is balanced after the sessions are over. It is necessary to make certain instrumental parts come out more than others. This is what we mean by balancing or "mixing" the parts.
8. **Orchestrators**—people who take the composer's piano sketches and assign the elements of the composition to the instruments of the orchestra and transfer this to a full score—are a necessary ingredient for most composers in Hollywood.
9. **Music copyists**—people who hand copy the individual instrument parts taken from the full score—also add to the budget. It is becoming more commonplace for music copyists to use a computer to write out individual parts.

8. Quoted in *Soundtrack* magazine, Vol. 1, No. 3, September 1982.

Determining the Music Budget for a Film

It has been estimated that an overall music budget for a film should be 1.5 percent to 2.5 percent of the film's total budget. That is, for a $100 million film, the music budget would be in the neighborhood of $1.5 to $2.5 million. Back in the 1940s and 1950s, music budgets were 3 percent to 5 percent of the film's overall budget.

How Much Do Film Composers Make?

The salaries of some of the top composers may vary according to the agreements made in their contracts, but, generally speaking, salaries range from $750,000 to amounts past $1.5 million per film for top composers. Some of these top composers can average anywhere from three to six films each year. The normal range averages $150,000 to $1 million per picture for film composers in general.

Sometimes a composer has a "**package deal**." This is when a composer has to pay some of the other people out of his salary. The production company will say, "Here is 'x' amount of dollars." Out of this money, the composer must pay the musicians, the cost of the recording stage, the cartage and rental of instruments, the orchestrations, the copying, and singers—if they're required; in fact the only thing *not* included would be license fees for source music, or the music editor, but everyone else must be paid by the composer. It can be both good and bad for the composer, depending on the circumstances.

Many producers or studios own the music rights of the original score composed for a film. Some composers will lower the fee in order to retain the music rights. This could be quite lucrative for the composer if the film is shown on television or in foreign countries.

ASCAP, BMI, and SESAC: Three Performing Rights Societies

Film composers and their publishers must belong to one of the following *performing rights societies:* American Society of Composers, Authors, and Publishers (ASCAP), Broadcast Music Incorporated (BMI), or Society of European Stage Authors and Composers (SESAC). It is important that the composer and the publisher belong to the same society, and they can only belong to one of the three groups at a time. ASCAP pays out royalties owed to its members on a quarterly basis. A blanket fee for use of the music in each society's catalogue is paid by TV and radio stations, restaurants, nightclubs, and companies, such as Muzak, which provide "atmospheric background music" (known as "elevator music" to some people). ASCAP collects these fees for its members and distributes them accordingly. These rights societies act as a way of providing composers financial payback and protection of their creations. It has been said that if a composer has written at least two hit songs, she or he will be financially set for life. One composer told me that he made $250,000 in royalties in 2000, just from one song, and he has written well over three hundred songs!

What do Orchestrators Do?

The orchestrator is someone who takes the composer's piano sketches (usually on a six- to twelve-stave page) and assigns the melody line and harmonic accompaniment to the instruments of the orchestra (i.e., violins, flutes, oboes, trumpets, etc.). The composer's sketch is a shorthand version of the full score that the orchestrator will generate from the notes given from the composer. Orchestrators write out all the different orchestral instrument parts on a full score of about twenty to thirty staves.

Composer's Piano Sketch

Flute part (done by music copyist)

Full score (done by orchestrator)

Orchestrators need to know:

1. The playing range of each instrument.
2. What instruments playing in various combinations will sound like. More technically, this means knowing how to voice instruments in harmonic textures.
3. The limitations of each instrument's playing capabilities (i.e., oboes have a difficult time playing softly in their lowest register, flutes cannot play very loudly in their lowest register, etc.).
4. That string players will sound better playing in certain key signatures for certain effects. Because of the fingering combinations of the string player's left hand, you can create certain feelings or emotions with "flat key" signatures versus "sharp key" signatures. In flat key signatures, the D♯ and E♭ are in slightly different fingering positions, giving you a less open sound. This will give you a more "muted," tentative sound. Keys such as A major (with three sharps in the key signature) will give you a very brilliant sound, good for excitement or victory. John Williams likes to write in A major.
5. Orchestrators need to know the characteristics of all musical styles, the capabilities of all instruments (both conventional and foreign or exotic), and should possess additional experience of knowing what works for a given scene and what doesn't work.

The orchestrator Robert Elhai (who works for composers such as Michael Kamen and Elliot Goldenthal) states, "First and foremost, an orchestrator must be facile. You must be able to work fast, and bring to the project a minimum of egotistical baggage, as well as a maximum of creativity. It is important to have the technical orchestral expertise at your fingers, especially when working with a composer who does not."

When asked what advice would you give a young person wanting to become an orchestrator, this is how the orchestrator Brad Dechter (who works for composers such as James Newton Howard, John Debney, Marc Shaiman, and Hummie Mann) responded:

> Knowing your musical craft is a given. Having the ability to orchestrate and arrange for various styles of music and types of instrumentations is essential. But remember that you don't have to show off everything you know in any given piece of music! There is a tendency for some younger orchestrator/arrangers to "flex" their musical "chops," which may be impressive from a musical standpoint but can actually hamper the recording process. For instance, spending undue amounts of time for a musical gesture that most likely will be unnoticed in the final mix can be costly, both in terms of time and money. Much of the success of a good orchestrator is knowing when and when not to add creative additions to a composer's sketch. I'm always reminded of what jazz arranger/composer Gerry Mulligan said: "The arranger's most important tool is his eraser." More important is understanding the process and the medium, whether it be film, television, jingles, live performances, or album recording. Each has its own unique demands and requirements. Get involved any way you can so as to gain as much experience as possible. But be willing to do the simplest of jobs. Pay attention to all aspects of the business around you; being able to see the "big picture" is very invaluable. That knowledge is learned through lots of experience in the studio, knowing who your musicians are and their capabilities, knowing how many minutes of music you need to record during a session (which is directly related to budget of course) and most importantly, understanding the intent and desires of the composer/director/producer. There are literally hundreds of "correct" ways to orchestrate a piece of music. It's the orchestrator's job to somehow synthesize all of the information he has in order to come up with the orchestration that best suits the situation.

Robert Elhai adds: "Listen with scores in hand and get to know the music of Mahler, Strauss, Shostakovich, Copland, and Holst—a large amount of film music is generally derived from these composers' work." He also feels it's important to get a graduate degree in composition at a university and "get to know composers, and try to get creative jobs with them that don't pigeonhole you as a player or a copyist. It helps to be detail-oriented, and to have a passion for how the orchestra works!"

Orchestrators must work under tight time schedules and must learn to expect the unexpected. Brad Dechter was called to work at an evening recording session for Barbra Streisand. As he relates, "About an hour into the session, I was asked to write a brand new arrangement of a song for her to sing for a movie soundtrack right there on the spot while an eighty-piece orchestra waited for me!"

Brad Dechter also said, "A couple of times I've had a director ask me to change a particular chord to another specifically designated chord in the composer's music (such request not making much sense musically). This would be akin to me telling the director how to frame his shot or what kind of film to use! There is a standing joke about how everyone in the filmmaking process knows his own craft AND music."

Most film composers know how to orchestrate their own music, but it is very tedious and time-consuming work. Because of the time pressures of delivering a score on schedule in a short amount of time, most Hollywood composers will hire one or more orchestrators. In England and many other countries, the film composers do their own orchestrations. But in Hollywood, the majority of the film composers use orchestrators. The composer James Newton Howard (1951–) said that it actually took longer for him to orchestrate his film music for the movie *Alive* than it did to compose the score itself (five weeks to compose and six weeks to orchestrate). He actually welcomes the "injection of additional personality dimensions" by using orchestrators.

The film composer Paul Chihara (1938–) feels strongly that orchestration is part of the score's final success or failure. It is another level or step of motivic development. Generally speaking, an orchestrator will make about *$400 per minute of music orchestrated*. For forty minutes of music in a major motion picture, that would account for a $16,000 fee. Complex orchestrations for a major release can exceed $30,000.

Music Copyists

After the music has been orchestrated, several music copyists come along and extract those parts from the full score for each individual player. These copyists can either copy these parts by hand on music manuscript paper with a manuscript pen or they can do it with today's computer software, such as "Logic" or "Cue Base" for PCs and "Performer" for Macs.

Music Librarians

The music librarian places individual parts on each player's music stand before a scoring session starts, and is responsible for making sure all parts are ready to go for each day's scoring session. Jo Ann Kane Music Service is one of the major music librarians in the business.

Music Contractors

A music contractor is a person who specializes in hiring the studio musicians. Early on in movie history, each major studio had its own resident in-house music department, along with staff composers, orchestrators, arrangers, music cutters (known today as music editors), librarians, and a studio orchestra. In the 1950s, things changed. Musicians became independent "free agents," with no loyalty to any one studio. This meant that someone had to make sure the musicians showed up for a particular session at a given studio. Music contractors became that "someone" needed to fulfill the task. For years, men dominated these positions. In the 1990s, things began to change, and women became the prominent music contractors in Hollywood. More recently, Tonia Duvall and Isobel Griffiths have paved the way for other women contractors in England.

Studio Musicians

The studio musicians are the personnel who will perform the composer's music, making it come to life for the first time. They will have never seen this music before; therefore, they must be able to *sightread* any style and level of music placed before them. Studio musicians are some of the finest musicians in the world and are masters of their individual instruments. Aside from rock and pop artists, they are among some of the highest paid musicians within the profession, earning $100,000 to $300,000 per year. The minimum pay for studio musicians averages a little less than $300 for each three-hour session per musician. Musicians are hired for a block of time, which is equivalent to a three-hour "call," known as a **session**. There could be two or three sessions per day (known by studio musicians as a "double" or "triple" call). Musicians are given a break (a rest period) of ten minutes every hour, or two fifteen-minute rest periods within a three-hour session. At no time is a musician required to perform for more than ninety consecutive minutes without a break. For those musicians who play more than one instrument during the studio session (called **doubling**), the studio musician makes an additional 50 percent above the basic scale for the first instrument doubled, with an additional 20 percent of basic scale being paid for each added double thereafter. For musicians who play oversized instruments, they receive an additional **Cartage fee**. This amounts to an extra $30 for the harpist (if transported by the musician) and an extra $12 for all other instrumentalists, for example, tuba players, cellists, and string bassists to percussionists, contrabassoonists, and musicians transporting all heavy or bulky amplifiers. Studio musicians get a "**special payments check**" from the Theatrical and Television Motion Picture Special Payments Fund (founded 1972) for the work that they have done. The money paid to each musician is

> **THE UNHERALDED PERCUSSION SECTION:**
>
> One part of the orchestra that most often goes uncredited in a discussion of film music is the percussion section. These instruments are crucial in providing the exciting pulse that is needed in so many scores. Throughout this book on film music, whenever we talk about a march within a movie, the reader is encouraged to notice that the crucial framework backdrop on which many march themes are displayed is the sound of snare drums, timpani, bass drum, and cymbals—the mighty percussion section!

calculated on how long the musician worked on the scoring project, whether it is one session or twelve sessions. A person who attended only one session would get a smaller check than a musician who worked on the entire run of sessions. These checks are mailed separately and are in addition to the fees made by working on the recording sessions. The studio musicians receive these checks once a year in the summer. For active musicians, the size of the checks can amount to $100,000 or more per year! To show you how much money goes into this fund, the contributions made for the fiscal year April 1, 1999 to March 31, 2000 were $50.1 million. This is divided out according to the formula explained above. In this case, the fund collected $50.1 million in revenue generated by musicians working on close to five thousand films over the years, making the average contribution $10,200 per film.

For television films, no more than five minutes of music shall be recorded per hour. For motion pictures, the average of about two to five minutes' worth of music is recorded per hour. The average recording schedule for a typical movie is four to five days. Many major motion pictures can have seventy or more minutes worth of music. Some of the really big productions could need ten to twelve three-hour sessions to complete a major score. The film *Waterworld* (1995) had about 140 to 150 minutes worth of music and took two weeks to record. The *Godzilla* (1998) score took almost a dozen days of recording to complete. According to the studio musician Charles Gould (bassoonist), they took three months to record the music for the film *Doctor Zhivago* in 1965! Some films are done in just two days. It all depends on the number of minutes of music needed to be recorded, the degree of difficulty of the music, and the type of film. Also, each composer works at a different pace. For a major motion picture with all of the costs added together in the complete package, the overall music budget could exceed $1 million per picture. Before the breakup of the major studio orchestras in the late 1950s, studio musicians who were members of the studio orchestra were contracted to receive an annual salary. Instead of having a three-hour block of time constituting a "session," as it is today, studio musicians could expect to work an eight-hour day, with a ten-minute break for every hour. If the studio musician puts in more than 520 hours in one year, they would be paid for extra hours on the job. Most of the older surviving studio players tell us that they always put in more than 520 hours and therefore made a handsome amount of money above their annual salary.

The majority of the film composers seem to think that the very best studio musicians are in Los Angeles and London. Certainly there are exceptions to this, but many composers have commented on their frustrations working in other locations. During a scoring session in Rome, one well-known American film composer went to cue the entrance of the harp player. She wasn't there. When asked where she was, he was told that she had left to "give a harp lesson!" Because of the high cost on the "back end" of using union musicians in Los Angeles, some producers have elected to have their composers record their scores in cities such as Seattle, Washington, or Phoenix, Arizona, which are nonunion orchestras. Hollywood studio musicians are paid "reuse" fees when a movie soundtrack is released. This costs the producer more money. Groups such as the London Symphony Orchestra, the Lyndhurst (England) Orchestra, the Philharmonia Orchestra (England), the Sinfonia of London, the London Philharmonic Orchestra, or the Graunke Symphony Orchestra (Germany) are engaged to record many scores for American-made films, to save money.

Music Supervisors

The music supervisor keeps track of all of the music used within a film. He or she is responsible for checking the clearance of rights, and therefore must have an extensive knowledge of the music business and some administrative, library, and legal skills.

Film Music Agents

The film music agent aggressively pursues assignments for certain film composer clients by negotiating with the producers of films. There was a time in Hollywood when film composers had little deal-making power. Back in the 1960s, composers were averaging around $17,000 per picture, with the top composers making only about $2,000 to $3,000 per picture more than their counterparts on the low end of the spectrum. This rather bleak condition continued into the 1980s. By 1985, a few of the top-flight composers of film music had demanded and received more than $100,000 per picture. Today, these same composers are making more than $1 million per picture, thanks to their agents. Some of the agents in Hollywood include people such as Michael Gorfaine and Sam Schwartz (of the Gorfaine-Schwartz Agency); Richard Kraft, Lyn Benjamin, and Laura Engel (of Blue Focus); and Vasi Vangelos (of Vangelos Management).

Film Music Publicist

Many of the famous film composers of Hollywood are dependent on a wonderful publicist named Ronni Chasen. Ronni and her extremely efficient staff distribute "press kits" on each composer client. A press kit consists of articles about the composer, a biography, and perhaps a brief filmography, as well as a current photo of the composer and anything else that might be pertinent.

Film Composers

Film composers are that rare breed of musicians who must work in a world in which, although they have certain freedoms, they must answer to people with little or no music education. They are restricted to specific timings within the film, yet they must be expressive. Their music cannot be louder than the dialogue, yet it must compete with the sound effects. They need to write music that immediately communicates to the filmgoer subliminal messages or shading, yet at the same time they must supply music that demands some kind of intellectual engagement. They need to write music that is coloristic or atmospheric, and make it coincide with the tempo of the action on screen. Yet, they should be able to write bombastic and thunderous climaxes at the appropriate time within the film to make the filmgoer reel with excitement. Finally, they must shade each nuance or innuendo with music that may seem "invisible" to many in the audience. In the hands of a master film composer, film music is magical. Yet, of all the personnel involved in making a movie, perhaps only composers (and songwriters) are the only ones judged by their work both *within* and *apart* from the movie itself.

If a composer's score is rejected, he or she will still be paid the full amount agreed on in the contract. Even if only a portion of the score is used, the composer will be paid their entire fee. It must also be said that *no composer, no matter how prestigious they are, ever has the final say-so on how their music is to be used within the film.* The filmmakers can take the music and do with it what they wish.

Schedules of Composers

Most people will agree that there is never enough time in life to do the things we want to do. The same definitely applies to film composers. As hard as it may seem, composer Max Steiner supposedly got only fifteen hours of sleep during the four weeks that he worked on the score for *Gone with the Wind*! He accomplished this superhuman feat under close doctor's supervision. He said that no one could be a Beethoven under those conditions.

Although this is not the norm, many composers of film music have horror stories to share regarding near-impossible deadline situations. Usually, this is due to last-minute editorial changes in the film.[9]

Filmmakers are always changing their minds. Whenever a film is reedited, this can lead to a major headache for the composer. Changes must be made to the musical score. This even can occur on the day of the scoring session. A successful film composer must be a master of his or her craft, or she or he will not survive the system.

Most film composers say that they are able to compose an average of about two to three minutes of useable music every workday. This might seem like an unusually slow turnout rate until one looks at the intricacies of film composing. In some extreme cases, several composers have boasted of composing twenty minutes of music in one night, but this is quite rare. Some composers may let a week pass by before writing a single note. Once an idea is formulated they might proceed at a speedy rate. Other composers peck along at a "snail-pace" rate, yet still manage to finish by the director's deadline. Some composers prefer to get up at the crack of dawn and finish by four in the afternoon. Others are workaholics, laboring well into the wee hours of the night for many days on end. Still others will work only an eight-hour day and no more to get the job done.

Before the 1960s, composers of film music had about ten weeks in which to compose and record their music. Today, the scheduling has shifted to a three- to six-week time frame, yet the filmmakers want the same high-quality scores that were turned out in the days of composers such as Korngold, Steiner, Waxman, and Newman.

Unfortunately, film composers tend to be judged *not* necessarily on the *quality* of their work. They are ranked according to the *box-office success* of the films that they do. How the score serves the film and the director is most important. The fact that the music may or may not accompany a hit film is a matter of good fortune. There are many fine film composers who go relatively unnoticed until they are associated with a "hit" film. On the Hollywood power ladder, composers tend to occupy the lower rungs of the ladder. Usually they are brought in six to eight weeks before the film is finished. This makes it very difficult for a composer to be stylistically experimental. If his or her score to a movie has a **"stand alone" quality** to it, the score may have lasting power to be around ten years from now as a favorite for soundtrack fans. By "stand alone," this means that the score possesses enough aesthetic and emotional charge to be enjoyed by the listener aside from the film images that they were originally designed to accompany.

To be a quick writer of music, to have a great sense of drama, and to work long hours for many days without adequate sleep are some of the qualities film composers say are helpful requirements to stay in the business. Additionally, composers should be successful in meeting and talking to producers and directors who, in most cases, will be the ones who will hire them. *They need to be able to "sell" their talents to prospective employers.*

9. There is a great deal of paranoia in the movie industry. People are afraid of committing to a decision. They feel as if their careers are going to die if they make one wrong move. This lack of decision can add to the stress of a composer and can hinder his or her ability to meet the final deadline.

Qualifications for a Successful Film Composer (Compiled from interviews with film composers; there are exceptions to this list)

1. Have knowledge of all styles of music. Know what works and what won't work in a particular situation.
2. Be a fast composer.
3. Possess a great sense of drama (be able to represent any human emotion by using music only).
4. Have great stamina. Film composers work long hours without much sleep.
5. Have good communication skills with filmmakers (be able to express your needs and concerns; don't be afraid to ask the director what it is he or she is trying to convey within a given scene).
6. Have the ability to change and adapt quickly on the scoring stage (a composer may have to change a musical cue "on the spot" at the whim of the director without a great deal of confrontation). A composer should leave his or her ego at home. "Stay humble and focused," according to John Debney. "Remember, none of us are Beethoven or Mozart."
7. Be able to accept rejection (have a "thick skin"). Almost every film composer has dealt with rejection in his or her career.
8. Feel comfortable promoting yourself to producers and directors, and be successful convincing these people that you would be the right composer for the job. This might be one of the most difficult parts of the job for many composers who feel out of their element doing this.
9. Know your strengths and weaknesses as a composer.

The true masters of film scoring are those composers who can move from one genre to the other with continued success. Herb Spencer (1906–1992) worked in Hollywood as an orchestrator for composers such as Alfred Newman, Alex North, David Raksin, Jerry Goldsmith, Leith Stevens, Johnny Mandel, David Shire, Cyril Mockridge, and John Williams. Spencer has some interesting comments regarding his work in Hollywood with composers. He stated in a 1988 interview that a person can be a very good composer, but if the music doesn't fit the picture, what's the use? "We used to say that the best composers for movies did not have to be the best composers, but had to be the best for what was going on. It's very hard to get good composers, because they have all these ideas about symphonic things instead of concentrating on what you have. The medium is very subtle, and when you get hold of it, you can feel it. Otherwise you sit there and you think, 'It's too bad this guy's wasting his time doing this because he's got one eye shut or something, he's not getting the idea.'"[10] *The Cue Sheet,* Vol.7, No.3, p. 95. At the time of his death (September 18, 1992), Herb Spencer was compared by his colleagues with preeminent international composers such as Maurice Ravel and Bela Bartok.

A Closer Look at Some of Today's Composers

There are many fine composers who are actively working in the business today. Following is some information on three composers who represent current trends.

10. *Getting Started,* p. 306.

ELIA CMIRAL

Elia Cmiral. Courtesy Chasen & Company.

Elia Cmiral is the award-winning composer of John Frankenheimer's *Ronin,* the cult classic *Apartment Zero,* the MGM thriller *Stigmata,* and *Battleship Earth.* He grew up in Czechoslovakia, where he took up playing drums and guitar for a hobby. He attended the Prague Music Conservatory from 1975 to 1979 as a composition and double bass major. He moved to Sweden, where he became a composer of scores for films and television and wrote three ballets for the National Theater of Sweden.

Cmiral moved to the United States to attend the University of Southern California's Film Scoring Program. After graduation in 1988, he met several key people, and this led to a job to score *Apartment Zero.* He composed a full-length tango-based score within the ten-day deadline.

In the mid-1990s, the actor Don Johnson produced a television series called *Nash Bridges.* Johnson singled out Cmiral's demo tape from several hundred that had been submitted. Cmiral scored the entire first season of the series. Veteran film composer Jerry Goldsmith had been hired to score the European thriller *Ronin,* but he had to leave because of scheduling conflicts. An executive at MGM (executive vice president of music Michael Sandoval) presented director John Frankenheimer with a copy of Cmiral's demo tape. Frankenheimer was impressed and invited Cmiral to compose a main theme for the film, one that evoked three dramatic requirements—sadness, loneliness, and heroism—to see if he was the right person for the job. Cmiral composed a wistfully determined minor-mode theme for strings and duduk (an Armenian reed instrument). Frankenheimer was impressed and Cmiral landed the scoring assignment. This score was the recipient of the first annual Movieline Young Hollywood Award for Best Soundtrack for 1998. Cmiral has been praised in *Variety, Entertainment Weekly,* the *Los Angeles Times, Film Score Monthly,* and the *Wall Street Journal.* His score for the supernatural thriller *Stigmata* illustrates his extreme versatility. This score is comprised of large orchestra, voices, synthesizers, and a variety of ethnic instruments. This score's complexities are enhanced by twelve-tone cluster writing, harshly chromatic textural figures, and cues that coexist in two different tempos.

In an interview, Cmiral described his approach as well as other aspects of his work:

1. How do you describe your approach to film scoring?

"I approach the film as a viewer. As the film is introduced to me, I ask myself what the film asks for—how I am moved emotionally and what am I missing as a viewer. I also do extensive research and emotional preparation by listening to a selection of soundtracks from films in a similar genre. Most of my listening time happens while driving to and from endless meetings needed at the beginning of the film's postproduction. Later on, I begin designing the structure and concept for the entire score. I group the cues into thematic families. The cues that best represent each thematic group are attacked first, even though I would rather start at the beginning and work my way to the end."

(continued)

2. *List some of the musical devices that you commonly use that make your score recognizable and unique as being written only by you.*

"These days I work very closely with the computer and my sequencer (Digital Performer). I do thematic writing at the piano—sometimes improvising to the computer, sometimes writing the theme straight down, sometimes playing with the notes until it is right—and then, all of a sudden, everything falls into place. I don't think I'm able to describe what is unique in my writing. I write what I feel is best—the best for the score and for the film. Of course, I have some favorite instruments, but mostly I like unusual sounds and combinations, both in orchestra and electronics. I like to surprise myself."

3. *Do you like spotting a film that contains a temp track?*

"I like spotting sessions in general. I enjoy discussing with the director the concept, seeing how he feels about the temp and what he expects from the music. Of course the temp is a double-edged sword. It helps to create communication and define a concept and approach to the whole score, but also the director can fall in love with the temp and then the composer is in trouble. It is very difficult to replace the music that the director knows, loves, and considers perfect for his movie. I have been lucky so far—it hasn't happened to me yet."

4. *In what film category do you like working the most? The least? Why?*

"I like writing for dramatic stories, fantasy, romantic, and epic adventure movies—probably because I enjoy them the most as a viewer. I'm not sure what I would write for a comedy, unless it is an absurd or black comedy."

5. *Is there a film genre that you haven't yet scored that interests you?*

"I would love to score a large epic drama or absurd black comedy, but all movies challenge and stimulate me to expand as an artist."

6. *Who has had the biggest influence on your career/style?*

"I think I have been influenced during my musical career in different periods by different people, music, and cultures. I've lived in many different places in the world and have always been interested in a wide variety of musical styles. If you asked me when I was twenty-one, I would have said Stravinsky and Dvorak. Later came Penderecki and musique concrète and so on and so on."

7. *Do you use an orchestrator and, if so, how much information do you give to your orchestrator in your sketches?*

"These days I like to use orchestrators. A knowledgeable person with a complete understanding of my music can bring additional ideas which I did not think of myself. Also, it's worth mentioning the sheer volume of music, which must be composed and orchestrated in a short time period. I give my orchestrator a transcription extracted from my demo MIDI files augmented with handwritten notes such as dynamics. These demos are completely orchestrated for full orchestra with all sections. I also typically give him three mixes on DAT of each cue-full mix, orchestra only, synths only—as well as the complete MIDI files for every cue. Before he starts, I meet with the orchestrator and give him verbal instructions and after he's done, we review his work, comparing it to my demo."

(continued)

4. In what film category do you like working the most? The least? Why?

"Drama tends to be the area of the most emotional depth and subtlety. Working on dramatic films is the best challenge. The category that I like the least is 'Bad'."

5. Is there a film genre that interests you that you haven't yet scored?

"I'd like to do a period film. I haven't done anything prior to the twentieth century so far."

6. Who has had the most influence on your career/style ?

"As a film composer, James Newton Howard. As a regular composer, I'd be flattered if someone were to say Bartók or Stravinsky. That would be what I'd hope to hear. And also Richard Strauss. He is someone that I listen to a lot."

7. Do you use an orchestrator and, if so, how much information do you give to your orchestrator in your sketches?

"I do use orchestrators. What they receive is a printout of a MIDI takedown. It is very detailed. The synth demos I do sound very much like the final orchestral recordings, except they don't have the depth that a real orchestra has. Usually every note is there. My comments are not meant to diminish the difficulty and expertise required by the orchestrator. These are magnificently talented people who are essential to the process. Just because I put a lot of detail in my sketches, it doesn't lessen their work."

8. Do you actively pursue most of your film assignments?

"There are often films that I really want to do that I don't get and then there are films that I didn't even know about that I get that I was given the opportunity to score. Sometimes I will see a new movie and say, 'Oh, I've got to work with this director.' "

9. Name two scores by other film composers that have moved you.

"The diversity and expanse of emotions that Leonard Rosenman expresses in his gorgeous score for *East of Eden* is magnificent, but today we really cannot express things that way. This is the same way that I think actors can't express things the way they used to. Today there is a degree of emotional expression that seems to be getting progressively more subtle. I think future scores will tend to project an emotion that really isn't involved in the scene at all. It is almost like a hue or a sheen being cast over the film. This is an entirely new concept. I think a good example of that is Thomas Newman's work in *American Beauty*. In that film, he is not responding to what's going on with every move of each character. He is creating and injecting an *emotional state* across the body of the film. I think that this is a *new trend* in scores and we might say that Tom Newman is responsible for that. I don't know if he would agree or not."

10. Do you see a time when we won't need live studio musicians, that is, everything will be done electronically?

"When that day comes, we won't need audiences at all. We will just have computers listening to the movies. I don't want to be around. I don't want to have anything to do with a planet where there are no musicians."

(continued)

11. What are several scores that you enjoy listening to?

"I never get tired of listening to Jerry Goldsmith's score to *Papillion.* I love Elmer Bernstein's score to *To Kill a Mockingbird.* It is spotted beautifully and is a model for film scoring. I also love all of the fascinating sounds of Jerry Goldsmith's score for *Planet of the Apes* as well as John Corigliano's score for *Altered States*."

12. Briefly list the various functions of film music.

"I think that the functions of film music are best described by the title of your book. I think that it is a *great* title! Film music does function like a *soul.* It makes a two-dimensional medium three-dimensional, first of all. And it's a universal language that can convey emotions when words can't. Film music also expands the power of emotions for a filmmaker within a film and is capable of expressing all of the dimensions of human feelings."

13. What qualities must a film composer possess in order to stay active in this business?

"You need tenacity. You also need a lot of personal skills dealing with being on a collaborative team. Politics is one word for it. You are dealing with a very difficult transformation of concepts that are often *verbal,* while later transforming those concepts into *musical* ideas. It's almost like being a psychologist and being able to interpret those notions that a director may have. I think that you have to understand human communications quite well. Also you must be imperious to rejection—to not even feel it. If you are married, make sure that your spouse understands the amount of space and alone time you need to compose."

MARK SNOW

Mark Snow, perhaps best known for his award-winning and effective scores for the long-running *X-Files* television series, is a very versatile composer with some innovative qualities that make him a pioneer in the world of electronic scoring. Although at home with the ability to compose for the orchestra, Snow realized years ago that there was a need for film and television composers to hone their skills in the art of *electronic scoring.* He followed that instinct with a fortunate degree of success. His large body of work encompasses lush orchestral scoring, state-of the-art electronics, pop album producing, classical performance, and cofounding of the legendary New York Rock 'n' Roll Ensemble (along with fellow film composer and Juilliard School of Music college roommate Michael Kamen).

Born August 26, 1946, in Brooklyn, New York, Snow came from a musical family His father was a professional percussionist and drummer on Broadway, while his mother was a kindergarten teacher who taught music and excelled at the piano. Young Snow took up the piano at age ten and then began studies on the drums and the oboe. He attended New York High School of Music and Art where he pursued composing. Snow went on to Juilliard for formal study from 1964 to 1968 alongside such notable classmates as Itzhak Perlman, Pinchas Zucherman, and Michael Kamen. His major teachers of composition included the *twelve-tone composer* George Tremblay and the television composer Earle Hagen. After a successful five-year tour with the New York Rock 'n' Roll Ensemble (Snow was this group's drummer), who specialized in performing both innovative pop and purely classical music, Snow and his wife Glynn moved to Los Angeles in 1974 so that he could score films and television. He has gone on to score over seventy television movies and miniseries in addition to the *X-Files* movie. Snow states that although he was an only child, that he is very team-oriented and loves the "collaborative nature of film music." He has an elaborate home studio where

(continued)

just a vehicle to sell records. I think the direction is going to be more electronic sample stuff and live performance combinations. I don't think that in ten years there's going to be something that we haven't done before."

8. *What are some of your favorite scores by other film composers?*

"Morricone's *Cinema Paradiso* and *The Mission,* with that great oboe piece called *Gabriel's Oboe*. [Snow is an oboist.] Goldsmith's *Alien* and *Islands in the Stream*. They're beautiful. The *Alien* score was just amazing. Goldenthal's *Interview with a Vampire* was great. Also, John Barry has been a big influence on me where he will have a 110-piece orchestra playing one of those long slow broad melodies. The main tune will be in the violins, the horns will play the counter-melody, and the celli will play an arpeggiated thing."

9. *By your definition, what makes a good or effective score? What is a score supposed to do?*

"I think first of all, it has to be a *subliminal message* that is sent to the audience that peaks their absolute submission into the film. And, on top of that, if you are lucky enough to write amazing music, then it is a slam dunk. That's why I think that the scores for *Alien* and *Islands in the Stream* are so wonderful. They stand as great *music* AND great *film* music!"

10. *Briefly list the various functions of music in films.*

"To me, that's an abstract question. I remember teaching a six-week thing at USC where the students wrote a cue for the two film selections. We all sat around and listened to them. It was truly a fantastic experience. What came out of this was that there are millions of ways to score the same sequence in a film. What separates a great film piece from something that's not is just sort of a personal thing. It's a real difficult thing to pinpoint. Obviously the stuff has to be mixed right and played well in tune and all that. If you are lucky enough to emerge from this and have some kind of a signature sound or style that people say, 'Oh, that sounds like John Barry or Mark Snow or Danny Elfman,' that's pretty great."

11. *What qualities must a film composer possess in order to stay active in this business?*

"You have to have an appealing, interesting, attractive personality. It's hard to say exactly what that is. Some of us are really flamboyant, really high powered, and have a good sense of humor. Then again, some people are very serious, some are very quiet and introspective. The best advice I could give is to be themselves as much as possible. When I first came to town, I remember hearing stories about how a certain composer acted when he went into meetings. I tried to be that way and I fell right on my rear. It wasn't until I was myself that I started getting successful.

12. *What advice would you give a young composer with aspirations of being a film composer?*

"Because of the advent of all this electronic gear, I feel that a person needs to learn how to use it. Going to a really good school with a serious film music program like Berkelee helps. You have to be trained in music whether you are a player or a composer. At the starting point of a career, *persistence* is way more important than *talent,* as far as I'm concerned. You've got to get your foot in the door. Maybe you have a relative or a friend in the business—any kind of connection. Then, of course, having talent is necessary.

Concert Hall Composer versus Film Composers

Some classical concert hall composers have stated that they felt that film composers have prostituted their talent in writing commercial music for movie soundtracks instead of serious music for the concert hall just to make a fast buck. *In actuality, more people will hear the music of a single film composer in one weekend than ever heard the music of Beethoven during his entire fifty-six years of life!* The film medium is an excellent way for a composer to have his or her talents reach a much wider audience than through the standard concert hall approach. The great film composer Bernard Herrmann said, "People who write for the cinema reach a worldwide audience." Very few modern-day concert hall composers can boast such a claim. Also, many modern classical composers might get that new work of theirs performed only once or twice in public before it is shelved for posterity, whereas the film composer's music will be heard by millions of people for generations to come.

Once everything has been established, the composer must calculate the number of days it will take him to compose the score in order to meet the established deadline, whether it is three weeks or six weeks. In the 1930s, 1940s, and 1950s, when major movie studios each had a music department, the composer would meet with the filmmaker, compose the score, and conduct the recording session. Now, things have changed. A composer must busy himself with additional details that can take away from his or her precious composing time. During the week after the spotting session, the composer needs to reserve a scoring stage (recording studio with motion picture projection facilities), hire his or her favorite recording engineer (scoring mixer), turn in a list of required musicians to play their score—many composers are loyal to their favorite studio musicians and will request their presence on his or her scoring dates—and hire additional personnel such as orchestrators and music copyists. Once these details are out of the way, the composer can begin to compose the needed music cues. The composer will use the timing notes as a guide along with a videotaped copy of the film. The composer has to realize that their score must interweave underneath the dialogue. *The dialogue must always reign supreme.* Because sound effects—such as laser blasts, gun shots, explosions, and car tires screeching—are so prominent in many action movies, composers have to anticipate how their music will fit into the final soundtrack mix. For delicate scenes, their score must always stay out of the way of the dialogue. The texture of the music must reflect the needs of the scene to enhance the elements and add another dimension to what is already present in the scene. The great film composer Elmer Bernstein put it succinctly. He states, "Music is art that begins where words and pictures end . . . the best use of music in a film should be to express what neither pictures nor words can."[11]

The Movie Trailer Composer

There is a special "breed" of film composer who specializes in composing music specifically for the movie "trailer" of coming attractions. Movie trailers are those two- to four-minute "coming attraction" previews from a movie that we see in movie theaters or on video before the feature film starts. If you watch a lot of television, chances are you have seen those short fifteen-, thirty-, or sixty-second commercials. Virtually all of these trailers rely on selling the product in a brief amount of time. In most cases, the original musical score hasn't been written yet and therefore cannot be used in these movie previews. And even if the movie score was available, many times the dramatic music written to underscore the movie may not be suitable to put a "hard sell" on the viewer, because the style or pacing may be slower than needed. In earlier days, many trailers were "tracked" with music from previous films or other sources. In recent times, it has become so expensive to get the "use" rights for much of this music.

11. Chris Willman, *Entertainment Weekly* No. 426, April 10, 1998, p. 70, "Sidetracked By Its Soundtrack."

Therefore, the marketing portion of a studio will hire a composer to write new music for their "coming attraction" trailer. Since most of these trailers undergo about six months of development, it would seem logical that the composer of music for the trailers would be given ample time for development of ideas. This is not so. In many cases, the marketing people will have temp-tracked the trailer material only to find that the music that they have used is not available for licensing reasons. Therefore, it is not unusual for a composer such as John Beal, who specializes in writing music for trailers, to be called at seven or eight o'clock at night and expect to have a completed two-minute score for a recording session at 6 A.M. the next morning. In some extreme cases, composers have been called at midnight with the intent of having music ready early the next morning.

Composing for trailers is not the same as writing for television and motion pictures.

1. You are dealing with a different kind of mentality. These people are into *marketing,* not *creating art,* as is the case with making films.
2. With a two-minute trailer, a film composer does not have the liberty to develop his or her musical ideas.
3. A trailer composer must be able to musically "hit" as many as 140 to 150 picture cues within the span of two minutes.
4. With trailers, most people are more aware of music than with movies or television because music is more "in-your-face." There are many examples of very poor films that had lucrative opening weekends because they were preceded with great, enticing trailers several weeks before. Next time you see the coming attractions for a movie, ask yourself if the music has little or no impact on you. Chances are you may have actually been attracted to a particular movie because you thought that it would contain the music that you "experienced" in its trailer.
5. Finally, a composer of trailer music should write music that grabs the audience's attention and makes them say, "Wow, I can hardly wait to see that picture!"

How is all of this done? Although there is no written formula, many trailers will start with a small beginning (with the occasional explosive start as an attention grabber for epic films or war movies). A gradual building of the music—perhaps an increase in tempo—will follow the small beginning that will move the action or drama forward. The music will increase in density—the texture of the music becomes more complex—to give the illusion that the viewer is actually falling into the complexity of the story. If the composer uses pounding drums for this effect, the trailer will almost always end with a low sustained note, with the drums stopping early. Going for the *emotional impact* is more important than going for *loud volume.*

Since many film scores are what we call "**song-driven scores,**" another approach to a film trailer is to temp it with *loud* pop music. In these trailers, loud is better. Of course, many of these films cater to an age group that is used to having their eardrums damaged. These song-driven scores contain a half dozen or more pop songs with only a smattering of dramatic underscoring from an original composer. If this kind of score is used, chances are good that the marketing department will not use a composer to write original music for the trailer.

There are rare times when the film composer hired for the feature film will actually write the music for the trailer. Most film composers don't like being involved in the marketing end of the film and therefore don't write the trailer music. It should be noted that once a film has been released and been in the theaters for a number of weeks, the studio will many times delete the original trailer music and substitute the recognizable music from the film's original score.

About 25 percent of movies from major studios get original music written for their trailers, so there really isn't enough demand to sustain an industry of composers of only trailer music. John Beal is one such composer who does this line of work exclusively. Since 1984, every major director and studio has turned to Beal. He has become the "guru of trailer music." When he first started back in the mid-1970s, the license fee for a section of a previous movie score to be used in a movie trailer was only $250 to $300. Now, it's usually $30,000 to over $50,000. Therefore, John Beal and several of his contemporaries are hired on a regular basis to give movie trailers an original music treatment. John Beal writes trailer music for forty to fifty films a year. Because of the vast exposure of these trailers, it is likely that his music is heard by more people than the music of most feature film composers.

It should be pointed out that many movie trailers are accompanied by film music from previous movies. When a film composer's music from their previous film scores are used in a trailer, he or she is paid quite handsomely.

Developing the Concept for the Score

We have all come to categorize the movies we watch into different classifications. How does a composer know what kind of music to write for each movie? Well, as we have already seen, the filmmaker's temp track score can be a big help in realizing what type of music would work best for the particular movie. In addition to this, there are several items to consider in order to arrive at the musical concept that will work best. These are several factors to consider in determining the type of music (the concept) that will work best for your film.

First of all, one must **consider the period of history of the movie**. If the action takes place during Shakespeare's day, we would probably expect to hear Elizabethan Renaissance music with lutes and madrigals. If it took place during the 1940s, we might expect to hear big band swing music. If a movie is set in the present day, we could feature almost any kind of music past or present to make it seem authentic. If a movie set is in the future, usually you would expect to hear some sort of modern "out-of-this-world" sounds never heard before.

Second, one must **look at the location and ethnic background of the movie**. If the film takes place in Brazil, it would be ludicrous to have the sounds of yodeling or bagpipes. A film composer will usually have to do a bit of research to study the various foreign styles of music needed in a picture of this type because most film composers don't have a handle on every international style of music in the world. If a film took place in the inner city in a predominantly African American neighborhood of a certain economic level, however, one might expect to have a rap-oriented score, as opposed to a classical orchestral score.

Third, one must **look at the major character or characters of the film**. In a movie such as *Jaws* or *King Kong,* composers enhance the fear factor of these creatures that are bigger than life through the use of leitmotifs scored in the lower musical range of the orchestra. It is common for composers to represent creatures that are bigger than we are by scoring themes in the lower instruments of the orchestra using tubas, string basses, celli, bassoons, contra bassoons, bass clarinets, and so on. If the main character is from England, as is the case of T. E. Lawrence in *Lawrence of Arabia,* the composer will write an English-sounding march.

It was said that Henry Mancini (1924–1994) chose a jazzy main theme for the detective Peter Gunn only because this detective liked to frequent jazz nightclubs. The opening episode of this 1958 television series takes place inside a jazz roadhouse called "Mothers." This is where Gunn is seen for five or six minutes, listening to jazz, as his girlfriend Edie sings the Johnny Mercer song *Day in–Day out*. Little did Mancini realize the profound effect that he would have on almost all movies and television shows dealing with private eyes, secret agents, and detectives. What happened was that most producers saw the success of the *Peter Gunn* series and naturally felt that it was the jazzy music that was the reason for part of the success. Therefore, jazz themes became the traditional type of music to accompany almost all movies and television shows dealing with this topic. Listen to the music for *James Bond, The Saint,* or other programs of this genre. Interestingly enough, Mancini admitted that the main title theme from *Peter Gunn* actually derives more from rock and roll than from jazz. To the layman's ear, the music sounds more "jazzy."

Finally, one must **look at the film's overall dramatic theme**. By this we mean, what kind of film is it? Is the film a horror movie, a comedy, a science fiction thriller, an erotic drama, or maybe a historic epic? We have conditioned ourselves to expect a certain type of music for each of these categories.

The Importance of Main Title Music

The music heard near or at the beginning of a movie, where we see the title of the movie and the credits that follow, is known as the **main title music**. If you have ever seen the opening of the movie *The Magnificent Seven,* there is little doubt in your mind that what you are about to see is a Western. Why? Because the music sounds like the music we expect to hear for a Western. Music has a certain sound, which you can analyze by looking in more detail at the orchestrations and compositional techniques used to make it sound that way. The music of the main title sequence helps to prepare us for the drama before it occurs. We usually know that what we are watching is a horror movie because of the threatening music. We feel the epic proportions of an epic film by its full-blown symphonic score or we experience the sentimental romance film by its reoccurring tender love theme. Main title music is crucial to setting the overall tone of the picture. If the composer misses the intentions of the director, the audience may have the wrong reaction to the film's overall message, thus creating confusion and destroying the director's film. The main title music is the one spot in any film where the composer can use strictly musical form to summarize the content of the film that will follow, that is, the composer has time to develop a theme without having to stay with strict timings.

Methods used for Music to Picture Synchronization

Have you ever wondered how the composer can line up the music so that it is in exact sync with the film? Very few composers have the ability to conduct a scoring session without using one of the following methods.

1. The Punch and Streamer method

The punch and streamer method is often used to mark visual cues on the actual film stock that are to coincide with the exact spot to be "hit" with the beginning and ending of a music cue. The **punch** is created by punching an actual hole in the film stock with a hole punch device. When projected on the screen, the punch will appear as a bright circular flash. The **streamer** is a long diagonal line placed on the actual film stock, which when projected, will appear as a vertical line moving from left to right. The streamer is created by using a device known as a **streamer board**. The film to be marked will be held in place by this device while the music editor can either scrape a one-eighth-inch-wide diagonal line in the film emulsion with a stylus (a sharp, pointed pen) or the music editor can use a grease pencil to draw the diagonal line. *The standard length of a streamer is three feet*. When projected up on the screen, *this length streamer will move across the screen from left to right in exactly two seconds*. It will appear not as a diagonal line, as one might expect, but instead as a vertical line. If the composer is using a copy of the film on videotape, these punches and streamers can be programmed into the video copy electronically.

When the composer is viewing the film, he will see a streamer run from left to right across the screen. If it is the standard three-foot streamer, it will take exactly two seconds to make its journey from left to right. This gives the composer a two-second warning for the "upbeat" preparation for the studio musicians to enter in on the downbeat (start of the music cue). Next, the punch will appear as a circular bright flash of light. This will be the exact starting point for the music to begin (the "downbeat").

PUNCH AND STREAMER METHOD:

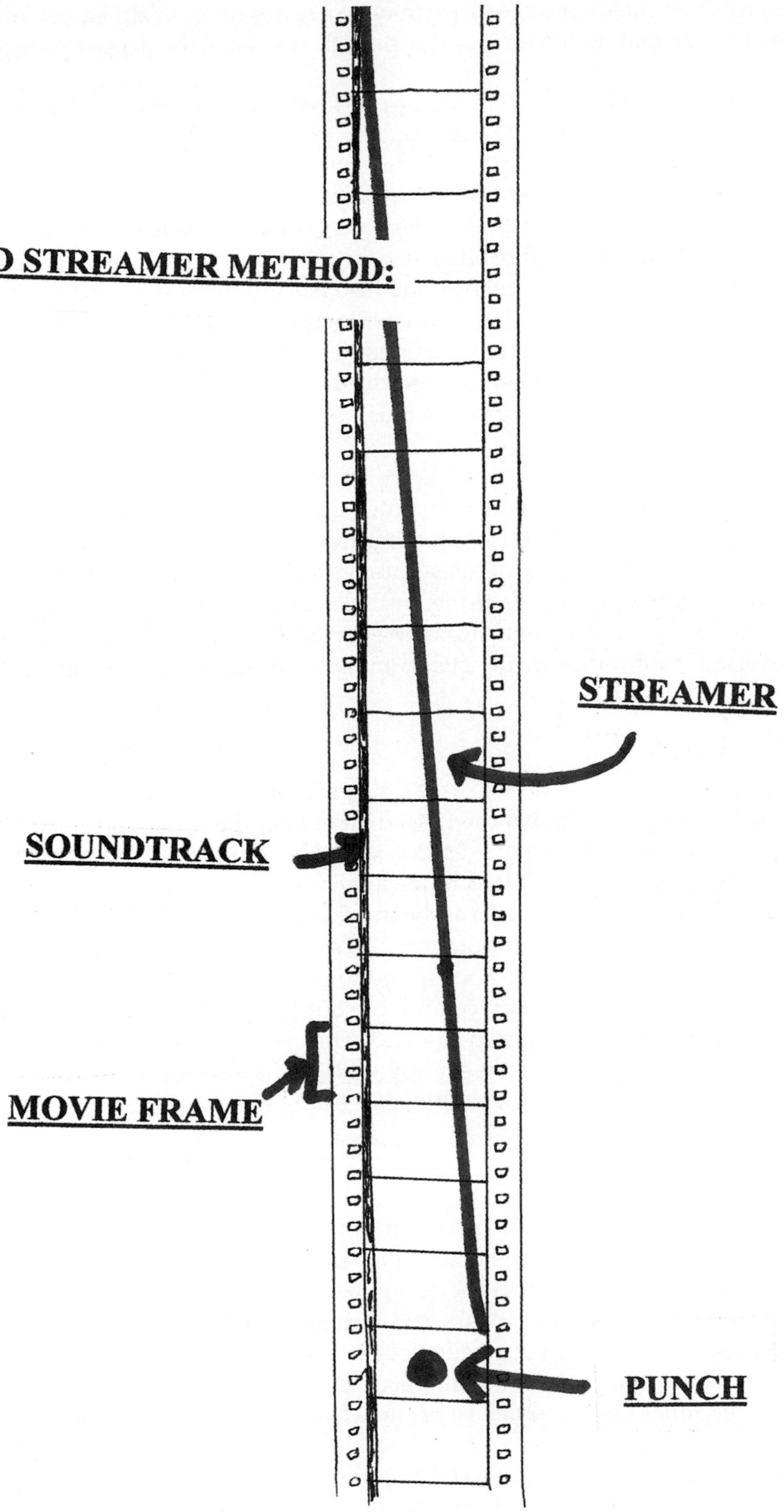

During the recording of the music cue, there may be a series of other streamers and punches as needed to assure the composer that he or she is performing the music at the proper pace to be in sync with the picture.

When the music cue is to end, there will be one final streamer followed by a final punch. The music will end precisely on that last punch. Some people refer to this method as **picture cueing**. Picture cueing requires quite a bit of practice to make it work correctly and is not something easily accomplished by the novice film composer. *Conducting an orchestra to a picture projected on a screen or television monitor is considered to be one of the most difficult aspects of the film composer's craft to master*. It does have several advantages: It allows the composer some flexibility or elasticity of tempo during the scoring session to give the effect of an expressive musical performance, and also lets the composer work with the rhythm and flow of the picture, to see how well his or her music will work in real time. The composer can make minute changes on the spot by making subtle variations in tempo. For this reason, the punch and streamer method (picture cueing) is also known as **free timing**. This method works very well in slower, freer moments in a movie in which the composer's music should sound very expressive.

The Newman System

The wonderful composer Alfred Newman invented a system—known as the **Newman System**—based on using a series of punches made on every other frame of film at certain key points for synchronization purposes. This group or cluster of visual punches (usually three, five, or perhaps seven of them) made on every other frame produces a flutter or flicker effect when the film is projected. Generally, this flutter effect is placed so that it will line up with specific downbeats of music so that the composer can pace himself in the performance of the cue to make sure that the music and picture will line up as planned.

2. The Stopwatch Method

Another method of free timing is known as the **stopwatch method** (conducting music to a large stopwatch). A large clock with a sweep hand is placed on or near the conductor's (composer's) music stand or podium. The music editor will have prepared several key "hitting points" that must be arrived at in the conductor's score by certain allotted times as represented on the clock. For instance, a cue may read: "Garden of Statues . . . faster tempo as the monkeys jump down from the statues 4:27.3." The timing as to when this was to occur (four minutes, 27.3 seconds into the playing of the music cue) would be marked on the conductor's score to correspond to the music and picture cue of the "monkeys jump down from the statues." The composer/conductor could check to see if he arrived at the right spot by watching for the monkeys to jump down at 4.27.3. This method also takes practice and skill. It is easy for the unskilled film composer to be off slightly with any of the above methods. With film music, the precision must be within a fraction of a second; otherwise, the viewer would notice the discrepancy.

3. The Click Track Method

It was said that the composer Max Steiner first used the click track method in the movie *The Informer* in 1935. Actually, he got the idea from Disney cartoon animators who supposedly used this method to line up the sound with the animated characters on screen. The click track method is very effective in fast action-packed sequences in which the composer has to "hit," with great accuracy, many visual cues with certain key points in the musical score such as accents and cymbal crashes.

The **click track** is a repetition of steady "clicks" heard by the composer and studio musicians in their headphones. These "clicks" sound similar to someone snapping their fingers. *The click track is prepared by the music editor and is created by using a digital metronome or a computer-generated click track system.*

This repeating series of clicks is locked to the picture so that, if the musicians are playing their musical parts in sync with the steady beat of the clicks, the result will be a perfect linking of picture with the music. Many composers whose conducting ability is limited will use this method for fail-safe

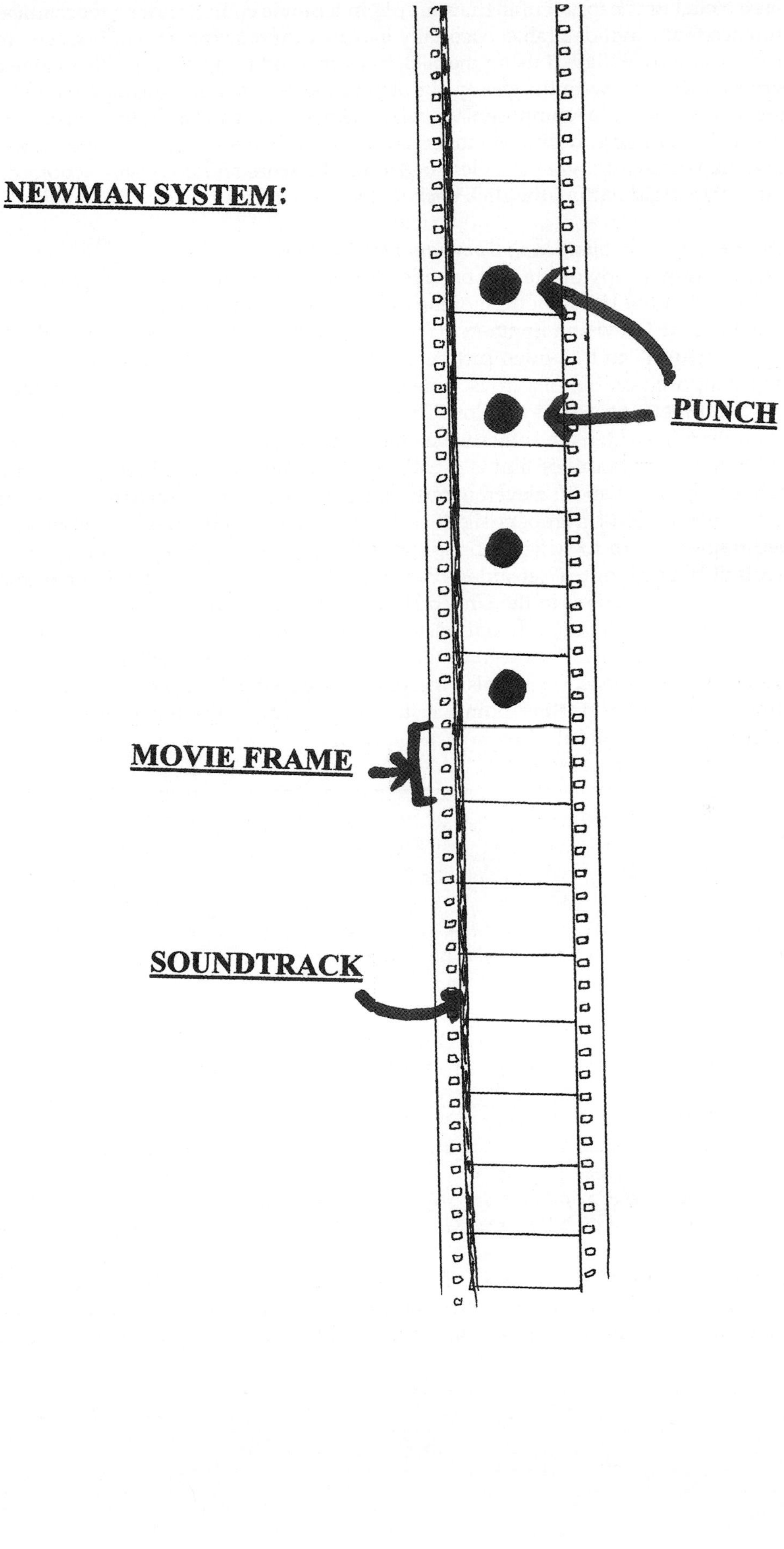
NEWMAN SYSTEM:
PUNCH
MOVIE FRAME
SOUNDTRACK

results. To use a click track for all of the music cues in a movie could render a mechanical, rigid, robot-like performance that is not desirable, especially in slow dramatic moments. However, the Hollywood studio musicians are so skilled at using the click track method that they are able to give an expressive, musical performance even with the steady popping of the clicks in their headphones.

There are times that film composers use what is known as a **variable click track**. This is when the steady clicks will fluctuate at dramatic moments or tempo changes. The recurring clicks will speed up or slow down depending on what is called for within the score and the visual action on screen. Obviously, because of its rigid nature, the click track method is *not* considered to be a method of free timing.

4. SMPTE Sync Pulse Timecode: Using Computers to Compose

If a composer is using a copy of the film on videotape, it will probably come with a **timecode** or series of numbers located at the top or bottom of the picture. This series of numbers is known as the Society of Motion Picture and Television Engineers (SMPTE; pronounced "simpty") sync pulse timecode. This timecode is "burned-in" to the video picture inside a rectangular-shaped window. This timecode of numbers superimposed on the picture is sometimes known as **window burn** or **window code**. There are four sets of numbers inside this window. The first set is in the hour position (many times referred to as the "reel number") and tells us either which reel of film we are looking at or which hour of film we are dealing with. A camera roll of film is usually one thousand feet in 35 mm or four hundred feet in 16 mm. Each reel of film is about eleven minutes long. The next set of numbers represents the number of minutes. The third set of numbers signifies seconds, and, finally, the last set of numbers tells us which video frame we are looking at. Simply put, SMPTE timecode is a running clock that counts hours (or reels of film), minutes, seconds, and frames. Movies travel through a projector at the rate of twenty-four frames per second. In the United States, Canada, Central America, Japan, and other parts of the world that use the NTSC (National Television Standards Committee) video standard, videotape moves at a rate of thirty frames per second. (Actually it is the rate of 29.97 frames per second, but our eyes cannot see the difference.) With this timecode, it is possible to locate any given picture or video frame within a movie as a starting point or stopping point for the music cue. As an example, the SMPTE time code might look like this:

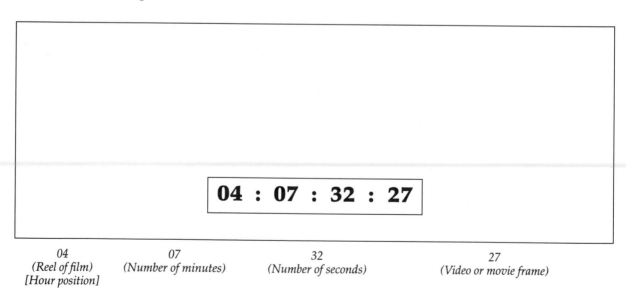

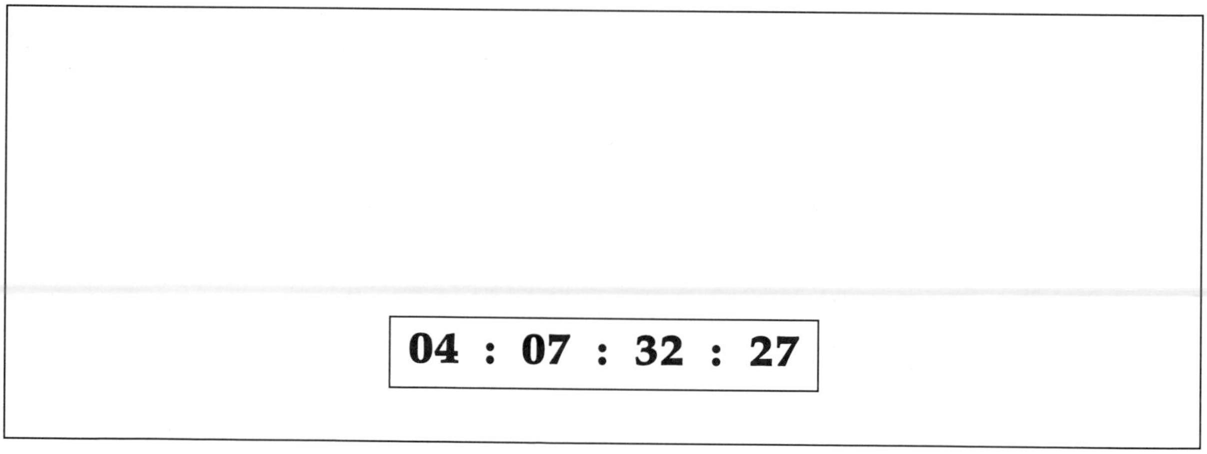

04 (Reel of film) [Hour position] — *07 (Number of minutes)* — *32 (Number of seconds)* — *27 (Video or movie frame)*

These numbers signify the following: The picture we are looking at is located in the fourth reel of film, seven minutes and thirty-two seconds into the reel, and we are looking at video picture frame twenty-seven. With this knowledge, it is possible to lock up the music with any given picture frame within the movie. Also present up on the screen will be a bar of numbers, which is the *footage counter.* This enables the composer to locate the exact frame of movie film to start or stop the music cue.

Using Computers to Compose Scores: MIDI

There are several computer music programs used by many film composers. As the music editor types in the timecode numbers or footage numbers, the computer program will automatically create timings to be used for the scoring of a given scene. A composer can write music cues on an electronic synthesizer while the videotape copy of the film will be locked in sync to the synthesizer or the film can be on the composer's hard drive. This way the composer can hear and see how their cue works against the picture with great accuracy. Thanks to the manufacture of MIDI (Musical Instrument Digital Interface), composers are able to allow their synthesizers and computers of any manufacturer to lock in and talk (interface) with one another. John Frizzell *predicts that many film composers will be composing their movie scores on their laptop computers in the not-too-distant future.*

There are different video standards used in various countries. Western Europe, England, Australia, New Zealand, and China use the PAL video standard, and the NTSC video standard is used in the United States. The PAL system, which has a higher quality video image (better picture resolution) than NTSC video, runs at exactly twenty-five frames per second (fps). SECAM, the video standard in France, Eastern Europe, Russia, Iran, and Iraq, also utilizes the twenty-five fps. Both PAL and SECAM video standards use 625 scan lines as opposed to NTSC's 525 lines.

5. Wild Recording

Wild recording is recording music for a movie without the benefit of seeing the movie projected on a screen or a video monitor. The composer might need music for a sequence that lasts two minutes and forty-two seconds. He will write three minutes worth of music that will be recorded in a simple recording studio versus a scoring stage. (The recording studio has no picture projection facilities, the scoring stage does.) Then this three-minute cue will be dubbed into the needed scene. At the cutoff point of two minutes and forty-two seconds, the sound mixer would simply fade the music away or even stop the music abruptly if necessary. This method is not effective in terms of lining up the music with the picture, because the composer sees no picture during the recording of the score. This is the cheapest method of providing music for a film but is also the least effective. It saves the producer money but rarely serves the film well unless the composer is well versed in this process. If wild recording is utilized, it is usually for low budget films such as television movies.

6. Tracking

There are times when filmmakers decide in advance that they wish no original score for their film. In this case, they will probably use what is known as **tracking**. Tracking is when a filmmaker uses prerecorded music cues from another source. Basically this is what is done when a filmmaker uses a temp track. The difference between tracking and temp tracking is that, with a temp track, the intended outcome is to use the prerecorded music on a temporary basis until the original score is ready. With tracking, the intent is to use the prerecorded music permanently. On the surface, one would think that tracking would be very reasonable financially—you don't have to hire a film composer, orchestrator, music copyists, or any of the usual personnel associated with traditional film scoring. *In reality, tracking can end up being quite expensive.* When music is "tracked" into a film, the filmmaker needs to get legal clearance of the "rights to reuse" of the prerecorded music. If the film uses songs of big-league recording artists the clearance rights could easily overtake the budget of a traditionally scored film. Even if a Beethoven symphony performed by the London Symphony Orchestra is used, the filmmaker must check the copyright clearance on the CD. The London Symphony Orchestra would have a copyright on its performance, the record company that recorded the music would have a copyright, and the publisher who printed the music would have a copyright that must be cleared before it can be used in the film. Each hurdle can cost money and must be determined if the filmmaker is going to track copyrighted music or songs. In 1981, Ralph Bakshi made an animation epic, *American Pop*. At the time, video was still in its infancy stages; therefore, Bakshi could not have seen his future need of getting clearance on all of the songs used in his film for future video release rights. He said, "At the time, I didn't know what the hell video was. The record label lawyer said, does Columbia want rights beyond the film? It was quite considerable, something like $3,000 a song extra and since I used more than fifty songs in the film, I thought it too expensive at the time. A few years later, rights for cuts by Dylan, Hendrix, and others on the pop soundtrack were now costing more like $50,000 a song! I should have gone with the original offer."[12]

A common practice for some studios is to replace some musical numbers in the theatrical release with different music heard in the home video release. Look on the video box to see if it says, "Home Video Version: Some Songs May Have Been Rescored (or replaced)." This was done for the video release of *Fast Times at Ridgemont High*. Some studios own prerecorded tracks of mood music that can be tracked without great cost to the filmmakers. Although this practice is not commonplace today, tracking was quite popular back in the 1930s, 1940s, and 1950s.

The Role of Music Editors and Orchestrators

The Music Editor

The music editor is present at the spotting sessions, and prepares the spotting notes that will be turned into timing or breakdown notes for the composer to use while composing the music cues. Music editors prepare click tracks, punch and streamers, or stopwatch timings on the conductor's score. The editor is present at the scoring sessions to make sure the composer's music is in sync with the picture both dramatically and technically. On low budget films, the film editor (picture editor) many times will function as the music editor, assisting the composer in getting his or her timings and laying in the tracks. This is especially true if there is very little music in the film. Many composers will select their own music editor with whom they have worked on many occasions. These "long-term" relationships between composer and music editor are not uncommon. There has been more than one instance where an experienced music editor has offered his or her expertise to a particularly difficult situation only to improve the quality of the outcome. It would probably be wise for a novice film composer working on one of his or her first assignments to request a music editor who has worked with many skilled film composers.

The Orchestrator

The orchestrator is the person who takes what the composer has written and expands on to a full score that music both melodically and harmonically using the various instruments of the orchestra. The film composer, because of a race for time, usually does not orchestrate his own music. He or she will sit down at the piano and write a piano sketch as to how the music should sound. They may or may not indicate which instruments should be used for the various notes in this piano rendition of the score.

If they do make indications, this will make things easier for the orchestrator. If no indications are made—as is the case for several "composers" who merely hum the tunes because they either can't write or even read music, or they have no knowledge of orchestration techniques—the orchestrators must create their own orchestrations and hope that they are acceptable to composer and filmmaker alike. Orchestrators should have a vast knowledge of the range and capabilities of the symphonic instruments. They usually know what sounds the best for various effects for a given scene because many orchestrators have worked with dozens of composers on countless films, and they know what works and what doesn't.

12. Chris Willman, "Sidetracked by Its Soundtrack," *Entertainment Weekly* 426 (April 10, 1998), p. 70.

Robert Elhai, one of Hollywood's busiest orchestrators, states that he likes "to think of the orchestrator as occupying the role of draftsman for an architect; filling out the details of the work while leaving the composer free to work out the conceptual big picture."

There is no typical work schedule for an orchestrator. Each assignment presents a variety of challenges. Brad Dechter, another extremely busy orchestrator, states that "most typical would be me getting some sort of sketch with which to work about two weeks (sometimes less) before the first day of recording. From that point until the last day of recording, I spend most of my waking hours (usually about eighteen a day) either on the phone, on the Internet, and occasionally orchestrating. It often seems that the necessary interruptions of dealing with the composer, copyists, other orchestrators, music editors, and the like often take more time than the actual music work itself. The pressure is often great and the days prior to the recording sessions are like nonstop whirlwinds." Elhai goes on to say that orchestrating "usually involves a lot of work and not very much sleep, usually over a period of about three weeks for a big picture."

Also when asked if there is a "winning formula" that orchestrators can count on to please most filmmakers, Elhai states that "it varies. Some filmmakers want the old-fashioned strings and horns soaring melody thing, 'a la James Horner'; others are more interested in more 'modern' (not necessarily 'orchestral') textures." He concludes, "I generally try to please the composer, and let him or her worry about pleasing the filmmakers." Both men agree that sometimes they would have written something differently had they been hired to compose a score. The truth of the matter is that an orchestrator is completely bound creatively by a composer's orchestral abilities (or lack thereof).

As the old saying goes, "A good score is one that you don't notice." Robert Elhai believes that "the best scores are those that are part of an audience's conscious experience of a movie. *Star Wars* is a good example."

It should be pointed out that in addition to being hired to orchestrate the score, there are many instances when the *primary* orchestrator is hired to be the "**booth person**." This is someone who sits in the booth "and watches the score to make sure that wrong notes, mistakes, and the like are caught and fixed." Elhai states, "Of course, it should also be said that the big payoff for staying up all night orchestrating a piece of music is to be able to hear it played the next day by some of the greatest musicians in the world!"

Recording the Music

There are three basic types of recording procedures done for motion picture music. You can record the music before, during, or after the picture has been shot.

Recording Music Before *the Scene is Shot*

In instances when there will be dance numbers or when an actor or actress appears to be singing or playing an instrument within the film, a technique known as **prerecording**, **prescoring**, or **playback recording** is used. The music is recorded *before* the picture is shot, which enables the performers to have the music beforehand so that they can rehearse for dance numbers or so the performers can have music to practice their lip sync abilities so they can appear to be singing on screen or perhaps to "side line" a musical instrument. "**Side line**" is the term used to describe looking like you are playing a musical instrument on screen even though you actually aren't. When we see performers in the background "playing their instruments," sometimes these are either real musicians called in all day to "side line," or they may be actors holding musical instruments and pretending to play them.

Recording Music During *the Shooting of a Scene*

The best way to lend an air of realism or authenticity to a musical performance on screen is to film the performance as it is actually happening. This second type of recording is known as **set recording** or

View of Paramount Scoring Stage as seen from the recording engineer's booth. Courtesy of David Ewart, Recording Musicians Association.

standard recording. This is when the music is recorded *during* the actual performance on screen. In the early days of sound films, this was the only method possible. Nowadays, this type of recording is not used as often. If an actor or actress is capable of actually playing the piano or violin it may be wise for the filmmaker to utilize this method for realism.

Recording Music After the Scene is Shot

The third and final type of recording commonly used in motion picture music is the most often used today. It is when the music is recorded *after* the picture is shot. This method is known as **scoring** or **underscoring**. Some people call it "recording to picture." Most film music falls into this third category. It is far more effective to add music after the picture has been shot, because it can be dubbed in with precision and state-of-the-art sound quality.

Dubbing: The Final Mix

At some point in the filmmaking process, it will be necessary to mix the three ongoing audio tracks—dialogue track, sound effects track, and music track—into one composite track. This is, in fact, three separate stereo mixes, known as **stems**. There will be a dialogue stem and a "music and effects" stem, known as an **M&E track** or **M&E stem**. Many foreign distributors will refuse to buy a film with an incomplete M&E track (or stem). By separating the music and effects track from the dialogue track, a foreign distributor will have the ability to dub in (loop or ADR) a foreign language to the M&E stem. Therefore, the foreign distributor can take the American-made film with the M&E stem and dub it.

The final mixing process is a long and tedious task. It takes great concentration and encompasses minute details. A ten- or twelve-reel film (standard length for many movies) might take as long as four to six weeks to premix and mix. **Premixing** is taking many different channels of sound and blending them down to only a few channels. In a standard motion picture, it is possible to start with as many as ninety different channels. This would be very complex to work with at the final mix, so it is better to premix to fewer channels. The **sound mixers**, sometimes called **rerecording mixers**, do this. On the east coast of the United States, this is usually done by one person. In Hollywood, three specialists are used to create the final mix. Sometimes there will be only two people: One in charge of the dialogue and music and the second to mix in the sound effects.

The Dialogue Mixer (rerecordist)

The dialogue mixer is considered the "captain in charge" (or supervisor) of the dubbing session, because *the dialogue must always reign supreme*. There are many instances in which the dialogue track—recorded live on the set, known as production sound—may not be adequate for use in the final dub. Perhaps there were extraneous sounds on the set that made the production sound unusable for the final dub. If this is the case, the actors in the scene in question will be called back to come into the recording studio to redub in their voices for a cleaner audio rendition of their voice. The actor will watch the scene several times to get the same inflection used in the original take. When he or she is ready, the sound engineer, known as the ADR recordist, will record the voiceover. This practice is known as **looping** or **ADR** (automated or automatic dialogue replacement). This can be a tedious process. Once the director is satisfied with the new cleaner audio dubs, the dialogue mixer has his or her final product for the final dub. It should be noted that when a scene is being shot, the on-set recordist person recording the production sound will usually ask for "complete quiet" so that he or she can record a few seconds worth of the room tone (ambiant sound). The **room tone** is the background "neutral sound" of the room. Stop and listen to the sound of the room that you are reading this book in at this very moment. Do you hear any background noises? When looping in an actor's voice, you must have a sample of the room's tone in order to lend a realistic quality to the dialogue track. Without this, the audience might notice that the actor's voice sounds too pure to have been recorded on the set.

The Sound Effects Mixer (rerecordist)

The sound effects mixer will balance in the sound effects in order to heighten the dramatic effects of the movie without overpowering the dialogue track. As you probably know, many sounds in nature—gunshots, explosions, tires screeching, and glass breaking—are not always as exciting as they seem in movies. Perhaps the sound of our main character walking on a cobblestone street late one night in foggy London might lack the spooky quality needed. During postproduction, a **foley artist** (also known as a **foley walker**) will be called in to "sweeten" the sound effects track. Originally, foley was defined as any kind of *body movement effect* recorded in a studio while watching the picture. Today, many kinds of sounds are recreated by this talented group of people. Foley was invented during the early history of sound films by Jack Foley. A **foley stage** is usually a large room containing several kinds of floors on which to walk, including dirt, sand, gravel, dry leaves, wooden floor, tile, and the like. This room may also include a water tank for splashing sounds, a bowl of soap flakes—by pushing down on the flakes, the sound of walking on snow will be recreated—and any number of props needed to complement the given film. The foley artist will watch the movie on a screen and synchronize the new sounds. The sounds that a foley artist recreates are exaggerated.

If the foley experts aren't able to recreate a given sound, that task may be passed on to the **sound designer**. This is a person who will either *customize the needed sound or use a prerecorded sound from a sound effects library.*

The Music Mixer (rerecordist)

The music mixer is the person who will dub in the composer's completed score. It is the responsibility of the music mixer to achieve the most effective results by dubbing in the music with the right dynamics and yet blend the music under the dialogue at all times. Some composers attend these final-dubbing sessions, others do not. There have been times when a music cue is dubbed into a scene at an inappropriate volume level only to seem out of place or lost under the sound effects or dialogue.

Review Questions

Discussion

1. Briefly describe why temp tracks are used.

2. Discuss the difference between spotting notes and timing notes.

3. What is meant by a "package deal"? List all inclusions and exclusions.

4. Name four qualities that film composers say are helpful requirements to stay in the business.

5. Watch three different types of films and discuss the role of the main title music and/or main theme (leitmotif) in each of the films.

6. Briefly describe the roles of a director and a producer.

7. Using terminology learned, what procedure would you follow as a music editor in working with the composer?

Short Answer

1. Music for film is usually written before or after the film is shot? ______________________.
2. Do directors ever produce their own films? ______________________.

   If yes, why? ______________________.
3. Which is usually longer, an assembly cut, or a rough cut, and why? ______________________

   ______________________.
4. What is an "answer print?" ______________________.
5. What is a spotting session and who is usually present at this meeting? ______________________

   ______________________.
6. What are two obvious decisions made at a spotting session? ______________________

   ______________________.
7. What is meant by "doubling?" ______________________.
8. What is meant by "cartage fee?" ______________________

   ______________________.
9. On the average, how many minutes worth of music are recorded per hour in the studio? ____

   ______________________.
10. How much useable music do most film composers write in a single day? ______________________

    ______________________.
11. What are four factors to consider when developing the score? ______________________

    ____

    ____

    ____

    ____
12. What is meant by main title music? ______________________.
13. Describe how the punch and streamer method is used. ______________________

    ____

____

____

____.

14. How long does a three-foot streamer take to cross the movie screen when projected? _______

    ____.

15. Name two advantages of picture cueing. ____________________

    ____

    ____.

16. During the mixing sessions, who is considered the "captain in charge?" ___________

    ____.

17. Who is the sound designer and how do they differ from the foley artist? ___________

    ____.

Define the following

Variable click track ______________________________.

SMPTE sync pulse timecode ______________________________.

Newman system ______________________________.

Free timing ______________________________.

Streamer board ______________________________.

Stopwatch method ______________________________.

Wild recording ______________________________.

Tracking ______________________________.

Playback recording ______________________________.

Set recording ______________________________.

Scoring ______________________________.

Underscoring ______________________________.

Looping ____.

ADR ____.

Music mixer ____.

Music copyist ____.

Orchestrator ____.

Music supervisor ____.

Temp track ____.

Fine cut ____.

Locked cut ____.

Rough cut ____.

Assembly cut ____.

Chapter Three

In the Beginning: Music for Silent Films (1895–1927)

When films were first exhibited, they generally ran for only twenty to thirty seconds. In order to view these early moving pictures, patrons would insert a coin into a slot machine. The films would move in a continuous loop inside the mechanism—called a **Kinetoscope**—allowing for an uninterrupted performance as the customer watched the moving images by looking down into a viewfinder of these handcranked machines. Sometimes, accompanying music would be supplied through earphones worn by the patron in these penny arcades. The year was 1894 and these early forerunners of the modern motion picture were usually simple scenes of a dancing girl or scenes representing some form of motion or movement.

Early Kinetoscope. Courtesy Deutsches Filmmuseum Frankfurt am Main.

One year later, two French brothers Auguste (1862–1954) and Louis (1864–1948) Lumière (pronounced "Lou-me-air"), would give the first known public performance of cinema accompanied by live music. The date was Saturday, December 28, 1895. The location was at the Grand Café at 14 Boulevard des Capucines in Paris, France. The Grand Café was at the street level of the Second Empire Grand Hotel. The room that they used was a room in the basement known as the Indian Salon. One hundred cane chairs were brought in from the café. The first day's admission numbered only thirty-three patrons, each being charged one franc for admission. Word must have spread because, by the second day, lines of people stretched down the street. Within weeks, mobs of people numbering more than two thousand each day were attracted to the Indian Salon. Police had to be called in to control the crowds, some of whom broke out into occasional fights. The program lasted about twenty minutes, and ten to twelve short films were projected up on the cloth screen. Patrons sat there open-mouthed, dumbfounded, astonished beyond belief at what they were observing. It was rumored that some were even frightened at the sight of a train coming toward them and that one man actually jumped to his feet and ran out of the room! They were amazed to see the images of factory workers moving up on the cloth screen as they exited the Lumière Factory in one of the short film clips. A pianist was hired to provide added excitement to the action being observed by the overwhelmed audiences. *The use of music in this way would start a precedent that would become a tradition throughout the entire period of silent pictures.*

The Lumières had rented this room for thirty francs a day. By the middle of the following year, they were averaging twenty-five hundred francs a day in receipts. The Lumière brothers were successful manufacturers of photographic equipment as well as capable amateur photographers. They wished to test the commercial value of some of their earliest films by test screening them before patrons at this coffee house. The Lumière's **Cinematographie**, the lightweight, handcranked camera that doubled as the apparatus that also projected their films, is the name from which the word "cinema" comes.

These early movie projectors were quite noisy and evidently distracting to the audience. The music provided by the pianist would help to cover the sounds made by this mechanical device. Eventually, movie projectors would be housed in their own soundproof projection rooms, but, until that time, *music served a multipurpose of providing additional emphasis to the moods and actions on the screen as well as providing a means of blocking out the unwanted mechanical sounds of the projector. It could also be argued that the three-dimensional quality of music in these early theaters provided a "hook" to scoop moviegoers into the action or drama as seen on the two-dimensional screen.*

Moving pictures were first shown to the public in locations such as cafés, university lecture halls, vaudeville theaters, fairgrounds, and in any vacant building available to the exhibitor. Over the next two to three decades, huge movie palaces would be erected for the purpose of public exhibition.

By February 20, 1896, the Lumière program was being shown to patrons in England. Later that year, in some of the theaters in Great Britain, film presentations were being accompanied by orchestras, instead of using the standard piano accompaniment. These early films *preserved history* in a way never seen before. For generations to come, people would be able to see what life was like back at the turn of the century. We can see now deceased political figures, architectural creations destroyed by fire, floods, or world wars. When the films were first shown in the late nineteenth century, they helped new immigrants understand the customs of the United States. A new art form had been born and was here to stay! The *motion picture camera* became one of the most influential inventions of the next century, affecting culture—hairstyles, fashions, sensitivity to violence, sexual acceptance, and other moral and ethical issues. As Kevin Brownlow states in his wonderful book *The Parade's Gone By*, "The secret of the silent film lay in its unique ability to conjure up a situation that closely involved an audience, because demands were made on its imagination."[1] It is true that the dreamlike world of silent images—whether a still photograph, a painting, or a silent film—opens the viewer's mind to unlimited interpretations, depending on the individual's state of mind. Some people can look at a photo of a river and can imagine a placid scenario. Other people can look at the same photo and can imagine a body of water filled with pollution. Filmmakers would soon realize the effectiveness of the world of silent images. *Music was added to help convey and amplify the moods represented in the various situations on the screen.*

As immigrants arrived into the United States, motion pictures were still in their infancy. However, it was this group of people that helped to make the motion picture industry a success. They provided a natural audience for these silent images . . . images that did *not* talk, images that were easily understood by *any* nationality regardless of any language barrier.

In the late nineteenth century, European filmmakers were technically far superior to their American counterparts. American filmmakers used crude sets and poor lighting. Stage actors were hesitant to appear in these early "flickers," as they were called. It was thought *undignified* to be seen as a movie actor in the early days of cinema. However, the $5.00 a day fee became attractive to unemployed actors during the summer months.

As improvements were made on the screen, film exhibitors began to get excited about trying to synchronize silent films with early phonograph recordings.

1. Kevin Brownlow, *The Parade's Gone By* (Berkeley: University of California Press, 1968).

In 1904, a device known as a **Chronophone** was first exhibited. This event took place in London, England, and was an attempt at lining up a gramophone recording (early forerunner of the modern LP record) with the picture up on screen. This device was invented by the Frenchman Leon Gaumont. Interestingly enough, the Chronophone was very similar to the Vitaphone, a device that would accompany the first successful feature film with spoken dialogue twenty-three years later. *This first known gramophone synchronizer* was not effective. Gunshots could be heard in places that were meant to be tender love scenes, because the speeds of the projector and the Chronophone were not lined up correctly. People such as Thomas Edison (1847–1931) in the United States, Oskar Messter (1866–1943) in Berlin, and Charles Pathé (1863–1957) in Paris were experimenting with developing the synchronization of the gramophone recording to the moving picture.

Meanwhile, during the first decade of the twentieth century, locations showing movies were springing up all over the country here in the United States. Almost every town had a place in which, as the movies were being shown, a keyboard player—usually a pianist or an organist—would follow the action up on the screen with their eyes and would improvise music to coincide with the action. Eventually, thousands of musicians were employed throughout the country. The largest theater in the United States at the time was the Capitol Theater in New York City. It employed six organists, but most of the smaller theaters throughout the country hired part-time pianists and organists who relied heavily on a collection of mood music so that they could have, at their command, a vast array of moods to match any conceivable event the filmmaker could invent. As time passed and as the larger cities began to build huge theaters, symphony orchestras were employed to accompany the silent images.

In 1903, Edwin S. Porter, a director for the Edison Company, shot a film across the Hudson River from New York City in Patterson, New Jersey, that would *change the way of thinking about movies*. The film was called *The Great Train Robbery* and lasted only about twelve minutes. Although this film is quite trite by today's standards, it made a great impact on audiences of that time. People in the audience shouted, "Play it again!" *It was the first smash hit.*

Most films up until that time were **single shot films**—the camera focused on only one scene for the entire film. In *The Great Train Robbery,* Porter took a series of separate shots and edited them together into a chain of images. This was the beginning of the "story" films. The plot was quite simple. A group of bandits attack the telegraph office at a train station. As the train pulls into the station, the bandits take control of the train. They rob the passengers of their valuables and dynamite the mail car's safe, killing the post office worker in the process. Then they ride off on horseback with their booty. The telegraph operator is rescued by his daughter, whereupon he alerts the men at the town's tavern. An exciting chase on horseback ensues between the bandits and the townspeople. When the bandits stop to divide up their loot, they are surrounded by the townsfolk and every one of the bandits is shot dead. According to David Parkinson, in his book *History of Film,* this film "established the basic principles of continuity editing and did much to widen the vocabulary of film's universal language."[2] At this point, original scores for an individual film were still a thing of the future. *The Great Train Robbery* and other films of this time could be accompanied by anything from a piano to a vaudeville/music hall orchestra. By 1907, there were approximately three thousand **nickelodeons**—theaters where shows cost a nickel for admission—throughout the United States. Programs lasted anywhere from fifteen minutes to one hour, and they changed every day. In the bigger cities, pianists were replaced by a live ensemble of varying size (chamber groups of three people to orchestras up to one hundred people). Many of these theaters had enormous theater organs capable of providing music, plus additional sounds such as thunder, gunshots, police sirens, and birdcalls. A **soundman** would sit down in the orchestra pit with the orchestra or behind the screen where he could add any array of sound effects to the action on screen.

Theater organists would amass impressive repertoires ranging from pop tunes of the period to the classics. It wasn't long before several men decided to collect and publish bound volumes of mood

2. David Parkinson, *History of Film* (London: Thames & Hudson, 1995).

music to be used by other musicians in the pit. Because many of these musical compositions were not yet in the **public domain** (that is, their performance use was not "tax free"), this became a financial goldmine for many composers. An organization known as **ASCAP** (American Society of Composers, Authors, and Publishers) charged each movie theater a fee of 10¢ per seat per year for access to the catalogue of fifty leading publishers.

One such volume of collected mood music, published in 1924, was *Motion Picture Moods for Pianists and Organists,* compiled by Erno Rapée. In this 678-page volume, Rapée assembled a collection of over two hundred themes representing fifty-two moods. Musical selections range from lullabies and love themes to exciting chase music and the sound of sinister and grotesque themes guaranteed to frighten even the strongest viewer. Rapée included anthems from over thirty countries to give films a certain nationalistic flavor as well as collecting various styles of dance music for each needed occasion. He noted that in most films of the time, one-third of the films depicted *action,* one-third depicted emotional or *psychological situations,* and the remaining one-third of the films dealt with *scenery* or *atmosphere.* This is how he chose the selections contained within this volume. Most of the musical selections were either one- or two-page keyboard pieces. In the margin of each page was a listing of each mood contained within the book, along with page numbers, for rapid-fire execution as the moment warranted. As movies lengthened from the ten- to twenty-minute running times to the six-reeler, lasting about an hour, the tunes in this book and similar collections would become ineffective.

Other volumes of mood music included the *Sam Fox Moving Picture Volumes* (seventy original pieces in four volumes published in the years 1913–1914, with the last volume appearing in 1923) compiled by J. S. Zamecnik, and the *Kinobibliothek* (known as the *Kinothek*), compiled by Giuseppe Becce. The *Kinothek,* first published in Berlin in 1919, was the best-known collection of the period.

Some movie directors would hire musicians to be present on the set, during the filming of the scenes throughout the silent period, specifically to inspire the actors or actresses into the needed moods required by the script. Several actors of yesteryear requested a particular song to be performed by the musicians to bring them to tears.

Victor Fleming (with hat) seen directing a silent film starring Clara Bow called Mantrap *(1926). Note: The live musicians in the right foreground used to set the mood. From the author's collection.*

Battle Music

Piano accompaniment Hugo Riesenfeld

Example of mood music

N° 8.

2 Minuten
ohne Wiederholung

Sturm

Storm, Tempest ✤ Tempête

Piano

Ernst Wiedermann Op. 15

Example of mood music

Camille Saint-Saëns. From the author's collection.

It would be inevitable that filmmakers would eventually realize that music arranged or even composed for a specific film would be overwhelmingly more effective than these snippets of mood music found in the above-mentioned volumes.

The Appearance of the First Original Movie Score

The first known original score written for a film appeared in 1908—*L'assassinat du Duc de Guise (The Assassination of the Duke of Guise*) by the French composer Camille Saint-Saëns (1835–1921), but it was not until the mid-1920s that original scores started to appear in abundance, as directors became more aware of the value of individually written scores.

The Birth of a Nation

The Birth of a Nation (originally released as *The Clansman*) had its opening night in Los Angeles on February 8, 1915. This movie had one of the earliest specially composed scores written for films made in the United States. The composer hired for the project, Joseph Carl Breil (1870–1926), wrote some original themes and used arrangements of well-known music for this massive three-hour epic about the American Civil War. The score was written for a forty-piece orchestra to be performed live in sync with 1,544 individual scenes. Because many Americans had never heard live symphony orchestra concerts, the classical music of composers such as Beethoven and Wagner, whose works were used in this score, helped to expose many people to some of the music classics. As a result, many moviegoers who first saw this great epic wrongly assumed that the entire score was exclusively by Breil. *In addition to borrowing from classical music, Breil also used music from American folk songs.* As an example, near the end of the film, as a group of white people are attacked in a log cabin by renegade ex-slaves, we hear the music from Richard Wagner's *The Ride of the Valkyries* (composed in 1870 for the opera *Die Walküre*). During this sequence, we see members of the Ku Klux Klan ride on horseback to their rescue. Moments later, as we see the "parade of the Clansman" on screen, we hear the well-known strains of the Civil War song "Dixie." The movie concludes with an arrangement of "The Star Spangled Banner." The Breil score was eventually made available in printed form, as were other scores of important American films.

The Birth of a Nation told an epic tale of the American Civil War and its aftermath by focusing on two families on opposite sides of the conflict. The father of the northern family pushes through legislation that gives rights to the freed slaves after the war, while the son of the southern family helps start the Ku Klux Klan in response to outrages committed by African American slaves in his town. This film caused great race relationship problems throughout the United States, and led to rioting in Boston and other American cities. The film was banned in several American cities because of this. This film, which glorified the Ku Klux Klan, *became the most successful silent film ever made,* grossing over $10,000,000 in its first run. *This is the film that launched the age of the full-length motion picture. It showed many people in the movie business the potential for great financial profit in full-length movies,* helping to start the fortunes and careers of people such as Louis B. Mayer.

D. W. Griffith. From the author's collection.

The man behind all of this was D. W. Griffith (1875–1948). According to Ephraim Katz in *The Film Encyclopedia,* Griffith is the "single most important figure in the history of American film and one of the most influential in the development of world cinema as an art."[3] The film historian Kevin Brownlow, in his book *The Parade's Gone By,* states, "*The Birth of a Nation* was the first feature to be made in the same fluid way as pictures today. It was the most widely seen production of the time and it had the strongest influence."[4] *This film became the first blockbuster in film history.* Griffith paid close attention to every detail in the filming of this epic. He brought in actual witnesses who were present in Ford's Theater in Washington, D.C., the night Abraham Lincoln was assassinated, to observe his recreation of this historic event within his film. Intimate details from Civil War veterans from both sides who were still alive helped to lay out the battle scenes used in the movie. To recreate the fierce power of General Sherman's March to the Sea, an entire city was built, only to be destroyed by fire on camera to lend an air of realism. All uniforms were recreated for historical accuracy by two hundred seamstresses working for two months. Replicas of military weapons used by both sides during the Civil War were also used. Five thousand works and reports on the history of the Civil War were researched for historic data. Griffith directed eighteen thousand people and three thousand horses in one of cinema's most-seen movies of all time. He labored for eight months without a break, at an estimated cost of $500,000, to make this milestone film, which even today *remains as one of America's most controversial cinema landmarks.* As a rather sad footnote, D. W. Griffith died in a Hollywood hotel room, a bitter, lonely, and nearly forgotten man, ravaged by alcohol in 1948 at the age of seventy-three.

Ben-Hur (1925)

Ben-Hur, the most expensive movie of the silent era (it cost about $4,000,000 to make [equivalent to $160,000,000 today]), was first shown on December 30, 1925, in New York City, at the George M. Cohan Theater. The audience was ecstatic with the excitement of the chariot race and the action of the naval battle sequences. The filming of the naval battle sequence took place in Italy using full-size ships. Many extras from poverty-stricken cities in Italy were used. Because these people needed the money, they had lied about being able to swim. One of the boats used in the battle sequence was covered in oil so that it would easily burn. Unfortunately, an unexpected wind blew violently during the sequence, the ship burst into flames, and many extras, wearing Roman armor, panicked and dropped to their knees in prayer. Others jumped over the side of the boat. Although there are differing accounts, some

3. Ephraim Katz, *The Film Encyclopedia* (New York: Putnam, 1979).
4. Brownlow.

witnesses stated that as many as eleven extras drowned. Naturally, fearing the worst in publicity, director Fred Niblo assured everyone that no one was killed. During the filming of the chariot race sequence in the Italian set of the Circus Maximus, a stunt man was killed when his chariot wheel broke and he was catapulted into a pile of rubble. The entire cast and crew were moved back to the United States where a new one hundred-acre Circus Maximus set was constructed to refilm the chariot race. The location of this set was on the present-day intersection of Venice Boulevard and La Cienega Boulevard in Los Angeles. The race started as forty-two cameras recorded the action. According to contemporary reports of persons present during the filming, the race was dull. In order to make the race more breathtaking, a $5,000 reward was offered to the winner of the race.[5] Now the race became a fight to the finish. So that a full-scale Circus Maximus did not have to be constructed, only the lower portion of the stadium was built. This held several thousand extras, while the rest of the structure comprised a hanging miniature suspended several feet away from the camera, in front of the real lower portion of the stadium. To match the movement of the real people in the stands, movable dolls on wooden dowels were used to simulate the rising and sitting cheering crowds. When photographed together, the effect is very believable.

The exciting Chariot Race from the silent version of Ben-Hur *(1925). Courtesy of Archive Photos.*

5. According to Bosley Crowther, in his book *The Lion's Share* (1957), a bonus of $150.00 was offered to the winner.

MGM had hired two composers to write the score for this great epic: David Mendoza and William Axt (1882–1959), a composing team who had worked together on other assignments, including King Vidor's film, *The Big Parade* (1925), and *Don Juan* (1926). *Don Juan* used the musical score recorded on disc to accompany the silent images, making it *the first film with a fully synchronized score.* One year later, this same system (sound-on-disc, called Vitaphone) would be the vehicle that Warner Brothers Studio would use in the groundbreaking film *The Jazz Singer* (1927). Although David Mendoza's career as a film composer ended in 1939, his real interest was back in New York writing music for radio and the theater. William Axt went on to compose over ninety more scores for MGM Studios between 1925 and 1939, and became the head of MGM's music department in the 1930s.

Today, we are able to view *Ben-Hur* with a completely restored pristine copy of the 1925 print, accompanied by a newly composed score by the modern composer, Carl Davis. Davis has made a distinguished career as the premiere composer of new scores for restored films from the silent era. Davis uses several leitmotifs for main characters such as Ben-Hur and Messala, and even bases portions of his score on certain elements of the original 1925 score of Mendoza and Axt.

As you view the naval battle, it almost seems as though you are watching a sound film with a modern soundtrack because Carl Davis's score is so effectively done. The chariot race is also greatly en-

CARL DAVIS

American composer Born: October 28, 1936

He now lives in England and has made an excellent reputation composing scores for old silent films that have been restored. These scores include: *Napoleon* (1927, restored 1980), *The Crowd* (1928, restored 1981), *Show People* (1928, restored 1982), *Flesh and the Devil* (1927, restored 1982), *The Thief of Bagdad* (1924, restored 1985), and other silent film classics such as *The Big Parade, Intolerance, Greed, The General, The Wind, Ben-Hur,* and *Phantom of the Opera.*

As a boy of nine, Davis used to study the scores to the classical compositions to be performed the following week on the radio. He would study what the composers had written. He was particularly fond of Gilbert and Sullivan operettas. He attended Queen's College in New York and the New England College of music. He was appointed piano accompanist with the famed Robert Shaw Chorale and did three nationwide tours with them. One day, at a music shop in Philadelphia, he looked down at a blank book of music manuscript paper and decided to fill it with music that he had in his head. It wasn't long before he became hooked as a composer. Jerome Robbins, the director of *West Side Story,* was impressed by Davis's work. Davis decided to move to Europe, and eventually settled in England in 1961. There he made a name for himself writing music for radio plays and the live theater. This transitioned into television music and finally film scoring projects. Davis's love of books and his strong feeling of drama have played a strong part in his success as a film composer. He said that he tries "to convey some of the excitement and drama that these books gave me."

In 1991, Carl Davis collaborated with Paul McCartney on the *Liverpool Oratorio.* He is also a conductor and has been conductor of the London Philharmonic.

Some of his more memorable film scores for modern films include: *The French Lieutenant's Woman* (for which he won the British Academy Award), *The Far Pavillions, King David, The Rainbow, The Girl in the Swing,* and *Widow's Peak.* As a composer, Davis is a great admirer of the music of Mozart and says that he could listen to his music all day long. He also enjoys the music of twentieth-century classical composers Bela Bartók, Igor Stravinsky, Sergei Prokofiev, and Dimitri Shostakovich. He states that he does not like the term "film composer": "I think that one should just be a composer and write for films as well as for other things."

hanced by the victorious trumpet fanfarelike motive for Ben-Hur, and the ominous, dark, and sinister-sounding musical motive for his enemy, Messala. The differing speed of sixteen frames per second back in the silent days versus the modern twenty-four frames per second standard has been accounted for in this restoration, to produce a natural-looking lifelike rendition of the action. This would explain why many of the older films, when viewed at the faster frame speed of today, appear to be jerky with rapid movement of action.

Battleship Potemkin

In 1925, the Russian filmmaker Sergei Eisenstein (1898–1948) made a silent film classic. Several international panels have voted *Battleship Potemkin* (pronounced: "Pa-chompkin") the greatest film of all time. The bold imagery and rapid rhythmic editing create a silent film that almost needs no musical score to

Scene from the film Battleship Potemkin *showing the infamous slaughter on the Odessa Steps. From the author's collection.*

accompany it. The viewer is able to feel the flow, rhythm, and texture of each scene, as though Eisenstein was a musical composer himself. The viewer feels the tension, the violence, and the horror of the concrete images on screen. Like modern music, which is harsh and dissonant to the listener's ears, the visual imagery of *Battleship Potemkin* clashes with the nerves and senses, leaving the viewer numb.

Potemkin, as American audiences know it, is a five-reel film that was made for the twentieth anniversary of the 1905 workers' revolution at Odessa Harbor. Although the film shows the mutiny on board the battleship during the earlier portion of the film, it is the "Odessa Steps" sequence that is forever ingrained in the minds of the viewer.

The citizens are carrying on their business as usual, around Odessa Harbor, when—without warning—the Russian czar's troops march down the outdoor steps, trampling and shooting every man, woman, and child in their path. At the bottom of this large set of steps were mounted Cossacks, who join the attack slaughtering people of all ages without mercy. Eisenstein's masterful montage has been accompanied over the years by the music of several composers. The score provided by German composer Edmund Meisel (1874–1930) was said to create an even greater impact on the viewing audience than Eisenstein had ever dreamed possible. *Potemkin* was banned in Berlin by government decree, if accompanied by Meisel's music, because it could cause an uproar. Composers such as Dimitri Shostakovich and Eric Allaman also composed newer scores for this silent classic.

The Rise of the "Feature Film"

From the earliest days of public exhibition in the 1890s to 1917, when the tide began to change on attaining respectability, the movie industry was now in full swing. By 1917, the length of films had grown from one reel (lasting about ten to twelve minutes) to one hour or even ninety minutes. The filmmakers were now making *"feature" films (adopting the term "feature" from the vaudeville usage of the same word to mean the program's main attraction).* Film directors had now mastered their ability to make longer narratives with more finesse. During World War I, the European film studios suffered disruption. Because of this, the focus of major filmmaking turned to Hollywood. Hollywood became the movie capital of the world, a distinction still held today.

The Coming of the Mighty Movie Theater

Moviegoers sat entranced in comfortable movie palaces instead of the cramped cafés and lecture halls of the earliest days of cinema. These movie palaces rivaled some of the greatest architectural creations of mankind. By the end of the silent era (1927), gigantic theaters capable of sitting over six thousand patrons had been constructed. The largest of these movie palaces was the Roxy Theater in New York City. These huge theaters were decorated with elaborate interiors of art work on the ceilings, on the walls, or wherever there was a need to impress the moviegoing public. In the Roxy, nicknamed "The Cathedral of the Motion Picture," sixty-two hundred seats had been installed with additional room for twenty-five hundred patrons standing in line formation in various foyers. The orchestra pit held one hundred musicians, with an enormous pipe organ equipped with a triple console (keyboard), capable of being played by three organists at the same time. It was the largest organ in the world. There were approximately three hundred people in the management corps to help the patrons to their seats.

The acoustics in this palatial theater were so fine-tuned that a person making an announcement from the stage, without the benefit of a microphone, could be heard hundreds of feet away in the remotest seat in the theater. An elaborate air conditioning system kept theatergoers bathed in purified clean air and at a consistent temperature, regardless of the air or weather conditions in New York. Each seat was richly upholstered and allowed plenty of room for people to pass before you to their seats without touching your knees. The architecture of these movie palaces was a triumph. No kings or emperors have wandered through more luxurious surroundings. Today, as we attend our generic multiplex movie theaters, very few of these great theaters remain. Only a handful have been historically preserved. Even the great Roxy Theater vanished into a pile of rubble at the crashing of the wrecking ball in the summer of 1960 to make way for "progress" . . . a new office building. As Ben Hall states in his wonderful account of these "shrines-of-the-make-believe" in *The Best Remaining Seats,* "Fallow ground . . . marked the realm where fantasy reigned, where romance and adventure flourished, where magic and charm united us all to worship at beauty's throne."[6]

There were basically four types of music during the silent period.

1. **Piano improvisation**—a pianist would follow the action up on the screen with their eyes and would attempt to reflect the mood and speed of the movie's action with their piano playing, becoming an "instant composer," as one contemporary put it. At first, pianists would have to rely on their own repertoire. Eventually, bound volumes of mood music were published by various people.
2. **Published musical extracts**—these, the second type of music used, became very important to musicians of the silent era. As films were sent out from Hollywood to all of the theaters around the country, "*cue sheets*" were sent with the cans of film. Unfortunately, many of these cue sheets were lost in transit from one theater to the next or they were mislaid by the management of the theater. These cue sheets were usually single pages of suggested music or extracts of musical selections that could be performed by either the pianist or pit orchestras. The lists of possible music to be used could range from a one-page piano piece to a more lengthy multipage piece for pit orchestra. The cue sheet would usually indicate the length of each cue to be used and would tell the musician what to look for on screen to enable them to change to the next musical selection. Also, many of these cue sheets would suggest possible sound effects to be utilized to coincide with the screen action. There was usually a soundman who would sit either in the pit or behind the screen to supply the necessary sound effects. On occasion, several people would sit behind the screen and would read the lines from a script to give the illusion, to members of the audience, that the actors on screen were actually speaking.
3. **Prearranged scores**—derived from familiar musical sources. The music director of a theater in a large city, working with a musical assistant, would view the film and would choose musical selections that would then be arranged to fit the action up on the screen. These musical arrangements usually lasted from thirty seconds to three minutes. At times, the cues would have to be ended abruptly if the action on screen suddenly changed. Because many of these theaters did not use the same music to accompany a film as it came out of Hollywood, the possibility of a wide variety of interpretations was forever present.
4. **Original score**—created for specific films. In the earlier days of feature films, original scores were not yet practical because many films were too short-lived, the distribution system too far-flung, and musicians too varied in ensemble and too uneven in talent to justify original scores. Today, the overwhelming majority of films use originally written scores, because filmmakers realize the impact customized music can make on their films.

6. Ben M. Hall, *The Best Remaining Seats* (New York: Da Capo Press, 1975).

Review Questions

Discussion

1. What are some of the reasons that music was used in the earliest days of cinema?

2. Can you think of a historically significant reason why cinema is helpful to us today when looking back at the turn of the century?

3. Discuss the four types of music used during the silent era.

4. If *The Birth of a Nation* were shown in theaters today, what would be the possible social and political ramifications?

Short Answer

1. How did we arrive at the word "cinema" for motion pictures?________________________________

   ____.

2. Where were movies first shown? ____

   ____.

3. Who were the Lumière brothers and why were they important? ______________________

   ____.

4. What is the Chronophone and was it effective? ________________________________

____.

5. Who were the people experimenting with the development of synchronizing the gramophone recordings to the picture and what was their country of origin? ____________________

   ____

   ____

   ____.

6. Why is Edwin S. Porter significant? ____________________

   ____.

7. What was the name of the "movies' first smash hit?" ____________________

   ____.

8. What is meant by a "single shot" film? ____________________

   ____.

9. What was the role of the soundman in theaters showing silent pictures? ____________________

   ____.

10. Why did some movie directors hire musicians in the silent days? ____________________

    ____.

11. What is the name of the first original score, who composed it, and in what year? __________

    ____.

12. What is the name of the most successful movie of the silent era? ____________________

    ____.

13. What is significant about the score for *Don Juan*? ____________________

    ____.

14. How did we get the name "feature film?" ____________________

    ____.

15. What world event caused a shift in movie production in Europe to make Hollywood the movie capital of the world? ______________________________.

16. What was the name of the theater that was able to accommodate sixty-two hundred seated patrons? ______________________________ .

Define the following

Vitaphone ______________________________

D. W. Griffith ______________________________

Joseph Carl Breil ______________________________

Kinothek ______________________________

ASCAP ______________________________

Kinetoscope ______________________________

Chapter Four

Music in the Early Sound Film (Late 1920s to 1933)

Even from the earliest days of public exhibition, films weren't ever really silent, as one might expect from the term "silent films." As we have seen, film exhibitors accompanied their films with music since the first days of the medium. Throughout the period of experimentation, when various inventors were trying their hand at synchronizing recorded music on discs with the picture up on the screen, another variable to contend with was finding an amplification system that would adequately boost the sound in the larger auditoriums and theaters. Also, the need to change the discs frequently during the showing of the film could easily throw the music and picture out of sync with one another.

In 1919, several German inventors (Josef Engel, Hans Vogt, and Joseph Massole) *devised a system that could photograph sound waves on the edge of the film.* This sound could be reproduced when the film was run through the movie projector. In essence, we now had "sound-on-film." This invention, known as the Tri-Ergon system, worked on the principle of using photoelectric cells to convert sound waves into light waves (electric impulses). As the celluloid film ran past another photoelectric cell in the head of the projector, there was synchronized sound on the film itself, as these light waves were converted back into sound waves. This also meant that we now had no need for live music in the movie theaters. In the future, dialogue, sound effects, and the music would all be self-contained on a part of the film that became known as the soundtrack. Another inventor, from France, worked on an early sound-on-film process back in 1910—Eugene Lauste. He was not able to get financial backing for his project because of World War I.

By 1922, a New Yorker named Lee De Forest (1873–1961) perfected a vacuum tube that greatly improved the sound-on-film process. This "audion" tube, invented in 1906, took the electronic sound signals and pushed the sound through speakers with much improved amplification for even the largest theaters. By adding this tube to a **sound-on-film system** invented by two men (Theodore Case [1888–1944] and Earl Sponable [1895–1977]) from Auburn, New York, De Forest gave us the crucial link necessary for the success of the sound-on-film process. It became known as the **"Phonofilm" system**.

During the period from 1923 to 1927, more than one thousand short sound films featuring opera singers, politicians, and vaudeville acts were made. During this same period, the new excitement of radio broadcasts posed a great threat to the advancement of motion pictures. A big radio broadcast had the capability of emptying movie theaters all across the country, much the same way as television can today. Ironically, had the movie moguls used Lee De Forest's "Phonofilm" system back in 1923, when it was first demonstrated, they might have won back their huge audiences away from radio. In 1923, Lee De Forest became the first entrepreneur to exploit the commercial possibilities of the "talking" motion picture by showing several short films throughout the East Coast of the United States. Unfortunately, De Forest was not a shrewd businessman, so his venture did not get a running start. Movie executives were leery of this new invention and were afraid of the cost of adapting each theater with this new sound system. The coinventor of the sound-on-film process, Theodore Case, negotiated a million-dollar deal with William Fox, head of the Fox Film Corporation. When De Forest found out about this, he sued Fox for patent infringement on his Phonofilm system. The Fox-Case Corporation was formed from this business venture, much to the consternation of Lee De Forest. The Case-Sponable sound-on-film system enabled this studio to make sound films. The result of this was the now-famous Fox Movietone newsreels. These were weekly accounts of the happenings-in-the-news from around the world, shown to movie patrons each week, before the start of their regular feature films. They were the first sound newsreels.

The *first hit song to come from an early sound film* came from a Fox Film Corporation movie, *What Price Glory?* (1926). The music was composed by Erno Rapée; the song was called "Charmaine." This would eventually trigger a trend of using pop songs to help sell movies, a trend that is still very much alive today in the marketing of films.

Since radio could give audiences live musical performances, comedians, and entertaining dramas, movies would have to make a drastic change in direction if they wanted to survive. That new direction came in the form of *sound* films.

The other sound system, **Vitaphone (sound-on-disc)**, was making strides—Warner Bros. exhibited *the first feature-length sound film without dialogue*. The principle involved a system by which electric signals picked up by the microphone on the set were transformed to seventeen-inch wax discs by disc-cutting machines that were locked in sync with the film cameras. On the evening of August 6, 1926, patrons at the Warner Theater in New York City witnessed history in the making at the showing of *Don Juan*. This film, starring John Barrymore, was released with a clever sound-on-disc format that showcased a prerecorded musical soundtrack, performed by the New York Philharmonic, complete with added sound effects. The music was that of the two men who had written the score for the 1925 version of *Ben-Hur,* William Axt and David Mendoza, with contributions from Major Edward Bowes. This performance was made possible by having the soundtrack on several large discs. The discs would be changed with each reel of film. Fortunately, after years of experimentation and failure, the day of success had finally come. This early sound film was impressive. However, it was still basically a silent film with recorded music, because *dialogue was still missing.*

In 1926, Sam Warner, one of the members of the famous Warner Bros. Studio team, was excited about the possibility of introducing films with complete scores that would be synchronized with the picture. He sold the idea to his other brothers that movies with musical scores in sync with the picture would improve business at the company's smaller theaters. Interestingly enough, Sam Warner had no vision of making "talking" pictures with these new innovations. Instead, he was overjoyed with the ability to have synchronized *musical scores* to enhance the films. One year later, the Warner brothers would change their minds and would drastically change the art of movie making forever, by making the landmark film that launched the age of the sound films.

The Jazz Singer

On October 6, 1927, *The Jazz Singer* premiered at the Warner Theater on Broadway and 52nd Street in New York City. This was the *first feature film to contain some spoken dialogue* and would be the film that would revolutionize the movie industry. *The Jazz Singer* was really a silent film incorporating a few

Opening night of The Jazz Singer *in New York City. Courtesy Marc Wanamaker/Bison Archives.*

inserts with sound; nonetheless, it still was enough to become the film that everyone remembers as the pioneer of sound in film. It used the Vitaphone system. As Scott Eyman states in his book *The Speed of Sound,* this premiere "proved to be the theatrical equivalent of the moon landing."[1]

The showing of *The Jazz Singer* was a magic moment in cinema history. The movie starred Al Jolson, deemed "the greatest entertainer in the world," and centered on the story of a Jewish cantor's son who was torn between the synagogue and show business.

In this movie, little Jakie Rabinowitz was supposed to follow in his father's footsteps and be a cantor in the Jewish synagogue, just as his father was, and just as all of his grandfathers had been going back five generations. Unfortunately, Jakie did not want to be a cantor and sing religious music; he wanted to be in the theater and sing jazz. One night, when Jakie was singing jazz songs at Muller's Café, his father burst into the theater and stormed up the aisle. Jakie turned ashen at the sight. He stopped singing when his father jumped up on the platform and dragged Jakie down by the collar. Now Jakie's face was red. He was ashamed before all of the people in the café who had been so supportive of his singing. Now, he could never go back there again because his father had found him

1. Scott Eyman, *The Speed of Sound* (New York: Simon & Schuster, 1997).

"performing music for the devil instead of for God." Back at their home, as the father prepared to punish Jakie, the little boy threatened "to run away if you whip me again." The inevitable happened. Jakie ran away much to the sadness of his parents. Years later, Jakie, now a fully grown man (and played by Al Jolson), returns to his parents' house. There he finds his father teaching young boys in the ways of the Jewish faith and finds his mother preparing something in the kitchen. It is when Jakie sits down at the piano and begins to play for his mother that we realize that the sound from the piano playing and the voices of the characters on screen are actually emanating from behind the screen. Sound in full-length motion pictures had been born and was here to stay. It is said that when Jakie's father enters the room where Jakie is playing and singing for his mother, and yells "Stop!" that this signifies the end of the silent era and the beginning of the sound age.

A musical score for this film was supervised by Louis Silvers (d. 1954), who went on to write scores for Warner Bros., Columbia Pictures, and 20th Century Fox until 1939. The premiere of this pioneering film was a resounding success according to audience members, who reportedly went wild at the sound of Jolson's improvised dialogue as he spoke the now immortal words, "You ain't heard nothin' yet!"

It is perhaps a cruel twist of fate that none of the four Warner brothers was able to attend this landmark premiere. Sam Warner, the man behind the Vitaphone experiment, died of pneumonia while recovering from surgery for a sinus infection at the age of thirty-nine (1888–1927), the day before the premiere. His three remaining brothers immediately left for his funeral in Los Angeles, missing this historic moment in cinema history.

The Jazz Singer was not only a milestone in cinema history because of its pioneering use of sound; it also marked the screen debut of Al Jolson. For ten years, motion picture studios had tried to entice him to the screen with fabulous salary offers. They failed. It was not until this Warner Bros. production that he went before the filmgoing public.

The Impact of the Addition of Sound to Motion Pictures

Although many people heralded the addition of sound to the motion picture with great excitement, not everyone in the industry welcomed the advent of sound with open arms.

Several Reasons Why the Advent of Sound Challenged Filmmakers

First of all, *since the music would now be part of the film itself, there would no longer be the need for live musicians in the movie theaters across the country*. This meant that over one hundred thousand musicians lost their jobs because of this new breakthrough in technology. This was a real tragedy, because in the 1920s the cinema had become the world's largest employer of musicians. Only a handful of the most enterprising musicians were wise enough to head West to become part of the recording studio orchestras. This could not have come at a worse time for many of these musicians, because looming around the corner was the great stock market crash leading to the Great Depression. Several cities around the country continued to use a core of live musicians as entertainment even after the advent of sound. These musicians would perform before the start of each feature presentation. In addition, Hollywood feared that *the arrival of spoken dialogue on screen would deprive silent stars of their ethereal appeal*. We all know what it is like to listen to a radio personality for several years and to comprise an imaginary composite as to what this person might look like based on the sound of their voice. We are usually surprised when we finally see that person to find that they usually look totally different from our imagined fantasy. The same was true for many of the silent stars, but in reverse. For years, women had swooned at the sight of the romantic leading man in the silent images up on the screen only to find that in the new sound films, he might have a high-pitched squeaky voice, or perhaps that a cowboy might have a thick Romanian accent. This crushed the careers of several silent stars whose talents were better suited to mime than to vocalization.

The addition of sound to movies also robbed the filmmakers of the dreamlike world of silent images. No longer could filmmakers make films in the same ways as the silent days. *Directors weren't able to shout instructions during a take.* Many felt that this made the smooth flow of a scene more difficult. *The introduction of sound posed artistic and technical problems primarily because of the inadequacy of the early microphones.* Actors had to be very near to the microphones because of their limited range. The awkwardness of the actors huddling around a concealed microphone in a flower arrangement meant that action was limited to staying within the range of the "mike." Scenes in which there were microphone placements on each side of the room also was no remedy. As actors would start out speaking within earshot of the first microphone, there would be silence as they moved across the room until they were within earshot of the second microphone. This problem was soon overcome by the invention of the **microphone boom** . . . the idea of fixing a microphone on a pole to make it more mobile. This meant that the cameras had to be placed in soundproof cubicles because the omnidirectional microphones would not only pick up the sound of the actors' voices but also the mechanical whine of the cameras. These large cubicles were clumsy and hindered camera movement permitting only thirty-degree tripod tilts. *The freedom of camera movement had been taken away.* In the early sound film, most of the action was filmed from a stationary camera. Also, the poor cameraman inside this hot, thickly padded "tomb" could not hear a thing when it came to the director's instructions or the actors' dialogue. In more than one instance, cameramen would pass out from lack of fresh air. The director would be excited by the performance only to later learn that the cameraman had collapsed on

For this shot outdoors, the microphone is placed on a long pole (called a boom). This microphone was enclosed within a megaphone to point it in the correct direction. This film was called Woman Hungry *(1931) and was filmed near Lone Pine, California. Courtesy Everett Collection.*

the floor of the compartment. Cameramen were eventually locked into these compartments after one unfortunate cameraman carelessly left the door open while hoping to get some ventilation, thus ruining the take. These camera cabinets created a claustrophobic quality to the openness once felt by the cameramen and their ability to film large panoramic vistas. Now they were by and large confined to sets at close range. As David Parkinson states in *History of Film,* "A concentration on the foreground meant that decor was neglected and space was robbed of its dramatic and psychological import."[2] By December 12, 1928, **cameras were "blimped"** in their own soundproof encasements, leading to absolutely silent camera operation. The large camera cubicles could now be done away with and the previous mobility of cameras in the silent era was now restored.

This sound camera was covered by sound-insulating material called a "blimp" and placed on a battery-operated dolly with rubber tires. This gave filmmakers more freedom of camera movement (from Lilies of the Field *[1930]). Courtesy Everett Collection.*

In the early days of sound films, the music had to be performed *at the same time* as the action was being shot, because at that time filmmakers did not have the ability to dub in music after the picture had been shot. This posed another problem. The microphones would distort easily if the orchestra was too close or if certain instruments were playing. The overall mix in the "mike" could be unusable because of the blurred quality of the actors' voices and instruments vying for prominence. George Eastman (1854–1932), one of the technical leaders of the film business who perfected the box camera designed for roll film, stated, "I wouldn't give a dime for all the possibilities of that invention [referring to sound movies]. The public will never accept it."[3] Harry Warner, one of the four Warner brothers, said, "Who the hell wants to hear actors talk? The music . . . that's the big plus about this."[4] In the early 1920s, studio executives were mostly apathetic to the attempts of adding sound to silent movies. Most executives felt that sound movies had been tried before but with little success . . . they simply did not work. Two movie moguls begged to differ about the promising prospects of sound movies, Sam Warner of Warner Bros. fame, and William Fox of Fox Film Corporation (later merging in 1935 with 20th Century Pictures to form 20th Century Fox). Warner would use the sound-on-disc sound system known as Vitaphone, whereas Fox opted for the sound-on-film system that later became the accepted format for all movie studios in the future. Both of these men had the faith and the vision to expand the horizons of movie making through the introduction of sound films. As Scott Eyman says in his book about the "talkie revolution," *The Speed of Sound,* "Sound made . . . movies less open to individual interpretation. Allusion

2. Parkinson, p. 86.
3. Eyman, p. 43.
4. Eyman, p. 70.

and metaphor were the bedrocks of the silent medium."[5] In a press release dated November 1, 1930, Charlie Chaplin, the great British-born U.S. comedian, stated that he detested the "talkies" and that he believes that they are only a passing fad. In an interview from *Silver Screen* magazine from that same year, Chaplin predicted "the imminent disappearance of pictures which are 100 percent talking. There is nothing that I could tell you about the talking pictures that would be more eloquent than my silence."[6]

From December 1926 to March 1927, a committee representing most of the major film companies in Hollywood evaluated the pros and cons of the various sound systems available. Their wishes were for adopting a universal sound system that could be used by everyone, making all equipment compatible. In May of 1928, the six major studios at that time entered into an agreement to adopt the *sound-on-film system* owned by *Western Electric*. Warner Bros. could see that their sound-on-disc system was on the way out, yet they continued its use until 1929. In that year, they reverted over to the sound-on-film system used by the other major studios, yet they still retained the name Vitaphone. The silent system had instantly become out of date, although the year 1928 was a year of transition. It took this year to refit the studios for sound productions and, for several months, sound films were released in alternate silent versions. By the end of the year, about eighty features with sound had been released.

Lights of New York

On July 8, 1928, *the first all-talking sound feature,* called *Lights of New York,* was released by Warner Bros. Later that year, Mortimer the mouse (later known as Mickey Mouse), made his debut in a clever animated cartoon with sound, called *Steamboat Willie.*

By the end of 1928, every major studio had talking pictures in production. *It was the novelty of sound pictures that enabled the studios to survive the Great Depression and the competition from radio.* By 1930, box office earnings had increased by 50 percent. The film industry had reason to be thankful for Warner Bros. in their timely pioneering into sound films, for it was this venture that helped to secure the future of the medium.

The Broadway Melody

In February 1929, MGM released *The Broadway Melody,* billed as "All-talking, all-singing, and all-dancing." This film set a milestone in the sound revolution, because, by the time it was released, many more Americans were able to see this particular film. This was because of the rapid installation of movie-theater sound systems throughout different parts of the country.

Blackmail

England's first sound feature was *Blackmail,* directed by the "master of suspense," Alfred Hitchcock. This was Hitchcock's tenth picture in England and his second thriller. It was hailed as the "First Full Length All Talkie Film Made in Great Britain," although another film, *The Clue of the New Pin,* was released several months earlier as a "talkie." The year was 1929, and by this time, Hollywood was responsible for

5. Eyeman, p. 20.
6. Robyn Karney, ed., *Chronicle of the Cinema* (New York: Dorling Kindersley, 1995), p. 220.

making more than three hundred sound films, a dramatic change since 1927. A year later, in 1930, the silent days would be nearly a thing of the past (except for a few Charlie Chaplin films made as silents). *Blackmail* was filmed in two different versions. The first version was a silent film with an M&E track, so that the film became a talking picture near the end. This version was released for the theaters that did not yet have the capability of showing sound films. The other version was an all-sound version using some of the original silent footage postdubbed with music and sound effects in addition to newly shot footage with dialogue sequences. It was this all-sound version that preceded the silent version by two months, opening on Friday, June 21, 1929. The music for *Blackmail* was compiled and arranged by Hubert Bath and Harry Stafford. Bath was an English composer who went on to compose at least seven more movie scores before his death in 1945, among them a score for Hitchcock's *The Thirty-Nine Steps* (1935). The music is used sparingly throughout most of *Blackmail*. The opening theme, heard as we see a spinning hubcap of a Scotland Yard police vehicle speeding through London's city streets on its way to round up a suspect, reappears several times in the movie to create unity as well as excitement in the final climax of the film, during the chase into the British Museum. This is a film about an ingenue who is invited back to an artist's studio after she had had a fight with her boyfriend. The artist wants to show off his etchings to the young girl. When his advances become a little too serious, she picks up a knife, for self-defense, and kills the artist. During this exciting murder sequence, Hitchcock refrains from using any music at all. The girl flees the artist's apartment, leaving behind a glove that will set up the opportunity for blackmail.

The Studio System

The 1930s marked the beginning of what has been referred to as the *classical era* of Hollywood cinema. The term *classical* in this case refers to the method of production and the aesthetic styles brought forth by those major studios who controlled production, distribution, and exhibition of the majority of the films being made. A "star system" was developed in which certain leading actors and actresses were under strict contract as a "contract player." This meant that, in most cases, each performer was "owned" by a specific studio for a term of seven years. The studios had the option to drop them before the end of the term, or the studio could lend the performer out to another studio for a profit. Performers could be suspended without pay for refusing a role. Publicity departments at each of the studios shaped an image for each star by leaking items of interest (good or bad publicity) to gossip columnists. Because some stars of the silent era had amassed huge fortunes, giving them considerable power, the movie moguls of the 1930s restricted the amount of money and power that these "stars" could have. Despite this, the 1930s is considered to be one of the most successful decades in motion picture history. Creatively and financially, the studios survived the Great Depression by creating a distinctive style at each studio, giving the public a variety of entertainment from which to choose.

MGM

MGM (Metro-Goldwyn-Mayer), claiming to have "more stars than there are in Heaven," was considered to be the flashiest and most glamorous of the studios. It boasted huge financial resources and specialized in family entertainment for the middle class. The studio had men such as Louis B. Mayer and Irving Thalberg at the helm. Mayer prided himself on "clean" pictures for family viewing.

Paramount Pictures

Paramount Pictures was a studio with a noble and opulent luster that encouraged a continental sophistication. It employed one of the greatest showmen in motion picture history, the mighty director, Cecil B. DeMille, considered by many to be the king of the epic filmmakers.

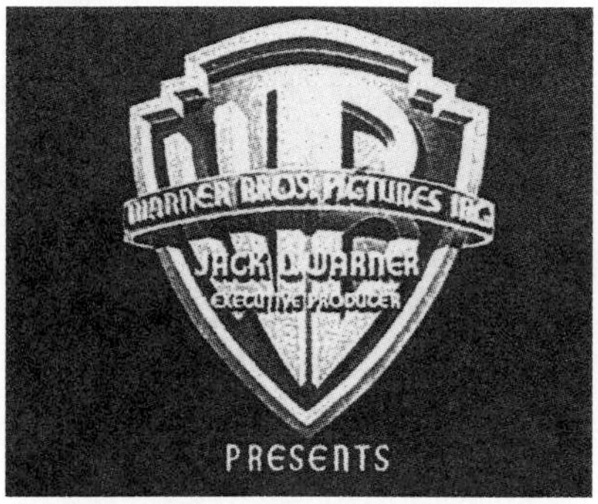

Warner Bros. Studio

Warner Bros. catered to the working class, showcasing a variety of films ranging from gangster movies (bringing stardom to James Cagney and Edward G. Robinson) to very entertaining musicals, complete with unequaled precision dance numbers by Busby Berkeley.

Universal Pictures

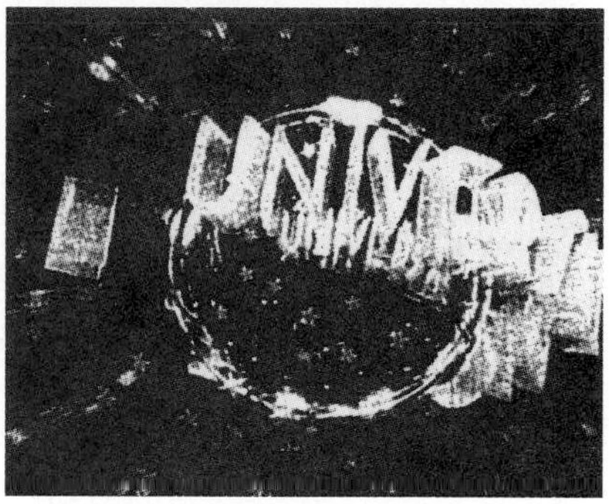

Universal Pictures made their mark in the public's eye as a producer of horror films, making films such as *Dracula* and *Frankenstein* (1931), and *The Bride of Frankenstein* (1935).

20th Century Fox Studios

20th Century Fox was formed in 1935, with Darryl F. Zanuck as production chief. This studio emphasized technical polish and visual gloss with a number of lighthearted musicals.

Columbia Pictures

Harry Cohn, known for his foul language, helped to make Columbia Pictures into a major studio. His colleague, Frank Capra, directed well-known films such as *It Happened One Night* (1934) and *Mr. Smith Goes to Washington* (1939).

RKO Radio Pictures

RKO Radio Pictures was instrumental in making stars of Fred Astaire and Ginger Rogers, as well as Katherine Hepburn and Cary Grant. However, its greatest success was the fifty-foot-tall ape, King Kong, who earned the studio almost $2 million at the release of the movie of the same name (*King Kong*) in 1933.

Each studio had a recognizable visual style, identified by colors used or the amount of excess grain or sharp focus in the black-and-white productions. Particular stars such as Clark Gable at MGM or James Cagney at Warner Bros. were identified with an individual studio.

Two Primary Approaches of Music in Early Sound Films

During the early years of sound films, there were basically two approaches to the use of music. The first approach was **to have music throughout the entire production**, from the main title sequence running continually through to the end of the film. This has been referred to as "wall-to-wall" music. Because many filmmakers were accustomed to music accompanying their silent films throughout, it seemed only logical to continue this tradition when sound was added to their films. It also is possibly a development of the practice of late nineteenth-century opera composers, such as Richard Wagner, who wrote his music dramas accompanied by "wall-to-wall" music.

The second approach was **to use music only as source music**, that is, only when the source of the music can be seen on screen. This may seem ludicrous by today's use of dramatic underscoring, but it was definitely favored by a number of filmmakers. A rather silly example could concern a movie depicting a young couple stranded on a desert island. If there was ever a love scene where they would kiss and embrace, the only way there could be a "love theme" present on the soundtrack at this point would be to have a strolling violinist come walking out of nowhere, playing a love theme on his violin! Otherwise, according to this second approach, we weren't supposed to hear any music of any kind if we couldn't see its source. A good satire of this occurs about twenty-five minutes into Mel Brooks's *Blazing Saddles* (1974). We see Cleavon Little's character riding on horseback through the desert, accompanied by the music of Count Basie. What makes this amusing is that Count Basie and his band are actually seen performing out there in the middle of nowhere.

Frankenstein

When *Frankenstein* was released in 1931, it was said that "women screamed, men trembled, and kids started crying." When the movie previewed in Santa Barbara, California, one patron phoned the manager's house every five minutes throughout the night, after having seen this film to say, "I can't sleep because of that picture and you aren't going to either!" *Frankenstein,* starring Boris Karloff as the monster, is one of Universal Studio's great masterpieces. The viewer of this film would expect an ample supply of dramatic music. On the contrary, the only music we hear at all is music during the main title and end credit sequences and on three occasions, as source music (roughly forty-seven, fifty-one, and fifty-six minutes into the story).

There is virtually no dramatic underscoring anywhere in the entire film. The main title music was composed specifically for the film by Bernhard Kaun (1899–1980). Kaun specialized in writing music mostly for horror-themed films. He died January 3, 1980, after having composed the music for at least fifteen films for Universal, Warner Bros., and Columbia Pictures. The end credit music was selected from a work called "Grand Appassionato," written in the 1920s by Giuseppe Becce (1877–1973).[7]

Boris Karloff, the man who played the monster, had started in American films way back in 1919, usually playing rather unnotable characters. As such, he was hardly a well-known actor. Karloff had to arrive at the studio in the wee hours of each morning for the intricate makeup required for the part of the monster. He had to wear an outfit complete with raised boots, which made him eighteen inches taller; with everything combined, the outfit weighed a total of between forty-two and sixty-five pounds. Karloff reportedly lost twenty pounds while filming *Frankenstein.* This film grossed about $12,000,000 on a $250,000 initial investment, and not only launched Karloff's career but also set a new standard in horror films.

Although other studios made horror films during this period, it was Universal studios that earned its reputation as the "home of horror." Over the next few years, Universal released movies such as *Dracula, Frankenstein, The Mummy, The Invisible Man, Murders in the Rue Morgue, The Black Cat, The Werewolf of London,* and *The Raven.*

The Hollywood Musical and Busby Berkeley

Another popular film genre was the Hollywood musical. This type of film evolved specifically for the purpose of escapism. Since many Americans were adversely affected by the Great Depression, movies, complete with elaborate musical numbers, appeared to be the best form of escapism. People needed to get away from the harsh realities of everyday life, even if for only two hours in a movie theater.

Several studios made musicals during this period, but musicals made under the direction of a man named Busby Berkeley (1895–1976) set a standard never again to be equaled. He was born in

7. The practice of composing music for only the main title sequence and perhaps the end credit sequence was quite common during this period of Hollywood history. Some composers worked in this manner on so many films that they lost count as to the number of films on which they worked.

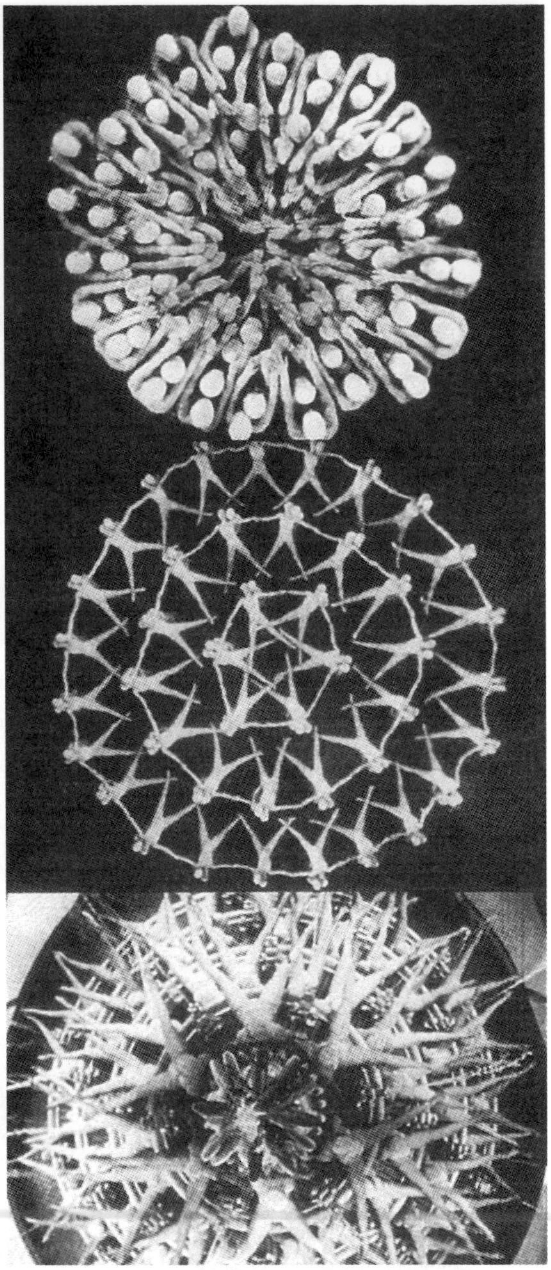

Berkeley's spectacular "top shots." From the author's collection.

Los Angeles. At the age of twelve, he enrolled in a military academy in the state of New York. During World War I, he enlisted in the army and was stationed in France. Since he was in charge of conducting the parade drills, he managed to get permission to use twelve hundred soldiers to march in unusual military formations designed by himself. After his tour of duty, he went back to New York City, where he became one of the major dance directors on Broadway during the 1920s. In 1930, he was invited to Los Angeles by Samuel Goldwyn, to start directing musicals. Movie musicals in fact had gone out of fashion by the second half of 1930, so it was rather daring of Goldwyn to invest $1.5 million in his first musical. This was the fast-paced and funny *Whoopie!,* staring Eddie Cantor, with music by Walter Donaldson and dance numbers staged by Berkeley. Berkeley requested to have one of the movie cameras mounted on a platform that could be lifted high up into the air enabling him to photograph the dancers from overhead. This became known as Busby Berkeley's "flying trapeze." At first, the filmmakers couldn't understand why anyone would want to photograph dance routines from above. After they had seen the dailies (the showing of the previous day's work in the screening room), they agreed that Berkeley was a master of his trade. These "top shots" high above the action enabled Berkeley to design geometric and abstract patterns in a kaleidoscopic fashion using hundreds of scantily clad young women. His routines have yet to be equaled by any other filmmaker. Berkeley was signed to a seven-year contract with Warner Bros., and he was responsible for daring and fantastic sequences in movies such as *Golddiggers of 1933* and *Footlight Parade* (1933). By the end of the 1930s, Berkeley left Warner Bros. and was immediately signed by MGM. He was quite successful with his musicals starring Judy Garland and Mickey Rooney and, later, Gene Kelly. By 1954, the heyday of the movie musical had basically come to an end. Many of the musicals on which he worked contained music by Harry Warren. Warren was a successful song and film composer for studios such as Warner Bros., Fox, MGM, and Paramount. He won three Academy Awards and was responsible for the music in many of Berkeley's greatest films.

Busby Berkeley was responsible for the revival of interest in movie musicals back in 1930. The Museum of Modern Art in New York deemed Berkeley the "Master of the American Musical." As you watch some of his musical numbers, you become aware of the great importance of the music to the success of this genre.

Review Questions

Discussion

1. Briefly discuss why the advent of sound was not universally welcomed by all the people in the industry (such as filmmakers and actors or actresses).

2. Compare the two early sound systems used in films.

3. In a paragraph, trace the evolution of Busby Berkeley's creative genius from an early age until he arrived in Hollywood.

Short Answer

1. What is ironic about Sam Warner's wish for a sound film? ________________.
2. During the period right before sound was introduced to motion pictures, what posed a great threat to the advancement of movies? ________________.
3. What is significant about *The Jazz Singer*? ________________.
4. Why weren't the Warner brothers in attendance at the premiere of the film mentioned in question 3 ? ________________.
5. Who was the world's largest employer of musicians? ________________.
6. What is meant by a "blimped camera?" ________________.
7. Which sound format became the standard? ________________.
8. Why did they make two versions of *Blackmail*? ________________

   ________________.

9. Which studio was known for its motto, "Home of Horror?" ______________________.

10. What was Busby Berkeley known for? ______________________.

Define the following

Soundtrack ______________________.

Phonofilm ______________________.

Hollywood musical ______________________.

Chapter Five

The Rise of the Symphonic Film Score (the 1930s)

The major studios survived the perils of the Great Depression (although Paramount declared bankruptcy in 1933, rebounding again in 1936 after a court-ordered reorganization, whereas the shortest-lived of any of the majors, RKO (Radio-Keith-Orpheum) went bankrupt in 1933, and did not recover until its reorganization in 1940). The movie palace was not so fortunate. Many theaters could no longer afford ushers to show patrons to their seats. Feeling the need to raise additional revenue, theater managers began selling popcorn, candy, and soft drinks in the lobby before and/or after the show. Because many potential theatergoers had limited funds to spend on movies, the double feature concept arose—occasionally even a triple feature would be the order of the day. This meant that patrons would get more for their money . . . two or three shows for the price of one. These additional features were often cheap "B" grade pictures lasting only about an hour and they were usually either a Western or an action-packed adventure. Theater owners could make more money by selling food and drinks between these shows, as patrons would purchase concessions during these intermissions. Movie patrons also were lured into the theaters with giveaway gimmicks such as "dish nights." This is where each member of the audience would receive a piece of chinaware with the purchase of a movie ticket. This encouraged weekly attendance by American families so that they might collect an entire set of china. Today, this "Depression china" is highly collectable.

On March 31, 1930, Hollywood released a Production Code, which gave a formal set of moral guidelines on what was acceptable and not acceptable in matters of sex, religion, crime, and violence in making motion pictures. In the previous decade, it was felt that the studios had lacked moral responsibility and leadership. There were arguments that the media had a profound effect on society. The Production Code, now known as the Hays Office, in 1933 asked Paramount Pictures to remove the line: "When I'm good I'm very good, but when I'm bad I'm better" from Mae West's movie *I'm No Angel.* The studio refused. By the middle of 1934, the Hays Office prohibited movie stars from endorsing alcoholic beverages. The Catholic Legion of Decency attacked indecent films, saying that they are "perhaps the greatest menace to faith and morals today." Initially, the code was voluntary. In 1934, because of pressure from the Catholic Legion of Decency, the production code was enforced.

In 1930, there were twenty-three thousand theaters in America, and 8,860 were wired for the showing of sound movies. By 1935, all theaters in America, even in the smallest towns, were capable of showing sound movies. The average weekly attendance at movies was ninety million people per week in 1930. This figure dropped somewhat during the Depression years, particularly in 1932 and 1933. Attendance at movies started a spiral upward, so that by 1939, the average weekly attendance was back up to eighty-five million people.

On May 27, 1933, Walt Disney studios released the cartoon *The Three Little Pigs,* which introduced the song "Who's Afraid of the Big Bad Wolf?" This song became the Depression fighting song.

The price of a movie ticket at the start of the decade was about 20¢ to 23¢ per person. This price peaked in 1936 at 25¢. By 1939, the average price was back down to 23¢. Only major productions such as *Gone with the Wind* would demand higher admission prices.

Music that accompanied films from 1927 to 1933 was by and large not apt to make a lasting impression on filmmakers or moviegoers. Dramatic films made during the early 1930s were basically comprised of dialogue only, with very little or no musical underscoring. Filmmakers feared that the added music under the dialogue might drown out the dialogue. In these early films, about all the music there is usually consists of main title and end credit music.

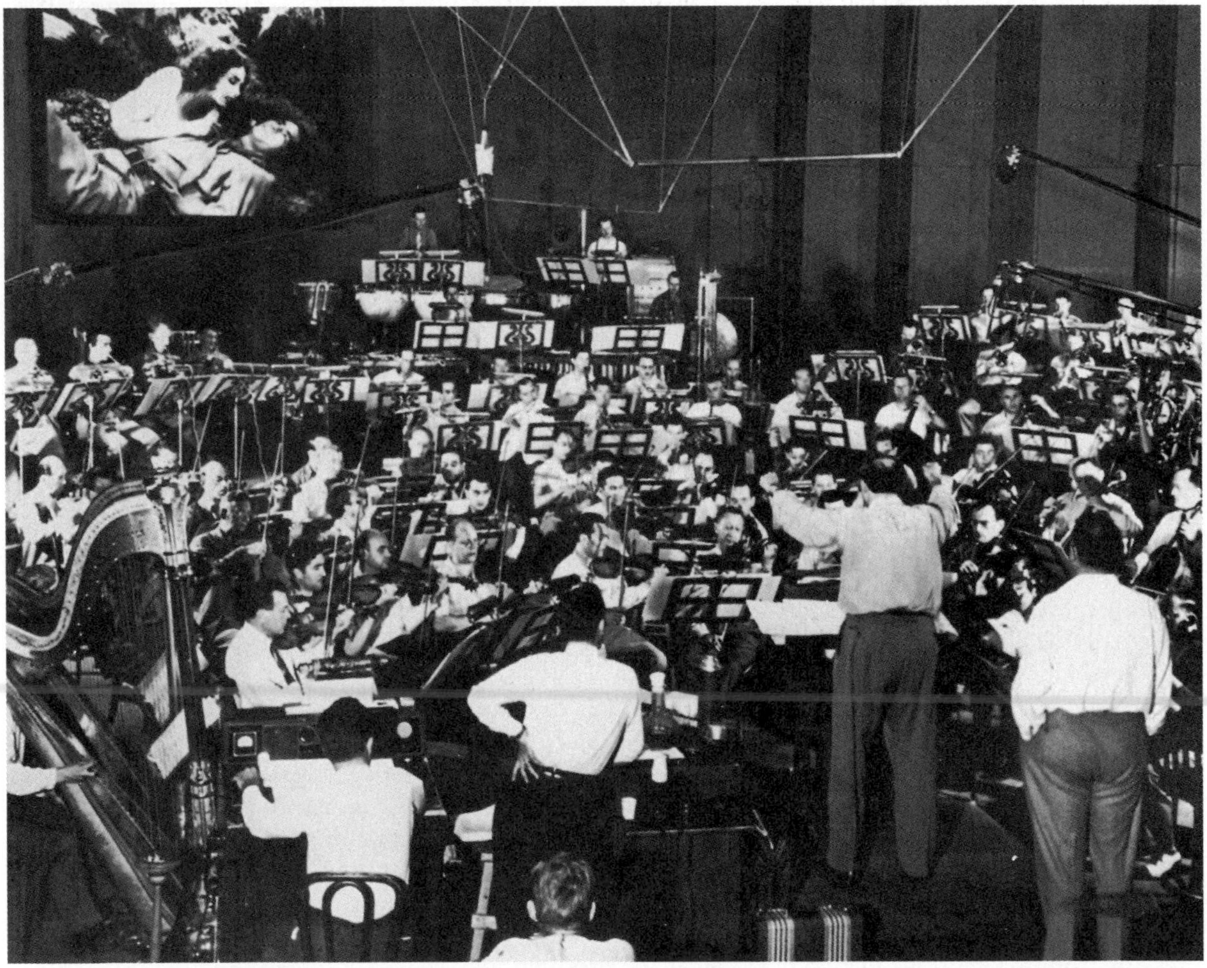

Composer Dimitri Tiomkin conducting the scoring session for Duel in the Sun *(1946) at the MGM scoring stage (now Sony Scoring Stage), where many of the world's most famous and successful film scores have been recorded. Note Gregory Peck and Jennifer Jones on the movie screen. Courtesy of David Ewart, Recording Musicians Association.*

Bird of Paradise

In 1932, Max Steiner was given free rein by RKO Radio Pictures to *create the first continuous dramatic music score*. Steiner received on-screen credit for this wall-to-wall music in the film about romance in the South Seas. The film, which contained a rather shocking skinny-dipping sequence by leading lady, Dolores Del Rio, was called *Bird of Paradise*. Then along came a groundbreaking score by Max Steiner for the movie *King Kong* in 1933. Movie music would never be the same again.

King Kong: The Beginning of the Dramatic Score

The score of *King Kong* plays such a much more major role in "creating and sustaining atmosphere, characterization, and pacing"[1] than any other score up to this point. Steiner's score single-handedly illustrated to other filmmakers of the time the incredible effect a custom score can have on the impact of a film. As John W. Morgan wrote in the liner notes to the soundtrack for the movie, "Created when sound film was in its infancy, the power, originality and importance of this score can not be overestimated."[2] Morgan goes on to state that the music for *King Kong* "is one of the key works of our cinematic heritage, one which furnished a sturdy foundation for the style and artistic principles of Hollywood's film music for many years to come."[3] When the film was in the final editing stages, the president of RKO Pictures was concerned about the public's reaction to the story of a huge ape who falls in love with a five-foot-tall blonde woman. Would this be a credible story and also would the special effects look too stupid to be believable? Max Steiner was told by the studio's president to locate some prerecorded music tracks in the studio library with which to accompany the action on the screen. Steiner told the executive that there was no music appropriate enough for such an unusual picture. Merian C. Cooper, the film's creator, producer, and director, told Steiner to go ahead and write an original score. Cooper stated that he would pay any costs involved. Steiner followed instructions, adding $50,000 to the film's overall budget. The score was composed for about forty-six musicians. This was considered to be a large orchestra in the early days of sound films. Max Steiner started work on this score on December 9, 1932. Working in close collaboration with Cooper, he finished the score about eight weeks later, in early February 1933. In a rather innovative twist, Murray Spivak—who was the film's sound effects technician and who had been a symphony percussionist—decided to alter the sound effects and their placement in the film so that they would conform to the pitch of the music, putting the sound effects in the same musical key as the music. To watch this movie without music is practically inconceivable. The score is a crucial and integral part of the film. Music is basically nonexistent in the first third of the film. This was Steiner's idea. He thought that "music would be brought in when"[4] the crew leaves Depression-torn New York on their way to Skull Island (Kong's island). This is when "reality gives way to dreamlike fantasy as the ship moves through the fog surrounding Skull Island."[5] From this point on, roughly twenty-one minutes into the film, music is heard underscoring most of the remaining portion of the film. In all, there is about seventy-five minutes' worth of music in *King Kong*, and Max Steiner said that this was one of his personal favorite scores out of his massive opus of over three hundred scores. *This score has been deemed film music's greatest achievement in the early 1930s.*

1. *King Kong* soundtrack (CD liner notes), Label X, recorded 1976.
2. *King Kong* soundtrack.
3. *King Kong* soundtrack.
4. *King Kong* soundtrack.
5. *King Kong* soundtrack.

The art of original scores was finally beginning to develop. *King Kong*—and Max Steiner—pioneered many visual and audio special effects techniques still in use today. Steiner's approach in the music for *King Kong* is an excellent example of the use of the leitmotif concept. Along with several secondary musical motives assigned to lesser characters, geographical locales, and dramatic situations, Steiner's score for *King Kong* contains three principal leitmotifs. The first is the Kong leitmotif, a group of *three descending chromatic notes,* suggesting this giant beast's overwhelming weight, fiercesome power, and size:

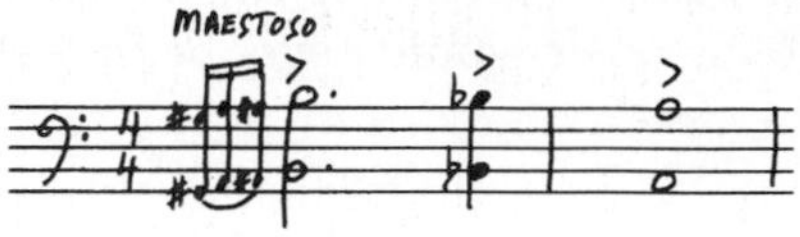

The second major leitmotif is for the female protagonist Ann Darrow (played by Fay Wray). She is the love interest of Kong himself. This is a pretty waltz melody with a strong Viennese flavor.

When Ann Darrow is in trouble, which is most of the time in this movie, Steiner uses a variation on this waltz theme, which is reminiscent of the three-note descending Kong leitmotif.

Variation of Ann Darrow theme:

The third principle leitmotif is a four-note motive, called the "courage motive."

This motive appears in several contexts throughout daring moments of the film. Steiner had the uncanny ability to write a score that, on the one hand, would illicit fear and danger to the listener and viewer, and, on the other hand, would convey the giant ape's love for Ann Darrow. Steiner's score is full of surprises. About forty-two minutes into the film, when Ann Darrow is being held captive by the island natives, we begin to hear the sound of giant footsteps as Kong approaches. What we are hearing are sound effects created by Steiner's orchestrations. These are loud dissonant brass chords equally spaced to coincide with Kong's walking.

Kong is eventually brought back to New York City and put on display as "The Eighth Wonder of the World." The stage that we see is supposed to be in New York, but it is really the Shrine Auditorium in Los Angeles. The music that we hear is implied source music coming from an assumed orchestra down in the orchestra pit.

Throughout the score, examples of Steiner "Mickey Mousing" (that is, catching almost everything in the action and paralleling it in the music) can be heard. This is a trademark of many of Steiner's scores. His contemporaries used to say, "Max liked to catch almost everything in his scores." His uncanny judgment of when and when not to use music is one of this score's most outstanding assets. At times, his music will build to a climax, only to drop out in order to accent the very next

Ann Darrow (Fay Wray) is the subject of Kong's interest. Courtesy of Archive Photos.

moment. Silence is also used effectively in the final scene when Kong, perched high atop the Empire State Building, is attacked by four airplanes.

The music stops at the moment that the first plane breaks formation and dives in for the attack. All we hear is the sound of the engines and that of machine gun fire. By not using any musical underscoring here, Steiner creates tension throughout the final battle, so that when the music reenters, it will have a marked effect on the audience. After being pelted by numerous bullets, Kong realizes that his death is imminent. The music enters in with a lamenting variation of the Ann Darrow theme, played passionately by the strings, followed by the Kong leitmotif. Throughout the film, these two leitmotifs have never resolved musically—that is, the music never felt like it came to a final resting place, it always gave the feeling of searching actively for a chord of rest without ever finding such a chord. Now, however, at this very moment in the film, the Ann Darrow theme is finally resolved, signaling the finality and resolution of her character's dramatic development. The Kong theme is also resolved by chords of rest or resolution, signaling his acceptance of defeat and the resolution of his dramatic development. It's in ways such as this that film composers can manipulate our minds and emotions so that we wonder how anyone can walk out of a movie theater and say, "Music, what music? I didn't hear any music in the movie."

King Kong held captive in New York City (actually the Shrine Auditorium in Los Angeles). Courtesy of Archive Photos.

Steiner wrote the main title music last. As the movie opens, the first thing we hear is the powerful descending three-note leitmotif representing Kong, followed by a brief hint of the Ann Darrow theme, and concluding with the very percussive aboriginal sacrifice dance:

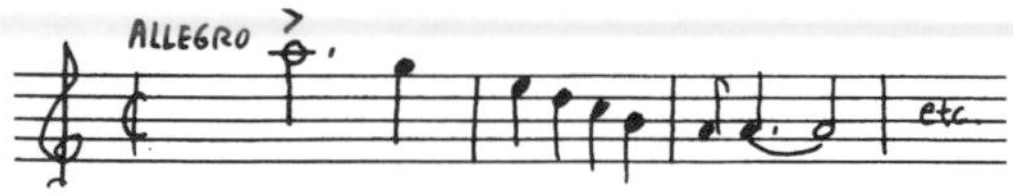

To achieve the effect of a huge ape, Willis O'Brien and his stop-action (also known as "stop motion" or "single-frame cinematography") photo technique brought an eighteen-inch model, made by model builder Marcel Delgado, to life. This model (actually two different models were used) was covered with rabbit fur, utilizing latex for Kong's skin. The movie camera would photograph the model, exposing a couple of frames of movie film each time, then O'Brien would move the Kong model a small amount between exposures. When projected on screen, the eighteen-inch model would appear to move, and, when combined with the live action actors, this created a believable illusion. The

Kong's fight to the death. Actually, there were really only four planes used in the film's finale. Courtesy of Archive Photos.

animated sequences were very time-consuming. They averaged about one hour of work for every second of film. Also a huge head, a gigantic hand, and a foot of Kong were used in the film for some of the scenes using live actors. As you watch the film, you will see two men in the cockpit of one of the four airplanes in the final confrontation when Kong fights for his life on top of the Empire State Building. These men are Merian Cooper and Ernest Schoedsack, the two men who produced and directed the movie. They both agreed that after all the hard work of making the film, they should "kill the S.O.B." themselves. These two men are the ones responsible for killing Kong. By firing enough bullets into him, this causes him to fall off the Empire State Building to his death 102 stories below. Some of the pioneering special effects used in this movie have been used in movies as recent as *Star Wars. King Kong* cost $650,000 to complete. It grossed $2,500,000. Fay Wray, the twenty-five-year-old actress who starred in the film, states, "Max Steiner's music was one of the greatest strengths of *King Kong*. If Kong carried me, Max Steiner's music carried much of the picture. And it is powerful in its own right."[6]

6. *King Kong* soundtrack.

MAX STEINER

Austrian-born composer (Vienna)
Born: May 10, 1888
Died: December 28, 1971

He was the major pioneer of original music for films and the first serious composer of the sound era.

He is sometimes called the father of film music.

His score for *King Kong* in 1933 was a landmark score, illustrating to future filmmakers just how effective a score can be and how it can greatly enhance the film, and one of the first times that a film composer received onscreen credit.

He was one of the first to use the click track method, first using it in *The Informer* in 1935, and using it most effectively in his score for *Gone with the Wind* in 1939.

Someone once said that the best kind of film music is that which you don't hear.

Steiner replied, "If you don't hear it, what the hell good is it?"

He was a very prolific composer, scoring over three hundred films to his credit.

Max Steiner with his many awards. Courtesy of Archive Photos.

He believed in "catching" almost everything, that is paralleling or "Mickey Mousing" the action.

Lieutenant Kije

The Russian composer Sergei Prokofiev (1891–1953) wrote the score for *Lieutenant Kije* (known in the United States as *The Czar Wants to Sleep*) in 1934. The music is remembered today not because of the film, which is rarely seen, but because of its concert suite that is played by symphony orchestras around the world.

The Bride of Frankenstein

In May 1935, one of the finest examples of the horror genre was released. This film also ranks as the masterpiece of director James Whale, who is considered to be one of the most distinctive filmmakers of the early 1930s. Although this film featured some memorable acting from all of its principal characters and included a groundbreaking score by Franz Waxman, not one of them received a nomination for an

Academy Award. This film, *The Bride of Frankenstein,* began shooting on January 2, 1935, and was completed on March 7. There was a sneak preview held the first week of April, after which the ninety-minute film was trimmed to its present length of seventy-five minutes. Nine of Waxman's seventeen musical cues suffered changes and were shortened. Numerous scenes and lines of dialogue were shortened throughout. Also, a happy ending was added to allow Dr. Frankenstein and his wife to escape from the exploding tower at the final scene of the movie. *The Bride of Frankenstein* premiered to rave notices at the Roxy Theater in New York City. With a budget of less than $300,000, Whale brought back a story of the monster that had terrified audiences in his film *Frankenstein* in 1931. *The Bride of Frankenstein* was originally titled "The Return of Frankenstein." Franz Waxman's score for this film was not an ordinary-sounding movie score, and contained some sounds that would pave the way for composers of future horror scores. Very few other scores of the mid-1930s rivaled this sophisticated score.

The largest cues for this score used approximately forty instruments. Waxman also uses the sound of the organ to achieve specific sound coloring in certain scenes. Word had it that he had planned to use a French electronic instrument called the **ondes martenot** (pronounced "ond marr-ter-no"). The music budget was not able to finance the use and importation from France of this esoteric and exotic sounding instrument.[7] Waxman's score employs the use of the **whole-tone scale**. A whole-tone scale has only six notes to the octave, utilizing the interval of a major second between tones. In film music, this can provide the feeling of a supernatural atmosphere and lends itself very effectively to a horror film scenario. This is an example of a whole-tone scale:

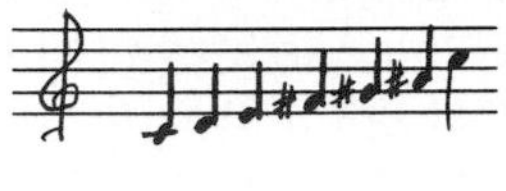

The score itself is comprised of several leitmotifs for some of the major characters. For the monster, we hear a five-note theme based on the interval of a minor third:

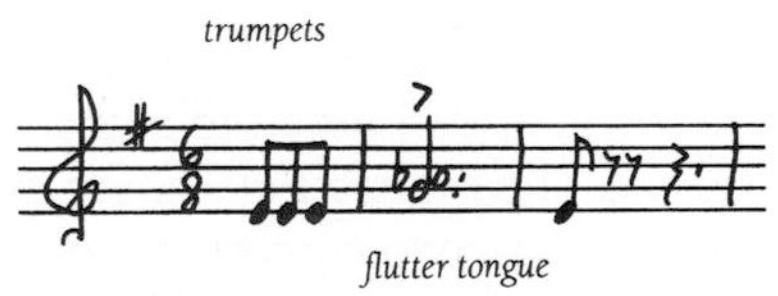

For the monster's mate, we hear a lyrical, almost subtropical sounding theme based on an ascending octave leap and a minor second descending, not unlike that of the song "Bali Ha'i" from the Broadway musical *South Pacific:*

7. Waxman had used the ondes martenot in his score for the 1933 film, *Liliom,* directed by Fritz Lang. We will study the use of the ondes martenot in more detail when we look at the score for *Lawrence of Arabia* by Maurice Jarre.

For the character Dr. Pretorious, who has the brainstorm to design a mate for the monster along with the help of Dr. Frankenstein, we have a leitmotif that is a descending arpeggio outlining a minor chord:

These three musical themes are heard at various times throughout the production, along with other less prominent motives. As you view this film you will notice several techniques such as string tremolos, woodwind trills, and flutter-tonguing brass, which add to the suspense. Although the use of **string tremolos** (this is an Italian term, meaning literally "trembling or quivering," it is produced on string instruments by rapid up-and-down movement of the bow on one of the strings causing continuous reiteration of a single pitch) dates back to music of the early seventeenth century, film composers owe a debt of gratitude to Waxman's score for pioneering string tremolos as a means for creating suspense in the horror film genre. Hundreds if not thousands of suspense scores have been composed using this time-honored technique. **Woodwind trills** (a trill is simply the rapid alternate playing of a single note and the note located above it) and brass **flutter-tonguing** (placing the tip of the tongue behind the gumline of the upper teeth, then rolling the letter "r" while playing into your brass instrument) are also effective means of soliciting suspense in a horror movie score.

In the opening main title sequence, there is a cymbal crash at the appearance of the phrase "Directed by James Whale." It was said that Franz Waxman was told that he would receive an extra $1,000 if he could emphasize Whale's name at the beginning of the film. This is apparently how he accomplished this.

The monster was supposedly destroyed in the original 1931 production *Frankenstein;* however, we are surprised to see that he is still with us as he takes his first two victims (the mother and father of the little girl Maria who was drowned in the lake in the original movie) to a horrible death in the underground chasm.

As we see the monster, we hear the monster leitmotif played by the trumpets. Later in the movie, the monster is caught, brought back to town, and chained to a chair inside a dungeon. We hear string tremolos as he breaks loose from his bonds. The monster clambers through the woods, where he sees a blind hermit living alone in a small cottage. Waxman cleverly takes the source music (Franz Schubert's "Ave Maria") being played on the violin by the lonely man and converts it to dramatic underscoring in the next scene as the monster enters the cottage. The blind man cannot see the hideous monster's face and the monster cannot talk. The hermit thinks that the monster is an answer to his prayers. He had prayed for a companion. As he tells his story to the monster we hear the "Ave Maria" again, but this time as dramatic underscoring with religious overtones played on the organ. The "Bride" does not make her appearance until late in the movie, and it is with the creation of the bride that we see Waxman's genius at work. Most film music aficionados will agree that the musical cue entitled "The Creation" is the best part of this score. Waxman introduces all three major themes in various musical settings. In addition to this, he uses the constant sound of the timpani pounding away as if to convey a human heartbeat. As the bride is lifted atop to the roof of the castle, a lightening bolt infuses life into the monster's mate-to-be. During this moment, we hear the "bride theme" in all its glory, as the new bride is lowered from the roof back down into the castle. Now the timpani is rapidly beating away the interval of a perfect fourth as if to convey a new life force inhabiting her body. To add suspense, the music and pounding timpani stop for a moment, creating total silence. With great anticipation, the bandages are removed from the bride's eyes, we hear a moan, her eyes open—at which point Dr. Pretorious exclaims, "She's alive!" This announcement by Pretorious is accompanied by a jolting

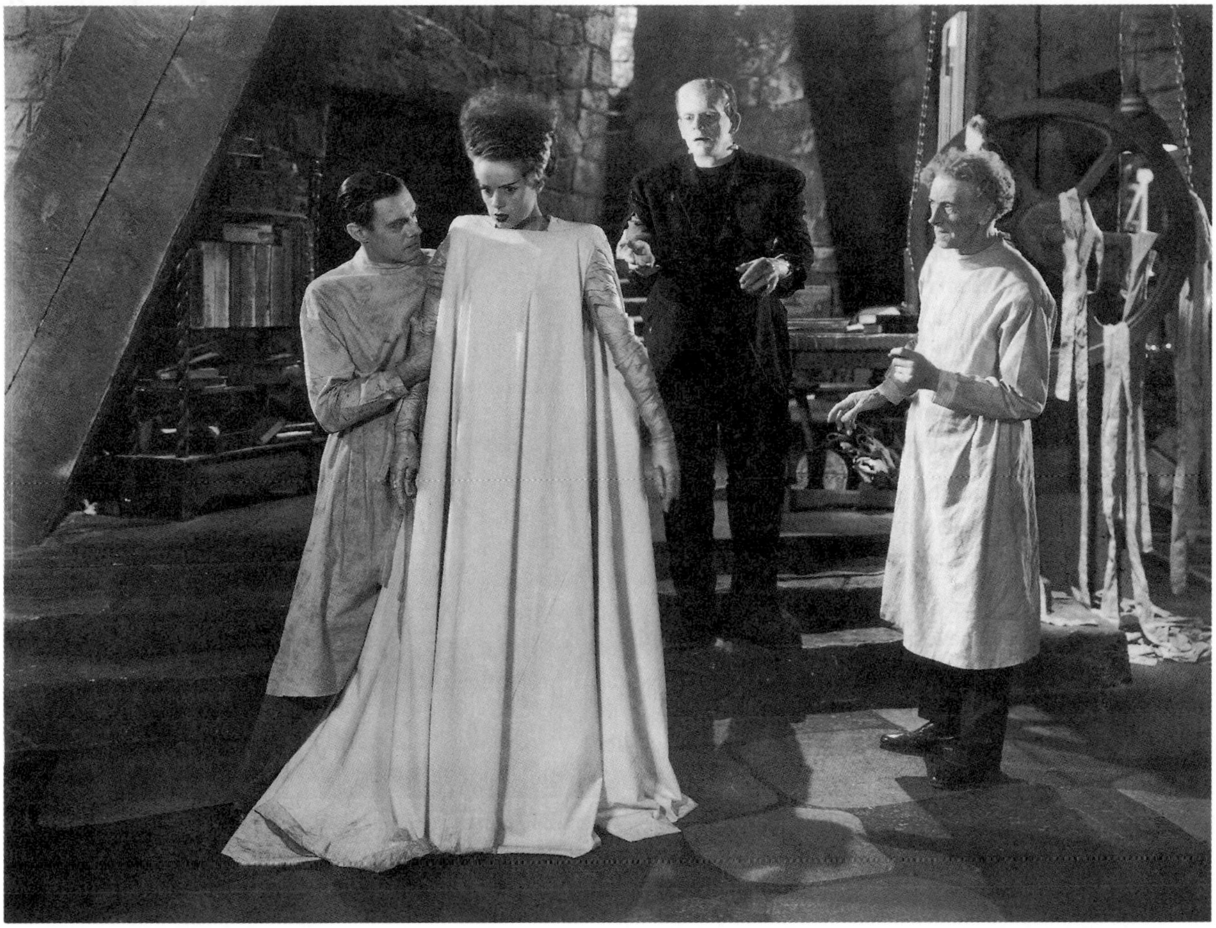

The Frankenstein monster meets his new mate in The Bride of Frankenstein *(1935). Courtesy of Archive Photos.*

dissonant chord in the brass. Their experiment was a success! Later the monster and his new mate meet face-to-face.

As the camera focuses on the bride, we hear her leitmotif. In turn, the same is true about the monster as he moves closer to court the new female creation. She is repelled and shrieks from the monster in horror. The monster goes berserk and pulls a lever, which causes the castle to explode. Before he does this, he signals to Dr. Frankenstein and his wife to leave. As they survey the mass destruction from afar, we hear a reprise of the bride theme (actually a repeat of "The Creation" climax, tracked in to underscore the newly added "happy ending" after previews). This is a score by a twenty-nine-year-old man who had fled Germany after having been beaten by a mob on a Berlin street the year before. With the success of this score, he was named head of the music department at Universal Studios. This masterpiece put him in the front ranks of Hollywood film composers, with one of the most perfect works of the formative period of the symphonic movie score.

performance. There is evidence to suggest that Stalin's office prematurely snatched the film from Eisenstein before it was polished, approving the film as it was. Although Eisenstein made several attempts to change the film, all attempts were denied by Stalin's office. One famous film composer (Andre Previn) stated that Prokofiev's score for *Alexander Nevsky* was "the best movie score ever written, trapped inside the worst soundtrack ever recorded."

Although a talented film composer, Prokoviev is best remembered for his concert hall music of the twentieth century. He, like his other Russian comrades, was a master orchestrator.

Hollywood's Golden Year: 1939

The year 1939 represents Hollywood's golden era at its peak, for no other year produced so many great films in one short period.

With films such as *Gone with the Wind; The Wizard of Oz; Goodbye, Mr. Chips; Mr. Smith Goes to Washington; Wuthering Heights; Dark Victory; Stagecoach; Ninotchka; The Women; The Private Lives of Elizabeth and Essex;* and *Juarez,* it was a spectacular year for entertainment.

Dimitri Tiomkin scored *Mr. Smith Goes to Washington* by using some well-known American folk songs and patriotic tunes, such as "Yankee Doodle" and "When Johnny Comes Marching Home."

Erich Korngold added to his roster of outstanding film scores by composing a well-rounded score for the Errol Flynn–Bette Davis historical drama *The Private Lives of Elizabeth and Essex.* In the true "Korngoldian" style, as later kept alive by composers such as John Williams, Korngold wrote a robust march leitmotif for Essex (Errol Flynn's character) and a dignified-heroic melody for Elizabeth (Bette Davis). For *Juarez,* Korngold had used a borrowed Mexican song called "La Paloma" as the leitmotif for Emperor Maximillian, the legendary leader of the Mexican Revolution. It was stated that "La Paloma" was the emperor's favorite song in real life.

The Dutch-born composer Richard Hageman (died 1966) won the Academy Award for best score of 1939 for his compilation of American popular songs used as the score for *Stagecoach,* the Western that made John Wayne a household name. Directed by legendary master John Ford, *Stagecoach* is still considered to be a classic and has been called the "Granddaddy of Westerns." It is unfortunate that the Motion Picture Academy chose this "compilation" score over some of the other, more worthy contenders that fateful year.

Wuthering Heights

Wuthering Heights became a landmark of Hollywood achievement. It had some of the greatest creative talents working in the movie business at that time. The film was directed by William Wyler, one of the most honored directors in Hollywood history, and had a script based on the novel by Emily Brontë prepared by Ben Hecht and Charles MacArthur, among some of Hollywood's most creative and brilliant screenwriters. *Wuthering Heights* was nominated for eight Academy Awards, although it would win only one, for Gregg Toland's magnificent cinematography. The score was by the most honored Hollywood composer of all time, Alfred Newman, who was paid $5,000 for the opportunity to write music for a genuine film classic. In the lead roles were Merle Oberon as Cathy and Laurence Olivier as Heathcliff. Principal photography began on December 5, 1938. Wyler wanted to shoot on location in England. This had to be rejected because of the expense, so Wyler choose a nearly five hundred-acre location northwest of Los Angeles in the hills of Chatsworth located in the San Fernando Valley to substitute for the

Cathy and Heathcliff in the heather fields in Wuthering Heights. *Courtesy of Archive Photos.*

Yorkshire moors of Northern England. To add realism to the idyllic rendezvouses between Cathy and Heathcliff at their special "castle out on the moors" (called Peniston Crag), Wyler stripped the California landscape of its usual vegetation and substituted one thousand heather plants, imported from England.

Wyler and Olivier did not get along during the shooting of the movie. Wyler demanded that each scene be photographed over and over again (as many as sixty takes on each scene!). Olivier, a great stage actor from England, felt it was unnecessary to have so many takes. In one bitter attack against Wyler, Olivier stated that he did a certain scene standing up, he did it sitting down, he did it with a smile, he did it with a smirk, he did it scratching his ear, he did it with his back to the camera. Olivier yelled, "How do you want me to do it?" Wyler stared at him in amusement and said, "I want it better." Years later, Olivier admitted that he had behaved like "a fool, a stupid, conceited, pompous little bastard." Wyler was right. Olivier felt grateful to Wyler for opening his eyes. Olivier also thought that Oberon was an amateur actress at best. He had wanted his love interest Vivien Leigh in the part of Cathy, but producer Samuel Goldwyn wanted Oberon. Olivier and Oberon were both guilty of tirades on the set. It was reported that Olivier accidentally spit in her face during one of the love scenes during a moment of passion. Oberon was infuriated beyond hope and fled in tears off the set. All of this aside, this film is considered to be a great example of romantic filmmaking and still holds its own as one of the screen's most beautiful love stories. Alfred Newman's lyrical and sensitive score brings out the passions of the tortured relationship so hauntingly portrayed on screen between Cathy and Heathcliff.

The leitmotif for Cathy is one of Newman's most poignant and beautiful themes of his film career. It begins with an octave leap (like that of the bride theme in *The Bride of Frankenstein*) to grab our emotions and continues lyrically to weave a pattern that eventually ends up back on the starting note, for a feeling of completeness:

This theme appears a countless number of times throughout the film in various guises, yet always recognizable to the listener's subconscience. When the film reaches its inevitable climax, Cathy's theme helps to tear us up emotionally. We have associated it with happier times of them meeting secretly out on the moors at Peniston Crag where Heathcliff was able to treat Cathy as his "Queen," without fear of ridicule. As Cathy lies dying, we hear the theme played by a solo cello and later by the high strings, as Heathcliff arrives at Cathy's bedside. We know that this will be their final time together. Cathy asks to be taken to the window for one final glimpse at their special place on the moors. Heathcliff obliges, taking Cathy in his arms, she appears almost weightless, almost as though she has already passed onto some other realm. As she utters, "I'll wait for you . . . till you come," the Cathy theme starts again, and after the first two notes, shifts to a chord that usually gives the listener the impression that the music will continue (an f minor chord with an added d natural as the sixth of the chord coming from the key of C Major). The music continues, but Cathy's lifeforce doesn't. She dies in Heathcliff's arms.

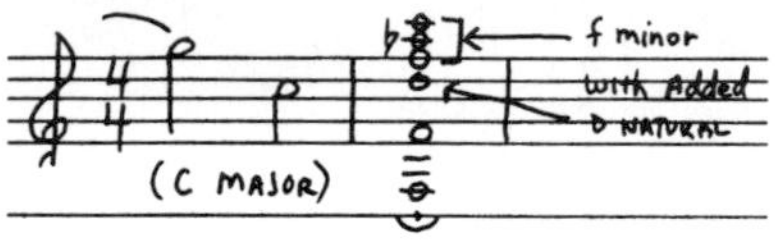

This may seem a bit unusual to place an "active" chord of unrest at a point in the story that cries out for closure. As Royal S. Brown states in his fine book, *Overtones and Undertones,* "The sense of closure provided by this normally nonclosure chord derives purely from the visually created drama of the narrative situation."[8] When the producer Samuel Goldwyn was shown a rough cut of the film, he was horrified with the ending, which showed the dead Cathy in Heathcliff's arms. He stated that he did not want to look at a corpse at the fadeout. Goldwyn demanded that an epilogue be added, which would show the two lovers reunited in heaven.

William Wyler refused to add the additional footage, and the principal actors were thousands of miles away. Wyler was placed on suspension. At the world premiere on April 13, 1939, at the Pantages Theater in Hollywood, Wyler was shocked to see that Goldwyn had secretly changed Wyler's original ending. By filming with doubles who looked somewhat like Cathy and Heathcliff, Goldwyn got his new ending showing the two lovers walking off into heaven. Wyler was furious. There was very little he could do at this point. To make matters worse, Goldwyn took full credit for the success of the picture, saying it was his greatest achievement. Goldwyn said, "I made it, Wyler only directed it."[9]

8. Royal S. Brown, *Overtones and Undertones* (Berkeley: University of California Press, 1994), p. 46.
9. Jan Herman, *A Talent for Trouble* (New York: G.P. Putnam's Sons, 1995), p. 199.

Wyler was not invited to either the Hollywood or New York parties celebrating the respective openings, yet he did attend the New York premiere at the Rivoli Theater. When Goldwyn saw him, he said, "What are you doing here?"[10]

Despite all the bickering during this film's production, what we have is *a masterpiece of romantic filmmaking helped in large part by Alfred Newman's lushly lyrical score*. Wyler had said that he considers a fine score to be an absolutely essential component to the full realization of the values in most films. He always fought to get the best composers available, and he knew precisely which scenes needed music and which scenes would be played out without music. He was always deeply involved during the final dubbing sessions. He stated that "if music was allowed to intrude itself into the consciousness of the viewer, even for an instant, the chain of enchantment was ruptured, and the drama had to start all over again, building from scratch."[11] Many people think that Wyler got the best composer for the job as proven by the success of the movie and its score.

Cathy's final moment before she dies in Heathcliff's arms. Courtesy of Archive Photos.

In 1939, Alfred Newman was named head of the music department and general music director for 20th Century Fox studios. His first love was conducting orchestras. He had said the loneliness of composing for films sometimes got to him, that he would sometimes spend hours looking at the blank music manuscript paper before writing a single note. *He considered* Wuthering Heights *to be among his three top scores when comparing his massive opus of 255 film scores*. As you listen to the music in this and other movies scored by Newman, it becomes apparent that he had an affinity for instrumentalists who performed with a fast **s** (a slight fluctuation of pitch and intensity). In string players, vibrato is created by a rocking of the left wrist as a finger from the left hand is placed on the string of the instrument as it is being bowed. This creates a slight "wobbling" of the tone. Wind players create vibrato by regulating the airflow as though whistling "Yankee Doodle Dandy"; on some instruments, it is created by a slight jaw or lip movement on the mouthpiece. Some brass players create vibrato by making a small repeated shaking movement (usually with their right wrist) as on the trumpet, or for trombones this is done by a slight in-and-out movement of the instrument's slide. Also present in this and other Newman scores is what we call the "**Fox string sound**," sometimes referred to as the "Newman string sound." Newman loved to write his scores that featured strings playing in their highest register. Because he was affiliated with 20th Century Fox studios, this became his trademark signature in his film music. Although the score for *Wuthering Heights* is highly praised today, there was one known negative review. James Shelley Hamilton, in *The National Board of Review*'s magazine, stated that the music for this film was "particularly unfortunate, syrupy and banal and completely missing the feeling it should heighten."

10. Herman, *Talent for Trouble*, p. 199.
11. Tay Garnet, *Directing: Learning from the Masters* (Lanham, MD: Scarecrow Press, 1996), p. 306.

ALFRED NEWMAN

American-born composer (New Haven, CT)

Born: March 17, 1901

Died: February 17, 1970

One of the most powerful and influential musicians in the history of Hollywood music.

His career spans forty years, covering the entire golden age of movies.

He was a prolific film composer, great conductor, and a respected executive.

He became music director for Sam Goldwyn and Darryl Zanuck at 20th Century Fox studios in 1934.

He wrote the 20th Century Fox theme music in 1935.

He was named music director (head of music department) at 20th Century Fox in 1939, where he stayed on as director until he resigned in 1960. He was a total perfectionist and ruled with a firm control and great authority. He continued to work as a freelance composer until his death.

Alfred Newman. From the author's collection.

He was nominated for forty-five Academy Awards and won nine Oscars.

He composed at least 250 film scores.

He created a style that became known as the "Fox String Sound" . . . strings playing in their high registers. He also wrote lyrical woodwind lines and sonorous brass parts. He favored instrumentalists with fast vibratos. He liked the intensity that vibrato gave to the musical line.

His forte was writing for religious-oriented pictures.

His favorite personal score was his score for *The Song of Bernadette* (1943).

His score for *Wuthering Heights* was instrumental in making this film a masterpiece of romantic filmmaking.

Gone with the Wind

Probably the most famous film from "Hollywood's golden year" (1939), and certainly the most successful, was *Gone with the Wind.* Based on a novel by author Margaret Mitchell, this movie was the result of several years of planning by the movie producer David O. Selznick. When the novel was first published in 1936, it became the fastest-selling book of all time. The publisher, Macmillan, could not keep up with the public's demand. Even *Publishers Weekly* stated that this was "very possibly the greatest American novel." Almost every American that was capable of reading had read a copy of this great Civil War drama. Several filmmakers and studios had considered buying the rights to the novel for film purposes. The head of MGM, Louis B. Mayer, was told by production head Irving Thalberg to "forget it. No Civil War picture ever made a nickel." Even Jack Warner of Warner Bros. had considered the film adaptation of the novel, but decided against it when told by film director Mervyn LeRoy that Civil War films were never successful at the box office. In July 1936, Selznick signed a contract for the film rights and began the huge task of turning a very well-received novel into the most popular movie of all time. One month before principal photography was to begin, Selznick decided to get a head start on the burning of Atlanta sequence. On the evening of Saturday, December 10, 1938, Selznick supervised the burning of many old movie sets, including the Great Gate set used in *King Kong,* sets from *King of Kings,* and *The Garden of Allah.* Forty acres of sets had to be cleared to make room for set construction on *Gone with the Wind.* Every Technicolor camera in existence (all seven of them) was used in the filming to capture this crucial sequence. Legend has it that on that fateful evening, Selznick's brother, Myron, arrived with his dinner guests Vivien Leigh and Laurence Olivier to witness the burning of Atlanta. At this point, David O. Selznick (the "O" in his name was added by Selznick himself, supposedly for flourish, rhythm, and production value) had not yet chosen an actress to play the part of Scarlett O'Hara. As the guests arrived on the set, Selznick turned to see Leigh's beautiful face glowing in the night's blaze. Supposedly Myron Selznick said, "Hey, genius, meet your Scarlett O'Hara!" Vivien Leigh got the much-coveted part. In mid-January 1939, after a search that had taken two years of screen tests with many hopeful actresses and had cost $92,000, Leigh was signed to play Scarlett. She would appear in about 95 percent of the movie's different scenes, so naturally Selznick wanted someone who could meet the demands of the role.

Principal photography started on January 26, 1939. Selznick knew that the task that lay before him would be a challenge, but he probably had no idea of the monumental headaches that would ensue. It was difficult enough just trying to find the best actors for the principal roles; the amount of money spent on screen tests alone would have financed another motion picture. After only three weeks into the filming, Selznick was unhappy with the way things were going with director George Cukor. Selznick felt that under Cukor, the production was moving at a snail's pace, and the lead male actors were bitter, as they thought that Cukor favored the female actresses. Finally, after Selznick realized that Cukor refused to listen to Selznick's ideas about the making of the picture, Selznick replaced Cukor with Victor Fleming, an MGM director who was just finishing directing *The Wizard of Oz*. Now the tables were turned. Clark Gable and the other male leads were much happier with Fleming, but Vivien Leigh and her female associates were extremely distressed at Cukor's leaving the set. (Cukor secretly continued to coach some of the female leads during the evening hours.) With the great demands of taking over this massive production, along with the added friction on the set, Fleming's health began to deteriorate. He stormed off the set on April 29, after yet another argument with Vivien Leigh. (Victor Fleming later admitted to entertaining the thought of suicide by driving his car off a cliff.) Selznick brought in a third director, Sam Wood. After two weeks of rest, Fleming was back on the set as director. As many as sixteen writers reportedly worked on the screenplay—including F. Scott Fitzgerald and Ben Hecht—yet only Sidney Howard received onscreen credit. Even after all the rewrites, there had never been a final script for the film editors from which to work. The final draft only existed in Selznick's head. The film editor Hal Kern had the Herculean task of taking nearly a quarter of a million feet of film and reducing it to about twenty thousand feet for the completed picture—that's about thirty hours of film reduced to four hours. Although the film saw three directors during its production (Victor Fleming even won Best Director at the Academy Awards), it was truly Selznick's vision that brought the completed film together. Hal Kern and Selznick spent four long months piecing together thousands of feet of film. The two of them worked together with no other outside distractions. What they accomplished in four months would normally take one year today, working under the best of conditions. One editing session lasted fifty hours! Both men were under medical supervision and were taking medications to keep going, many times working twenty-three hours a day!

Clark Gable and Vivien Leigh in Gone with the Wind *(1939). Courtesy of Archive Photos.*

Selznick planned a sneak preview on September 9, 1939, at the Fox Theater in Riverside, California. It would be several months before the scheduled gala premiere in Atlanta, Georgia, on December 15. Because the now-famous main title sequence along with Steiner's music had not yet been filmed, Hal Kern dubbed in a temp track with music from Alfred Newman's score to *The Prisoner of Zenda* (1937). No one had told them in advance what the name of the movie was that they were about to see. Because most moviegoing Americans knew that the film adaptation of *Gone with the Wind* was imminent, the preview audience went wild with anticipation when they saw the name Margaret Mitchell up on the screen.

Selznick had wanted Max Steiner to compose the music for the picture, yet Steiner was busy on other projects and was not sure that he could meet the deadline. Selznick had hired two other composers to be on call in case Steiner couldn't meet the demands in time. (Franz Waxman and Herbert Stothart were both notified. Although Waxman had written a small amount of material for the film as a backup plan, it was not used in the score. Stothart had written nothing for the score, although he was ready to begin at moment's notice.) Max Steiner composed a huge score of over three hours of music in about four weeks. Steiner claims to have gotten only fifteen hours of sleep during these four grueling weeks! He had the help of five orchestrators: Hugo Friedhofer, Maurice de Packh, Bernhard Kaun, Adolph Deutsch, and Reginald Bassett. Because of the enormous time pressures, Friedhofer, Deutsch, and Heinz Roemheld composed a small amount of material in the style of Steiner. As late as November 21, just a few weeks before the premiere date, Selznick was ordering changes in the score. Steiner's completed score contained eleven principal themes (the most famous being the "Tara theme" heard at the opening of the movie's main credits and concluding the movie's final scene, as well as being heard throughout portions of the film). The bulk of the score was based on American folk songs by composers such as Stephen Foster and including songs popular at the time of the American Civil War, such as "Dixie." There were two short cues, totaling fifty-three seconds, by Franz Waxman that were used, as well as one cue by William Axt (cocomposer of the 1925 score for *Ben-Hur*). These borrowed cues were selected from the MGM library, and had come from earlier film productions—the Waxman cues were from the film *His Brother's Wife* (1936) and the Axt cue was from *David Copperfield* (1935).

The "Tara theme," the most famous theme from the movie and quite possibly Steiner's best-known movie theme, begins with a soaring octave leap of grand proportions. It isn't too long that we begin to associate this theme with the Tara plantation, the land on which the O'Hara family's future rests. As Scarlett's father says, "Land is what lasts, it's the only thing worth dying for." Steiner himself said in 1939 that, "more important than all these individuals is Tara, the O'Hara family plantation. I can grasp that feeling for Tara, which moved Scarlett's father and which is one of the finest instincts in her, that love for the soil where she had been born, love for the life before her own which had been founded so strongly. That is why the Tara theme begins and ends the picture and permeates the entire score."[12] We hear another octave leap in the second and third measures of the Tara theme music as well. The power and excitement of this music is quite apparent. One needs only to see the movie from beginning to end to become "hooked" on this recurring theme. As we have seen in earlier scores (*Bride of Frankenstein* and *Wuthering Heights*), the use of an octave leap in a main theme is not uncommon.

Tara theme from Gone with the Wind.

All of the principal characters have their own themes as do the main supporting characters. Steiner also wrote two love themes, and he used patriotic tunes of the time of the Civil War as well as Southern songs and military pieces. This is by no means Steiner's greatest or most important score. As a matter of fact, it has been called a "patchwork score" by several critics. It is, however, a score accompanying the most popular movie of all time. Some of the music written for the film was not used in the final version.

At the time of its gala premiere on December 15, 1939, in Atlanta, Georgia, *Gone with the Wind* was the longest, most expensive, and most widely publicized movie to date. Selznick wrote in a letter to Al Lichtman, vice president at MGM, "This picture represents the greatest work of my life, in the past and very likely in the future." After three days of festive celebrations, several years in the making at a cost of over $4 million, *Gone with the Wind* opened. The premiere was attended by all of the principal people, except the director Victor Fleming, who was conspicuously absent. He had been insulted by the edict from Selznick that credit should be given to the other directors who also had worked on the film. Fleming also was infuriated by a comment in the program that the film directors had all been "supervised personally by David Selznick." The two men never spoke to one another again. *Gone with the Wind* won the award Best Picture for 1939 at the Academy Awards ceremony, but Max Steiner did not walk away with the Oscar for this score, nor did Alfred Newman for his lushly romantic score for *Wuthering Heights*. Amazingly, Newman made film music history that year as being the only film

12. *Gone with the Wind* soundtrack (CD liner notes by Rudy Behlmer), Turner Classics, 1996.

composer to be nominated for four different scores in the same year for Academy Award consideration. It is unlikely that this record will ever be broken, because since 1946, it has become customary to limit the number of nominations in the Best Score category to five. For one composer to have written four of the top five scores in the same year is unlikely. Prior to 1946, there was no limit to the number of allowable nominations up for grabs in each category.

The Wizard of Oz

Herbert Stothart at a scoring session. From the author's collection.

The winner for best original score of 1939 was Herbert Stothart (1885–1949), for his work on *The Wizard of Oz. Stagecoach* won for Best SCORE of 1939, not Best ORIGINAL Score. Although Stothart wrote a multitude of music for the film, much of it was based on music composed by Harold Arlen (1905–1986). Arlen was not a film composer by profession and had never written a film score. Herbert Stothart, by contrast, was quite an accomplished film composer, with sixty-five film scores to his credit. Stothart worked on 116 movie scores. Sadly, about half of his scores were lost after his death when a water pipe burst in the basement of his home, rendering all of this priceless material unsalvageable.

Stothart took the original music of Arlen and adapted it for this movie, along with the help of about a half dozen orchestrators, including Murray Cutter, the chief orchestrator; George Bassman; George Stoll; Leo Arnaud; Bob Stringer; and Paul Marquardt. Conrad Salinger orchestrated a sequence not used in the final release of the film called "The Jitterbug." The lyrics for the songs were by E. Y. "Yip" Harburg. Both Arlen and Harburg were chosen to write the songs and lyrics for the film, although other people such as Jerome Kern and Ira Gershwin had been considered for the film project. Harold Arlen and "Yip" Harburg were hired on May 9, 1938, on a fourteen-week contract, by which they would be paid $25,000. By late that summer, they had finished the songs needed for the film. Among the songs written for the film and definitely the most popular song is "Over the Rainbow." L. Frank Baum, author of the book *The Wizard of Oz,* never mentions a rainbow in the text. However, he does mention the "gray" qualities of a drought-cursed Kansas landscape in the opening pages of the book. Harburg felt that to introduce the colors of a rainbow into Dorothy's life would be appropriate in such a drab existence. Harburg's first title to the song was "Over the Rainbow Is Where I Want to Be." When this didn't work, Harburg tried several other titles such as "I'll Go Over the Rainbow," "Someday Over the Rainbow," and "On the Other Side of the Rainbow." He claims that it was a long time before he came up with the idea of the title that was finally used, "Over the Rainbow." To make matters worse, after spending more than ample time working on this signature song, several of the executives at MGM wanted to delete the song from the finished film. They felt that the song "slowed the forward pace" of the film or that the melody (once again beginning with a mighty octave leap!) was "too powerful for a little farm girl to sing." Even the music publisher Jack Robbins protested and said that this piece sounded "like a child's piano exercise.

Nobody will sing it—who'll buy the sheet music?" Fortunately for the fate of the song, the associate producer Arthur Freed, who was in good with the studio boss Louis B. Mayer and who would make the final decision, stormed into Mayer's office and insisted that "either the song stays or I quit!" Mayer was grooming Freed for future film projects and did not want to loose him, so naturally the song stayed in the picture. This proved to be a prudent decision, for it won the Academy Award that year as the best song!

Herbert Stothart won the Academy Award for Best Original Score in 1939, which was no small feat, considering he beat out eleven other nominated scores. The musical score for the film had to go through several different transitions, because the length of the film was undergoing changes during its preview period. There were six recording sessions (utilizing orchestras ranging from thirty-seven to fifty-four players) to underscore the film. Amazingly enough, Victor Fleming worked on filming *Gone with the Wind* by day and cutting (editing) *The Wizard of Oz* by night. He ended up with a version of the film that lasted almost two hours, much longer than most standard movies of that time. After several sneak previews in Santa Barbara and Pomona, the film was cut down to 112 minutes. After another sneak preview in San Luis Obispo, some additional minutes were trimmed from this rough cut to get the film down to its running time of 101 minutes. Final adjustments were made to the music in one additional scoring session on July 9, using a thirty-seven-piece orchestra. Now the film was ready for general release. It premiered at the Grauman's Chinese Theater in Hollywood on the night of August 17, 1939. Much was made of the fact that the studio had originally wanted Shirley Temple to play the part of Dorothy, but that 20th Century Fox would not loan her out (she was a contract player) to MGM. Another factor, not as well known, is that a screen test was done with Shirley Temple, and her singing abilities were less than admirable for the part. The movie proved to be a wonderful vehicle for the career of the bright new prodigy Judy Garland. Many people have said that it was the music that made *Oz* such a hit and an enduring classic for the entire world to enjoy over the years. Incredibly, the whole score was written in two months. In addition to many changes in the last weeks of previews, there had been changes in the leadership of the film production as well. This entertaining family film actually saw five different directors during its creation. Norman Taurog had started as the original director, shooting only a few test scenes, after which time he was assigned to another picture. Principal photography for the actual production started on October 13, 1938, with the director Richard Thorpe. Thorpe shot scenes in the cornfield and in the witch's castle. The producer, Mervyn LeRoy, was unhappy with the results, and replaced Thorpe with George Cukor on October 25. Cukor was unable to stay but only a few days because he was in the preproduction phase of directing *Gone with the Wind*. On November 4, Victor Fleming came in to direct the project, and it was Fleming who got the onscreen credit in the movie as its director. Actually, just when the production was nearing its final phase, Victor Fleming left *Oz* to go salvage the production of *Gone with the Wind,* once again replacing Cukor to save another "dying" production. Fleming did not want this new task, and left *Oz* under protest and duress. The fifth and final director to be brought in was King Vidor, who filmed the "Over the Rainbow" sequence and the Kansas scenes, including the cyclone scenes and the "We're Off to See the Wizard" sequence. The last day of shooting was March 16, 1939, six months after shooting had started. Victor Fleming was still involved with *Oz* right to the very end, as he returned in the evenings from the Selznick studios back to MGM to edit. Fleming must have thought that the extra effort in working on both films was warranted, because on looking back in history, film historians would be hard-pressed to think of other instances in which one director worked simultaneously on two great classic films that still appear on the top-ten-films-of-all-time lists.

Review Questions

Discussion

1. View a film from 1927 to 1933. Discuss the use of music in the film. Tell how the same film today would be scored differently.

2. Compare Max Steiner's score for *King Kong* to a more recent monster film.

3. Compare the music in *The Wizard of Oz* to a modern-day musical.

4. Discuss how Max Steiner used leitmotifs in his score for *King Kong*.

Short Answer

1. Why were many of the giant movie theaters in need of raising extra revenue by selling food and drink in the 1930s? ______________________________.

2. Why were double and triple features created? ______________________________.

3. What impact did double and triple features have on concessions? ______________________________

______________________________.

4. What gimmick did theater owners use to bring people back in the theater during the 1930s?

______________________________.

5. Which 1933 score illustrated to other filmmakers the powerful effect a custom score can have on a film? ______________________________.

6. Who wrote this score? ____.

7. How does the composer create tension in the final battle of Kong high atop the Empire State Building? ____.

8. Why do you think Steiner wrote the main title music last for *King Kong*? ____________

____.

9. Name two sounds that Alfred Newman liked in his soundtrack, according to our text.

____

____.

10. Did Max Steiner have any help on his score for *Gone with the Wind*? ____________

____.

11. Why did some of the executives at MGM want to delete the song "Over the Rainbow" from *The Wizard of Oz*? ____

____.

Define the following

symphonic score ____

whole-tone scale ____

string tremolos ____

vibrato ____

"Fox string sound" ____

Chapter Six

The Golden Age of Film Music (the 1940s and 1950s)

Part One: The 1940s

In this chapter we are going to look at representative scores and their composers and see the maturing of film music by pioneering masters whose works reached a pinnacle of achievement and style, setting a high standard to which all other scores would be compared for years to come. This is a time when giants of the field of film music such as Bernard Herrmann, Erich Wolfgang Korngold, Hugo Friedhofer, and Miklos Rozsa became prominent and innovative figures in film music history. We could call this chapter "When Film Music Comes of Age."

In the 1940s, a higher percentage of the population attended movies on a weekly basis than in any other decade in the history of cinema. At the peak of attendance, in 1946, ninety million people attended movies on a weekly basis—approximately 65 percent of the United States population. To put that in perspective, in 1994, there were about twenty-five million theatergoers every weekend, less than 10 percent of the population. In addition, in the 1940s, people went to the *movies.* Now people go to a *particular movie.*

At the beginning of the decade, the average cost of a movie ticket was twenty-four cents. By the end of the decade, the price had nearly doubled, to forty-six cents.

HUAC: House Un-American Activities Committee

In 1947, the House Un-American Activities Committee (HUAC) began investigating Communist infiltration within the motion picture industry. This eventually would have a negative impact on ticket sales. The major stars, under contract to the studios, suddenly found that their contracts lapsed. Anyone known or suspected of being a member of the Communist Party or anyone who was a sympathizer would not be permitted to work on any Hollywood film.

The Coming Threat of Television to the Industry

In 1949, MGM introduced wage cutbacks and massive layoffs. To make matters worse for the studio industry, there was *the coming threat of television.* By 1949, there were only one million television sets in American households, but within three years, that number had grown to ten million. By the end of the 1950s, that number had grown to fifty million! Just as the movie industry had to weather the threat from radio in the 1920s, the movie studios would go through some tough times worrying about their future because of the rise of television. Interesting enough, although television was a threat to the future of cinema during the 1950s and 1960s, it was television that helped the financial woes of the major studios in the latter part of the twentieth century. By offering their inventory of films on video, the movie industry realized that they were sitting on a potential goldmine. By selling or renting their titles on video, the industry was able to add greatly to their income. *The motion picture industry was prudent to take a once-feared opponent (television), and turn its existence around for its own financial gain.*

Film Music in the 1940s and 1950s

1940 was the year that the filmmaker Alexander Korda brought the composer Miklos Rozsa to America from Hungary to score *The Thief of Bagdad.* This was a very colorful Arabian Nights fantasy, enhanced by Rozsa's equally colorful score. Rozsa's score for this Technicolor film already showed signs of the more mature Rozsa who would eventually become the most sought-after composer of Hollywood spectacles. Complete with brass fanfares and catchy melodies, this also was Rozsa's first Oscar nomination.

Following the immense success of *Gone with the Wind,* the producer David O. Selznick summoned the director Alfred Hitchcock from England to direct his first American-made film. The project was the film adaptation of a Daphne du Maurier novel, *Rebecca.* The composer Franz Waxman provided an effective score to enhance the drama of the ending of the movie in which the lavish Manderly estate is destroyed by a raging fire.

Suspicion: Franz Waxman

In 1941, Hitchcock hired Waxman to score the film *Suspicion.* The story (based on the novel *Before the Fact* by Frances Iles) tells how a young woman's imagination and overly dramatic fantasy causes her to live a life of terrifying suspicion about the man she loves. Joan Fontaine gave an Academy Award–winning performance as a young bride who fears that she has married a murderer. Her character, Lina, is a vulnerable, delicate socialite who wants very badly to defy her parents because they have said that she is their "old maid daughter . . . definitely not the marrying kind." Johnny (played by Cary Grant) provides the excellent opportunity for this defiance by showing interest in Lina, a woman who appears to lack romance or excitement in her life up until the time of their first meeting. In defiance, she decides to exploit Johnny's charm for her purposes and he in turn will exploit her family's wealth. He is a lazy, lying, irresponsible spendthrift who refuses to go to work, yet relies on others for his income by constantly borrowing without ever planning on repaying his debts. The musical score by Waxman greatly enhances the emotions shown on the screen. Roughly thirteen minutes into the film, we find Lina seated at the dining table with her parents. She receives a phone call from Johnny. As she leaves the

Also in the same year, the Russian-born composer Dimitri Tiomkin (1894–1979) composed a dramatic score for Alfred Hitchcock. The film was called *A Shadow of a Doubt*. The main function of this score was to provide a distorted version of the waltz theme from Austrian composer Franz Lehar's (1870–1948) operetta *The Merry Widow* (1905). The actor Joseph Cotten plays the part of Uncle Charlie, who is later found out to be the dreaded "merry widow" murderer.

The Chicago-born composer Victor Young (1900–1956) composed a Spanish-flavored score based on the story of Ernest Hemingway's *For Whom the Bell Tolls*. Featuring an oft-repeated love theme, the film also shows a solo guitarist as source music playing various Spanish idiomatic flourishes throughout the film.

Laura

In 1944, the composer David Raksin (1912–) wrote a score for a film noir classic called *Laura*. The main love theme in this film became one of the most recorded movie themes of all time—as of the writing of this book, it has been recorded by more than four hundred separate recording artists! (The most recorded of all is "Stardust" [1929] by songwriter Hoagy Carmichael [1899–1981]. Carmichael contributed songs to motion pictures and even acted and appeared in fourteen films.) Cole Porter (1891–1964), one of the greatest composers of American popular music, said that of all the songs ever written, he wished that he would have written the love theme from *Laura*. The entire score is based on this single melody. Not only does every musical cue within the film make reference to the *Laura* theme, so does the source music in most cases. This was one of the first film scores to be so monothematic.

The story about how David Raksin came up with this love theme is now legendary. Basically, the director of the film, Otto Preminger, had stated his wish to use Duke Ellington's (1899–1974) song, "Sophisticated Lady." As much as Raksin had respect for both Ellington and this song, he told Preminger of his objections to using the song. Preminger reportedly said, "Okay, this is Friday. If you cannot give me a song that we like by Monday, we use 'Sophisticated Lady.'" As it turned out, Raksin spent a grueling weekend composing dozens of various melodies. On Sunday night, he remembered a letter that he had received from his wife on Saturday, the day before. It suddenly became apparent, as he reread the letter that she was asking for a divorce. He put pencil up to the page and began to write, only this time, something clicked. This was going to be *Laura*'s theme! He took the theme into the studio office on Monday morning and played it for Preminger. The rest, as they say, is history.

David Raksin. From the author's collection.

By the way, Raksin is connected to another legendary film music story. When Alfred Hitchcock was filming the 1944 movie *Lifeboat*, at 20th Century Fox, Raksin was told by a friend that Hitchcock had decided not to use music in the film. After all, explained Hitchcock, "since the action in the film takes place out at sea in a lifeboat, where would the music come from?" Raksin snapped back with his usual dry wit, "Ask Mr. Hitchcock to explain where the cameras come from that photographed the film, and I'll tell him where the music comes from." Hugo Friedhofer wrote the score for this Hitchcock film.

Hangover Square

In 1945, Bernard Herrmann created a rather clever score for a bizarre character who strangles his victims. Laird Creger plays the part of a pianist/composer named George Harvey Bone in *Hangover Square.* Herrmann composed a piano concerto that would feature a variety of moods that could double for dramatic underscoring during the murders within the story. In the climax of the movie, one of Bone's students is seen performing a piece for piano and orchestra called *Concerto Macabre.* As the police realize that Bone is the murderer, they surround the concert hall that accidentally catches on fire. As his young student leaves the piano to flee for safety, Bone goes to the piano and continues performing his piece as though nothing unusual had happened. Herrmann had written this dramatic piece to end without orchestral accompaniment, a rather unique approach in the history of piano concertos. This was so that it would fit into the ongoing drama, as the entire hall is overcome by flames and the orchestra members had left, leaving only Bone to perform his new work.

Miklos Rozsa

According to Royal S. Brown in his fine book, *Overtones and Undertones,* the Hungarian composer Miklos Rozsa was "the composer who most visibly brought the classical film score into the modern era . . . during the 1940s."[1] Rozsa started by scoring films for Alexander Korda on several fantasy films including *The Thief of Bagdad* and *Jungle Book;* but it was in 1945 that he wrote two important and effective scores, one for Alfred Hitchcock, and the other for Billy Wilder. These scores were for two psychological dramas dealing with the dark side of the human mind.

Film Noir

Because of their dark and gloomy nature, both films would be classified as **film noir**. This is a term (translated as "dark" or "black" film) applied by French critics in 1946 to a group of U.S. films made during the 1940s and early 1950s. This type of film is usually replete with lighting that emphasizes dark shadows, main characters who are insecure loners unsure or apathetic about their future, and stories that feature an abundance of night scenes, usually with dingy realism. Some people say that this stylistic and narrative tendency started with the now-classic film *The Maltese Falcon* (1941) or perhaps a year earlier with Boris Ingster's film *Stranger on the Third Floor* (1940). The Hitchcock film was called *Spellbound* and dealt with an amnesia victim and his obsession with the color white. The other film, *The Lost Weekend,* was directed by Wilder and dealt with one man's struggle with alcoholism. Each of these films needed unconventional scores.

1. Brown, *Overtones and Undertones,* p. 19.

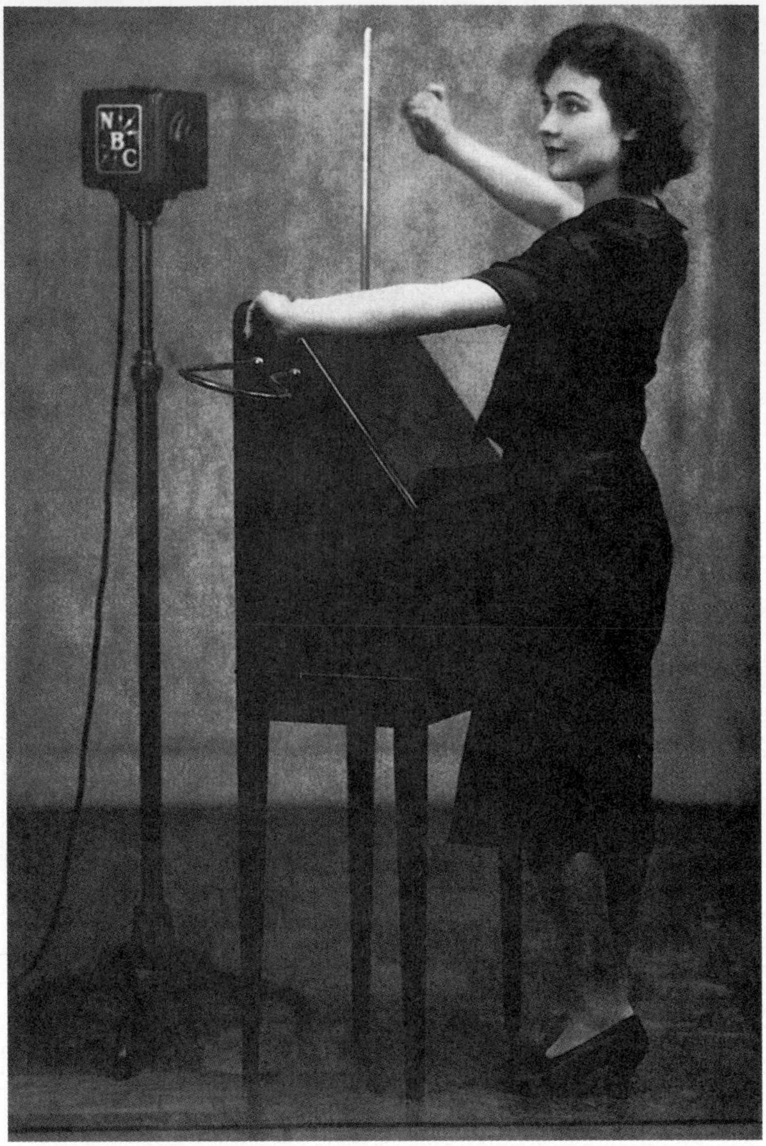

Alexandra Stepanoff playing the theremin. Courtesy of the George H. Clark Radioana Collection, Archives Center, National Museum of American History, Smithsonian Institution.

The Theremin: An Early Electronic Instrument

David O. Selznick, who produced *Spellbound,* and Hitchcock, who directed it, both agreed that Rozsa needed to come up with some "new sound" for their film. That sound happened to be in the form of an early electronic instrument called a **theremin**. The theremin, invented by the Russian Lev Theremin, was first demonstrated in 1920. It works on the principle of the player moving his/her hands near two antennae, one controlling pitch, the other volume, as two radio frequency oscillators create the sound.

The result is very eerie and, as heard in each of the following scores, started a trend of association for films dealing with insane people, and scenes of nightmares or hysteria. Rozsa himself said that his use of the theremin in these two film scores was responsible for making the theremin the "the official Hollywood mouthpiece of mental disorders."[2] Eventually, the theremin was used for science fiction films (and television programs) in the 1950s and 1960s.

The Lost Weekend

Regarded by many to be one of the all-time great dramas in movie history, *The Lost Weekend* has lost none of its bite or power in its uncompromising look at the devastating effects of alcoholism.

The main character, played by Ray Milland, was so convincing that he actually fooled a lady who happened to be walking by during the filming of a scene shot on the actual streets of New York. In this scene, Milland was looking for a pawn shop where he might hock his typewriter in order to purchase more alcohol. Wilder and the camera crew followed close by in a bakery truck. Milland, appearing sick and unshaven for his movie character, was seen rattling the gates of a pawn shop. A female pedestrian

Ray Milland in The Lost Weekend *(1945). Courtesy of Archive Photos.*

2. Miklos Rozsa, *Double Life: Autobiography of Miklos Rozsa* (Kent, TN: Midas Books, 1982), p. 129.

came up to Ray Milland and said, "Hey, aren't you Mr. Milland? Please give me your autograph." Milland, not wishing to ruin the "take" [each day was costing $30,000 in production costs] said, "I'm not Mr. Milland, I'm just a guy who needs a drink bad and trying to pawn my typewriter." She went on to say that she did not believe him, that she had been a fan of his for years and that if he really wanted a drink, she had a quart of Seagram's Seven back at her place to which he was invited. Still not believing him, he had to take her over to the hidden camera in the truck. Still not being able to be rid of her, his only recourse was to get her name and address and offer her a screen test.

When the film was completed, Paramount held a sneak preview in Santa Barbara. Unfortunately, the audience reacted with giggling and laughter; many even walked out early. For those who stayed, their comments were that *The Lost Weekend* was putrid, disgusting, and boring. Hollywood had never made a movie that struck such a sensitive nerve in the minds of many. The truth be known, many in the theater probably had a friend and maybe even a relative who had a drinking problem. Who wanted to be reminded of this family "secret"?

Was this supposed to be someone's idea of entertainment? For years, movies had depicted drunks as jovial partygoers who enjoyed a good time. Wilder now had to convince audiences that the life of a real drunk was nothing to laugh at. Part of the problem was the temp track music used in the opening scene. According to Rozsa, the temp material led the audience to expect a comedy and was the chief reason for the film's poor reception. After he applied his original score, which was "intense, impassioned, and dramatic," the audiences began to appreciate the drama in the manner envisioned by Wilder, that of "the odyssey of a serious drunk." With Rozsa's original score now in place, the audience gave an ovation at the end of the movie and it became a box office hit. The distillery industry became nervous. Prohibition had been repealed only twelve years earlier. The liquor interests had feared a resurgence of propaganda against alcohol. The mob boss Frank Costello, who had considerable interests in the liquor industry, offered Paramount $5 million "under the table" to buy all copies of the film to block showings of the film in the United States. Paramount president Barney Balaban, realizing that the film had cost the studio $1.1 million, decided that it was futile to make expensive films and then shelve them, so he went ahead with its release. The film not only became one of the year's top money makers, it garnered Academy Awards for Best Picture, Best Actor (Ray Milland), Best Director (Billy Wilder), and Best Screenplay. Rozsa's score also was nominated, but he lost out to *himself* for his score to *Spellbound*. The morning after the Academy Awards, as Billy Wilder was driving his Buick on to the studio lot, he noticed that from every window of every office of the Writers' Building there was suspended a bottle of whiskey! (In the opening scene of *The Lost Weekend,* there is a bottle of whiskey dangling by a rope from the apartment window of Ray Milland's character.) We might say that it was also Rozsa's powerful score, with the eerie obsession theme played on the theremin, that not only saved the picture (the movie could have been retitled *The Lost Film*) from extinction but also helped to make it the dynamic classic drama that it remains today.

Obsession theme (played by strings and theremin)

As you watch the film, you can hear different variations on this theme dominating the score, just as the main character's craving for alcohol dominates him. The film viewer becomes conditioned to equating Milland's character's mad, delirious cravings with the obsession theme each time it appears. By the end of the movie, the viewer can almost feel Milland's desperate struggles with liquor by merely hearing the recurrence of this haunting obsession theme, in much the same way that we are conditioned to equate the expected appearance of sharks when hearing John Williams's two-note *Jaws* motive.

Spellbound

Although Alfred Hitchcock finished most of the principal photography on the Selznick-produced *Spellbound* in 1944, the film was not released until after *The Lost Weekend* in late 1945. Several reasons were given for the almost one-year delay: First, there was the slow retake schedule on a dream sequence designed by Salvador Dali, augmented by the rather difficult special effects needed and the fact that Selznick had plunged into a deep depression after the death of his brother Myron. Selznick also saw Rozsa's pioneering use of the theremin in his film to be an exploitable gimmick. Selznick's office phoned Rozsa after the premiere of *The Lost Weekend,* asking him if it were true that he had used the theremin in *The Lost Weekend* as well as *Spellbound* (as though Selznick had a monopoly on the use of the theremin). Rozsa, not to be outdone by Selznick, responded with, "Yes, I had used not only the theremin, but also used the piccolo, the trumpet, the triangle, and the violin . . . goodbye!"[3] Relations between the two men became strained after this incident. When Rozsa won the Academy Award for his music for *Spellbound,* Selznick sent him a one-word telegram that simply stated, "Congratulations." Even though Rozsa won his first Academy Award for his work on *Spellbound,* he had always personally preferred his score to *The Lost Weekend,* and thought that it should have won for Best Original score, being "an infinitely stronger score."[4] Nonetheless, the score for *Spellbound* is considered a landmark in film music because it is the first time that a theremin had been used in a motion picture score supported by a full orchestra. *Spellbound* was made for about $1.7 million and grossed about $4.7 million at the box office.

This motion picture, about psychoanalysis, was made at a time when the press was preaching the advantages of psychological counseling to GIs returning from World War II. Selznick's timing could not have been better. The screenwriter Ben Hecht and Selznick had both been in psychoanalysis and each man was able to bring a special quality to the project. Alfred Hitchcock had envisioned Joseph Cotten in the male lead role. Unfortunately, Cotten wasn't available. With the advent of the war, many possible leading stars were away serving their country. Other contenders were either tied up with competing studios in contract, or, if they were freelancers, could afford to do only two films a year, because of the income tax structure. This left Hitchcock a small list of male actors from which to choose. Since the newcomer Gregory Peck had starred in *The Keys to the Kingdom* in 1944, and the advance reviews on his performance had been good, Peck was hired. By hiring an insecure, inexperienced male lead, Selznick and Hitchcock created an atmosphere of tension . . . a desirable quality in this case.

The story of *Spellbound* weaves an intriguing plot of mystery, suspense, and madness—an amnesia victim (Gregory Peck) must recall events that will clear his name of the murder that he fears he has committed. Peck shows up as the new head of Green Manors, a psychiatric institution. Everyone on the staff is impressed by his credentials, but each remarks that he appears much younger than they had anticipated for a man of his amazing accomplishments and reputation. Dr. Edwards (Peck's character) is introduced to Dr. Constance Peterson (played by Ingrid Bergman), who is on the staff of Green Manors as one of their distinguished faculty. They are immediately drawn to one another as though each was struck by lightning . . . an instant attraction. Throughout various plot twists, we learn that Peck is not the real Dr. Edwards; he has been murdered, and Peck feels that he must be the one responsible for the murder. We also learn that Peck is suffering from amnesia and that he has an obsession with the color white and parallel lines.

This buildup alone is enough to whet the appetite of any suspense fan. All the circumstantial evidence tends to incriminate the man. The film becomes a chase drama on two levels, physical and mental. Peterson and the fake Dr. Edwards are led on a journey where they try to always remain one step

3. Rozsa, *Double Life,* p. 128.
4. Rozsa, *Double Life,* p. 130.

"Terror on the ski run" from Spellbound. *Courtesy of Archive Photos.*

looming over the bed with his razor blade and at the same time the music heightens to its dramatic arc in the trombones and pounding percussion.

What will happen to Bergman? This very memorable moment in this film helps to showcase the end result of two great geniuses at work (Hitchcock and Rozsa). The "terror on the ski run" cue, which occurs about ninety-three minutes into the movie, is probably the music of Franz Waxman, although it goes uncredited. As mentioned earlier in this chapter, the music in this part of *Spellbound* is the *identical* music heard in the movie *Suspicion,* when we see Johnny driving Lina to her mother's house along the sea cliff road, toward the end of that movie. This was a rather frequent practice (the utilization of music from previous films, going uncredited) during this period of cinema history. What follows the end of the ski run is sure to stay in your memory forever, for it is at this point that we see why Peck has had such a rough time dealing with his paranoia.

Once again not wishing to give away the ending to this great classic, let it be said that this movie will hold your attention right the final frame of film. Sadly, this would be the only film Rozsa would score for Hitchcock. The two men never really clicked, and Rozsa felt that Hitchcock showed little, if any, interest in his music. Even after it won for Best Score, Hitchcock never congratulated Rozsa. When Rozsa reached his eightieth birthday, his friend Dr. Marvel Jensen compiled a beautifully bound

MIKLOS ROZSA

Legendary film composer Miklos Rozsa. From the author's collection.

Hungarian-born composer (Budapest)
Born: April 18, 1907
Died: July 27, 1995

Composer of both concert works and film music.

He did not like to be known as only a film composer.

Highly respected intellect and composer. He became a professor of film scoring at USC (1945–1965).

His film composing career can be broken up into four creative periods:

1. His **exotic, fantasy period**, in which he scored films that had exotic locations. Films include *The Thief of Bagdad, Jungle Book*, and *Sahara.*
2. His **psychological period**, in which he scored films that represented the dark side of the human mind or the world of mental disorder. These films usually dealt with the lives of people who were suffering from some kind of obsession or phobia. Films include *The Lost Weekend* and *Spellbound.*
3. His **gangster film period**, in which he scored movies that were hard-hitting and brutal films noir. Films include *Brute Force, The Killers*, and *Naked City.*
4. His **historical-epic period**, in which he became known as the master at this craft in composing for large-scale productions, particularly movies dealing with the Roman Empire or great heroes. Films include *Quo Vadis, Ivanhoe, Julius Caesar, Knights of the Round Table, Ben-Hur, King of Kings*, and *El Cid.*

He won three Academy Awards for Best Score: *Spellbound* (1945), *A Double Life* (1947), and *Ben-Hur* (1959).

He composed ninety scores during his forty-four years in Hollywood.

Fellow Hungarian Eugene Zador was his usual orchestrator.

The film composer Ennio Morricone's uncle was Rozsa's music copyist while he worked in Rome.

His music always contained a dark Hungarian folk influence that was easily recognized.

He signed a long-term contract with MGM, from 1949 to 1962.

He suffered a stroke during the last years of his life.

volume of letters from many people associated with him over the years. Contained within was a letter from Gregory Peck, which sums up Rozsa's contribution to this now classic work:

> Since you composed the score for *Spellbound,* I have been more or less identified with your music. The score is so immediately recognizable, so unlike any previous film music, that

it has given an ongoing vitality forty years after it was made. The music still evokes images of Ingrid and me, struggling to cope with the snares and obstacles Hitchcock put in our way.[6]

Erich Wolfgang Korngold

Another leading composer during the golden age of film music was Erich Wolfgang Korngold. Korngold has the unique distinction of being the first composer of international reputation to accept a Hollywood contract.

Prior to coming to Hollywood, Korngold had established himself as an *outstanding opera composer* in Vienna, Austria. It would be a somewhat natural transition to compose for operas and then for films, because the two mediums are so much alike. Each is a drama where music helps to enhance the story. Korngold's intention was to write music for films that would serve the purposes of the picture and yet still be music when heard away from the movie. This requires a composer with the ability to write music that is appropriate, understandable, and appealing. *During Korngold's twelve-year tenure in Hollywood, he composed music for only eighteen original scores.* Because of his clout, he was able to pick and choose his film assignments.

His music for films was inspired by the Romantic composer Richard Strauss (1864–1949). Just listen to the tone poems of Strauss, then close your eyes and listen to the film music of Korngold. There is a striking stylistic resemblance. One might even say that Korngold was an extension of Strauss, that Korngold's style is that of the late Romantic period composers. At the age of nine, Korngold was taken to perform on the piano for the Romantic composer Gustav Mahler (1860–1911). Korngold played his first dramatic composition for Mahler, who afterwards pronounced the young Korngold to be "a genius!" Richard Strauss himself said of Korngold, "One shudders with awe when one realizes these compositions are by an eleven-year-old boy." The great Italian opera composer, Giacomo Puccini (1858–1924), is reported to have said that ". . . the boy has so much talent he could easily give us some of it and still have enough left for himself." Amazingly enough, Strauss lived well into the twentieth century, yet he never wrote any film scores. One noticeable trait in several of Korngold's better-known scores is a main title theme that starts off with a brass fanfare followed by a sweeping melody in the strings. Listen to the opening of Richard Strauss's tone poem, *Don Juan* (1888). Compare that with the opening titles of films such as *The Sea Hawk* or *King's Row*. Each has an opening brass fanfare followed by a sweeping melody in the strings.

From 1935 to 1939, Erich Wolfgang Korngold composed several outstanding scores for films produced by Warner Bros. He won the Academy Award for his score for *Anthony Adverse* (1936). His score contained over forty different leitmotifs for the variety of characters and situations within this movie that was nearly two and one-half hours long. In 1937, he penned a lightweight score for *The Prince and the Pauper,* but it was his 1938 score for *The Adventures of Robin Hood* that left a permanent mark on the film-scoring world. Future film composers such as John Williams, John Debney, David Arnold, and a handful of others have emulated the heroic-adventure style laid down in this score. Some people feel that this score and his score for the *Sea Hawk* (1940) are among his two greatest contributions to film scoring.

To prove that the Strauss/Korngold style is not dead, listen to the opening main title sequence of any of the *Star Wars* trilogy films, each scored by John Williams. Once again, we hear the brass fanfare

6. Rozsa, *Double Life,* p. 226.

followed by the sweeping melody in the strings. This exciting style of composing lends itself very well to the types of films on which Korngold was to work. Actually, of the various categories of film genres available, Korngold limited his output to but two types.

The Swashbuckling Adventure Film

The swashbuckling adventure film includes films such as *The Adventures of Robin Hood* and *The Sea Hawk*. A swashbuckling adventure is one dealing with a mighty swordsman who also happens to be a daredevil. Each of these films soared to great heights in entertainment value, due in part to the legendary star Errol Flynn, and certainly, without argument, because of the massive contributions of Korngold's thrilling scores.

The Romantic Drama

The other type of film that Korngold mastered was the romantic drama, including films such as *King's Row* and *Anthony Adverse*. These were films that dealt with melodramatic story lines complete with a variety of human emotions. Korngold loved it when he found a really good screenplay dealing with this type of challenge.

Korngold had been a child prodigy, and as such had been hailed as "the second Mozart"! As a film composer, he possessed several extremely useful gifts: (1) He had a great instinct for the dramatic. This great sense of drama is a necessary ingredient for any successful film composer, as stated earlier in this book; (2) Korngold was able to synchronize his music to the picture on the screen without the benefit of a click track or stopwatch. He also used a highly developed leitmotif style, as did his colleague, Max Steiner.

Warner Bros. studio was indeed fortunate to have on its roster of staff composers, at the same time, three mega giants of the film music industry: Max Steiner, Franz Waxman, and Erich Wolfgang Korngold. What a coup! Leading man Errol Flynn was later to say that he owed part of his career's phenomenal success to the fact that most of his most successful pictures were scored by the legendary Korngold.

The Sea Hawk

From the swashbuckling category, we find perhaps the best adventure on the high seas of its kind, the classic film, *The Sea Hawk*.

This film was released in 1940 and set a high standard in action entertainment. Today, filmmakers such as George Lucas and Steven Spielberg pay homage to this bygone style of filmmaking in their modern-day film creations. As you watch the film, it will be noticeable that there are parts of this film that contain wall-to-wall music. One hour and forty-six minutes of music had been recorded for the original running time of the film, which came in at two hours and six minutes. The film was later cut down to a final running time of 109 minutes. Korngold sat at a piano provided for him in a Warner Bros. projection room, where separate reels of this film were run for him over and over again so that he might create the necessary music to the images and dialogue coming from the screen. After seven weeks, Korngold was ready to record the score. For this score, one of his longest, Korngold relied on the services of four orchestrators. These men—Hugo Friedhofer, Ray Heindorf, Milan Roder, and Simon Bucharoff—each used Korngold's detailed sketches, which usually contained clear instructions

Errol Flynn starring in The Sea Hawk *(1940). Courtesy of Warner Bros./Archive Photos.*

as to the wanted instrumentation. Korngold discussed the work minutely with each orchestrator, after which he would come back in and add his own corrections and modifications to the orchestrations. A fifty-four-piece orchestra at Warner Bros. worked a total of fifty-eight hours over a period of several weeks to bring us this now classic score.

The story starts in the year 1585, as Spain is trying to conquer the known world. King Philip II of Spain is frustrated that the one thing that stands in his way is the power of England and Queen Elizabeth I. Don Jose, ambassador from the court of Spain, is sent to England to persuade England's "Sea Hawks" to lay off the Spanish fleet. Queen Elizabeth I is convinced by Don Jose that King Philip II wants the best for England. One of the "Sea Hawk" captains, Captain Geoffrey Thorpe (Errol Flynn), doesn't trust the king. Thorpe has a plan to sail with the "Albatross," his English ship, down to Panama to secretly attack the Spanish secret stash of treasures and bring the treasures back to the queen. Thorpe and his men are captured by the Spaniards and chained for life as slaves on one of the Spanish galleys. As Thorpe and his men are providing the power for a Spanish galley on its way to the harbor of Cadiz, they suddenly stop rowing. We are aware of this, not by physically seeing the men stop. We know because Korngold's accompanying score slows down. While docked in the harbor, the men break free. They sail back to England to warn the queen that the Spanish armada plans to attack England.

This is a film of swashbuckling richness, of piratry and gallantry, of queens and kings, when England ruled the world and Spain was a close second best. The opening fanfare theme is that of Captain Thorpe's leitmotif. It will be used throughout the movie in various contexts and guises:

There is a leitmotif for the beautiful niece of Don Jose, Donna Maria, who is the lover of Captain Thorpe:

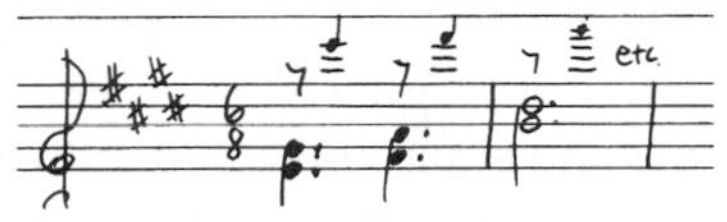

There is the love theme that binds the two together:

There is even a theme for the "Sea Hawks," that gallant group of British sea captains to which Thorpe belongs:

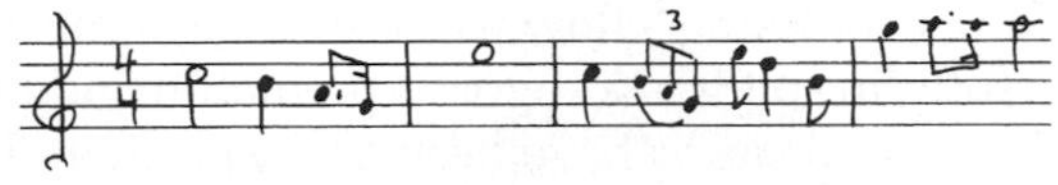

Some say that this is the best nautical adventure film ever made, and it is generally regarded as Erich Korngold's *best film score*. Nonetheless, it was his last score for a historical, swashbuckling film, and it was his sixth film in this genre with leading man Errol Flynn. As George Korngold, the son of Erich Korngold, so aptly put it, "Warner Brothers was a remarkable studio at that time. Everything was geared to a unified end, drama and emotion were beautifully acted and photographed, and musical scores not only complemented but enriched the pictures."

King's Row

The main title theme for *King's Row* is considered by many to be Korngold's *best-known melody* from his film scores. It starts with two measures of a string and woodwind trill followed by a brass fanfare in alternating meters of $\frac{4}{4}$, $\frac{3}{4}$, and $\frac{2}{4}$, progressing to a four-measure string melody:

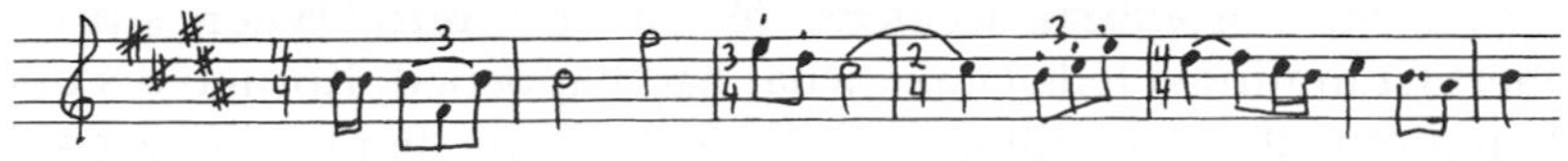

Erich Wolfgang Korngold with his son and wife Luzi. Courtesy of UPI/Corbis-Bettmann

ERICH WOLFGANG KORNGOLD

Czechoslovakian-born composer (Brno, Czechoslovakia)
Born: May 29, 1897
Died: November 29, 1957

He was a child prodigy like Wolfgang Amadeus Mozart (1756–1791).

Because of his great gifts, he was hailed by critics as a "second Mozart."

His father, Julius Korngold, had been the major music critic for Vienna, Austria, at the time. He named his son Erich after Mozart, using Mozart's first name for Erich's middle name. Erich Korngold also had a brother named Robert, named after his father's other favorite classical composer, Robert Schumann.

He became the first composer of international reputation to accept a Hollywood contract (with Warner Bros.).

During his twelve years working in Hollywood, from 1935 to 1947, he wrote only eighteen original film scores. He had an exclusive contract that allowed him to pick and choose his assignments. He was given a royal treatment afforded no other film composer. He became the highest paid film composer of that period. He adapted the music of other composers for two additional films, *A Midsummer Night's Dream*

(continued)

(music of Felix Mendelssohn) for Warner Bros. in 1935 and *Magic Fire* (music of Richard Wagner) for Republic Pictures in 1956.

He received four Academy Award nominations, winning twice, for *Anthony Adverse* (1936) and *The Adventures of Robin Hood* (1938).

His total film scoring output was limited to just two types of film categories: the swashbuckling adventure film and the romantic drama.

He used Hugo Friedhofer to orchestrate fifteen of his eighteen scores.

As a very successful opera composer in Europe, he possessed a great sense of drama.

He had the ability to synchronize his music (while recording) to the picture without the use of any mechanical means (such as a click track or stopwatch).

He saw movies as "operas without songs."

His film composing style is that of the late Romantic period composers. One major influence was the music of Richard Strauss (1864–1949).

Many of his scores started with a symphonic overture featuring a brass fanfare followed by a sweeping melody in the strings.

His music has been a major influence of other film composers.

Hugo Friedhofer

Hugo Friedhofer, that marvelous orchestrator of Korngold's scores, became a first-rate composer of over eighty film scores. Nominated for the Academy Award eight times, he won for his score for the now-classic film, *The Best Years of Our Lives,* in 1946.

The Bishop's Wife

One year later, he would be nominated for his lighthearted, **quasi-baroque-oriented score** for the Christmas classic, *The Bishop's Wife*. The score lost out to Miklos Rozsa's score for *A Double Life* (his second of three Oscars that he received during his career). *The Bishop's Wife* is based on the novel by Robert Nathan and involves a misguided bishop whose priorities are in the wrong place. Dudley, an angel played by Cary Grant, is sent down to earth to show the bishop, played by David Niven, that the building of a new cathedral on Sanctuary Hill is not as important as his attention to his wife, Julia (played by Loretta Young) and their daughter Debbie. Unfortunately, Julia doesn't realize that Dudley is a heavenly angel and she begins to fall for his charms in the absence of her husband's affections. Orchestral arrangements for the film were done by Jerome Moross and the musical score was conducted by Emil Newman, brother of Alfred. Although Friedhofer did not win the Academy Award for this score, it is one of his most enjoyable. Fred Lau won for his wonderful sound recording work and the film was photographed by one of the masters of black-and-white cinematography, Gregg Toland. The film opens featuring the vocal talents of the Mitchell Boychoir singing an arrangement of "Hark! The Herald Angels Sing." This sets the time and place of Christmas. The musical score evolves into a quasi-baroque rendition of the piece, as we see Dudley looking into the department store windows. After helping a blind man cross the street, we hear the "Dudley theme," which was first heard in the main title credits.

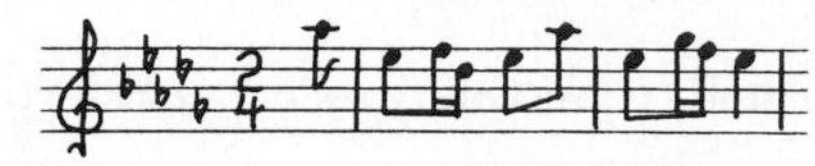

The Dudley theme

The next theme we encounter is the "Professor theme." Professor Wutheridge is a old friend of the bishop and Julia. He has supposedly been working on a book about Roman history, yet we later learn that he has yet to write a single word.

The Professor theme

Friedhofer wrote a lush theme for Julia, which we first hear when the bishop and Julia are seated at the dinner table. This theme is later heard throughout various parts of the film, usually when Dudley and Julia are together.

Julia's theme

When the bishop stands in his study and asks God for help in the building of his new cathedral, suddenly we hear religious-sounding music as he looks up at the painting of the proposed cathedral. This is created by the lush string chords enhanced by a **wordless choir**.

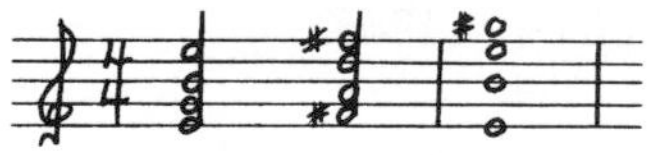

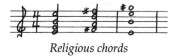

Religious chords

At this point, Dudley enters the bishop's study and we hear the "deeds of an angel theme" played on the alto sax. We had heard this same theme toward the beginning of the film, as Dudley helped a blind man walk across a busy street.

Deeds of an Angel theme

This particular theme is heard throughout this film, sometimes in variation. A rather clever use of music is achieved when Dudley takes Julia to lunch at the exquisite restaurant called Michel's. The scene starts off with the expected "Muzak"-like source music heard in restaurants like this. As Dudley looks at Julia's hand, in order to read her palm, Friedhofer transforms the moment into a nearly romantic interlude for Julia by quoting the "Julia theme" once again. The source music disappears momentarily, yet returns when Julia notices that Dudley hasn't looked at her hand at all. This magical moment

Cary Grant as Dudley charms Julia (Loretta Young) at Michel's restaurant in The Bishop's Wife *(1947). Courtesy of RKO Pictures/Archive Photos.*

for Julia is interrupted by the nosiness of three old ladies who are members of the cathedral committee and who happened to be sitting behind Dudley and Julia, assuming them to be having an affair.

In another interesting use of music, we hear a variation of the "deeds of an angel theme" played by flutes and glockenspiel. This takes place as Dudley and Julia visit the professor at his place. Just when the professor goes to pour more sherry, Dudley secretly "fills" the glasses and eventually the sherry bottle itself. Each time this happens we hear a variation on the "deeds of an angel theme." Friedhofer takes these leitmotifs and quotes them at times overlapping one another and sometimes with variations on the original rhythms.

Hugo Friedhofer became a master because he worked with the best. In addition to being Korngold's major orchestrator, he also orchestrated at least fifty of Max Steiner's scores. To have apprenticed with such stellar superstars is quite unique in the world of film composing

Although *The Bishop's Wife* is now considered to be one of the best-loved holiday movies, it had a rather shaky early production. Several weeks of the movie were originally filmed with a different director and Cary Grant was playing the part of the bishop, whereas David Niven was playing the role of the angel! Producer Samuel Goldwyn was not happy with what he saw in the rushes, so he replaced directors and reversed the roles of the two leading men. The results were much improved and another classic was born.

HUGO FRIEDHOFER

American-born composer (San Francisco, California)
Born: May 3, 1902
Died: May 17, 1981

Hugo Friedhofer. Courtesy of L. Tom Perry Special Collections, Harold B. Lee Library, Brigham Young University, Provo, Utah.

Because of circumstances, he may be one of the best "schooled" of all film composers.

He started by playing cello in silent movie theaters.

He later became the main orchestrator for some of the "giants" of the film music industry.

He worked alongside Steiner as his orchestrator on more than fifty of his scores.

He worked with Korngold as his orchestrator on fifteen of his eighteen original scores.

Leo Forbstein, head of Warner Bros. Music Department, knew how Korngold and Steiner were happy with Friedhofer's orchestrations for their scores, so Forbstein kept Friedhofer from getting a composing job at Warner Bros.

He also orchestrated scores for Newman and others.

He was a utility (ghost) writer for several composers who got credit for his work.

Between 1930 and 1943, he composed portions of the scores of around sixty films.

Alfred Newman gave him his big break by offering him a contract as composer at 20th Century Fox in 1943.

Nominated for five Academy Awards, he won the Oscar for Best Score for *The Best Years of Our Lives* in 1946. This score was influenced by the music of Aaron Copland (1900–1990).

He was a meticulous composer and sometimes took more time than producers liked on some of his scores.

He was a master orchestrator with few peers.

He was not widely recognized in his lifetime by the masses as were other composers. He stated with some degree of wit, "Yes, I am a false giant in a community of genuine pigmies."

His approach to film scoring was to watch a film through and determine which portions are the peaks in the story and save up for that. He thought of a film as an architectural whole.

He composed over eighty original film scores.

Bernard Herrmann

One of the leading innovators of film music had his cinematic start in the 1940s. Described by one of his contemporaries as "a mastodon of divine conceit," Bernard Herrmann's stubborn genius and high expectations of himself and all those around him led to a reputation of being a bitter, abrasive, and

Bernard Herrmann composing at home in the 1940s. Courtesy of Bernard Herrmann Collection, Davidson Library, University of California at Santa Barbara.

nearly impossible man with whom to deal. He held the highest of standards that he demanded of his musicians and coworkers. If they couldn't meet the demands, he often became obnoxiously impatient and verbally abusive. Nonetheless, Herrmann remains one of the premiere film composers of any age.

He wasn't afraid to vary the size of the orchestra if that's what a movie needed, at a time when other composers continued to always write for the full studio orchestra. His unorthodox instrumental combinations have since become legendary, as we shall see in our study of the Herrmann scores throughout this book. Many composers working today in the business owe some of their inspiration to the innovative qualities of this giant. He may have been eccentric, but so, too, were composers such as Mozart, Brahms, Wagner, and Beethoven. Herrmann usually started the first scoring session for one of his movies with complaints about the type of mallets used by the timpani player or comments that the strings were using too wide a vibrato. He liked an almost cold, dead sound, without vibrato in the strings; just the opposite approach of composers such as Alfred Newman who, as we have seen, loved the fast and intense vibrato. On one occasion, there was an intricate pattern of repeated notes in the orchestra part. All of the string players assumed that the pattern repeated itself. On close scrutiny, it was realized that some of the notes changed. Herrmann's response to the situation was, "Gentlemen, you are not playing wallpaper!" After several tense hours of caustic comments, Herrmann usually began to enjoy himself, and by the end of the day was cracking jokes with the studio musicians.[7]

Bernard Herrmann worked as a composer for CBS radio dramas in New York City in the 1930s. His assignment was working for Orson Welles and his talented Mercury Players acting entourage. What better training for a future film composer, who will need to paint emotions with colors of musical sounds, than to start off in radio, as Herrmann did? In radio, there is no picture. The composer has to be very good at painting pictures in the minds of the listeners.

The filmmaker Brian De Palma said, "Herrmann was the master of giving a whole emotional subtext to the characters" within a film.

Citizen Kane

When Orson Welles came out to Hollywood to make *Citizen Kane,* he remained loyal to his buddy, by asking Herrmann to come as his composer. In retrospect, it was a wise move for Herrmann. Many consider *Citizen Kane* to be one of the greatest, if not *the* greatest movie ever made in America. For a young

7. Several studio musicians who worked with Herrmann were interviewed for this book. All said that he was a tyrant at times, yet each said that he was a brilliant musician for whom each held the utmost respect.

composer to have his start in the business by being affiliated with such a high profile film is an incredible stroke of providence. Shortly before his death in 1985, Orson Welles told a movie director friend (Henry Jaglom) that Herrmann's score was responsible for 50 percent of the artistic success of *Citizen Kane*. Herrmann stated that he usually didn't like using the leitmotif technique in his scores. For *Citizen Kane,* it was a near necessity, because of the nature in which this story unravels in a series of flashbacks. The main character, Charles Foster Kane, dies in the opening moments of the film. His last dying word was "Rosebud." Wishing to find the meaning of this word, the story is told in flashback by those who either worked for him or lived with him. Herrmann wrote two main leitmotifs. One is the "Rosebud" motive:

Rosebud theme

This theme goes through various guises in different parts of the film, offering clues to its identity along the way. It becomes a clue to the final identity of Rosebud itself.

The other theme is called the "Power" motive, which represents Kane's unstoppable thirst for success and power, no matter what the cost.

Power theme

This motive is also transformed during the progress of the film. If you listen carefully, it is heard in the style of ragtime, later as a polka, and at the end of the film, it becomes a commentary on Kane's life. We hear both major leitmotifs (Rosebud and Power) in the opening moments of the film. Herrmann's use of low-pitched instruments (bassoons and contrabassoons, alto and bass flutes, contrabass clarinets, trombones and tuba) in this score's opening sequence, signals a style that would become one of Herrmann's trademarks in most of his movie scores—the use of low-pitched, "dark" sonorities. His love for this rather sinister sound would reach a high point in some of Alfred Hitchcock's films. Bernard Herrmann was given twelve weeks, working with a forty-five-piece orchestra, in which to complete the score. For this, his first film score, Herrmann worked on the film, reel by reel, as each was being shot and cut. *Many of the scenes were actually tailored to match the music.* Early in the film, when we see the various duties of the running of Kane's *Inquirer* newspaper, Herrmann accompanies this with a variety of dance forms popular in the 1890s, such as the French *can-can,* the German *galop,* and the Bohemian *polka.*

A couple of scenes in *Citizen Kane* stand out because of their use of music. During the memorable "breakfast table scene" montage, we spy on Kane and his first wife in a sequence that on screen takes only about two minutes, yet represents a much longer period of time. As we see the rise and fall of affection of the young newlyweds, Herrmann's score becomes increasingly less sentimental and evolves into an icy, calculating musical underscore. By the end of this sequence of events, the two lovers have lost all communication, choosing to read the newspaper across from one another in silence, instead of trying to save what they once had. Herrmann said that what he used to underscore this scene was a waltz in the style of the prolific waltz composer Emile Waldteufel. This French composer enjoyed an international fame in the 1870s and 1880s for his output of nearly three hundred dance tunes, and "The Skaters' Waltz" (1882) is one of his most famous creations. Herrmann took the theme of his own waltz melody through a series of variations, with each breakfast scene being represented by a separate variation.

Orson Welles in the breakfast table scene from Citizen Kane *(1941). Courtesy of Photofest.*

The major musical moment of the film is the massive opera sequence that Herrmann wrote for Kane's second wife, an aspiring opera singer. The script for the movie called for her to be an amateur singer with a feeble voice. Her husband, Charles Kane, builds an entire opera house for her debut in Chicago. In order to give the impression of a weak sounding voice, Herrmann wrote the opera sequence in a late-nineteenth-century French-Oriental manner. The range of the soprano part was pitched to go too high, beyond her singing abilities, and the orchestral accompaniment was too thickly orchestrated so that it would cover up her voice, giving the impression of a feeble singer straining her voice to be heard. As Herrmann put it, "Our problem was to create something that would give the audience the feeling of the quicksand into which this simple little girl, having a charming but small voice, is suddenly thrown." A real-life soprano singer from the San Francisco Opera, Jean Forward, was hired to sing the vocal parts of actress Dorothy Comingore. The desired effect was explained to Miss Forward and it worked; this "simple little girl" fell into the "quicksand," and fell hard!

Herrmann's score for *Citizen Kane* was revolutionary in several respects:

1. At the onset of the movie, we notice his innovative orchestration techniques. Herrmann was quite comfortable using rather bizarre instrumental combinations to achieve the necessary colors. His use of the low-pitched instruments of the orchestra to create the smell of death at the beginning of the film was to set a precedent that would be used by many composers throughout film history.

2. Herrmann's pioneering method of using short musical cues of only a few seconds to help tone down the sharp and sudden scene changes was innovative. As a former radio composer, Herrmann mastered this bridging device in telling the listener that the scene is shifting. For *Citizen Kane,* music is often used as a "linking device," bridging scenes together.
3. This score was instrumental in illustrating the effectiveness of using music sparingly, not like the common practice of constant "wall-to-wall" nonstop music, a technique so prevalent at that time.
4. *Finally,* as Steven Smith states in his wonderful biography on Herrmann, *A Heart at Fire's Center,* this score had a unique approach "in its blend of dramatic scoring and its incorporation of indigenous American music."

BERNARD HERRMANN

American-born composer (New York City) — Born: June 30, 1911; Died: December 24, 1975

He got his start as a composer for radio dramas for CBS in New York in the 1930s.

It was here that he worked with Orson Welles and the Mercury Theater Acting group for radio.

Welles brought Herrmann to Hollywood to score *Citizen Kane* (1941).

Herrmann was awarded an Academy Award for Best Score for *All That Money Can Buy* (from the Stephen Vincent Benet story *The Devil and Daniel Webster*) in 1941.

He used the theremin in his score for *The Day the Earth Stood Still* (1951).

He used nine harps in *Beneath the 12 Mile Reef* (1953).

He scored his first Hitchcock film, *The Trouble with Harry,* in 1955, and continued to work for Hitchcock until *Marnie* in 1964.

He made his only cameo appearance in the Hitchcock movie *The Man Who Knew Too Much,* released in 1956. He appears conducting the London Symphony Orchestra at Royal Albert Hall during a performance of Arthur Benjamin's *Storm Clouds Cantata.*

He wrote a main title theme in the style of a Spanish dance called a Fandango for *North by Northwest* (1959).

He used five organs (one large cathedral and four electronic) in his score for *Journey to the Center of the Earth* (1959). This score also featured the ancient "serpent."

He composed his magnum opus, the score to *Psycho* (1960), using strings only to create a "black-and-white" sound to match the black-and-white picture.

He eventually became disgruntled with the Hollywood way of life and moved to England.

Several young American directors, such as Brian De Palma and Martin Scorsese, hired Herrmann for their early films.

Herrmann died the night of his last recording session for Scorsese's *Taxi Driver* (released 1976).

Herrmann was known for his abrasive temperament, although he was greatly respected for his talents as a composer.

(continued)

He always orchestrated his own scores as he composed.

He was a master orchestrator and tone colorist.

He never signed a long-term contract with a major studio; he operated as an independent composer.

His output represents a very distinguished and impressive body of work when compared to many other film composers.

He was very innovative and tried to create new colors of sound through pioneering methods of orchestration.

He revolutionized film scoring in at least two distinct ways: (1) He customized the size of the orchestra (instrumentation) to fit the needs of the scene. He did not believe in using the same instrumentation from one film to the next. (2) He used short chord cues at times instead of long melodic lines, feeling that wall-to-wall music was not always as effective.

Herrmann strived to write music that will suggest what is not visually apparent.

He had a special ability for depicting the dark and sinister side of man.

He had a fondness for ultra "dark" sonorities (sounds) and achieved these effects by scoring for low brass, low woodwinds, and low strings.

It is now widely known that the movie *Citizen Kane* was very loosely based on the life of the newspaper tycoon William Randolph Hearst. As Harlan Lebo states in *Citizen Kane: The 50th Anniversary Album,* "The Hearst organization . . . made a monumental effort to stop *Citizen Kane,* first by trying to destroy the film, then by working to suppress distribution, and finally by attempting to ignore its existence."[8] Hearst's representatives felt that the movie painted an unfair and ugly picture of Hearst's life.

Principal photography for the film started on June 29, 1940, and was completed on October 24. Hearst used his power to squash all publicity for the film. Not one of the Hearst-owned newspapers reviewed or bothered to mention the movie. *Citizen Kane* was completed at a cost of around $800,000. Because of the Hearst boycott, the picture lost $160,000. *The film was an artistic success, not a commercial success.* Orson Welles's first film still managed to receive nine Academy Award nominations. On May 1, 1941, the film opened at Broadway's RKO Palace in New York City. Its release was planned for February 14 but was postponed because of the negative campaign waged by Hearst. Other major studio-owned theaters boycotted the showing of *Citizen Kane.* Not until several decades passed would the film enjoy its place as one of the greatest masterpieces of American film. The film was resurrected in the art house theaters of the 1950s. Here, patrons saw *Citizen Kane* on grainy 16 mm prints. In the 1960s, a group of international film critics unanimously agreed that the "number one film of all time" was none other than *Citizen Kane.* The results of a similar poll in the early 1970s and then again in 1982 came up with the same results. In 1989, the National Film Registry began an annual task of choosing twenty-five films needed for restoration and permanent preservation. *Citizen Kane* was on the list. In the early 1970s, an untimely fire in a lab in New Jersey destroyed *Citizen Kane*'s original camera negative. This physical artifact of American film history was lost forever. A 1940s-era fine-grain nitrate positive print was located, which enabled duplicate prints to be made. Today, the film stands as a masterpiece, thanks in large part to the camera work of Greg Toland and the innovative score of Bernard Herrmann.

8. Harlan Lebo, *Citizen Kane: The 50th Anniversary Album* (New York: Doubleday, 1990), p. 134.

As David Cook states in his monumental study, *A History of Narrative Film,* "The influence of *Citizen Kane* upon the cinema has been enormous and nearly universal."[9] Cook goes on to say that it was not until after World War II that "the film's impact . . . began to be felt . . . when its use of low-key lighting and wide-angle lenses to achieve greater depth of field influenced the visual style of American *film noir* and its flashback narrative technique began to be imitated in more conventional films like Robert Siodmak's *The Killers.*"[10]

The Killers

The Killers, which was released in 1946, is told in the same flashback style as *Citizen Kane.* This movie starts off with the gunning down of Swede, a failed boxer, whose past deeds finally catch up with him. As Swede waits in the bed of his boarding house, smoking a cigarette in the darkness, we can feel the tension build as Rozsa accompanies this scene with a long sustained harsh and dissonant chord in the brass. Our anticipation builds to a breaking point. As Christopher Palmer states in his book *The Composer in Hollywood,* "We know that the dissonance cannot last, that something must happen to break the tension, the suspense achieved so simply (with a simple dissonant chord) is impressive."[11] The next thing we see are the two "killers" who enter the bedroom and blow Swede away. Swede is played by Burt Lancaster in his first starring role. Edmond O'Brien plays insurance investigator James Reardon, who tracks down the friends and enemies of Swede and pieces together Swede's story from their flashback memories. *This movie inaugurated Miklos Rozsa's third creative period in film composing.* He had already had his "fantasy, oriental" period with films such as *The Thief of Bagdad* and *Jungle Book,* and his dark "psychological" films such as *The Lost Weekend* and *Spellbound.* Now he joined the ranks as perhaps the foremost composer for gangster films. Rozsa's producer friend, Mark Hellinger, hired Rozsa to score a set of three now-classic gangster flicks, *Brute Force, Naked City,* and *The Killers.* In *Music for the Movies,* Tony Thomas states that "Rozsa's thickly textured scores for these pictures, full of sharp accents and terse rhythms and tension chords, is unlike any he had written for the screen previously or would write later."[12] The music that Rozsa wrote for this genre of film suits the brutal quality of each film's theme. As the late Christopher Palmer (a Rozsa scholar) writes, Rozsa's music is full of "jagged, asymmetrical rhythms, sharp accents, pulsating ostinati, bitonal harmony . . . and an obsessive use of quick, nervous, repetitive figures."[13] In essence, the music is powerful and brutal. This hard-hitting music is perfect for the actions of the cold-hearted characters on screen. Films might be more violent now than back then, yet few composers have equaled the driving force of Rozsa's gangster scores during this period. The repeating "dum, da-dum, dum" figure in the low brass right at the beginning of *The Killers* not only becomes the main musical motive of the film; it later evolved into the now famous Dragnet theme from the television show of the same name.

Robert Siodmak, who directed *The Killers,* earned his only Academy Award nomination for best director. Miklos Rozsa's score was also nominated for best dramatic score, although it lost out to Hugo Friedhofer's score for *The Best Years of Our Lives.* One of the highlights of Rozsa's score comes at the climax of the picture. The insurance investigator agrees to meet with Swede's girlfriend, Kitty (played by Ava Gardner—also in her film debut), at the Green Cat nightclub. This meeting was planned so that

9. David Cook, *A History of Narrative Film* (New York: W.W. Norton & Co., 1990), p. 425.
10. Cook, *History.*
11. Christopher Palmer, *The Composer in Hollywood* (London: Marion Boyars Pub., 1990), p. 203.
12. Tony Thomas, *Music for the Movies* (Beverly Hills: Silman-James Press, 1997), p. 122.
13. Palmer, *The Composer,* p. 202.

she could tell "all she knows" about Swede's past. At the nightclub, we hear the source music from the club's pianist. He changes from a rather romantic piece of music into a jazzy, "boogie-woogie" style. A moment later, the two hit men who had killed the Swede enter the nightclub. At that moment, we hear Rozsa's now famous four-note "dum, da-dum, dum" leitmotif power over the pianist's source music. As "the killers" begin shooting at the insurance agent, Rozsa's dramatic underscoring, complete with violent syncopated chords from brass and strings, add to the excitement of the moment as patrons in the nightclub begin to scream in panic. Meanwhile, Kitty manages to elude the authorities until the end of the film. Miklos Rozsa's music, throughout this period of the 1940s, established him as a leading composer of *film noir.*

Henry V: William Walton

In 1944, the great Laurence Olivier brought the story of Shakespeare's *Henry V* to life on the big screen. He hired the esteemed English composer Sir William Walton (1902–1983) to write the score. The score is quite versatile in that it features a contrast of styles from conventional orchestral music to a Renaissance band. The film was released in America in 1946. Because the film was made during World War II, the powers-that-be demanded that movie studios limit the production of color films to those that had propaganda value to help the populous improve morale. England supplied the money for this production because it was felt that it would enhance the Englishmen's sense of courage to help in fighting the war.

During the long buildup before the fateful Battle of Agincourt in France, we are brought into the excitement of the scene with the help of Walton's score. Many miles away, we see the French troops as they begin their long march forward to meet the English forces of King Henry V. As the French close in, moving closer and closer, Walton provides an underscore of music that *parallels* the increasing speed of the men on horseback by building the music in tempo (speed) and intensity. Waiting on horseback with his hundreds of men is Henry V. At the right moment, he will signal his men to release their arrows into the sky. Meanwhile, we continue to see the French getting closer and closer. The music has now reached an exhilarating pace, as there are only seconds before the French come into view. After an almost two and one-half-minute musical buildup, Henry V drops his raised sword to signal his men to release their arrows at their enemy. At that signal, Walton's music stops and all we have is silence, followed by the almost indescribable *swooshing sound* of hundreds of arrows being released into air to fall down on the enemy seconds later.

During the death scene of the character Falstaff, Walton underscores this sequence with a **passacaglia**[14] melody that is repeated during his lonely soliloquy. This somber musical approach is extremely effective in reaching the emotions of the viewer.

In the movie's final moments, as the end credits are rolling by, Walton combines the *Agincourt Song,* an old melody that is affiliated with this famous battle, with his own original material. This creates a stirring ending.

The U.S. premiere was in New York City on June 17, 1946. This film ran for forty-six weeks at that theater.

William Walton's score was nominated for best score, but lost to Hugo Friedhofer's score for *The Best Years of Our Lives.*

14. In this usage, a passacaglia is a classical music term used to denote a set of variations above a repeated bass line.

The Ghost and Mrs. Muir

One year later, in 1947, Bernard Herrmann wrote a score considered by many to be his *most romantic. Herrmann himself considered this to be his finest score.* The story, based on a popular novel by R. A. Dick, proved to be a delightful and compelling story as envisioned by screenwriter Philip Dunne. It is about a widow named Lucy Muir who moves into a seaside cottage in order to escape her pestering in-laws. She discovers that this cottage is haunted by the ghost of a sea captain who once lived there. It was said that he committed suicide there, yet we later learn from the captain's spirit that he died accidentally. After much plot development, Captain Gregg, as he is called, and Lucy eventually fall in love with one another. Herrmann composed about fifty-two minutes' worth of music for the movie. Although he used an orchestra of sixty-seven players, much of the time the instrumentation required fewer players for different needs in each of the scenes. The score is filled with many leitmotifs, more than any other of his scores. Herrmann supposedly called this his "Max Steiner score," in reference to Steiner's prolific use of leitmotifs throughout his career. There is a theme for the sea, one for the haunted house, a beautiful leitmotif for Lucy, and a strange "ghost" theme played on the piccolo. Two particularly noticeable features of this score are the soft palette of musical colors and textures that Herrmann chose, and the fact that Herrmann avoided using the typical "ghost music" one would expect from a Hollywood movie. One needs only to listen to Claude Debussy's impressionistic work

Lucy Muir (Gene Tierney) and Captain Gregg (Rex Harrison) in The Ghost and Mrs. Muir *(1947). Courtesy of Archive Photos.*

for orchestra called *La Mer* (*The Sea*) (1905) or perhaps parts of Benjamin Britten's *Peter Grimes*, an English opera that premiered in 1945, to see how much influence works such as these may have had on Herrmann for this memorable score. The haunting tale of *The Ghost and Mrs. Muir,* which takes place in Victorian England, still holds its own as another classic romance of the screen. The evocative score of Herrmann helps to make this film a fable of eternal love.

It was during this time that Herrmann was filled with desire and mixed emotions, himself. He was trying to find recognition as a concert hall composer and a successful symphony orchestra conductor, outside of the glamour and glitz of Hollywood. Unfortunately, Herrmann never realized these ambitions. Also at this time in his life, Bernard Herrmann was falling in love with his wife's cousin, Lucy Anderson. Was it made all the more difficult that his wife's name also was *Lucy* (Lucille Fletcher) and that the female lead in *The Ghost and Mrs. Muir* was *Lucy* Muir? Nevertheless, Herrmann left his wife and two children two years later and married Lucy Anderson.

Gene Tierney, who played Lucy Muir in the film, broke a bone in her foot the day before principal photography was to start. Because she appeared in almost every scene of the film, the filmmakers started with scenes in which she didn't have to walk. The cast on her foot was cleverly hidden or eliminated from each shot. She finally had her cast removed two weeks early, against the doctor's orders, and finished her walking scenes in aching pain. Her husband, Oleg Cassini, designed all of her outfits worn in the film.

Review Questions

Discussion

1. Discuss why Herrmann's score for *Citizen Kane* was revolutionary.

2. If Herrmann would have scored *Spellbound,* how would it have been different?

3. View a film from the 1940s and analyze the use of the music in the film.

Short Answer

1. What instrument did Rozsa use in *Spellbound* to come up with the "new sound" requested by Selznick and Hitchcock? ______________________.

2. In *The Lost Weekend,* the main character had mad cravings for what substance? ______________________.

3. What is significant about Rozsa's score for *Spellbound*? ______________________.

4. Why was Gregory Peck chosen for the lead role in *Spellbound*? ______________________.

5. Which is considered by many to be Korngold's best film score? ______________________.

6. Which film is said to contain Korngold's best-known melody? ______________________.

7. Who was the chief orchestrator for Korngold? ______________________.

8. Which composer was described as "a mastodon of divine conceit?" ____.

9. Compare the string sound of Bernard Herrmann to that of Alfred Newman. ____.

10. What did Orson Welles say about Herrmann's music in *Citizen Kane*? ____.

11. What "sound" became one of Herrmann's trademarks? ____.

12. Was *Citizen Kane* a commercial success at its opening? Why? ____.

13. Who became the leading composer of *film noir*? ____________________.

14. Which score did Herrmann consider to be his finest? ____________________.

15. Name two noticeable features about Herrmann's score for *The Ghost and Mrs. Muir.* ____.

Define the following

1. Theremin ____________________.
2. Swashbuckling adventure ____________________.
3. Romantic drama ____________________.
4. *Film noir* ____________________.

Chapter Seven

The Golden Age of Film Music Continues

Part Two: The 1950s

The 1950s saw the waning of the Hollywood musical, the *breakdown* of the Hollywood studio system as it had been, the advancement of television, the arrival of "rock 'n' roll," and the development of the independent productions and the industry's attempts at luring their audiences back into the movie theaters.

During the 1950s, the movie industry introduced the 3-D motion picture experience, which was short-lived because audiences did not like having to wear the cardboard eyeglasses that were needed to capture this effect. Also, the novelty of "seeing objects come out of the screen at you" soon wore off, and this new trend in movie-making suffered a quick demise. Even Alfred Hitchcock, who had filmed his 1954 movie *Dial M for Murder* in the 3-D process, withdrew the idea and released the film in the standard two-dimensional process of normal motion pictures. (Actually the 3-D movie concept had been tried as early as 1922. Filmmakers continue to release movies from time to time in 3-D to this day.)

The Widescreen Motion Picture

The next lure to get audiences back into the theater was the giant curved screens of **Cinerama**. This was achieved by filming the images with three movie cameras locked in position that were side-by-side. When projected (originally by three corresponding movie projectors and one extra projector used for six-track stereophonic sound) the images would engulf the audience with the feeling that the movie images wrapped around them on the sides of the theater as well. It worked on the impression of

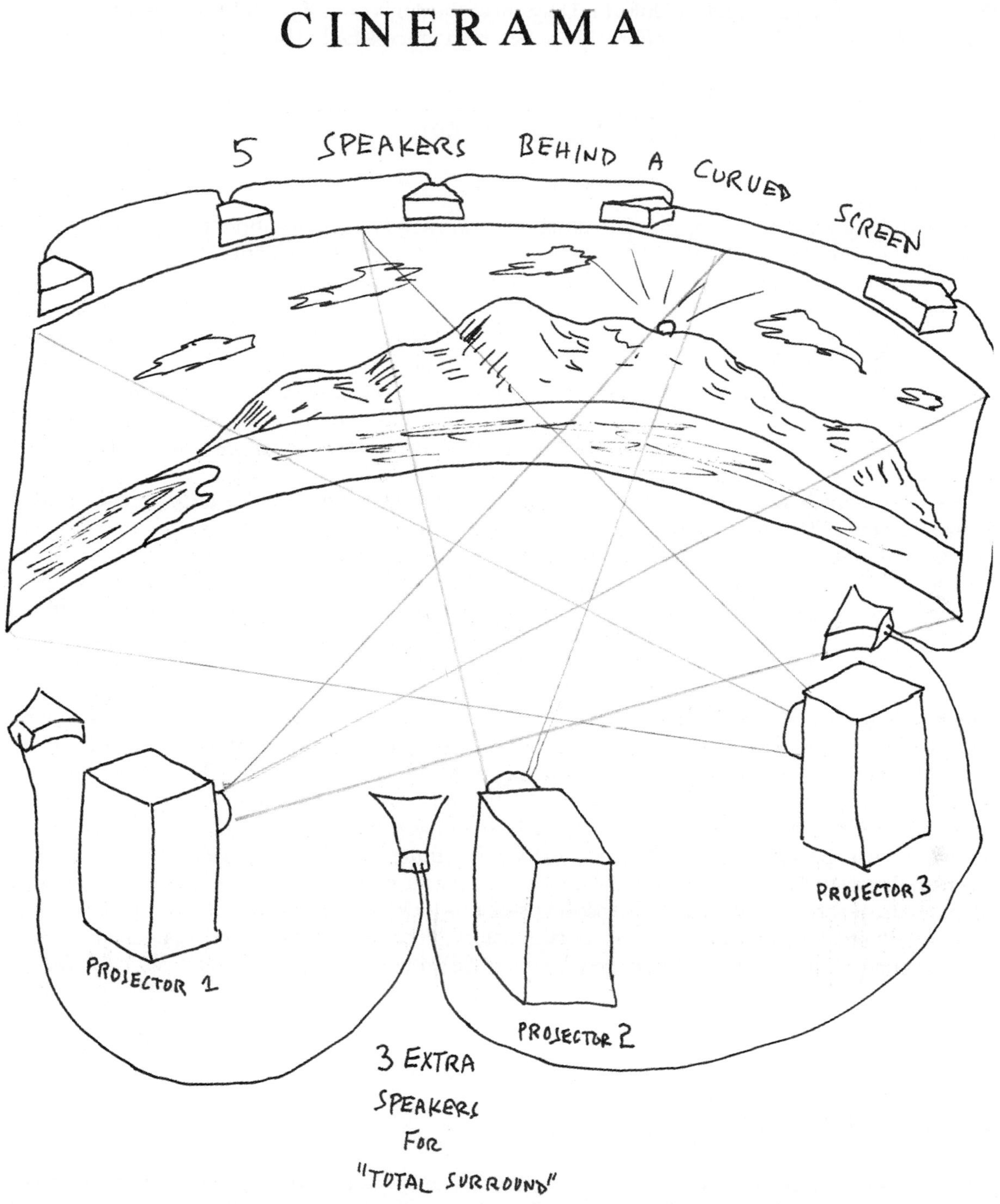

peripheral movement. Movies such as *This is Cinerama* in 1952, and eventually *The Wonderful World of the Brothers Grimm* (1962), *It's a Mad, Mad, Mad, Mad World* (1963), *How the West was Won* (1963), *2001: A Space Odyssey* (1968), and *The Greatest Story Ever Told* (1965) were examples of films that showcased this extra-wide curved screen process. Unfortunately, most theaters could not afford this new moviegoing experience. Because of this, a more affordable widescreen process had to be developed.

The Robe: CinemaScope and the Score of Alfred Newman

In 1952, 20th Century Fox studios purchased the rights to use a French invention that became known as **CinemaScope**. The executives at 20th Century Fox had obtained this invention from Henri Chretien (1879–1956), a French scientist who had developed and exhibited an anamorphic lens in 1927. Chretien had called this lens the Hypergonar. A year later, French filmmaker Claude Autant-Lara (1901–2000) had filmed a short film, *Construire un Feu,* that was the first film to use this new invention (Autant-Lara is best remembered for his 1946 film, *Devil in the Flesh*). This new widescreen process worked on the principle that the picture images would be photographed onto 35 mm film using a special anamorphic lens that would squeeze the picture horizontally from the sides to fit the standard 35 mm film width. When projected, the resultant picture would stretch out to its desired rectangular ratio of over two-to-one on the newly widened movie screen.

The Robe, which was released in 1953, was the movie that introduced this new process to the moviegoing public. This film was instrumental in convincing the industry that this widescreen process, CinemaScope, was workable and affordable for theaters around the United States.

The musical score for *The Robe,* written by Alfred Newman, is considered to be one of his finest scores from this period and proves his versatility as a composer. Newman came to the assignment with plenty of experience in this genre, having scored films such as *The Song of Bernadette* (1943), *The Keys to the Kingdom* (1944), and *David and Bathsheba* (1951).

Because *The Robe* opens with the newly introduced widescreen CinemaScope process, complete with multichanneled stereophonic speakers behind the screen, Newman wanted "to blow the roof off" of the theater with a bombastic beginning. We hear a huge orchestra accompanied by a wordless choir that sets the religious-sounding mood of this telling of the crucifixion story of Jesus Christ. This same music returns during the Crucifixion scene with a great impact. This score encompasses everything one might expect from a story such as this. We hear Roman-sounding marches, we hear solo songs accompanied by "period instruments" such as the harp, flute, and oboe, and we are overcome by the passionate drama of the "Hallelujahs" that are sung by the large studio chorus at 20th Century Fox studios for the final scene of the movie. The scoring sessions took place in July and August of 1953.

In an interesting footnote for film music history, Franz Waxman actually resigned from the Motion Picture Academy in protest because they had failed to nominate Newman's score for *The Robe* as the best score that year.

More Widescreen Formats

Other studios tried out various widescreen processes, such as VistaVision at Paramount, Warnerscope at Warner Bros., Technirama, MGM Camera 65, and, by actually widening the film from 35 mm to 70 mm, a process known as Todd-AO. At the end of the decade in 1959, the majority of the studios abandoned all of these widescreen inventions in favor of a process in wide use today called Panavision. Super Panavision (also known as Panavision 70) was first used in the filming of MGM's 1959 version of *Ben-Hur*. It uses 65 mm film without the distortion of the anamorphic lens. Ultra Panavision uses 65 mm film and an anamorphic lens.

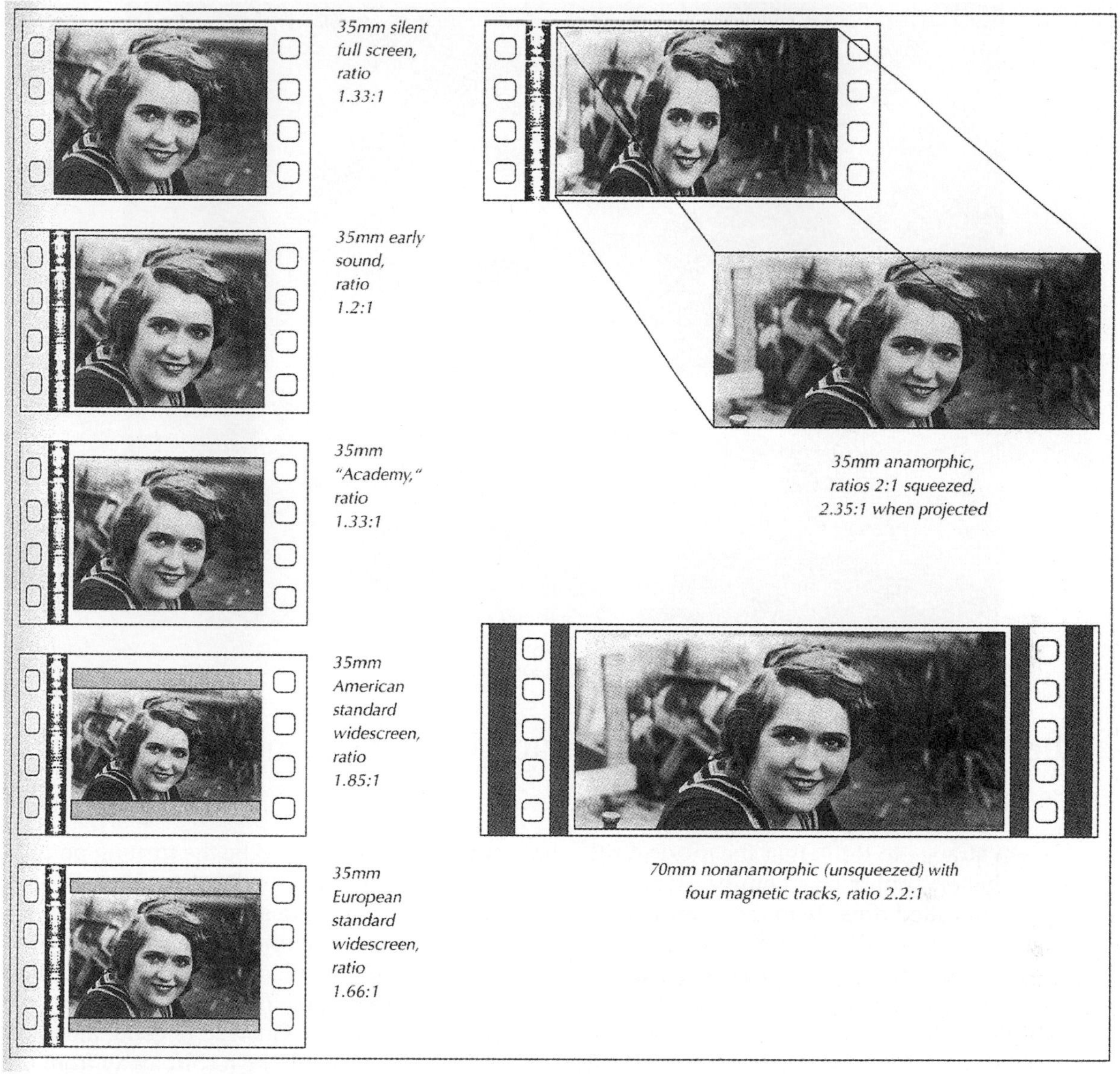

The Hollywood Epic

Another method of reviving audiences in the theaters was the advent of the big epic films. Miklos Rozsa composed a landmark score for *Quo Vadis* in 1951 by doing a great deal of research on music of the period to give the score a more authentic sound. Dimitri Tiomkin gave filmgoers a special treat with his score for *Land of the Pharaohs* in 1955. The young film composer Elmer Bernstein (pronounced "Bern-steen) would make his mark in Hollywood by scoring Cecil B. DeMille's mighty epic *The Ten Commandments* in 1956 and William Wyler's remake of *Ben-Hur*—featuring Miklos Rozsa's spectacular score—would break all Academy Award records.

The years 1950 and 1951 were very good for Franz Waxman, who won an Oscar for best score for *Sunset Boulevard* in 1950 and *A Place in the Sun* in 1951.

Dimitri Tiomkin at a scoring session. From the author's collection.

The Demise of the Golden-Age Symphonic Film Score; Tiomkin's *High Noon*

It may seem strange to think that the music written for a simple Western would be the turning point in film music history, but it was Dimitri Tiomkin's groundbreaking music for the Western *High Noon* in 1952 that contributed directly to the demise of the golden age symphonic film score. Tiomkin had written a Western ballad called "Do Not Forsake Me" that was heard at the beginning of the film and used throughout the movie. Because of the success of *High Noon* and Tiomkin's ballad sung by Tex Ritter, film music was about to undergo a dramatic change. The success of this song in *High Noon* sparked a new trend of film producers wanting to have composers write songs for their films instead of using the traditional golden age symphonic approach of past years. Eventually, there would be a shift away from the more serious approach to film scoring as seen up until now. By the 1960s, the symphonic score was replaced in favor of the pop, rock, and jazz scores that utilized smaller ensembles of players to make the music come to life. Producers liked this because it usually meant that there could be less money spent on the music budget. It was the 1977 score for *Star Wars* by composer John Williams that rekindled interest in the big symphonic scores once again.

High Noon does have several memorable moments that are enhanced by the score. The plot involves a smalltown Western marshal who will eventually confront four bad men as the clock strikes "noon." The marshal (played by Gary Cooper) had helped to send a gunman to prison. Now that bad man had been released from prison and was arriving back in his town on the train at twelve noon. Three of his mean gang members were waiting at the train station to help the gunman settle his feud with the town marshal.

The score builds in rhythmic synchronization to the view of the swinging pendulum inside the wall clock as the dreaded moment draws nearer. At precisely twelve noon, the music stops and is followed by the sound of the train whistle. The film music historian Roy Prendergast has called this musical buildup "one of the finest, most unnoticed moments in film music" history. As the four gunmen begin their trek into town to seek the marshal, Tiomkin accompanies this with dramatic marchlike underscore that includes variations of the film's opening ballad melody. In a rather innovative approach to film scoring, Tiomkin ends the final scene of the movie with music that *diminishes in volume* as the victorious marshal and his new bride ride off into the distance. This musical approach to the ending of a dramatic film was contrary to the typical loud and bombastic orchestral ending that seemed to be in vogue at that time in film history.

High Noon won the Best Score and Best Song Oscars (the ballad "Do Not Forsake Me Oh My Darlin'"), and Tiomkin gained great success in Hollywood. At the same time, his score for *High Noon* became a landmark score.

Two years later, Tiomkin's memorably whistled theme from *The High and the Mighty* (1954), a John Wayne movie, became an enormous success and spent over four months on the Top Ten charts.

During the early fifties, Elmer Bernstein (1922–) gained experience scoring very low-budget films such as *Robot Monster* (1953) and *Cat Women of the Moon* (1954).

Leonard Bernstein's (1918–1990; pronounced "Bern-stine," no relation to Elmer Bernstein) *On the Waterfront* was a worthy contribution to the world of film music. This 1954 film won the best picture Oscar and was nominated for the best score, although it lost out to Dimitri Tiomkin's *The High and the Mighty*. This score had the double distinction of being the only *original* score composed by Leonard Bernstein and yet being recognized by the Academy by garnering an Oscar nomination for Best Score. In spite of its distinguished recognition, there were some critics who felt that Leornard Bernstein's score was too loud and overpowering. In fact, in one scene, the director Elia Kazan had to reedit the volume of Bernstein's dramatic love theme as it became too pretentious for actor Marlon Brando's mumbling dialogue. Even great concert hall composers such as Leonard Bernstein, who also won critical praise for his Broadway musicals such as *West Side Story* and *Candide*, cannot excel in every form of musical composition. His score had some elements of jazz, but it was two other scores from the 1950s that paved the way for a unique approach to jazz music in motion pictures.

A New Approach to Jazz in Films

Although films had used jazz music in many of the 1940s musicals, two scores from the 1950s are both landmark scores for their early *use of jazz in a dramatic sense*. The first is Alex North's 1951 score for the steamy New Orleans drama *A Streetcar Named Desire*. The other innovative jazz score is Elmer Bernstein's effective music for *The Man with the Golden Arm* in 1955.

A Streetcar Named Desire (1951)

Alex North (1910–1991) had never before created a film score. His use of the solo alto saxophone in *A Streetcar Named Desire* was helpful in providing the seedy side of sexual longing set in hot and humid New Orleans. Not surprisingly, North was nominated for his first Oscar, although he did not win. In fact, he would be the recipient of twelve more Oscar nominations during his distinguished career and would never win for a single film score. In 1986, five years before his death in 1991, *North became the first film composer to receive an honorary Academy Award for his lifetime achievement*.

The Man with the Golden Arm (1955)

As Elmer Bernstein clearly states in the book *Film Music: From Violins to Video* (edited by James Limbacher), "The score for *The Man with the Golden Arm* is not a jazz score. It is a score in which jazz elements were incorporated toward the end of creating an atmosphere." Elmer Bernstein stated in an interview in Tony Thomas's book *Music for the Movies,* "For example, in *The Man with the Golden Arm,* the main character . . . wanted to be a jazz drummer, so I therefore tried to make that broad jazzy theme speak for his ambition, and by giving it a sad quality it also implied his frustration. He was a tormented man, a narcotics addict, and there are sounds in jazz—blues, wails, trumpet screeches—that are perfect for expressing anguish."[1]

United Artists studio, which released this groundbreaking film, withdrew from the Motion Picture Association of America (MPAA) because that organization refused to grant the necessary production seal of approval. The MPAA felt that *The Man with the Golden Arm* broke the code in its forbidden portrayal of drug addition. This was a strictly taboo subject for films to illustrate at that time in film history. The action taken by the studio would eventually lead to a modification in the code.

Herrmann's Return to Film Scoring

Several years would pass after Herrmann's score for *The Ghost and Mrs. Muir* before he would create another outstanding contribution to the world of film scoring. Although he had written "Jennie's theme" for David O. Selznick's *Portrait of Jennie* in 1948, Herrmann would not return to scoring films again until 1951 for the 20th Century Fox film *The Day the Earth Stood Still.*

The Day the Earth Stood Still

As usual, true to Herrmann's philosophy of creating custom-made instrumentation for each film assignment, his score for this movie was no exception. The score for *The Day the Earth Stood Still* consists of thirty brass instruments, four pianos, four harps, electric violin, electric bass, and the eerie sounds of the electronic theremin (in this case *two* theremins). Herrmann employed Dr. Samuel Hoffmann as theremin performer, the same man that Miklos Rozsa had used on his two classic scores of the mid-1940s, *The Lost Weekend* and *Spellbound.*

The Egyptian: Herrmann and Newman Work Together

In 1954, a rather unusual collaboration in the world of film composing took place. Alfred Newman had been hired by Daryl F. Zanuck to score the epic film *The Egyptian;* however, the filmmaker had pushed

1. Thomas, *Music for the Movies,* p. 254.

up the release date, making it virtually impossible for Newman to meet the demands of the new deadline. Bernard Herrmann recommended to Newman that he cowrite part of the score to make things easier on his friend. Newman accepted the idea. The amazing thing is that neither composer met during the entire time to discuss what each was doing for the film. Although each section composed by Herrmann has his distinct style, as could be said for Newman's creative work, the score works very nicely.

East of Eden: Leonard Rosenman's Innovative Score

Leonard Rosenman (1924–) started his long distinguished career scoring the Elia Kazan film adaptation of John Steinbeck's lengthy novel, *East of Eden*. Rosenman had been born in Brooklyn, New York. He had been a music theory and composition student of the innovative composer Arnold Schoenberg, who rocked the traditional world of musical composition by presenting the world with the twelve-tone row technique. While living in New York, Rosenman had a group of piano students. Among these students was a young man named James Dean. Dean had just been contracted by Kazan to star in *East of Eden*. As luck would have it, Kazan and Dean attended a concert given by Rosenman at the Museum of Modern Art in New York. After an introduction by Dean, Kazan asked Rosenman if he had any interest in writing music for films. Since Kazan was both producer and director of *East of Eden,* he was at liberty to ask Rosenman if he would like to score his next project, starring his young piano pupil, James Dean. The rest is history. The film opened on March 9, 1955.

The music that Rosenman provided is both beautiful at times and modernistic and unusual sounding. *This combination of a lyrical, singing melody with contrasting modern harshness was foreshadowing a style of film scoring that would be tried by many film composers over the years to come.*

The Cobweb: Pioneering Use of a Twelve-Tone Row in a Movie

Later that same year, Leonard Rosenman would shock the ears of filmgoers by using a new innovative style of film composing based on the 1923 pioneering twelve-tone row technique of his composition teacher, Arnold Schoenberg. The score that Rosenman composed for *The Cobweb* is considered to be the earliest film score to use the **twelve-tone row**. This is a method of composing (invented by Arnold Schoenberg around 1923) in which all twelve chromatic tones (meaning every white and black-keyed notes are sounded going up or down the scale on a piano) are used in such a manner as to preclude tonality as we know it. Because this creates a *lack* of a tonal center as in conventional music, and because with a twelve-tone row we basically have each of the twelve tones sharing equal importance, we say that this kind of music is **atonal**. (Conventional music, that is, most of the music we listen to in the world, is tonal.)[2]

2. David Raksin contends that he used the twelve-tone row in a 1949/50 film called *The Man with a Cloak*. The first five notes of the row spelled out *Edgar*. (The letter "r" was represented by D♭.) It was during the last minute of the movie that the audience realizes that the man in the cloak was none other than Edgar Allan Poe.

Picnic: Clever Use of Pop Melody and Original Scoring

In the 1955 film *Picnic,* the American-born film composer George Duning (1919–2000) achieved an amusing effect in film scoring history by combining a well-known popular melody called "Moonglow" with a love theme that he had written for the film. The scene starts with William Holden's character Hal (a former football hero) dancing with a young girl who appears to be having a difficult time keeping the proper rhythm of the 1930's hit song "Moonglow." Next we see the young Kim Novak as Madge enter in the scenario to take over by dancing with Holden's character. When their eyes meet, Duning superimposes his love theme over the popular song "Moonglow." They fit together beautifully. By *superimposing* the two together in this crucial scene, he was able to give the impression of uniting the two main characters in a relationship that would be cemented together at the film's end when Madge runs off to join Hal.

This combining of the two songs made a very popular hit that remained as number one on the Top Ten charts for a month and a half. He later stated that it took him about four or five days to work out the combination of the two tunes for this film sequence.

By combining these two songs together, George Duning would cement a permanent place in film music history for himself with this innovative touch.

The Trouble with Harry

The year 1955 was a turning point in Bernard Herrmann's career. At the advice of composer Lyn Murray (who scored Hitchcock's *To Catch a Thief* in 1954), Alfred Hitchcock hired composer Bernard Herrmann to score his new black comedy *The Trouble with Harry* (1955). Although Herrmann and Hitchcock had previously met one another on several occasions, this union would mark the beginning of one of the most brilliant and effective collaborations between director and composer in the history of film music. These two men would create some of the most memorable "dabblings" into the macabre the moviegoing public would ever see. This partnership, which lasted more than a decade, started with *The Trouble with Harry* and ended with *Torn Curtain* (1965). Herrmann's score for *Torn Curtain* was not used because it supposedly lacked commercial appeal. Herrmann wrote a score for large orchestra, including the "terrifying" sound of twelve flutes along with a greatly augmented brass section of sixteen horns, nine trombones, and two tubas! Because Universal Studio executives felt that Herrmann's approach to scoring was old fashioned and out of date, Hitchcock was forced to use the British composer John Addison, whose score was still unsuccessful in salvaging this box office bomb. Herrmann had thought that he and Hitchcock were good friends. Having his score rejected by Hitchcock totally devastated Herrmann's spirit. Neither man ever spoke to the other after this unfortunate incident. A brilliant team parted their ways over the insane concept that for a film score to be successful, it must cater to the youth market with a hit song as opposed to serve the film with effective underscoring. Unfortunately, that same philosophy continues to drive the film music business to this day, much to the detriment of several veteran composers, who have had their expertly written scores rejected in favor of a more youth-oriented pop score.

The Trouble with Harry is about the film's main characters' stumbling on Harry Worp's dead body; each person feels that they might have been responsible for Harry's death. Hitchcock was later heard to say that this, along with *Shadow of a Doubt,* was among his personal favorite movies. The film deals with two of America's chief preoccupations . . . *sex* and *death* (violence). The unique nonchalant approach to the film's handling of these two taboos helps to support Hitchcock's philosophy that "understatement is important." It appears that no one really liked Harry, so the discovery of his death came as no real tragedy. As it happens, Harry's body is casually buried and then disinterred at least three times. We finally learn that Harry died of natural causes. In the meantime, it was Hitchcock's taking the "melodrama out of the pitch-black night" and bringing "it into the sunshine" of the Vermont forest that helped to relax the viewers in dealing with the subject matter. Also adding to this lighthearted approach was the *somewhat comical score supplied by Bernard Herrmann.*

What we see in the film as the Vermont countryside during its famous fall season colors, is in many cases somewhat deceiving. Hitchcock had relocated in Vermont to catch the change of seasons. Due to an unplanned set of rainstorms, it became necessary for Hitchcock to move his cast and crew inside an interior set, built inside of a school gymnasium in Vermont. Because the roof of the gym was constructed of tin, the heavy pounding sound of the rainfall prevented the crew from being able to use the synchronous sound taken on this set. The dialogue had to be rerecorded back in a studio in Hollywood, much the same way as it is done on many films today. Even though a few hours of sunshine finally appeared, Hitchcock and crew had already decided to relocate back at Paramount studios in Hollywood to finish the shooting of the film. For some of the outdoor shots that we see in the film, this was actually done by having the actors stand in front of a large screen in the studio, on which the outdoor shots (actually shot during the few hours of sunshine in Vermont) were projected from the rear. This technique is known as *rear projection*. For other scenes shot inside Paramount's sound stages, the sets were constructed of plaster trees on which actual leaves from Vermont were individually attached.

One wonders how Herrmann and Hitchcock could have been so successful in their years of collaboration. As Donald Spoto states in his definitive biography on Hitchcock, *The Dark Side of Genius,* "Each of these men was stubborn, often intractable, [and] not given to the patient endurance of complaints from temperamental associates or subordinates or studio bosses. But beyond their proud and gifted personalities lay common bonds. Hitchcock and Herrmann shared a dark, tragic sense of life, a brooding view of human relationships, and a compulsion to explore aesthetically the private world of the romantic fantasy."[3] The score that Herrmann wrote for *The Trouble with Harry* sounds as though it was intended for an animated cartoon. Each time one of the main characters stumbles upon Harry's dead body, we hear a four-note leitmotif:

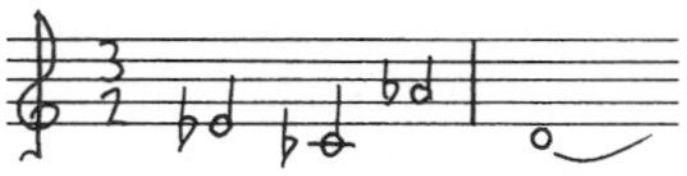

This theme is recognizable in most of its entrances throughout the movie. Occasionally, Herrmann places these notes in variation, disguising this theme somewhat, as when Miss Gravely first sees Harry's dead body, as Captain Wiles drags the corpse through the leaves for burial. The score contains interesting musical motives for most of the film's characters, including a memorable recurring theme for the nearsighted doctor, who appears oblivious to Harry's dead body each time he stumbles over his corpse, as he walks through the woods. We also hear a wide-sweeping pastoral theme for the local abstract painter, played by John Forsythe.

The Man Who Knew Too Much

Later that year, Hitchcock started production on a remake of one of his earlier films of the same name, *The Man Who Knew Too Much.* In comparing the two versions, Hitchcock said it best: "Let's say that the first version was the work of a talented amateur and the second [the subject of our study] was made by

3. Donald Spoto, *The Dark Side of Genius* (Canada: Little, Brown & Co., 1983), p. 335.

a professional." The first version, released in 1934, starred Peter Lorre and became Hitchcock's first international success.

The 1955/56 remake version starred Doris Day and Jimmy Stewart. The plot involves an American family who vacations in Marrakech, Morroco. They become involved in a complicated plot in which their son is kidnapped and they must stop a possible assassination attempt. The movie's climax takes place at a concert in Royal Albert Hall in London. Although this is not one of Herrmann's great scores, the movie is discussed here primarily for two reasons. First, Herrmann makes his only "cameo" appearance in a motion picture during the Albert Hall sequence and, second, the music being performed during this concert is *extremely* crucial to the outcome of the movie. We see Bernard Herrmann conducting the London Symphony Orchestra in a performance of Arthur Benjamin's *Storm Clouds Cantata*. This work is scored for chorus, orchestra, and vocal soloist. In a rather unusual dual function, Benjamin's music acts as both source music and dramatic underscoring, all at the same time. As you watch the movie, it becomes obvious just how important this work becomes to the plot. At the precise moment, toward the end of this piece, there is a loud cymbal crash. It is during this crash that an assassin must shoot his one shot in order not to be noticed by members of the audience. His target is the prime minister, who is seated directly across from this "hitman," in his royal box seat. As Donald Spoto states in his book *The Art of Alfred Hitchcock,* "The great sequence at Albert Hall is a perfect summary of Hitchcock's method and one of the most astonishing episodes in film. . . . To create and sustain tension, he employed all the counterpoints, balances and juxtapositions at his disposal."[4] His rhythm of crosscutting (cutting between two or more independent actions to show their relationship to one another) during this nine-minute musical performance is highly effective. As the music builds closer to the cymbal crash near the end of the piece, Hitchcock maintains suspense by rapid-fire editing back and forth from seeing the assassin, to seeing the prime minister, to seeing Herrmann conducting the performance, to seeing Doris Day's character writhing in anxiety as to how to handle the situation. If she alerts the authorities, her son could be killed, but the prime minister's life will be spared. If she does nothing, her son's life may be spared, but the prime minister will be assassinated! The entire Albert Hall performance of the *Storm Clouds Cantata* lasts around nine minutes in length, and Hitchcock has filmed the entire performance. Hitchcock has very carefully orchestrated his *montage* (the process of placing film images in a specific sequence) to work alongside the Arthur Benjamin piece in building suspense. From the time Bernard Herrmann gives the downbeat to the fatal fall of the assassin, there are over 120 edited scenes, some lasting only one or two seconds in length. As you watch this sequence, note the length of each shot, and how each seems to fit what is happening in the music. On a side note, the actress Doris Day was upset that Hitchcock didn't seem to be very friendly to her on the set. It was a "cool, remote and uncaring" relationship on the part of Hitchcock. This bothered Day. She had a personal meeting with him and told him that she felt that she was not pleasing him. If he would like to replace her on the picture, she said that she would understand. He was dumbfounded. Hitchcock stated that if he didn't like what she was doing, he would have told her. He went on to reveal that "he was more frightened of life, of rejection, of relationship . . . than anyone. He told me [Doris Day] he was afraid to walk across the Paramount lot to the commissary because he was so afraid of people."[5] The actress Thelma Ritter remarked, "If Hitchcock liked what you did, he said nothing. If he didn't, he looked like he was going to throw up."[6]

4. Donald Spoto, *The Art of Alfred Hitchcock* (New York: Doubleday, 2nd ed., 1992), p. 249.
5. Spoto, *Genius,* p. 364.
6. Spoto.

The Ten Commandments

One of the great epic films of all time is Cecil B. DeMille's *The Ten Commandments*. This was his most ambitious production and it certainly dwarfed all others that had gone before. Costing over $13 million to make (a colossal amount for that time), this 1956 production used a reported twenty-five thousand extras in some of the massive sequences. The film, made by Paramount Pictures, was the top-grossing film in Hollywood following *Gone with the Wind*. Before premiering this mighty epic in New York, Cecil B. DeMille insisted on testing this film with Mormons in Salt Lake City. He felt that, being as devoutly religious as this test audience would be, if they liked it, so would everyone else. The film opened in Los Angeles on October 5, 1956.

During the shooting of the film, DeMille was known for making rather loud comments, sometimes being rather rude in nature, to members of the crowd or crew. These announcements were made with a large megaphone so that everyone within earshot could hear these sometimes embarrassing remarks. However, it was said that DeMille was usually respectful of the major cast members. He was a showman and a taskmaster. He loved spectacle. Anyone who has seen this film will forever remember the crossing of the Red Sea sequence or the mass Exodus of Moses and his people from the Pharaoh Rameses. DeMille had worked with the composer Victor Young (1900–1956) on several films before this, and he really wanted Young for this scoring project. As it turned out, Young became very sick and felt that he would not be able to carry out this massive project, so Young recommended the young composer Elmer Bernstein. Although this was an unfortunate turn of events for Young, as he died of a heart attack later that year, it was the score Bernstein needed to launch his illustrious career. Bernstein was not given a long-term contract; he basically was asked to compose each cue and play it for DeMille on a week-by-week basis. At first, Bernstein would play an elaborate piano arrangement of the section of the score in question. However, according to Bernstein, DeMille would eventually ask him to perform a more simplified "one-finger" demonstration. This was a difficult yet rewarding experience for Bernstein.

In the mass exodus scene in which literally thousands of extras are seen leaving Egypt for their "Promised Land," Bernstein noticed that the pace at which the people were walking was rather slow. He, accordingly, wrote music (a quasi-Hebraic anthem) to underscore this section of the film at this slow speed. When DeMille heard what Bernstein had written for this cue, he began to wonder what Bernstein was trying to do. The producer was afraid that Bernstein's music would cause the scene to become too lethargic for the viewer, making the exodus almost unbearable and boring to watch. Afterall, Moses' people had just been let go after four hundred years in bondage. They should be *rejoicing*, not lamenting. DeMille told Bernstein that what he should do is write upbeat music that moves at a *faster* tempo. This technique, he said, will give the audience the impression that the people are walking much faster than they actually are. It worked! Now the Jews, through the change in music, appeared to be feeling excitement and hope for the future instead of solemn lethargy. Bernstein learned a valuable lesson from this veteran master and would later reuse this technique for his score to *The Magnificent Seven* in 1960.

Bernstein said that DeMille had very strong opinions as to how he wanted the music to sound and function within the completed film. DeMille's approach was that of using leitmotifs for the many characters within the film. This explains the reason why there are a number of musical themes within the film. Bernstein's own approach, had he been left alone to score this great epic, was based on the premise that the story of a film can work on its own, without the need for identifiable leitmotifs . . . that the best thing that music can do is add another dimension to the film. Bernstein had to create some authentic-sounding Egyptian source music of the period. Since there are no existing examples available (it predates musical notation), Bernstein created his own, knowing that certain woodwind and percussion instruments did exist at that time. According to Bernstein, "The only 'tricky' effects employed were in the burning bush sequence in which the string choir was reinforced by a novachord [similar to an electric piano] and in the sequence of the pestilence in which several electronic devices were used to help impart the feeling of terror."[7] The score was written for a seventy-one-piece orchestra that included the use of eight horns as opposed to the usual four found in most orchestras.

During the opening of the Red Sea sequence, Bernstein introduces a Hebrew-sounding march intertwined with some of the musical themes heard earlier in the movie:

Red Sea march theme

The most prominent musical theme in the film, first heard right at the onset of the movie, returns throughout the picture and deals with the idea of deliverance out of bondage:

Deliverance theme

Elmer Bernstein said, "It was a very complex problem since the composition [score] had to express Scripture, history and drama in music."[8] The entire movie was on a grand scale and dealt with the life of Moses and his people and their relationship to God.

One of the biggest questions asked was who would be the "voice" of God? Later, when asked, DeMille said that a political speechwriter friend of his by the name of Donald Hayne would have this job. For years, people had credited Hayne with the "voice" of God. It was not until 1978, when it was revealed that the real "voice" was none other than Charlton Heston, who was also playing the role of Moses. Evidently, Heston was able to convince DeMille for this dual role. So as not to be recognizable as the same voice, especially in scenes where Heston was talking to God, his voice was recorded and played back at a slower speed.

In order to create authenticity, DeMille was able to get away with certain scenes because this picture had a biblical theme; therefore, the censors of that time would leave some rather risqué subjects intact. In the sequence where the people made a golden calf to worship while Moses had gone up atop Mount Sinai to receive the Ten Commandments, DeMille staged an orgy in which scantily clad girls are seduced by the men behind rocks. In a rather unusual twist of protocol, one exhausted girl supposedly went to one of the assistant directors on the set and asked, "Who do you have to sleep with around here to get *out* of this picture?"

Elmer Bernstein had almost a year to work on the score, and because of a twist of fate, he got the job instead of his capable colleague, Victor Young. With the success of this score, Bernstein's career took off. He became one of the most sought-after composers of the 1950s and 1960s. Although Elmer Bernstein remains an active film composer even into the twenty-first century, his most memorable scores were from this earlier period.

It is interesting to note that Bernstein wondered why DeMille would entrust a completely unknown composer like Bernstein to score the most ambitious film ever made up to that time. *The Man with the*

7. James L. Limbacher, ed., *Film Music: From Violins to Video* (Metuchen, NJ: Scarecrow Press, 1974), p. 155.
8. Limbacher.

Charlton Heston as Moses in Cecil B. DeMille's The Ten Commandments *(1956). Courtesy of Archive Photos.*

Forbidden Planet: The Era of Electronic Music in Films Begins

The year 1956 also ushered in a new era in film music. This would be the year that we have *the first totally all-electronic score*. Although instruments such as the theremin and the ondes martenot had already been around, the electronic synthesizer was still in its infancy stage, and was therefore not utilized in film composition at this time. A young team of artists in the new field of electronic music was hired to provide some new sounds to a MGM production of the science fiction fantasy *Forbidden Planet*. This film needed a score that would match the uniqueness of the sets and special effects. The music department at MGM was baffled as to how to score a film like this with the traditional symphonic sounds; that's why Louis and Bebe Barron were hired as the creators of a new type of movie score—the electronic score. They were a husband and wife team who would go on to cowrite the scores for *The Very Edge of the Night* (1959) and *Spaceboy* (1979). Their landmark score for *Forbidden Planet* launched the era of electronic music in cinema. The sounds on this score were emitted by a series of cybernetic circuits. These circuits were conceived, designed, and built by Louis and Bebe Barron. These "electronic tonalities," as they were credited on screen, were so effective that members of the Motion Picture Academy nominated this score for an Academy Award. It has been said that this movie inspired future filmmakers to make the *Star Wars* and *Star Trek* films.

The Spirit of St. Louis

The composer Franz Waxman, that German master of film composing, was given an extremely challenging assignment in 1957. Billy Wilder had been fascinated with making a film version of Charles Lindbergh's heroic flight from New York to Paris. The actual event had taken place back in 1927. Because much of the action in the film was confined to one man all alone in a narrow cockpit, the main drama was represented by one airplane pilot battling against the elements. No one had ever successfully crossed the Atlantic Ocean in a single engine airplane before. The whole film project was a gamble for its screenwriters as well. Because the story was factual, being based on Lindbergh's Pulitzer Prize–winning autobiography, they could not invent episodes or characters. Could the story hold the audience's attention for two hours and fifteen minutes? Wilder knew that this was not the type of film that would make a lot of money. He was right; Warner Bros. lost $6 million on this film. A young stage actor by the name of John Kerr was the first choice for the part. He turned it down because he did not like Lindbergh's political beliefs during World War II. The actor Jimmy Stewart, who had been the pilot of a bomber during World War II, stormed into producer Leland Hayward's office, insisting that he play the role of Lindbergh. Stewart at forty-eight was too old to play the part of Lindbergh, who was only twenty-five at the time. Nevertheless, after much tenacity, Stewart convinced Hayward that he was the right man for the part. Jimmy Stewart gave a convincing portrayal of this great American hero, or, as a writer for *The Hollywood Reporter* put it, "one of the most remarkable in screen history." Three exact working replicas of the original Lindbergh plane were built to be used in the movie. Seven thousand extras were used in the final landing sequence as Lindbergh heroically lands "the Spirit of St. Louis" airplane after the thirty-six-hundred-mile journey, lasting thirty-three hours, thirty minutes, and 29.8 seconds. To add realism to the scene, producer Hayward had an exact life-sized Le Bourget airport built several miles outside of Paris, as it looked in 1927.

Waxman's task before him was to musically fill in the absence of dialogue during the many sequences that took place in the cockpit of Lindbergh's plane, as he spans the width of the North Atlantic from New York to Paris. Scored for an unusually large studio orchestra, Waxman added *five*

Actor Jimmy Stewart as Charles Lindbergh in The Spirit of St. Louis. *Courtesy of Archive Photos.*

female vocalists for an ethereal "out-of-this-world" airborne sound. The film opens on the eve of Lindbergh's solo flight. Through a series of flashbacks, it tells the story of a young aviator who eventually becomes a world hero. We notice the music right at the beginning of the film's story as we see a small plane sailing through the air. The main title sequence is suggestive of the feeling of being airborne or flying. We hear the music weaving in a constant upward direction, particularly in the high strings. This "rising" musical motive will dominate the whole score and could be called the "Spirit" theme. Later in the film, as Lindbergh's flight gets underway, we see Lindbergh falling asleep. Notice how Waxman accompanies this sequence with a monotonous repeating ostinato pattern. We, too, begin to feel fatigue from this minimalistic repetition of notes. Finally, the ostinato pattern stops at the moment Lindbergh plunges into a deep sleep. As Lindbergh's plane spirals downward, the plane's crashing into the ocean seems unavoidable. Fortunately, as Lindbergh's plane winds around and around, a ray of sunlight pokes through the cockpit window, beaming across his face. Each time this occurs, Waxman supplies a dissonant brass chord (a leitmotif for the sun's rays). Eventually, this awakens Lindbergh just in the nick of time so that his plane does not plummet into the ocean. This is a very effective scene and really shows the power of film music as used by a great master such as Waxman. Imagine this scene without

Opening main title Spirit theme (note the rising direction of the musical line).

music. It is for this cue that Waxman puts to good use his five female vocalists (three soprano singers and two mezzo-sopranos). They help create a surreal atmosphere for this scene. As Lindbergh finally reaches land on the other side of the Atlantic, we know it before he does, that the land he is over is Ireland coming into Dingle Bay. This information is relayed to us via music in the manner of an Irish dance form known as a gigue. Another clever use of music, or should we say, *lack* of music, comes during the final minutes of the movie, when it appears that Lindbergh has less than an hour to go before he reaches Paris.

First, we hear music snippets of "La Marseillaise," telling the viewer that Lindbergh has finally reached France. Then, with only ninety-eight miles to go before landing the plane, the music builds on a variation of the opening "rising" or "Spirit" theme. Suddenly, the music stops! So does his plane's engine! He is out of fuel. Fortunately, he finds a reserve fuel tank left, designed to bring him safely into Paris. As he finally arrives over Paris, he encounters one more unexpected dilemma. The music that underscores his arrival over Paris sounds majestic and victorious. This will soon change, however. Because he has been awake for over three days, flying the plane for over thirty-three hours, his eyesight is too blurred in order to see his map. Lindbergh cannot find Le Bourget airfield. He begins to panic. As Lindbergh becomes more and more disoriented, so does Waxman's underscore, which accompanies this effective sequence. Listen carefully and you will note that the music in this section bounces around in a chaotic fashion, mimicking Lindbergh's confusion. After a brief cry for help from God, Lindbergh brings the plane in for a safe landing. We hear one final quote of the opening "rising" motive that concludes the score—and the movie—on a note of optimism for the future.

This score ranks as one of Waxman's finest musical achievements. Because there were long stretches in the film without spoken dialogue, music was the necessary panacea. Also significant in this score was the way in which Waxman utilizes musical nationalistic references to countries over which Lindbergh flies (i.e., the Irish gigue and the French "La Marseillaise"). Part of the completed score had to be rewritten by two people other than Waxman. After Waxman had finished recording the score, he left for Paris to work on his next score for the movie *Love in the Afternoon*. Jack Warner, head of Warner Bros., decided to have a preview of the film in San Francisco to see the response by an audience. Because the results were somewhat disastrous, Warner ordered changes in the film and wanted them done quickly. Because Waxman was in Paris, and therefore not available, music rewrites were handled by the music director Ray Heindorf and the staff composer Roy Webb.

The Bridge on the River Kwai

A somewhat strange thing occurred in film music history at the Academy Awards for 1957. The English composer Malcolm Arnold (1921–) won for his work in the Best Score category, although many people feel that this award was given because of the popularity of a march song contained within the film that was actually composed by someone other than the winning composer.

Anyone who has ever seen this movie cannot help but notice the "Colonel Bogey March." It is perhaps one of the most memorable tunes that is easily whistleable by most moviegoers from any war movie. What many people don't realize is the fact that it was not written by Malcolm Arnold; it was composed in 1914 by Kenneth J. Alford (1881–1945).

The Big Country

The year 1958 saw a very important landmark score created by a composer who was basically known as a concert hall composer who just happened to compose some film music. The composer was Jerome Moross. He had started in the business as an orchestrator for various film composers. You might remember seeing his name on the credits of *The Bishop's Wife* as an arranger/orchestrator for Hugo Friedhofer. Moross was born in New York in 1913 and continued to live in New York. He chose to commute from New York to Hollywood when he had a film to do or, as he put it, "when I needed the money." A film concentrating on the grandeur and sweeping panorama of the great Western frontier was *The Big Country*, directed by William Wyler. Moross was hired to provide a score that would not concentrate on individual leitmotifs for each of the major characters, a style of film composing that had become standard fair for many of the Hollywood composers. Instead, Moross wrote a nearly seventy-minute score that broke traditions by creating musical cues that were complete compositions rather than fragments. This innovative score is considered by many, including the composer himself, to be the prototype Western score.

Jerome Moross. Courtesy of the Tony Thomas Collection.

This was certainly not the first Western score. Many had come before. Composers such as Victor Young and Dimitri Tiomkin had given the film world several memorable scores. It was perhaps the high quality of this score that helped to separate it from earlier scores of this genre. The extremely exciting main title sequence starts with a flashy, knee-slapping hoe-down-like ostinato in the strings that signals a "Western" flavor.

Hoe-down ostinato in strings

The Pentatonic Scale

Moross mixed his score with ethnic American folk idioms along with traditional symphonic writing to give us the sound that makes this such a landmark Western score. His use of the pentatonic scale for many of the tunes in this movie helps to give this score its Western sound.

The pentatonic scale uses only five notes per octave. A good way to describe the sound of the pentatonic scale is to play a tune on the piano using only the black keys.

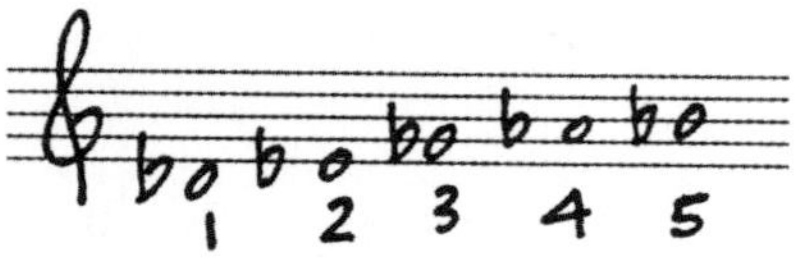

This type of scale has been around since the most ancient of times, dating way back to ancient China. It is how these tones are arranged that makes them sound Scottish, Chinese, or Western.

Chinese theme

Scottish theme

Western theme

Moross masterfully penned a style of writing using the pentatonic scale and triadic melodies (a triad is a group of three notes that outline the intervals of thirds) that would influence future composers of Western scores.

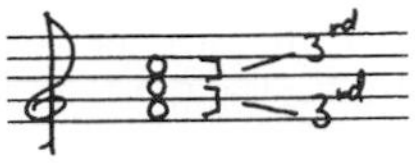

A triad

The use of jazzy syncopated rhythms in some of the tunes may be the influence on Moross of the music of George Gershwin (1898–1937).

Syncopation

Syncopated rhythms or "*syncopation*" occurs in music when the musical notes do not always fall "on the beat." This creates the "jazzy" bounce feeling and can create tension, suspense, or excitement.

Prior to writing the score to *The Big Country,* Moross had been the pianist for the touring production of Gershwin's American folk opera *Porgy and Bess*. Listen to the music from *Porgy and Bess* to hear striking similarities.

Moross used three different pianists on the scoring sessions for *The Big Country*. One of these pianists was none other than Johnny Williams, better known today as John Williams, the film composer who has scored most of Steven Spielberg's films.

Jerome Moross started work on this outstanding Western score in the spring of 1958. He wrote a total of forty-two musical cues, comprising about seventy minutes' worth of music. One of these cues illustrates the powerful use of an ostinato pattern (repeated notes) to build suspense. As Gregory Peck's character (James McKay) rides through Blanco Canyon, we hear a repeated pattern played in the horns and strings as the trumpet plays a variation of the "welcoming" theme heard earlier in the movie.

Blanco Canyon ostinato:

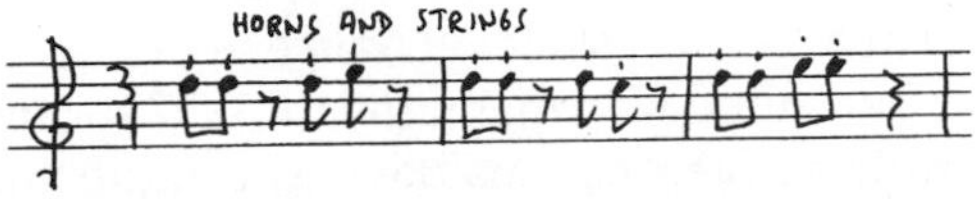

"Welcoming" Theme variation:

Peck's character rides on horseback through the white-rock canyon, seemingly oblivious to the dangerous riflemen who lurk in the hills around the canyon. The above ostinato theme *builds tension* for the viewer who is definitely aware of the danger. At any moment, one of the gunmen could shoot and kill Peck's character.

Although a master orchestrator, Jerome Moross used four orchestrators on this score—one of them was Alexander Courage, who went on to write the famous *Star Trek* television theme. Because the scoring stage #7 at Goldwyn Studios was always in heavy demand, it took Moross four months, from April to July, in which to record the complete score. It was written for a large studio orchestra of around one hundred players. Moross was able to hire the cream of the Hollywood studio musicians crop. In the string section alone were several top-rate concertmasters—the principal violinist in an orchestra who plays all of the violin solos and who is in charge of marking all of the phrasings, known as "bowings," for the other members of their sections—from other orchestras.

The Seventh Voyage of Sinbad

The late 1950s brought another change in Bernard Herrmann's life, as he began to work on what we might call the fantasy film genre. In 1958, Herrmann scored *The Seventh Voyage of Sinbad*. This was followed in 1959 by *Journey to the Center of the Earth. The Seventh Voyage of Sinbad* displays Herrmann's mastery of orchestration. Written at a time in his career that might be classified as being the height of his orchestral genius, Herrmann utilized a large symphony orchestra with additional brass, woodwinds, and a larger than normal percussion section. John W. Morgan, in the liner notes of the CD recording states, "Most of the composer's stylistic traits are evident [in this score]: moving minor chords played by various choirs of the orchestra; a penchant for low woodwinds; repeated rhythmic and harmonic sequences and a pulsating sense of orchestral dynamics."[9]

The plot involves Captain Sinbad and his crew who must sail to the island of Colossa to find a piece of an eggshell from a giant bird known as a roc. This will help in restoring the beautiful Princess Parisa back to her normal size. She was reduced to a tiny person by the evil magician Sokurah. Along their journey, Sinbad and his men encounter a giant one-eyed, one-horned beast known as a cyclops. Herrmann accompanies this cyclops attack with pounding percussion and powerful brass. The fierceness of the music evokes the feeling of helplessness for Sinbad and his men. They are up against something bigger than life. The cyclops seems undefeatable. The strong masculine quality of the music here makes the thick-skinned creature seem almost unpenetrable.

Later in the film, Sinbad is attacked by a human skeleton who is brought back to life by the evil Sokurah's black magic. As we see the skeleton slowly coming to life, we hear Herrmann's "trademark" low woodwind accompaniment, particularly in the bassoons. As the duel between the two gets underway, Herrmann cleverly accompanies the action with an instrument often associated with skeletons, the **xylophone**. This instrument can depict the sound of human bones clanking together.

Added to this are the sounds of a whip, wood blocks, and castanets as well as a tuba and several horns and trumpets, who perform a devilish skeleton dance.

Producer Charles Schneer had hired Herrmann in late 1957 for the scoring assignment of *Sinbad*. Schneer had admired Herrmann's music since his days as a radio composer. Ray Harryhausen, the film's special effects man, had originally wanted either Max Steiner or Miklos Rosza for the job. Herrmann was shown a rough cut of the film in black and white. He wanted nothing to do with the project, saying that he had never scored a film such as this. It took about six months of negotiations before

9. *The Seventh Voyage of Sinbad* (CD liner notes by John W. Morgan), Varese Sarabande, 1980.

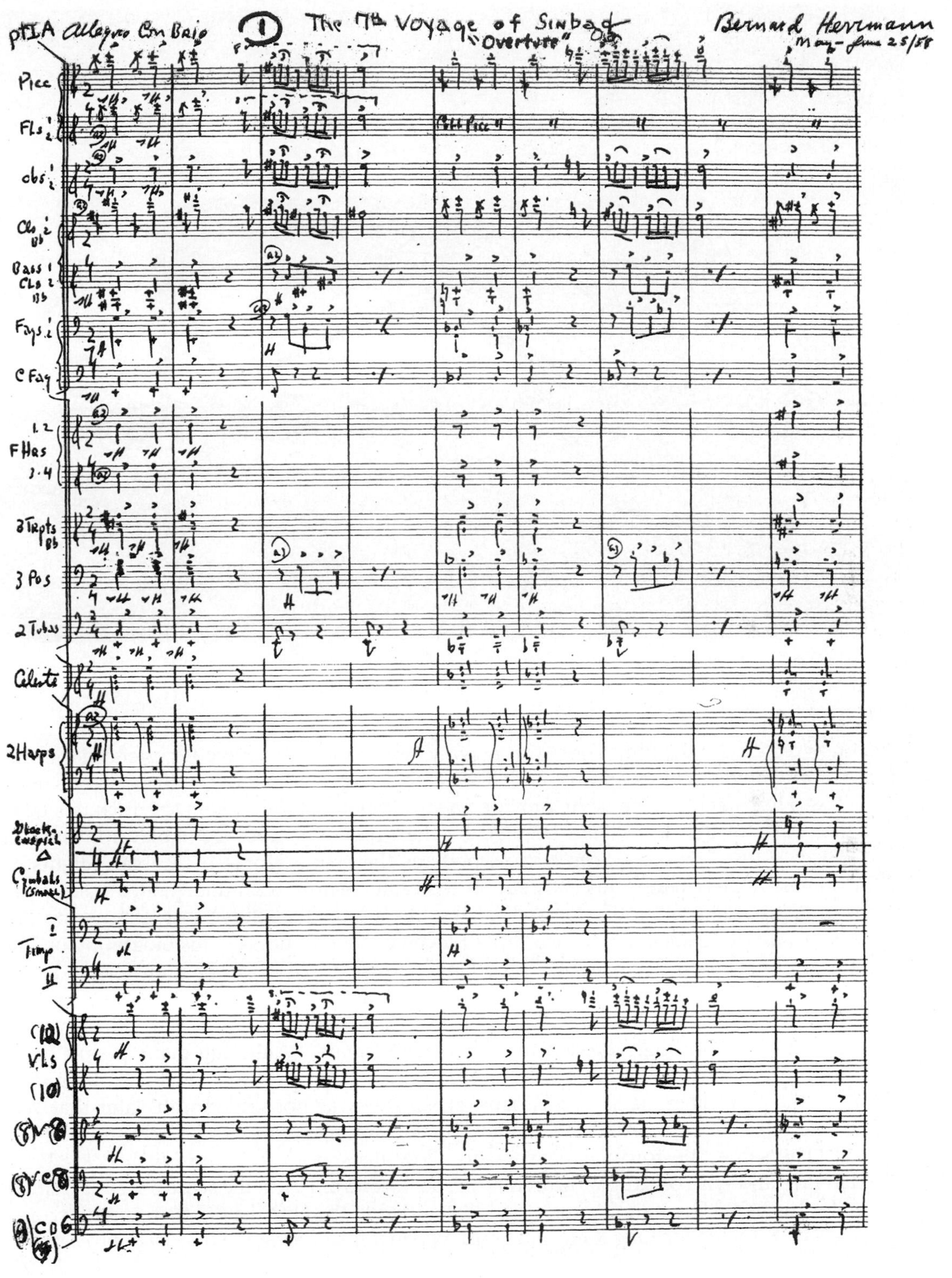

Actual main title page of The Seventh Voyage of Sinbad *in Herrmann's handwriting. Courtesy of Bernard Herrmann Collection, Davidson Library, University of California at Santa Barbara.*

The Xylophone. From the author's collection.

Herrmann agreed to do the film. There was no way Herrmann could have experienced the sharp vivid brilliance of the movie's colors and the added effect that they would have on the viewer's impressions. Nevertheless, Herrmann's score alone provided a large palette of tone colors to enrich this tale. It could be said that parts of the score were inspired by the Russian composer Nikolay Rimsky-Korsakov's (1844–1908) colorful showpiece *Scheherazade*, perhaps the best example of Arabian Nights orchestral color for orchestra. Herrmann musically supported each creature with unorthodox instrumental combinations and provided leitmotifs for each of the film's key characters in order to wrap "the entire movie in a shroud of mystical innocence."[10] As Steven C. Smith quotes in his biography on Herrmann, "Orchestral timbre is used to create both mood and a sense of scale [for the monsters and creatures], a world in which evil is characterized by low, 'heavy' instruments and in which heroism and beauty are depicted through light or traditionally balanced textures. Herrmann gives Harryhausen's creatures a sense of gigantic scale through the density of his orchestration." Although many people consider this score to be one of Herrmann's most colorful efforts for cinema, he was unable to be present at the recording of the score because of a musicians' strike that was not settled until later that year (1958). Therefore, the music was recorded in Germany by the Graunke Symphony Orchestra with a different conductor. (The same fate forced Herrmann to allow his score for Alfred Hitchcock's *Vertigo* to be recorded in England with conductor Muir Mathieson in control.) With the score for *The Seventh Voyage of Sinbad* under his belt, Herrmann's music could be added to the elite list of other fantasy scores such as Max Steiner's 1933 score for *King Kong* and Franz Waxman's score for *The Bride of Frankenstein* in 1935.

10. Quote from Smith, *A Heart at Fire's Center*.

Vertigo

The year 1958 also saw Bernard Herrmann composing a masterful score for the now-classic film, *Vertigo. Herrmann considered this score to be his own personal favorite of those scores he wrote for Alfred Hitchcock. Vertigo* contains one of cinema's most memorable romantic moments of longing, thanks in part to Herrmann's dramatic paraphrase of Richard Wagner's *Liebestod* ("Love–Death") aria from his opera *Tristan und Isolde* (1865). By linking together one musical phrase after another, with no apparent letup, both Wagner and Herrmann were able to create in their music an unequaled endless feeling of yearning and longing for a loved one. *The impact that Wagner's music has had on succeeding generations of composers can scarcely be measured,* particularly his music for this opera. It was Max Steiner who had said, "If Wagner had lived in this century [the twentieth century], he would have been the number one film composer." Even Richard Wagner said, "My music speaks the unspeakable."

In *Vertigo,* Herrmann has to create an intense yearning feeling of the main character Scottie (played by Jimmy Stewart) and his unquenchable love for Madeline (played by Kim Novak). In a rather twisted necrophilia-like sequence, Scottie spies a beautiful woman whom he dresses up to look like the supposedly dead Madeline. Herrmann's music captures the surging power of the moment so beautifully that it is nearly impossible to imagine a better approach of underscoring this moment by any other composer. This scene is one of the most powerful of its kind in cinema history, thanks in major part to Herrmann's incredible scoring talent.

Journey to the Center of the Earth

It has been said that this period in Bernard Herrmann's life—from 1958 to 1963—is probably his *greatest period of creativity*. Herrmann was hired by 20th Century Fox to score a Jules Verne adventure called *Journey to the Center of the Earth* (1959). In this score, Herrmann has nearly done away with thematic material. This is replaced by short two-, three-, or four-note cues. In this film, Herrmann uses his favorite two-note semitone motive that dominates most of this film's score (an "f" natural resolving to an "e" natural). Herrmann wanted to create a score that gave the impression of a world in which explorers delve "with absolutely no human contact." To capture the eerie feeling of the inner Earth, Herrmann chose a rather interesting combination of instruments. He eliminated all strings from the main portion of the score and substituted five organs (one large cathedral organ and four electronic ones). We hear an array of bassoons, a clarinet choir, a vibraphone, and a cluster of harps to provide the *atmosphere* of the descent into the inner world.

On discovery of the lost city of Atlantis, we hear a supernatural organ chorale accompanied by the chanting of a vibraphone. This is a color created by Herrmann like no other in a movie score. It is moments like this that support the feeling by many that Herrmann was perhaps the master of creative orchestral color in motion pictures. This also enhances his philosophy that he was not afraid of using unorthodox combinations of instruments to fit the needs of a given scene. Herrmann "unearthed" an instrument, invented around 1590, called a **serpent**, for inclusion in this motion picture during the scene involving a giant chameleon. This was a bass member of the cornett family whose shape is that of the letter "s." Its tubing was about two meters long and was played at one end with a cup mouthpiece similar to that of a bass trombone. Although obsolete today, the serpent was widely used in the eighteenth and nineteenth centuries. In this score, its sound is reminiscent to that of a sick cow. Herrmann had used the serpent on an earlier score of his called *The White Witch Doctor* (1953).

Main title page in Herrmann's hand of Journey to the Center of the Earth. *Courtesy of Bernard Herrmann Collection, Davidson Library, University of California at Santa Barbara.*

Bassoonist Don Christlieb playing the serpent with Bernard Herrmann at scoring session for Journey to the Center of the Earth *at Fox Studios. Courtesy of Bernard Herrmann Collection, Davidson Library, University of California at Santa Barbara.*

North by Northwest

James Bond movies have been popular since the early 1960s. It may seem hard to believe, but it was Bernard Herrmann who scored a film that some people say established the prototype for James Bond style glamour, action, and romance—Alfred Hitchcock's *North by Northwest*. This was Herrmann's only score done at MGM. Herrmann started the score for *North by Northwest* on January 10, 1959, immediately after completing music for the pilot episode of the new television series called "The Twilight Zone." He completed the score, including orchestrating every note (his standard practice), in fifty-one days. The scoring sessions took place on April 23 and 24. Because of quite a bit of time spent reediting by Hitchcock, two additional sessions were done on May 14 and 15. The filmmaker Francois Truffault (1932–1984), who interviewed Hitchcock, regards *North by Northwest* as the zenith of Hitchcock's work in America, a feeling shared by Hitchcock himself.

The film opens with a very energetic and exciting Spanish dance of South American origin in the form of a **fandango**. This type of dance propels itself in alternating $\frac{3}{4}$ and $\frac{6}{8}$ time. The action moves from New York City to Chicago to South Dakota, concluding on the stone faces of Mount Rushmore. This fandango main title theme is used to "kick off the exciting rout that follows" Cary Grant's character as he is tracked down by both good authorities and evil men because of mistaken identity. This rowdy theme is heard throughout the film in various guises as Roger Thornhill (played by Cary Grant) is constantly hunted.

In perhaps the film's most memorable sequence, known as the "crop duster sequence," Herrmann and Hitchcock play the scene out *without* music to build *unbearable tension*. Thornhill is to meet someone out in the middle of nowhere on a dusty highway in Illinois, surrounded by desolate farmlands and cornfields. Hitchcock had stated in an interview that when we see a character in a dark warehouse or dark alley, we expect something rather unfortunate to happen to them. The audience would never expect any harm to come to our main character standing out in the open cornfields during the light of day. But that is exactly what happens! Suddenly, swooping down out of seemingly nowhere is a crop duster airplane. Thornhill is almost immediately suspect when he becomes the target of a madman on board the plane, who begins shooting a machine gun at Thornhill. As this scene transpires we expect to hear the restatement of the now-familiar fandango motive. But wait! Where is it? This scene is played out with *no* music, hearing only the real sounds of the situation, such as the plane's engine and machine gun noise. Only at the last possible moment (as the crop duster crashes into the tanker truck on the highway) do we hear the return to a variation of the fandango. The music provided a much-needed emotional release at this moment. This is a film with both wit and suspense, and Herrmann's score provides a wonderful backdrop for the unfolding of this fast-paced comic-thriller.

The film went on to make a $6.5 million profit and played to recordbreaking crowds at Radio City Music Hall in New York City. The title comes from Shakespeare's *Hamlet:* "I am but mad north-northwest; when the wind is southerly, I know a hawk from a handsaw." This film also became Hitchcock's most popular and successful film to that date.

Herrmann busied himself on two other scoring projects plus the start of a now-classic television series. "The Twilight Zone" television series premiered on October 2, 1959. Herrmann was instrumental in providing music to this series, particularly in its first year (it ran for five years). One needs only to listen to the music on these episodes to determine Herrmann's uncanny ability to bring the most out of the world of fantasy, horror, or the grotesque.

The Diary of Anne Frank

Earlier in this book, when talking about Alfred Newman, we described his "Fox string sound." A very effective example of this—that is, the scoring of strings in the high register—can be found in the highly acclaimed film *The Diary of Anne Frank* (1959). This powerful drama, based on a true story, chronicles the day-to-day existence of two Jewish families who are forced to live in hiding in an attic in Amsterdam, Holland, during World War II. Anne is not quite thirteen when they are forced to go into hiding. The other family has brought along their sixteen-year-old son, Peter. For the next two years, the two families live in constant fear of discovery by the Nazis. As Anne experiences her first yearnings of love for young Peter, Newman has composed very poignant music to accompany this.

In a very memorable moment in the film, when the camera pans over the roof tops of the city, Anne starts off by saying that she feels that spring is coming, that she feels it in her whole body and soul. She goes on to say that she is utterly confused, but that she is longing, longing for everything. We see Peter playing with a small sailboat in a tin wash tub, as Anne advances closer to Peter. She lays her head on his shoulder. At first, he seems oblivious to her affections. Anne walks away. Peter soon realizes what is going on. He hurriedly moves toward her and affectionately rubs his face against her hair.

This entire scene is done without dialogue. It is Newman's music that carries the power of the moment, as well as featuring Newman's famous "Fox string sound." Newman was able to add another dimension to this scene by getting inside the characters' emotional feelings for one another. Although it looked as though these two were destined for a wonderful future together, the Nazis discovered their hiding place, and all were taken away. Anne was not allowed to take her diary with her to the concentration camp where she died, two months before the liberation of Holland. Somehow her diary managed to survive for the rest of the world to read.

The Nun's Story

Like Bernard Herrmann, Franz Waxman was a pioneer in his methods of writing film scores. He placed great emphasis on orchestral color. *The Nun's Story* (1959), a story about a young nun and her ordeals, led Waxman to decide that his thematic material should be based on the music of the Roman Catholic church. Waxman traveled to the papal library in Rome, where he was able to find Gregorian chant source material that would later become the framework on which this score would be based. In the opening main title sequence, we hear these six notes played in the trumpets and glockenspiel:

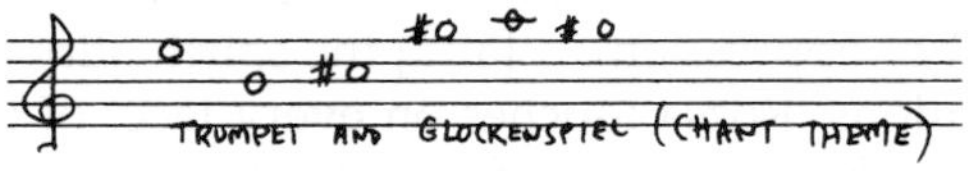

These notes will be heard throughout the score in the various cues. Waxman has also written several cues that sound like church chorales. It is here that we hear quotations from actual chant melodies.

When the young Sister Luke has to depart for the Congo to work with the natives, Waxman provides the necessary African atmosphere by using music in an African tribal drum beat idiom.

The most memorable musical sequence in this movie, and certainly the most innovative for its day, is the scene that takes place in an *insane asylum.* It is here that Waxman utilizes the **twelve-tone row technique**. In this scene, one of the inmates asks for a glass of water, because the fish that she had eaten was so salty. The young nun, against her better judgment, obliges by bringing her some water. As she opens the door, the female inmate yanks the nun into the cell with her and begins to tear off the nun's habit. The poor nun is nearly paralyzed with disbelief and fear. This atonal (music without a tonal center) tone-row music heard during this sequence, *emphasizes* the nun's confusion and panic. **Pizzicato** string parts ("pizzicato" is when string players pluck out the notes with their fingers instead of playing with their bow) and muted horns (French horn players mute or dampen their sound by placing their right hand inside the bell opening of the horn) create chaos. Today, it's not unusual to hear film music with sections of tone-row material or harsh dissonant chords. ("Dissonant" means not pleasing to the ears, as opposed to "consonant," which is pleasing). Back in 1959, this was still quite innovative in motion picture scores. *This was certainly one of the earliest scores to use the twelve-tone row technique.* This technique had been used by other composers such as David Raksin (1912–) in several films and Leonard Rosenman (1924–) in his score for *The Cobweb* in 1955. Seven years later, Waxman would employ this system of composition in his dramatic song cycle *The Song of Terezin.*

4. How did Elmer Bernstein "speed up" the exodus in *The Ten Commandments*? ______________________________.

5. Which film contained the first totally all-electric score? ______________________________.

6. How did Waxman give his score for *The Spirit of St. Louis* an ethereal quality? ______________________________.

7. What is a good way to describe the pentatonic scale? ______________________________.

8. How does Herrmann depict the inner earth in *Journey to the Center of the Earth*? ______________________________.

9. Who is the master of orchestral color? ______________________________.

10. Why does Herrmann use the fandango in *North by Northwest*? ______________________________.

11. What new technique did Waxman use in his score for *The Nun's Story*? ______________________________.

12. How long did Rozsa have to write his score for *Ben-Hur*? ______________________________.

13. Who became the most recognized authority on writing film scores that dealt with historical settings? ______________________________.

Define the following

1. Triadic melodies ______________________________.
2. Serpent ______________________________.
3. Twelve-tone row technique ______________________________.
4. Atonal ______________________________.

Chapter Eight

The Age of Versatility (the 1960s through the 1990s)

The 1960s, the Beginning of a New Age

During the 1960s, the attitude toward cinema was changing. There was more of an appreciation for the importance of film and filmmakers. There was rapid growth in university film courses and books and magazines related to film were more numerous than before. Directors such as Alfred Hitchcock were given more respect and were highly rated. Music used in films would become more versatile as filmmakers discovered new avenues to explore in their search for creativity. Also, the Hollywood studio system was no longer in power, as it had been for several decades. This was the beginning of a new age of independent productions. The studios remained as overseers and distribution giants, helping to finance these independent productions. As such, the once full-bodied orchestrations of the 1930s through the 1950s were being replaced by a trend in cost-saving smaller instrumental combinations or by songs.

The lure of money by producers to hire song composers such as Burt Bacharach (1929–) in the 1960s and Marvin Hamlisch (1944–) in the 1970s brought a new sound to the contemporary filmgoing experience. Bacharach's song "Raindrops Keep Fallin' On My Head" from the film *Butch Cassidy and the Sundance Kid* (1969) not only won the Academy Award that year but also helped to sell the film and made the bicycle montage that it accompanied more memorable. Bacharach also had a smash hit for the title song he provided for the film *Alfie* in 1966.

European Composers at Work

European composers such as John Barry, Maurice Jarre, Ennio Morricone, George Delerue, Francis Lai, Michel Legrand, and several others worked on films released in the United States.

Performers and Songwriters

Performer-songwriters such as Simon and Garfunkel were a smash hit with their music accompanying *The Graduate* in 1967. Composer-performer-songwriter Henry Mancini (1924–1994) is still remembered today for his work on films that gave us immortal songs such as "Moon River" (*Breakfast at Tiffany's* [1961], the title song from *Days of Wine and Roses* [1962], and the theme from *The Pink Panther* [1964]). Mancini also wrote the very popular music for the *Peter Gunn* television series that debuted in the fall of 1958.

The Jazz Trend Continues

The jazz trend continued in the 1960s with memorable contributions from composers such as Andre Previn (1929–)—*The Subterraneans* (1960); Leonard Bernstein and his powerful jazz score (music adapted for the movie by Irwin Kostal [1911–1994]) from his hit Broadway musical *West Side Story* (1961); and Elmer Bernstein continuing to show his command of jazz in *Walk on the Wild Side* (1962). Two African American composers, Quincy Jones (1933–) and Herbie Hancock (1940–), wrote scores for two landmark films—Jones's effective work for the controversial film *The Pawnbroker* (1965) and Hancock's contribution for the equally provocative *Blow-Up* (1966). French composer Michel Legrand (1932–) provided a jazz score for *The Picasso Summer* (1969).

Other Changes During the 1960s

The 1960s started off with Doris Day and Rock Hudson as the biggest box-office draw and the average price of a movie ticket set at sixty-nine cents. Members of the Screen Actors Guild (SAG) went on strike over the issue of residual payments made to them for films sold to television. Ronald Regan had to resign as president of SAG because he had now become a producer. The strike was settled within a month. During the 1960s, major Hollywood studios began financing more and more foreign-made productions. The studios also began shooting more films overseas primarily for economic reasons. Airlines began showing in-flight movies. United Artists studios signed a contract for a series of films based on Ian Flemming's character, James Bond.

The New Ratings System: G, M, R, and X

In response to an audience outcry that violence (in movies such as *Bonnie and Clyde* in 1967) and nudity (in movies such as *Blow-Up* and *The Pawnbroker*) were running rampant, the movie industry unveiled a new ratings system on October 7, 1968. The designations were: "G" for general audiences, "M" for mature audiences, "R" for no one under 16, and "X" for those 16 and older, without exception. Less than a year later, *Midnight Cowboy* (with a score by John Barry) became the first and only X-rated film to win the Academy Award for Best Picture of the Year. This score contains a song, "Everybody's Talkin'," sung by Harry Nilsson, that became a huge hit on radio.

By the end of the decade, Paul Newman and John Wayne were the box-office champs and the price of admission averaged $1.42. Also, weekly attendance at movies had dropped off considerably because of the competition of television. In 1960, there were forty million people attending movies. By 1969, that figure had dropped to 17.5 million.

Psycho

It may seem appropriate then to usher in a new age of film music with one of the most famous and recognizable scores ever composed—Bernard Herrmann's most famous score, which in turn accompanied Alfred Hitchcock's most famous and successful motion picture, *Psycho* (1960).

Perhaps no other film changed Hollywood's perception of horror films as much as *Psycho* did. Although audiences today are somewhat jaded by the gore and violence of films made now, no one had ever seen anything quite like it in 1960. *Psycho* contains a Herrmann score that is, on the one hand, quite typical of preceding scores composed by the master, yet, on the other hand, it is unique. According to Graham Bruce in his book, *Bernard Herrmann: Film Music and Narrative,* "It is characteristic especially in its use of small clusters of notes, developed and modified to provide narrative links across the film. Its uniqueness lie in its scoring for strings alone."[1] Alfred Hitchcock filmed the movie using black-and-white film because he felt that the gore of the shower scene would be too much for the audience to take if it were in color. Because Hitchcock had made the movie with black-and-white film, Herrmann decided to give his score a colorless "black-and-white" sound by using strings only. There would be no woodwinds or brass to add orchestral colors that were so familiar to moviegoing audiences. Hitchcock paid such close attention to detail; he even had Janet Leigh appear in a *white* bra during the film's opening love scene. Later in the movie, after she steals the $40,000, she is seen in a *black* bra, a very obvious switch in wardrobe to reflect the change from good (white) to evil (black). As a black-and-white film, *Psycho* became one of the highest-grossing black-and-white movies in motion picture history. It cost $806,448 to make, yet by the end of 1966, it had taken in $14.3 million. By today's inflation dollars, that would be the same as roughly $133.7 million!

Psycho was more than a B-grade "quickie." It has become one of the most analyzed films in cinema history and has become a textbook case at universities of how to make a classic thriller/suspense/horror film. This film has been a powerful force, making quite an impact on filmmaking. It has often been imitated, yet never equaled for its originality. The stars of the film still received fan mail several decades after the film's release. During the filming of the movie, Hitchcock insisted on a closed set. Many people felt that this was a publicity ploy to build advanced interest in the movie.

Hitchcock started a groundbreaking tradition with *Psycho* that was truly bold and controversial for its time. Prior to *Psycho,* a movie patron could purchase a theater ticket and enter the theater at any time. With *Psycho,* Hitchcock started a promotional campaign that insisted that theatergoers were not allowed into the theater once the film had started. Today, this is rather commonplace with some of the big blockbuster films. Patrons have to wait in long lines outside the theater until about ten minutes before the start of the movie. Although this created long lines outside of theaters for people waiting to see the next showing of *Psycho,* Hitchcock's basic reason for this policy was to make sure that people would see Janet Leigh before she was killed off a little over one-third through the film. (She is murdered forty-seven minutes into the 108-minute film.) It was her unexpected and sudden demise that caught the audience off guard. The audience thought that nothing could happen to her because she is the star. The sense of security is shattered with her slaying. The murder shocks the audience for a few minutes, but it is the fear and anticipation of not knowing when the next murder might occur that really scares the audience.

1. Graham Bruce, *Bernard Herrmann: Film Music and Narrative* (Ann Arbor, MI: University Microfilms International, 1985), p. 183.

Anthony Perkins stars as Norman Bates in Alfred Hitchcock's Psycho. *Courtesy of Archive Photos.*

Psycho was also innovative in its pushing the moral code as far as possible in terms of showing nudity, a more graphic depiction of violence than before, and abnormal behavior with a perverted view of mother love. Although audiences by and large were receptive to the movie and it became Hitchcock's greatest hit, about 60 percent of the reviewers were negative. The *New York Times* said that *Psycho* was a "blot on an honorable career." *Esquire* magazine went so far as to say that this film was "merely one of those television shows padded out to two hours by adding pointless subplots and realistic detail . . . a reflection of a most unpleasant mind, a mean, sly, sadistic little mind." Actually, *Esquire*'s description almost became a reality. Hitchcock was evidently not too pleased with the final cut of *Psycho*. He therefore was contemplating cutting the completed film to one hour in order to be used on his weekly television show.

Of course, missing from this rough cut viewed by Hitchcock was the musical score, yet to be realized by Herrmann. Hitchcock was known for giving detailed instructions to his composers and soundmen as to where music should be placed, as well as instructions on what sounds the audience should hear and when. Herrmann was given a copy of the film to take home. Herrmann felt that Hitchcock didn't realize that with the right music this film could become a masterpiece. All of the other elements were in place. He thought that Hitchcock was crazy for wanting to butcher the movie down to a one-hour television episode. The last thing that Hitchcock had said to Herrmann was, "There should be *no* music at all through the motel sequence, *especially* the shower scene." Herrmann said, "Wait a minute, I have some ideas. How about a score completely for strings?"[2] The detailed instructions to Herrmann and the two soundmen still survive. They shed some light on Hitchcock's wishes:

> Throughout the killing, there should be the shower noise and the blows of the knife. We should hear the water gurgling down the drain of the bathtub, especially when we go close on it . . . during the murder, the sound of the shower should be continuous and monotonous, only broken by the screams of Marion.[3]

As it turned out, Herrmann did *not* listen to Hitchcock's instructions for the murder sequence. Instead, he wrote a very innovative effect to represent the sharp jabs and blows of the knife. He achieved this by asking the string players to play rapid ascending **glissandos** on their stringed instruments. The first violins were asked to glide their finger over the string with their left hand up toward their chin until they reached high "E flat." The second violins did the same thing until they approached high "E natural." The two pitches (E and E flat) clash together to give an unsettling destruction of tonality, or as Herrmann put it in one word, "Terror." These "slidings of the finger" are the glissandos. Herrmann and Hitchcock had watched this sequence together without his music in the dubbing studio. Then Herrmann said, "Let's try it again, but this time with my music." After that Hitchcock said, "Of course, we will use your music there." Then Herrmann said, "But you requested no music for the murder sequence." Hitchcock replied, "Improper suggestion, my boy, improper suggestion."[4] The effect was so powerful that it pleased Hitchcock. He doubled Herrmann's salary from $17,500 to $34,501. Hitchcock was amused by Herrmann's "screaming violins," as these glissandos were called.

It is equally interesting to note that Herrmann was able to further show his great knowledge of orchestration by creating these glissandos to evoke the sound of *shrieking birds* as well as the screams of the murder victim (Janet Leigh). If you note in the story, *bird imagery abounds in this film*. Norman Bates's hobby is taxidermy. He likes to stuff birds. We even see pictures of birds up on the walls in the background. The last bird he stuffed was a crane from Phoenix. Janet Leigh's character's name is Marion *Crane*. Norman loves to eat Kandy Korn and he is shown from a low angle, "eating like a chicken." Norman Bates remarks to Marion Crane that she "eats like a bird." The shower scene took an

2. Quote attributed to various sources passed down as part of the *Psycho* legend.
3. Stephen Rebello, *Alfred Hitchcock and the Making of Psycho* (New York: W.W. Norton, 1990), p. 138.
4. Smith, *A Heart at Fire's Center*, p. 240.

This is the infamous thirty-seven measure murder cue from Psycho. *Courtesy of Bernard Herrmann Collection, Davidson Library, University of California at Santa Barbara.*

(17)
page ~2~
Pizz
Arco
Vls
Violas
V.C.
CB
17 18 19 20 21 22 23 24 25 26
(Pizz)
(Sust)
27 28 29 30 31 32 33 34 35 36 37
58

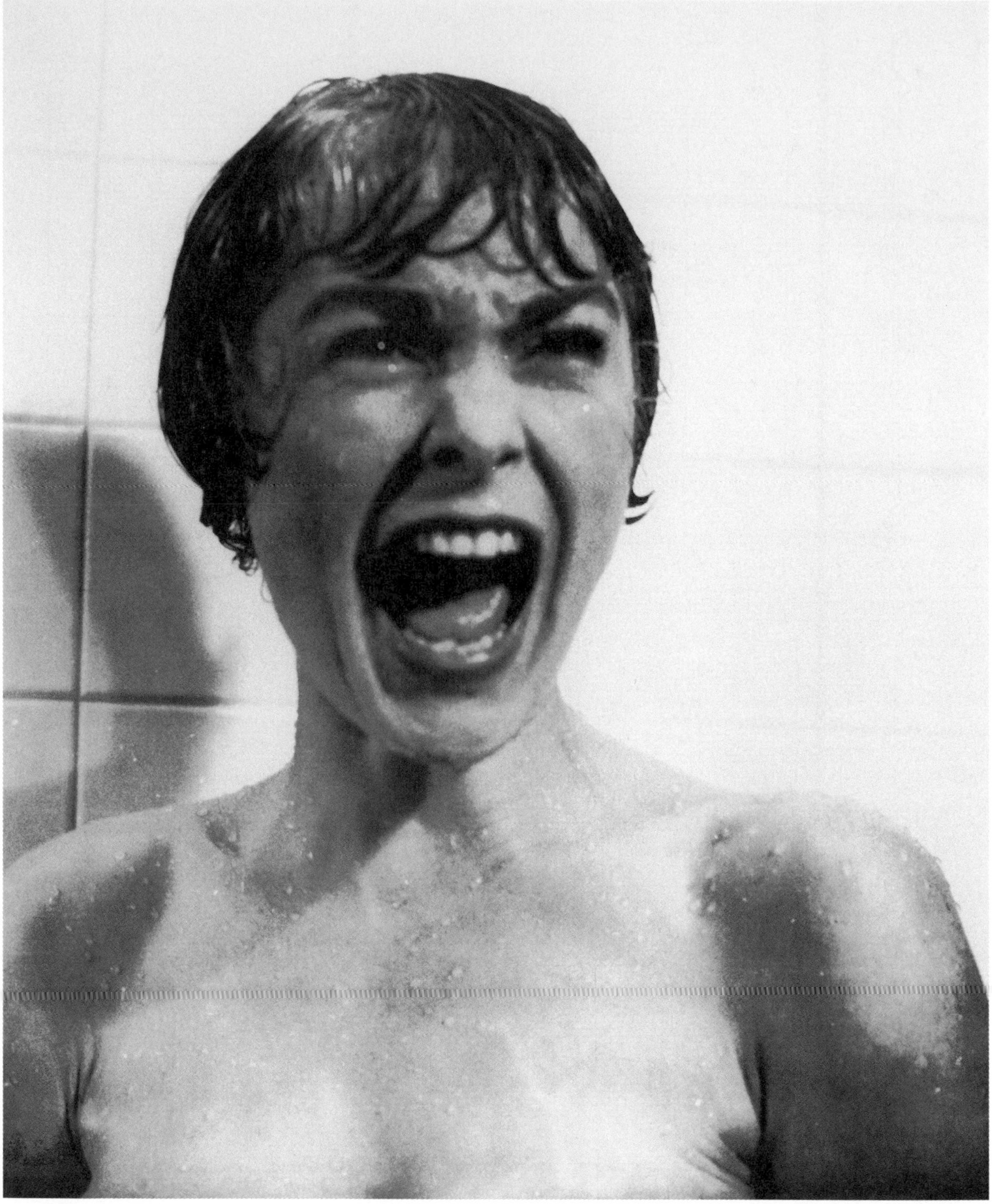

Janet Leigh in the famous shower scene from Psycho. *Courtesy of Archive Photos.*

entire week to shoot although it lasts for a little less than three minutes. Because of Hitchcock's rapid editing of shots, which practically last only the blink of an eye, the viewer assumes that he sees more than he really does. From the time Marion flushes the toilet right before her brutal murder, to the spot in the film where the camera pans back away from her open eye after the murder, about two minutes and thirty seconds have elapsed and fifty-six different camera shots have whizzed by on the screen.

Herrmann's cue for this scene lasts only fifty seconds, but probably has moved more filmgoers to shear frightfulness than any other minute-long cue in the history of cinema! As you watch this now-famous murder scene (perhaps the most famous murder scene in the movies), note the method of editing. During the actual attack, the length of scenes moves by in such rapid-fire succession, lasting only a fraction of a second each, that they alone cause a very uneasy feeling to the viewer. Immediately before and after the murder, the length of scenes is much longer. Hitchcock was once criticized for spending a week on the filming of this sequence, and was asked why he wasted so much time on such a short scene. He returned the question by asking what part of the movie did the inquisitor remember the most at which time he stated, "The murder, of course." At no time does the knife actually touch or go into Marion Crane, although it would appear to the viewer that it does. Also, much of the nudity is very discreetly done, yet we feel that we see more than we actually do. Hitchcock was told to reedit the nude scenes for approval of the Hays Commission—that group that administered the film industry's self-censorship code. He cleverly resubmitted the *identical* footage that was approved as being acceptable the second time around. The blood that we see is actually chocolate sauce. Tony Perkins, who played Norman Bates in the film, said, "Not many people know this, but I was in New York rehearsing for a play when the shower scene was filmed in Hollywood. It is rather strange to go through life being identified with this sequence knowing that it was my double. Actually, the first time I saw *Psycho* and that shower scene was at the studio. I found it really scary. I was just as frightened as anybody else."[5] One moviegoer later complained to Hitchcock that his wife had not been able to bathe or take a shower since she saw *Psycho,* and he wondered what he should do. Hitchcock replied, "Have you ever considered sending your wife to the dry cleaners?"

We've seen how Herrmann utilizes the string glissandos to create the right atmosphere for the murder of Marion Crane. How does Herrmann create suspense and atmosphere in other parts of this now-classic motion picture? A device that Herrmann uses in *Psycho*—as well as in *Vertigo, North by Northwest,* and *Marnie*—is the use of the **seventh chord**. The seventh chord *creates the feeling of restlessness and dissatisfaction.*[6] This harmonic device gives us the craving for resolution, but it never does, hence the suspense. If one were to play an ascending scale on the piano, but play only the first, third, fifth, and seventh notes in the scale, this would make a seventh chord.

Example of a seventh chord:

Comprised of four tones, each a third apart

This effect can be heard at the beginning of the movie *Vertigo:*

Broken seventh chords

5. Robert Harris and Michael Lasky, *The Films of Alfred Hitchcock* (Secaucus, NJ: Citadel Press, 1976), p. 220.
6. Concept based on Bruce's book information.

In this example, the broken seventh chord produces the uneasy feeling of disorientation, of whirling about aimlessly. In *Psycho,* Herrmann makes an unforgettably strong statement at the onset of the main title sequence with four sharp and aggressive seventh chords:

Opening music to Psycho *(clustered seventh chords)*

To represent Norman Bates's withdrawn personality, Herrmann employs the device of using mutes placed on the strings. A string mute is a three-pronged device that clamps down on the bridge, absorbing some of the vibration and creating a relatively veiled or "muted" sound. This dampened sound is very effective in conveying Norman Bates's mental condition.

It is interesting to note that although Herrmann set out to give us a colorless, black-and-white score, the single tone color of the string orchestra emits a wide variety of timbres. This also sets a new style of writing for certain film scenes that has been copied by other composers to this day. The "shrieking" **string glissandos** used during the shower sequence later became one of the most often imitated musical devices used in "slasher" movies by the next generation of film composers—*and may be the most imitated film music cue in the history of cinema.*

Herrmann composed the score, written for fifty performers, between January 12 and February 12, 1960. Here is the breakdown:

fourteen first violins
twelve second violins
ten violas
eight cellos
six string basses

There were no woodwinds, brass, or percussion. Everything that we hear was done by strings alone. Hitchcock later remarked that basically 33 percent of the success of *Psycho* was due to Herrmann's moody score. Although the movie was nominated for several Academy Awards, the Academy failed to recognize Herrmann's creative genius in this powerful score, so he was overlooked at awards time. As hard as it is to fathom, *Herrmann's entire output on all of his Hitchcock film scores was never nominated for an Academy Award!* In fact, the members of the Academy never nominated him for the last twenty-nine years of his life, from 1946 to 1975. Sadly, the Academy finally nominated Herrmann posthumously for his two scores, *Taxi Driver* and *Obsession,* in 1976, the year after his death. Both scores lost out to Jerry Goldsmith's score for *The Omen.*

The Magnificent Seven

1960 also saw the emergence of another Western score prototype. We have already looked at Jerome Moross's 1958 score for *The Big Country,* yet some people think that the quintessential Western score was the one that was composed by Elmer Bernstein for *The Magnificent Seven* in 1960. The main title theme (once used in television commercials as the musical theme for Marlboro cigarettes) is certainly one of the most popular and recognizable themes to come from the world of movies. The score sets a

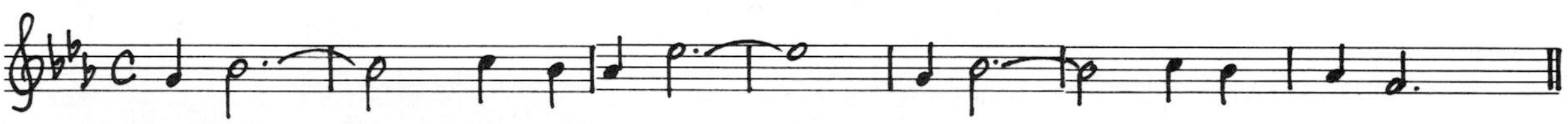

Main title theme from The Magnificent Seven

musical style that has since been the inspiration for many film and TV composers, who are called on to compose music reminiscent of the American West.

The plot involves the people of a small Mexican village who are periodically terrorized by a group of outlaws. The villagers hire seven gunmen to help them against these thugs. The screenplay is a reworking of Akira Kurosawa's major hit, *The Seven Samurai* (1954). Because of its locale, Bernstein thought that the score should have "a definite Chicano sound, a blending of many elements of American and Mexican music."[7] He used a variety of instruments associated with this type of atmospheric setting such as solo guitar, a Mexican log drum, castanets, marimba, conga and bongo drums, and solo trumpet and English horn playing solos to create a Spanish flavor. His music contains syncopated starts and stops, heavy on percussion and brass. Bernstein said that he was faced with a similar dilemma to that which he encountered while writing the score to *The Ten Commandments*. Bernstein states in the liner notes, "The purpose of the music was primarily to increase excitement, but it also served in a quite specific way to provide pacing to a film which would have been much slower without the score. When next you see the film, observe that the music is often faster in tempo than anything actually happening on the screen [as in the mass Exodus scene in *The Ten Commandments*]. The film needed music to help give it drive."

Spartacus

Alex North (1910–1991) was hired in 1960 to score the large-scale epic *Spartacus*. He supposedly studied the script for several months and ran the film eighteen times before he wrote a single note. North had a total of thirteen months to work on the score. The norm at that time was more like a ten-week contract for a movie score.

The story takes place about two thousand years ago, and is about a slave named Spartacus who was instrumental in leading thousands of other men out of the bondage of being held captive by the Roman Empire. The slave revolt took place in 73 B.C. Although defeated by their Roman masters, there were still six thousand survivors of the ninety thousand men that took part in this historic revolt. Unfortunately, Spartacus and his survivors were eventually crucified along the Appian Way (the road to Rome).

7. *Elmer Bernstein by Elmer Bernstein,* CD liner notes, Denon Records, 1993.

AARON COPLAND: ORIGIN OF "AMERICANA STYLE" USED IN WESTERNS

Aaron Copland. Courtesy of the Hearst Newspaper Collection, Department of Special Collections, University of Southern California.

Born in Brooklyn, New York, on November 14, 1900. Died on December 2, 1990. He was a great influence on many film composers. His style has been deemed the ultimate in the "Americana" style. This style comprises melodies and harmonies built on perfect fourths, perfect fifths, and octaves. This creates an "open" sound that lends itself well to creating the grandeur of expansive vistas or the color and flavor of the old American West. His music from *Appalachian Spring,* music written for ballet, is an excellent example of this style. He wrote several film scores including *The Red Pony, Of Mice and Men, Our Town,* and *The Heiress,* for which he won the Academy Award. His score for *Of Mice and Men* was written to depict the lifestyle of being on a California ranch, complete with folksong-like melodies and containing a pastoral quality that would become part of his Americana style. His next score, written for Thorton Wilder's *Our Town,* is considered to be his definitive example of "Americana." In this film, Copland is able to capture the atmosphere and moods of smalltown life. Probably his most famous film music was written for a John Steinbeck story, *The Red Pony.* This film, which came out in 1949, featured a story of a ten-year-old boy growing up on a California ranch. Music in this film was needed to provide many of the unexpressed feelings of daily living. Copland liked the music that he had written for this score so much that he adapted it into a concert suite. This suite is among his most famous music for the concert stage. His final film score for a Hollywood movie was for *The Heiress,* also in 1949. The producer-director William Wyler decided to remove the powerful and moody main title music and substitute an arrangement of the song "Plaisir d'Amour," which also happened to be featured during the course of the film. This score has two firsts in film music history. First, it is the first time that a film score won the Oscar without the winning composer's main title music. After all, it is the main title music that contains the musical theme or themes that the audience may remember best from a film. Second, this is the only film score written by Copland in which he utilizes the leitmotif technique. This is something he had never done in any of his other scores. He was not fond of this approach in scoring films but thought that because this film dealt with a series of character studies, particularly the main character's transformation from innocence to bitterness and reclusiveness, it was inevitable. In this Academy Award–winning score, Copland also used music of the 1850s, popular in New York at that time, as well as composing new "period" music in that historic style. He is known primarily as a concert hall composer, despite his own film scores and his powerful influence on other film composers. It was in his compositions for *Fanfare for the Common Man* (1942), and his ballet music for *Billy the Kid* (1938), *Rodeo* (1942), and *Appalachian Spring* (1944) that he carved his niche in American music.

North wanted part of his score to show a cold, brutal, and barbaric quality. This hardhitting sound is apparent right at the beginning of the main title sequence. Here we hear heavy brass and percussion. In one sequence, in which the gladiators rebel against their Roman masters (about fifty minutes into the film), notice the low volume of the music. In this case, the director (Stanley Kubrick) must have wanted the sound of the men's voices yelling to be more prominent than North's powerful music. North purposely waits until the thirteenth reel of the film to introduce the sweet sound of the violin, when the love between Spartacus and Varinia blossoms. North introduces a variety of leitmotifs for various aspects of the story. One such leitmotif is a beautiful love theme played by the oboe.

This score contains wide contrasts in both style and in terms of instrumentation. One such instrument was brought over from France by North, making its debut on American soundtracks with this particular film. This instrument was called an ondioline. It is basically an electronic instrument resembling a miniature piano. It is played using only one hand and emits a unique sound: sort of a combination of woodwinds, mandolin, and percussion. North also used a variety of rare instruments not usually heard on a movie score. He employed a sarrousophone (a brass instrument invented in 1856), a Roman string instrument called a kythara, a dulcimar (a string instrument in the box zither family), a Chinese oboe, an Israeli recorder, a mandolin, a Yugoslavian flute, and bagpipes.

To see how effective North's music is, look at the "training to kill" sequence, about twenty-four minutes into the film. The music enhances every movement of the slaves who are training to be gladiators. If we didn't know better, we would think that the men have been choreographed to move with the music. North has written a very emotional death dirge, heard about forty-five minutes into the movie, as four gladiators enter the ring to fight to the death. Three minutes later, as Kirk Douglas fights his opponent, North's music catches every lunge, jab, and blow, as each man "fights to the death" to provide entertainment for the amusement of the Roman citizens. This $12 million epic was scored by North using an eighty-seven-piece symphonic orchestra. It premiered October 6, 1960. North had said that he found it difficult to compose for large-scale spectacles. His reasons have to do with his love for identifying with the individual characters through his music. The massive epics pose more of a problem in this respect. North says, "Spectacles call for writing that is objective in character. I prefer to be subjective. I write best when I can empathize."[8]

The total cast numbered 10,500 (including eight thousand Spanish soldiers as extras). The battle scenes were shot in Spain, near Madrid. The remaining parts of the film were shot on and off the sound stages of California. This huge epic was shot in 167 days. Both *Spartacus* and *Cleopatra* (1963) (also scored by North) employed unusual instrumentation.

Exodus

The score for *The Magnificent Seven* and *Spartacus* were among those considered in 1960 for the Best Score Oscar. It was a score by Viennese-born Ernest Gold (1921–1999), for *Exodus,* that captured the covetous award. This movie dealt with the creation of Israel after World War II and the struggles involved by the Jewish emigrants to Palestine. Gold's main title theme for this movie was not only his most memorable theme of his career, it became a smash hit on the pop charts as well.

Never on Sunday and *Zorba the Greek*

Two fellow Greek composers brought a new ethnic sound to the shores of America with their charming scores for two classic films. *Never on Sunday* was a comedy about a fun-loving prostitute who had the

8. Tony Thomas, *Film Score* (Burbank, CA: Riverwood Press, 1991), p. 190.

Both films depicted the Nativity, the Way of the Cross, the Crucifixion, and the Resurrection. In the scenes in which Jesus performs miracles, the music carries the drama, because there is virtually no spoken dialogue from the characters on screen. The music says it all! Rozsa wrote his *only* twelve-tone theme of his career for the Devil, heard during the temptation of Jesus in the desert sequence. Rozsa's main theme, heard throughout the movie, is the Jesus theme. It features a wordless female chorus. He also wrote a theme for John the Baptist. For the birth of Jesus, he wrote a wordless chorale setting in a $\frac{6}{8}$ time. In addition to this, Rozsa wrote one of the most seductive dances ever composed for Salome's dance of the seven veils. The young girl chosen to play the part was neither a dancer nor an actress. Some of the acting was so bad that the filmmakers decided to add voiceovers explaining things that ought to have been in the film but weren't. *This was the last and the most challenging of Rozsa's religious film scores.*

El Cid

Because of the commercial success of *King of Kings,* Bronston hired Rozsa to score his next project of 1961, *El Cid,* which became Rozsa's own personal favorite score of his ninety movie scores, and Rozsa's last major score.

The story, which is almost as well known in Europe as the King Arthur legend, centers on the life of Rodrigo Diaz de Vivar (1043–1099), Spain's national hero. He fought to bring together the Christian and Moorish kingdoms of Spain to ward off the would-be Arab conquerors. Although his goal of unifying Spain was never realized in his lifetime, his legend has been carried down for centuries and has been beautifully told in this lavish, colorful, and pageantry-filled epic motion picture. Rozsa had been called to work on *Mutiny on the Bounty* for MGM at the same time Bronston wanted him for *El Cid. Mutiny on the Bounty* was to have been a very big and important movie. Rozsa was under contract with MGM, but Bronston, the independent producer, made arrangements for Rozsa to be back in time to score *Mutiny on the Bounty* if they would lend him out for *El Cid*. As it turned out, Rozsa was still in the middle of working on his score when MGM called him back to score *Mutiny on the Bounty.* Bronston once again was able to get Rozsa out of his binding contract with MGM so that he could complete *El Cid.*

Another composer, Bronislau Kaper (1902–1983), who was from Poland, finally wrote the score for *Mutiny on the Bounty*. Rozsa went to Madrid and did a month's worth of research to find out more about the Spanish music of the Middle Ages. With the help of Nobel Prize–winning historian Dr. Ramon Menendez Pidal, Rozsa was exposed to dance music of twelfth-century Spain as well as Spanish folk songs of the period. This provided the impetus for this score's wonderful Spanish flavor. Rozsa sifted through illuminated manuscripts of church music of the period in addition to examining surviving examples of music used for the entertainment of ladies and gentlemen of the court. The Battle of Valencia sequence was inspired by an eleventh-century Castilian folk song, whereas the movie's beautiful love theme is drawn from surviving Moorish music.

Because Bronston had employed several Italian actors and many Italian artists who worked on the crew, the production was able to benefit from some very generous financial help from the Italian government. This was a real help to this production; however, not all things went smoothly. Four hours after Sophia Loren completed her shooting schedule, she fell down a flight of stairs, breaking her arm and shoulder.

The Italian composer Mario Nascimbene (1913–2002) originally had been hired to score *El Cid*. Nascimbene had written some dance cues used for the beach scenes. When Nascimbene met with Bronston, he found out that Bronston had hired Nascimbene not to write an original score but to adapt the music of Jules Massenet's (1842–1912) 1885 rendition of the story called *Le Cid*. Nascimbene and Bronston did not get along well in their meeting, so Nascimbene tore up his contract and quit work on the picture. As a result, Bronston phoned Rozsa and told him that he did not like Nascimbene's music, and asked Rozsa to be the new composer. In all fairness to Nascimbene, he really hadn't composed any themes yet for the movie to be criticized, except for the beach music, so Bronston had misrepresented the truth to Rozsa.

Barabbas

When Mario Nascimbene was hired for his next big project, he tried a new approach to scoring Roman Empire films, very different from what Rozsa and North had done in their scores. When asked to score the film *Barabbas* in 1962, he approached the Crucifixion scene in a unique way. He realized that the total eclipse that took place in this sequence would have been a supernatural event that would have put fear in the minds of the people who lived in the Judean age, because many of the people didn't understand what was really happening. He therefore could not use a typical orchestral sound, so he devised a "gimmick," whereby he recorded parts of this music cue at half the tape speed. When played back, it would have an eerie quality—a high pedal-point (sustained sound) sustained by sopranos and contraltos singing a tone apart. This dissonant clash was doubled by the first and second violins. This created a constant high pitched "drone," over which were added thick, ponderous chords played by tuba, bassoon, contra-bassoon, timpani, piano, and the distinct resonance of a tam-tam (gong). Nascimbene took the tape of the above combinations and played it back. During the playback, a chorus sang and recorded the theme of *Barabbas,* based loosely on the Miserere section of the Catholic Mass. The effect is unforgettable.

The score that Nascimbene wrote for *Barabbas* is not only considered to be his greatest achievement in film scoring, but also it continues to impress people today for its inspirational power. In addition to this, *the "new sounds" he employed in this score undoubtedly encouraged the upcoming new generation of film composers to be innovative*. His music for this score was unlike anything that had ever been heard before. It assured him a position as a composer of great originality. Nascimbene also developed a sound-mixing console combining twelve stereo cassette tapes coupled together to give a variety of sounds based on all the notes on the musical scale, performed by a range of instruments and voices, running at different speed. He called this a *mixerama.*

In order to give the Crucifixion scene its authentic quality, this scene was supposedly filmed during an *actual* total solar eclipse!

Lawrence of Arabia

The French composer Maurice Jarre won widespread critical acclaim for his epic-proportioned music for *Lawrence of Arabia* (1962). Jarre created an opening main title sequence that contains the film's two primary themes. First, we hear a British-sounding march for the main character, T. E. Lawrence. The other primary theme, or "B" theme as we might call it, is a sweeping, panoramic Arabian-sounding theme for the Arabian desert. This theme dominates the movie and is the more often recognized of the two: so we have the "British" theme and the Arabian "desert" theme.

Jarre uses the **ondes martenot** to provide atmospheric shadings for scenes that take place in the Arabian desert. The scene showing the morning sun rising over the desert landscape is extremely effective. At first we hear the exotic metallic sounds of the ondes martenot, adding an eerie ethereal quality to the transition from night to dawn on the desert floor. As the sun rises, we hear the music evolve into the Arabian "desert" theme once again.

Jarre also used two other unusual instruments not normally heard in a Hollywood film, the cithare (a companion electronic instrument with a more idealized tone quality than the ondes

Composer Maurice Jarre receiving Hollywood Walk of Fame recognition. Courtesy of Reuters/Fred Prouser/Archive Photos.

MAURICE JARRE

French-born composer (Lyons, France) | Born: September 13, 1924

He studied composition at the Paris Conservatory with Arthur Honneger, among others.

In his early years (the 1950s), he wrote scores for director Georges Franju, along with other avant-garde scores. His big break came when he was given the opportunity to score *Lawrence of Arabia* in 1962 for David Lean. He continued with other epic scores for films for Lean such as *Doctor Zhivago* (1965), *Ryan's Daughter* (1970), and *A Passage to India* (1984). He has been awarded the Oscar three times for Best Original Score (for *Lawrence of Arabia, Doctor Zhivago,* and *A Passage to India*).

He frequently uses electronic and ethnic instruments in his scores.

He has used the ondes martenot in several of his scores, along with other exotic instruments.

He is a very prolific composer of both television and feature film scores.

His score for *Witness* (1985) is an excellent example of a powerful all-electronic dramatic score.

His sweeping epic style scores have been imitated by other composers.

martenot) and the darbuka (a goblet-shaped small hand-drum from North Africa or a clay kettledrum from Turkey). The producer of the film needed a composer who could translate "into musical terms the amazing enigma of T. E. Lawrence, the loneliness of the desert and the wild drumbeat of the nomad Bedouin tribes lead by Lawrence."[9]

David Lean, the esteemed director of the film, had wanted Malcolm Arnold to compose the score, along with Sir William Walton (1902–1983). These two men sat down to watch the film after having had a bit too much to drink for lunch. They barely saw two hours of the film, and each man thought it was "terrible," or, as Walton put it, "a travelogue needing hours of music." Much to the surprise of David Lean, they turned him down. Jarre had originally been hired to orchestrate and conduct the music of Arnold and Walton. With them both out of the running, Jarre told Lean that if he wanted a specialist in writing Eastern music, he should contact his good friend Aram Khatchaturian (1903–1978). The next thing you know, the producer Sam Spiegel had invited the British composer Benjamin Britten (1913–1976) to write British Imperial music for the film along with Khatchaturian who would write the Oriental music, and finally Jarre would provide the dramatic underscoring and would coordinate the music of the other two men. Spiegel telephoned Jarre to say that his friend Khatchaturian could not leave Russia and that they could not use Britten because he had asked for a year to do the score. So, with four composers out of the picture, Spiegel went to New York and supposedly signed a great deal with the composer of *Victory at Sea,* Richard Rodgers (1902–1979). In the middle of September, Rodgers met with Lean to play some of the thematic material that he had written. Lean rose from his chair and said, "Sam, what is all this rubbish? I am supposed to be editing and you take up my time with this nonsense?" Then Spiegel turned to Jarre and asked him if he had written anything for the movie. When Jarre had played a little portion, Spiegel said, "Maurice, *you* are going to do it!"[10] Jarre worked very hard on the score, sleeping only about two or three hours a night during the six weeks that he had been given to compose the score. Jarre had the London Philharmonic record the score at

9. *Lawrence of Arabia* CD soundtrack liner notes, Varese Sarabande, 1990.
10. Kevin Brownlow, *David Lean, A Biography* (New York: St. Martin's Press, 1997), pp. 472–473.

Shepperton Studios in London. Even though Sir Adrian Boult's name is on the screen as conductor, Jarre did the whole thing himself. Because of his work on this and other scores for David Lean, Jarre became recognized as a pioneer in the field of using exotic and electronic instruments in his scores. *What most people don't realize is that it was director David Lean who encouraged Jarre in the use of these electronic and ethnic instruments.*

In 1992, when *Lawrence of Arabia* was rereleased in a restored director's cut version with an additional thirty-five minutes reinstated, over three tons of film had to be sifted through in order to find missing scenes that were cut in 1962 and 1970 for politically sensitive reasons. Unfortunately, ten minutes of the dialogue track appeared to be lost forever. Fortunately, the actors in the key scenes were still alive and were therefore called back into the studio to dub in their missing dialogue tracks. Because their voices had matured, their voices had to be electronically enhanced to give them their original more youthful quality.

Doctor Zhivago

Although Jarre's music for *Lawrence of Arabia* is well known to many people, it was his extremely popular score for the 1965 film, *Doctor Zhivago,* with its lovely theme song for "Lara," that became his most well-known score.[11]

According to Jarre, his arrival of coming to an acceptable theme had a rather interesting history. Jarre came to Lean and said, "David, I want you to hear something that I have written." After hearing it, Lean said, "Well, Maurice, I think that you can do better." Jarre said that he was very disappointed. Jarre rushed back to his room to write another theme. This time Lean said, "This theme is too sad." Jarre wrote a third theme. Lean said, "This theme is too fast." Finally, seeing that Jarre was getting quite frustrated, Lean said, "Maurice, forget about Zhivago, forget about Russia. Go to the mountains with your girlfriend and think about her and write a love theme for her." So Jarre went to the mountains with his girlfriend and on Monday morning he wrote the theme that became Lara's theme. Jarre wanted to give Lara's theme a Russian sound, so he explored using balalaikas (a long-necked fretted lute with a triangular-shaped body and one of the most popular of Russia's folk instruments). Since there were no balalaika players in the MGM orchestra, Jarre was finally able to locate twenty-two players at a Russian Orthodox church in Hollywood. There was one major problem. None of them knew how to read music! So, on the day of the scoring session, Jarre had to quietly mime or dictate each note change to this ensemble to coincide with the performance of the MGM studio orchestra.[12]

Taras Bulba: The End of a Distinguished Career for Franz Waxman

Although he went on to score two more films after *Taras Bulba* (1962), Franz Waxman was nominated for best score for his work on this rather poorly done film. His recognition by his peers in the Academy, during the last years of his creative life, is a great testimony to the high caliber of work that he achieved throughout his career. From *The Bride of Frankenstein* in 1935 to *The Longest Hundred Miles,* his last completed score done for a television film for Universal TV in 1967, the year of his death, Waxman left a legacy not to be forgotten in the world of film music.

11. This song broke records for a popular song taken from a movie; it was on the pop charts for more than two years.
12. Taken from an interview on laserdisc of special deluxe thirtieth anniversary edition, Turner Entertainment, 1995.

Days of Wine and Roses

The composer Henry Mancini (1924–1994) tackled the delicate subject of alcoholism in the 1962 film, *Days of Wine and Roses*. Although Maurice Jarre won for his impressive score for *Doctor Zhivago* as best score, it was Mancini's stirring song "Days of Wine and Roses," with words by Johnny Mercer, that walked away with the award for best song.

Henry Mancini. From the author's collection.

The film is tied together by this single tune that eventually comes back to tear the viewer up emotionally as Jack Lemmon's character tries to convince his wife (played by Lee Remick) to accept her addiction to alcohol and get help as he had done through Alcoholics Anonymous. The music is very powerful and effective in this film. Because the film is so monothematic, the viewer is haunted by this single tune long after being exposed to it.

Dr. No: The James Bond Saga Begins

One of the most recognizable music logos in movie history was first heard in the film *Dr. No* in 1962. This marked the beginning of perhaps the most successful film series in motion picture history: the James Bond films.

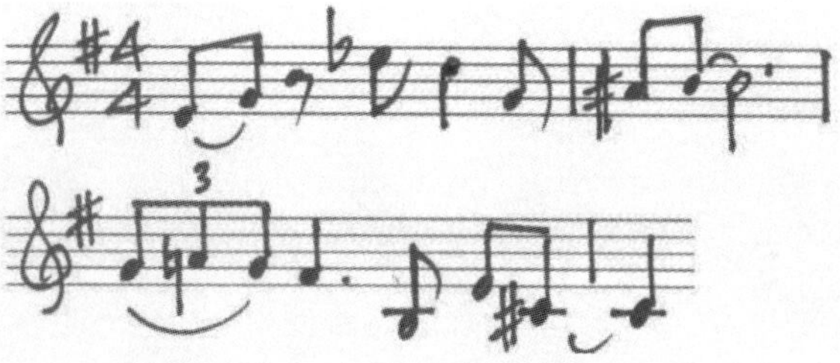

James Bond theme

The authorship of this now-famous James Bond theme is shrouded by some controversy. Producers Albert R. "Cubby" Broccoli and Harry Saltzman had hired Terrance Young to direct this film. The English songwriter Monty Norman (b. 1928, his credits included only one film before this, *House of Fright* [1960], also known as *The Two Faces of Dr. Jekyll,* for which he cowrote the score along with composer David Heneker) had been their choice to score *Dr. No.* It has been said that Norman wrote the basic theme. After some discussion, John Barry (1933–) was brought in to "liven" up the theme by making it "jazzier." The contract supposedly read that Norman was to get *exclusive* credit for the theme (including collecting all of the royalties all of these years), with Barry getting *only* an "arranged by" credit and £250. In an interview, Barry contends that it was he alone who wrote the now-famous theme. After all, as he says, "Who continued to work on the series, Monty Norman or me?" He went on to state that the James Bond theme was an outgrowth of a fragment from one of the tunes he had written for a 1959 film called *Beat Girl* (released as *Wild for Kicks* in England).

On Monday, March 19, 2001, Monty Norman was awarded £30,000 libel damages from the High Court in London over a London *Sunday Times* newspaper article that said that Monty Norman did *not* write the James Bond theme, saying that John Barry wrote the theme. John Barry told the jury during the two-week hearing at the High Court that "Mr. Norman's claim that he, and he alone, wrote the tune . . . which first gripped the public's imagination in the 1962 film *Dr. No* . . . was *absolute nonsense.*" Although we may never know the entire story, it is clear and very obvious that John Barry has gone on to become one of the premiere film composers of his age, and certainly one of the best loved.

The Herrmann-scored film *North by Northwest* greatly influenced the direction the James Bond films were to follow. *The popular formula was* to take a charming, witty, and handsome leading man, surrounded by elegant locations and beautiful women, and place him in hair-raising situations. The James Bond producers took this prototype one step further by adding high-tech gadgets and state-of-the-art special effects, along with unbelievable stunts that, in turn, has become the "blueprint formula" for the contemporary action movie.

Cape Fear

1962 also gave us the film *Cape Fear,* with a Bernard Herrmann score for a frightening movie about a released ex-con who returns to haunt the lawyer who was responsible for keeping him in jail for many years. What is unique about this score is that some of the original material, including the powerful four-note leitmotif heard in the 1962 version, was used once again in the 1991 remake of *Cape Fear*. This time, Elmer Bernstein took basic elements from Herrmann's music and created a new structure.

Actually, Bernstein ended up with only about six minutes of Herrmann's original material in this new score. Both the original and the remake have top-notch acting. According to Bernstein, the remake "is rife with booming sound effects and head-bashing melodrama. . . . Bernard used his score as an engine to push the film along, but Martin's [Scorcese] version didn't need that kind of drive." The remake "is a lot more intense, complicated, and violent than the original, which was basically a thriller about good and evil."[13]

As you watch the original, a notable scene is the one involving Max Cadey (the ex-con played by Robert Mitchum) terrorizing the lawyer's (Sam Boden, played by Gregory Peck) teenage daughter as she sits in the car listening to the radio. Note Herrmann's music. He writes for a small chamber ensemble, not a large symphony orchestra. All he uses are flutes, horns, and strings. He also uses much repetition in a minimalistic sense, using small nonmelodic cells, techniques heard in previous scores such as *Psycho*. When Sam Boden's daughter runs from Cadey, we hear horns, flutes, and strings. When she stops running, we hear her breathing accompanied by dissonant string chords. This psychological thriller is a forgotten classic made even more memorable by Herrmann's dynamic score. Watch both versions and see how the returning four-note leitmotif is used in each film. This would be the only film scored by Herrmann for Universal Pictures outside of his affiliation with Hitchcock.

To Kill a Mockingbird

Although Elmer Bernstein may be better remembered for his music for *The Ten Commandments* or *The Magnificent Seven,* one of his all-time personal favorites among his own output is his *incredible* score for *To Kill a Mockingbird* (1962). Many other film composers have said that Bernstein's score for *To Kill a Mockingbird* is certainly one of the very best examples of *how* a film score should work within a film. *It is almost the perfect "textbook" example for this kind of film.*

This score helped to launch a type of music that uses a more intimate relationship with the characters on screen by using a smaller ensemble of players. Instead of the full-blown full orchestrations of a large orchestra, Bernstein was able to poignantly say what he had to with small, intimate chamber-sized ensembles. Rarely do we hear more than a few instruments providing the dramatic underscore.

The various members of the cast and crew, including Bernstein, were interviewed for a thirty-fifth anniversary rerelease of the movie. They were unanimous in their praise and high acclaim for the project and its outcome. Many had stated that it was one of the most satisfying films on which they had ever worked. When the star Gregory Peck was asked if he would star in the film, he said that he could hardly wait to call back the next morning and say, "If you want me, I'm your boy." According to the director Robert Mulligan, he said that when he and the producer Alan Pakula had sent a copy of the book to Peck, that he said yes immediately, in an instant. He loved the story and could identify with many of the qualities of the main character that he would play, the lawyer Atticus Finch. Later, Gregory

13. *Soundtrack* magazine, March 1992, Vol. 11, No. 4, Luc van de ven, Belgium.

Elmer Bernstein. Courtesy of Adriana Getz/Kraft-Benjamin Agency.

Peck would go on to say that his being called on to play this part ended up being one of the luckiest days of his life. Alan Pakula felt that the film captured the soul of Harper Lee's book. The story, based on the Pulitzer Prize–winning novel by Harper Lee, unfolds in a small southern town in the 1930s. Peck plays the role of a lawyer who is trying to defend an African American man wrongly accused of raping a white woman in a racially divided small town. Atticus (Peck) prepares his defense while trying to raise his two small children.

According to Bernstein, "It was a particular film. There has never been another film even remotely like it, in my opinion. It had to have an individual language. We were seeing an adult world and really serious adult happenings *through the eyes of children*. One approaches it in terms of what would address itself to children."[14]

Bernstein decided to *use the piano to represent the innocence of children*. Later in his career, Bernstein would use the piano in his score for *The Good Son* (1993), a movie about an evil boy. His tender piano theme tends to lead the viewer astray into believing that maybe this boy really isn't bad.

The movie starts off with the sound of a simple childlike music box melody played on the piano. This is immediately followed by the sound of a little girl humming. Mulligan and Pakula had wanted the opening of the film to convey the mysterious and secret world of childhood. Stephen Frankfurt, who designed the opening title sequence, had wanted it to play as is, without music. As we see the Universal International logo, we hear Bernstein's innocent piano melody, which dies away leaving only the child humming. We see her open a cigar box full of childhood playthings, from crayons and jacks to marbles and small dolls. Then we hear a beautiful theme played on solo flute, accompanied by harp and clarinet arpeggios, violin tremolos, and broken chords in the celeste and vibraphone. As one marble collides with another, we hear a more fully orchestrated version of the flute theme, this time in the strings, horn, and woodwinds.

One of their mysterious neighbors was a character known as Boo Radley, played by Robert Duvall in his screen debut. Bernstein's music helps to convey the sense of mystery as to "who was Boo Radley and what was going on inside his house?" Boo was the children's "Bogeyman." About twenty-five minutes into the film, the three children in this story decide to see if they can sneak up on Boo Radley's house at night so as to get a peek at him. The scene starts with the piano, accompanied by a trill in the strings with intermittent solo passages in the woodwinds. The piano disappears for awhile. Next we hear the horns and woodwinds. As the piano returns we hear the addition of the xylophone. This is about as good as masterful film scoring will ever get. Three minutes into this sequence, as the older boy manages to sneak on to the front porch, we have the eerie combination of piano and vibraphone. Then, as we see the shadow of Boo Radley against the wall of the porch, the childlike piano music now drops down several octaves, and along with the trombones, horns, and trumpets, the music suddenly becomes terrifying. The kids are frozen in place from fear. We hear a repeated ostinato pattern in the piano and low voices of the orchestra. Then, as the children suddenly flee the scene, the orchestration, somewhat reminiscent of the music of Aaron Copland, becomes about as fully blown as any other scene in the movie.

Elmer Bernstein said this was a difficult movie to score. It took him six weeks before he hit on the approach for the music. Once he realized that the real function of the score was to deal in the magic of a child's world, he was able to proceed, composing in a definitely American-sounding ambiance, influenced by his former teacher, Aaron Copland.

Gregory Peck won the Oscar for best actor. Bernstein's score was nominated for best score, but lost to *Lawrence of Arabia*.

14. Taken from interviews of special thirty-fifth anniversary commemorative edition, 1998, Universal Studio.

How the West Was Won

Although we give credit to Jerome Moross and Elmer Bernstein as the composers of the two quintessential Western-score prototypes, the score for *How the West Was Won* (1963), composed by the veteran composer Alfred Newman, has been admired and imitated. When we say score, we really mean the main title theme for this larger-than-life epic of the old West.

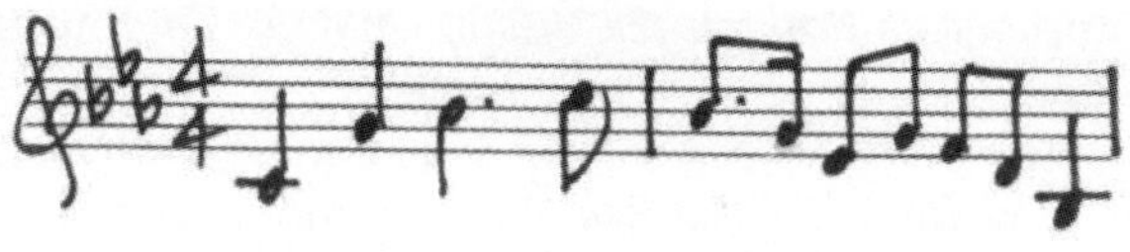

How the West Was Won: *Main Theme*

The opening main title theme starts with an expansive interval of a perfect fifth followed by a minor third played by the horns to create the feeling of the open vistas of the American West. This is followed by a rousing up-tempo rodeo roundup kind of feel with the full seventy-five-piece studio orchestra playing the same theme.

How the West Was Won was the first major feature film to be filmed in the impressive ultra-widescreen Cinerama. It traces the lives of several families throughout several generations as they try to tame the American West as they move across the frontier. Along the way we hear borrowings from various American folk songs as used for both source music and to create the time and place of nineteenth-century Americana. Newman even borrows from one of his own main title themes from the 1939 John Ford film, *Young Mr. Lincoln,* when we see Raymond Massey in the role of the great American president.

To add additional musical backdrop color for the Americana flavor, we hear the Ken Darby Singers performing songs such as "Shenandoah," "When Johnny Comes Marching Home," and the

Ken Darby (1909–1992) was a loyal and devoted friend of Alfred Newman. He was born in Hebron, Nebraska, on May 11, 1909. His family moved to California when he was seven years old. As he grew older, he took composition lessons at Santa Monica Junior College, while making money playing organ in the local movie houses and augmenting this with a part-time job as a gas station attendant. In 1929, he was offered a job singing in a male quartet that became the King's Men Quartet. This group was offered a contract to appear in movies and be heard on radio programs throughout the 1930s. Decca records offered them a contract, most notably as a backup group for Bing Crosby. He began to do all of the arrangements for the group and also did some choral directing jobs. In 1939, MGM hired him as the vocal arranger and supervisor for *The Wizard of Oz*. The next year, Disney hired him for *Pinocchio*. It was his arrangement for "When You Wish Upon A Star" that helped that song win the Oscar for best song. He did a five-year stint as Disney's vocal director of the Disney music department. In 1948, Alfred Newman, who was head of the 20th Century Fox music department at the time, gave Darby a call, with an offer to come to 20th Century Fox studios as their vocal supervisor and choral director. Although the contract was for only seven years, the Newman–Darby team was so successful that it continued until Newman's death in 1970. Two of the nine Oscars won by Newman were shared by Darby. They were for the musicals *The King and I* and *Camelot*. The two men were also nominated for their work on *South Pacific* and *Flower Drum Song*. Darby won an additional Oscar for his work on the film of *Porgy and Bess*, shared with Andre Previn. He was also a song composer. One of his most famous songs has become a famous standard, "Love Me Tender."

emotion-stirring "Battle Hymn of the Republic." Alfred Newman used about 125 studio hours to record this long score over a period of about a year and a half! The movie opened in America on February 21, 1963, and had its actual world premiere in the United Kingdom on November 1, 1962.

How the West Was Won also was notable for at least two other reasons. It was made by three different directors (John Ford, Henry Hathaway, and George Marshall) and, with a running time of almost 165 minutes, it qualifies as one of the longest Westerns ever made.

Jason and the Argonauts

Bernard Herrmann's final venture into the world of fantasy, as created by Ray Harryhausen, the master of special effects at the time, was for *Jason and the Argonauts* (1963). Herrmann scored four films for the filmmaker Charles Schneer and Harryhausen: *The Seventh Voyage of Sinbad, The Three Worlds of Gulliver, Mysterious Island,* and *Jason and the Argonauts.* A fifth fantasy film, *Journey to the Center of the Earth,* involved a different studio.

What the film may lack in great substance, Herrmann more than makes up for with another "tour de force" of masterful orchestration techniques. True to his philosophy, he once again customizes the size of the orchestra to fit the needed moods and colors of the movie. The score is written for a larger than normal brass section that is accompanied by a heavy, pounding percussion section. The score contains no strings. Woodwinds are added for color and emotion.

With the amazing computer graphics (CGI) that are available to our modern filmmakers, think of the mindbending experiences Herrmann could have taken us on if only he would have lived long enough to score some of today's fantasy films.

Cleopatra: The Last Hollywood Epic

Alex North's two scores for *Spartacus* (1960) and *Cleopatra* (1963) both employed unusual instrumentation. For *Cleopatra,* North composed for sistrum (an ancient jingling rattle common in Egyptian worship, particularly in the cult of Isis), crotales (small cymbals that can be tuned to a definite pitch and date back to ancient Egypt, Rome, and Greece), small dinner bells, tuned cowbells, five suspended cymbals of different pitches, five suspended triangles also of different pitch, five small gongs, and gamelon. In another sequence, he used the entire family of saxophones, from the contrabass to the sopranino, each playing straight—without vibrato for a unique sound. This was the largest group of instrumentalists ever assembled for a film score in the history of 20th Century Fox studios.

The opening main title sequence features the seductive sound of an alto flute to represent the very seductive Queen of the Nile. North wanted to simulate as closely as possible the instruments that were known to have been prevalent during this historic period. *He even had replicas of the ancient instruments made to appear in various scenes to lend a feeling of authenticity to the movie.*

One of the most spectacular individual sequences ever put on film has to be the amazing entry of Cleopatra into Rome to resume her role as Caesar's wife. She was coming to conquer by spectacle. There were twenty-six thousand extras in complete costume present. Elizabeth Taylor (playing the role of Cleopatra) is seen wearing an outfit made of twenty-four-carat gold. The total cost back then of her elaborate wardrobe of sixty-five different costumes was $194,800. This is the highest sum ever spent on costumes for a single performer in any one film. What started off as a $3 million production to be filmed in England at Pinewood Studios quickly escalated into what was to become the biggest and

Autograph of main title for Jason and the Argonauts. *Courtesy of Bernard Herrmann Collection, Davidson Library, University of California at Santa Barbara.*

most expensive film in motion picture history. As a matter of fact, *Cleopatra* was the most expensive movie ever made for many years to come (surpassed by films such as *Waterworld* and *Titanic*). The production was moved to Rome, and the sets were constructed near Anzio Beach. The length of the film grew to six hours. The director Joseph L. Mankiewicz pleaded with the executives at 20th Century Fox to release the film as two three-hour films. It was eventually trimmed to its present four-hour length.

Cleopatra recreated four major battles with uniforms and weapons all made to order and used seventy-nine separate sets. For the scene of Egypt in and around the Alexandria palace of Cleopatra, workers built an enormous set that used more cement than was used in building Italy's new Olympic Stadium at that time. There were fifteen thousand bows and 150,000 arrows to distribute to the thousands of extras on the set. It could take hours to assemble the thousands of people needed for a scene that lasts only minutes on screen.

Alex North. Courtesy of the Tony Thomas Collection.

At the New York world premiere of *Cleopatra,* those in attendance to represent the world of music included composer Richard Rodgers (1902–1979, composer of such Broadway hits as *Oklahoma, South Pacific,* and *The Sound of Music*) and Leonard Bernstein (1918–1990), former conductor of the New York Philharmonic and composer of *West Side Story*). *Cleopatra* was booked to play in mid-June at New York's Rivoli Theater. The film was so eagerly awaited that there were no seats left for the first four months!

It earned an impressive $26 million at the box office at a time when the average ticket price was less than a dollar. Unfortunately, *Cleopatra* cost over $40 million to make. Eventually the film would clear $5.5 million, but it was too late. Because of *Cleopatra,* all of the studio's cash was going out instead of in. The studio was virtually bankrupt. Darryl Zanuck, head of the studio, sold off acres of studio property and closed down the entire studio laying nearly everyone off from work.

Fortunately, *The Sound of Music* (1965) saved the studio. It played in many theaters for two straight years and went on to make nearly $160 million in its first domestic release. It was the phenomenal success that Fox needed to regain its strength.

Mondo Cane

A rather bizarre and graphic Italian documentary film called *Mondo Cane* (1963) featured a main title theme song entitled "More," which was extremely successful—it became a number one hit on the pop charts for eight weeks. The score was written by the Italian composers Riz Ortolani (1926–) and Nino

The "mature" Bernard Herrmann, taken during the last years of his life. Courtesy of Bernard Herrmann Collection, Davidson Library, University of California at Santa Barbara.

The Fall of the Roman Empire

It was stated by Mark Walker, editor of the *Gramophone Film Music Guide,* that although Dimitri Tiomkin's music for *The Fall of the Roman Empire* (1964) was "lively, stirring, romantic, [and] filled with grand fanfares . . . there is little to suggest to the ear that we are . . . in Imperial Rome." Walker goes on to state that "audiences would have to wait until *Star Wars* in 1977 before they were to hear anything even remotely approaching this magnificence again." These comments aside, it is true that this is considered by many to be one of Tiomkin's greatest scores. It is also true that Tiomkin did not approach scoring for ancient Rome with the same degree of scholarly insight as Miklos Rozsa. Nevertheless, his music is effective for what it does for the film.

The most memorable aspect of the film score is probably the powerful main title sequence, complete with a blasting pipe organ in the mix of sound.

The Agony and the Ecstacy

There are times when more than one film composer will work on the same film at the same time (see, for example, *The Egyptian*). In 1965, Alex North wrote the main score for *The Agony and the Ecstacy,* but Jerry Goldsmith was in charge of writing underscore to the opening prologue to this movie. To add to the realism of the period, North studied the music of the sixteenth-century composer Giovanni Gabrieli (1557–1612). As might be expected, both North and Goldsmith did an admirable job.

Alex North received an Academy Award nomination for best score, although the Oscar went to Maurice Jarre for the *Doctor Zhivago* score.

The Sound of Music

The Sound of Music (1965) was the salvation of 20th Century Fox, following the *Cleopatra* fiasco of 1963. The interest in Hollywood musicals had finally come to an end in the 1950s, yet several musicals that had made their debut on Broadway and then were made into movies in the 1960s did very well at the box office. These included *West Side Story* (1961), *My Fair Lady* (1964), *The Sound of Music* (1965), and *Oliver!* (1968).

The phenomenal four-octave singing range of English actress/singer Julie Andrews helped to make *The Sound of Music* one of the top-grossing films of all time.

The Greatest Story Ever Told

In 1965, Alfred Newman wrote one of his (arguably) greatest scores for a mighty religious epic, *The Greatest Story Ever Told.* The director George Stevens had wanted to make this the film of all films, with a large production including many cameos of Hollywood's finest and best-known actors. Stevens had wanted Newman to use the "Hallelujah Chorus" from George Frideric Handel's (1685–1759) *Messiah,* which was written in 1742. Alfred Newman had already written his own "Hallelujah Chorus" and had hoped to use it instead. Stevens had said that he would keep in Handel's music no matter who criticized it. After several test screenings, the critics around the world had stated how Stevens had used bad taste by quoting part of Handel's *Messiah* in the film. Newman got a call saying to reinstate his chorus back into the picture.

The sequence in which Jesus raises Lazarus from the dead is an excellent example of Newman's talents in religious-themed film. As Jesus, standing at the tomb, says, "Lazarus, come forth," everyone standing around looks on in disbelief. At first, Newman accompanies this with strings and a wordless chorus. This evolves into Newman's "Hallelujah," based on the "great journey theme," heard earlier in the film as we see Jesus and his disciples spreading the Word of the Lord to new believers. This leads to some transitional material that goes right into Handel's "Hallelujah Chorus."

The main title theme from this movie is reminiscent of Samuel Barber's *Adagio for Strings*. This score has some wonderfully lush orchestrations in a religious style. We also hear some colorful double reed choirs featuring instruments in the oboe and bassoon families. According to MGM Music Department statistics, the total number of musicians called to work on this monumental score was 1,057! The number of singers was 386, and there was a total of twenty-three days of double sessions (six hours of work per day—each "session" is three hours in length). The grand total recording time for the whole film project, including recording sessions for the record album, is 140 hours of work! The film was reedited and forty-seven minutes was trimmed from the final film. Unfortunately, this caused twenty minutes of the 142-minute score to be butchered in an offensive way. As a result, Alfred Newman requested that his name be withdrawn as the composer of the score. George Stevens did *not* grant his wish. Fortunately, for those who wish to hear this extra music, the entire score has been released in a special three-CD package for us to savor.

Alfred Newman's score also received an Academy Award nomination, but lost to Maurice Jarre's *Doctor Zhivago*.

Who's Afraid of Virginia Woolf?

In 1966, Alex North was called on to score a film directed by Mike Nichols, *Who's Afraid of Virginia Woolf?*, based on a play by Edward Albee. This was the first film to receive a Production Code seal of approval from the MPAA, despite the presence of four-letter words (profanity). Warner Bros., which made the film, had to promise to limit admission to people over eighteen years of age. Richard Burton and Elizabeth Taylor star as a middle-aged married couple at odds with one another. Taylor won an Oscar as best actress for her portrayal in this film.

North felt that the story had no need for music, at first. Nichols disagreed, and he badgered North to come up with a musical solution. Because the dialogue was so intense, North had a real challenge as to what kind of score would best serve the scenario. Because of the extreme tension between the two main characters, North tried a jazz approach at first, to play against the action and tone down the friction between the two. This didn't work. Perhaps a twelve-tone score to enhance the tension? No, North felt that this would make the film unbearable to watch. He finally settled on the appropriate solution, a quasi-baroque score. This style of music *played against* the violent outbursts in the story and directed the viewer more in the direction of the human relationship represented on screen. It was a triumph of wisdom for North, earning him an Academy Award nomination. (John Barry's score to *Born Free* won, however.) In order "to remind the audiences of the play's abrasive tone, North often incorporates dissonance into the score's warm, lyrical flow."[16]

16. Quote from CD liner notes.

By 1966, the average price of a movie ticket had risen to $1.09. Perhaps more importantly, the moral code that had dominated the ways movies were made was beginning to break down, and this was one of the crucial films that pioneered that change.

A Man and a Woman

Francis Lai was born in Nice, France, on April 26, 1932. His parents were market gardeners. He learned how to play the accordion and after a time he learned jazz. He eventually moved to Paris, where he made his home. He became a songwriter for Edith Piaf, Juliette Greco, and Yves Montand. Well-known celebrities such as Maurice Chevalier loved his work and praised him highly. With the success of his score for *Love Story* (1970), he became an international sensation and gained recognition as one of the world's great contemporary film composers.

He does all of his composing at night. According to composer-arranger Hal Shaper, his "melodies are so engaging they seem to have been plucked out of the air of Paris. There is a great deal of Paris in this modest and endearing man. He is basically a piano accordion player, whose feet are in the gutters of Montmartre, but whose soul is somewhere among the stars and whose music runs through the heart of Paris like a lover's tears."

Lai (1932–) became very popular after *A Man and a Woman* (1966) achieved recognition, by winning the Best Foreign Language Film Oscar. The main title of *A Man and a Woman* became a smash hit. Four years later, Lai's score for the ultrapopular 1970 movie *Love Story,* won the Best Score Oscar.

Lalo Schifrin

Argentinian-born Lalo Schifrin (1932–) became a member of the rising stars of film composers who had a strong influence in changing the sound of movie scores in the late 1960s. He had started in Hollywood as a television composer and gravitated to full-length feature films in the mid-1960s. He may be remembered best for his *Mission Impossible* TV theme, the very catchy *musical meter [beat pattern] of five recurring beats per measure.*

In a waltz, the triple meter of "*one* two three, *one* two-three, *one*-two-three" is heard over and over again, with a strong accent or more emphasis on beat "one." In a march, a duple meter of "*one*-two, *one*-two, *one*-two" is heard over and over again, with an accent or more emphasis on beat "one." For *Mission Impossible*'s main theme, Schifrin used the combination of the two meters together: *one*-two-three-*one*-two, *one*-two-three-*one*-two.

Lalo Schifrin's score for *The Cincinatti Kid* (1965) has been marked as the "real start of my career in movies." He was concerned about being typecast, as so many creative people are in Hollywood, into one category of film genre. This eventually happened to him

Lalo Shifrin. Courtesy of the Tony Thomas Collection.

after his success with the high-adrenaline car chase movie *Bullitt* (1968), starring Steve McQueen. One of the things that added to the excitement of this movie was the fact McQueen was a car-racing fanatic in real life, so he was able to do his own stunts.

Schifrin's music was so effective that other filmmakers sought him out for similar assignments in this "car chase" movie genre. After *Bullitt,* he scored movies such as *Coogan's Bluff* (1968), *Dirty Harry* (1971), *Magnum Force* (1973), *Sudden Impact* (1983), *The Dead Pool* (1988), and *Rush Hour* (1998).

Schifrin was trained as a classical musician, but soon acquired a love for jazz and improvisation. Additionally, he became acquainted with the sophistication and technology of electronic music, at a time when many of his other colleagues were stagnating with the conventional, more "old-fashioned" methods of scoring. This quickly put him in great demand, both as a television composer and a feature film composer. At one point in his career, he was scoring as many as five or six films a year. His output is approaching two hundred scores for television and films.

Although his scores are quite versatile, with many experimental sounds and meters, incorporating elements of jazz, mixed with electronics and conventional instruments, Schifrin has a firm grasp of his role in scoring a film. He believes that a film is like a human body. He feels that the brain of the film is its director. The lungs would be the producer. As one might expect from this analogy, the cameraperson represents the eyes, and the composer represents the ears. He thinks that we should not be aware of any one part of this "body" too much. He states that "the music shouldn't overplay any more than an actor should overact, but neither should it be so subtle it is almost nonexistent." He has helped the sound of film scores change over the years because of this philosophy. His scores are "characterized by sparse, modernistic lines" of music that showcase a variety of styles, rhythms, and tone colors in a more contemporary sound (taken from elements of jazz, rock, electronics, and orchestral colors).

Cool Hand Luke

Lalo Schifrin earned his first Academy Award nomination for the comedy-drama about a prison chain gang in the South, *Cool Hand Luke* (1967). Veering from the usual full orchestral sounds of movie scores, Schifrin painted a believable and effective score for a southern landscape by using individual instruments such as a banjo, a harmonica, a xylophone, and a guitar. It was apparent even in his earlier years of film scoring that Lalo Schifrin would be an innovative leader, taking film music in a new direction.

Quincy Jones

The Chicago-born jazz trumpeter and arranger Quincy Jones (1933–) got his start in the business by arranging music for some of the greatest names in the world of jazz (Lionel Hampton, Dizzy Gillespie, Count Basie, Frank Sinatra, and Tony Bennett). He eventually rose to several executive positions with certain recording companies. Like Lalo Schifrin, he started his film-scoring career in the mid-1960s.

It was his score for the controversial film *The Pawnbroker* (1965), directed by Sidney Lumet, that helped to establish his career as a film composer.

Two of his scores from this period drew praise from critics. *In the Heat of the Night* (1967) featured a R&B (rhythm and blues) style, along with honky-tonk themes showcasing several artists from Nashville. One such artist was a young man who rose to stardom over the years. His name was Glen Campbell. The music that Jones supplied for this film has been praised as being some of the best scoring work ever done for a film dealing with a racially biased southern town at the start of the civil rights movement.

The other score, for the movie *In Cold Blood* (1967), was nominated for an Academy Award. It accompanied a gruesome murder story penned by Truman Capote that Jones felt needed some innovative sounds to accompany the eerie plot. Quincy Jones "composed" for a set of bottles that were tuned to play specific notes of the musical scale. Although he does have some of his trademark jazz elements in this score, he also creates atmosphere with various clusters of orchestral sounds and percussion as well as the creepy use of a pipe organ during a flashback to the gruesome murder.

He has written for several successful television shows, including *Ironside* (1967). He won an Emmy Award for the critically acclaimed television miniseries *Roots* in 1977. He continues to wear several hats as record producer, arranger, composer, and conductor. In 1985, he earned his second Oscar nomination for the movie *The Color Purple*.

Quincy Jones. Courtesy of the Tony Thomas Collection.

Ennio Morricone

The Italian composer Ennio Morricone made his first fame as the composer for a group of films known today as "spaghetti Westerns." Many of these are films directed by Italian writer-director Sergio Leone (1921–1989). Interestingly enough, both men had actually gone to grammar school together and were seen sitting next to each other in an old photograph owned by Leone.

When these men first worked together, there was some concern that people in America might criticize any movie about the old American west made by a group of foreigners. Therefore, both Leone and Morricone used pseudonyms that each man felt would make their work more acceptable and legitimate to American filmgoers. Leone took on the name Bob Robertson, whereas Morricone used either Dan Savio or Leo Nichols. As it turned out, this change of names was not necessary. The public went wild over this group of films (although panned by critics). These films also made an unknown actor by the name of Clint Eastwood an instant star.

The Italian "Spaghetti" Western

Three Films by Leone

A Fistful of Dollars
The Good, the Bad, and the Ugly
Once Upon a Time in the West

For these film scores, Morricone and Leone used a rather unorthodox approach. Before writing the script and then shooting a scene, director Leone would describe to Morricone the kind of music that he had in mind for a character or a particular situation. After each character had received his or her leitmotif, these themes would be recorded with a few instruments. Leone would then play these recordings

ENNIO MORRICONE

Ennio Morricone. Courtesy of the Tony Thomas Collection.

Italian-born composer (Rome, Italy) Born: October 11, 1928

Perhaps the most prolific of all film composers, he has written nearly four hundred scores.

He was classically trained at the Conservatorio di Santa Cecilia in Rome.

He also is a successful composer for the concert stage.

He has scored films for a host of international directors.

He has worked for film companies in France, Belgium, England, Germany, Canada, Spain, Italy, Mexico, and the United States.

He got his start by scoring a series of Italian Westerns, known today as "spaghetti Westerns" (*A Fistful of Dollars, For a Few Dollars More*, and *The Good, the Bad, and the Ugly*).

He has yet to win the Academy Award, but has been nominated about a half-dozen times.

He has won at least five British Academy Awards: *Days of Heaven* (1978), *Once Upon a Time in America* (1983), *The Mission* (1986), *The Untouchables* (1987), and *Cinema Paradiso* (1988).

He won the Golden Globe Award for his scores for *The Mission* (1986) and *The Legend of 1900* (1999).

His philosophy is to orchestrate all of his own scores.

He is a very versatile composer, capable of different sounds and styles.

His scores are full of experimental sounds and colors, such as using sounds from animals and birds, and whistling and grunt noises from humans.

on the set with very effective results. According to Leone, "Ennio is my best scriptwriter, because when I don't have too much dialogue going on, I throw in a musical theme or two: it fulfills the same basic function, since it speaks instead of the characters, and it helps stress their feelings, their emotions."

Morricone used new or interesting sounds in his scores for these three Westerns directed by Leone. The use of the harmonica for the movie *Once Upon a Time in the West* (1969) was cleverly done in a simplistic style that was effective for what was needed to convey the atmosphere of the old West. For *The Good, the Bad, and the Ugly* (1966), he incorporated the various sounds made from animals and birds. He tried something a little different for the film *A Fistful of Dollars* (1964). Although whistling themes had already been heard in movie music, Morricone had the performer Alessandro Alessandroni whistle the main title theme over a guitar accompaniment. To make it more unique, this theme is also supported by voices that sometimes shout or grunt various words. This was definitely a different approach to scoring a Western. As a matter of fact, the music that he composed for this series of Westerns made him the new master of Western scores. Although Tiomkin, Moross, and Elmer Bernstein had written very important music for this genre of film, it was Morricone's music that became better known to a new generation of filmgoers during this decade.

The Lion in Winter

The English composer John Barry won his second Oscar for his cleverly done score that is based on a play by James Goldman who also wrote the screenplay. *The Lion in Winter* (1968) is about the twelfth-century king, Henry II of England, and his queen who are at odds with one another as to who will be his successor when he is gone. The story takes place during Christmas 1183.

Barry had recently become acquainted with a new recording of the Zoltán Kodály (1882–1967) Hungarian Girls Choir. He thought that they produced a wonderful sound and told the producer of the film that he wanted to use them in his score. Before Barry had begun writing music for films, he had spent time with Dr. Francis Jackson, who was the organist and choirmaster at York Minster in England. For three years, Barry had studied a huge amount of choral literature and then wrote a massive amount of music for choir himself. This would be the first time that he had ever written choral music for one of his film scores. As it turned out, Barry decided that he needed more than the sound of sixty young Hungarian girls singing, so he added men to the mixture to give the score the full dramatic range that it needed.

The score for *The Lion in Winter* contains brass fanfares, unaccompanied choral pieces, beautiful lyrical musical lines for the strings, and combinations of the above, all inspired by the sounds of medieval chants. This score is considered by some of Barry's admirers to be among his best film scores.

Romeo and Juliet

Once in a while, a film comes along that contains a song that becomes as well known as the movie itself. In 1968, the filmmaker Franco Zeffirelli (1923–) made a now-classic film version of Shakespeare's *Romeo and Juliet*. The love theme from the Zeffirelli movie, written by the Italian composer Nino Rota (1911–1979), went on to be a bestselling recording under the title "A Time For Us." Although there have been other popular movies made based on Shakespearean themes, this movie set the record for the highest number of sales for a movie soundtrack that accompanies a story based on Shakespeare. People went crazy for this recording and its love theme. Many stores could not handle the extreme demand for the soundtrack and quickly ran out, leaving fans dismayed. Zeffirelli is perhaps best remembered by some television viewers as the director of the very popular *Jesus of Nazareth* television drama, first released in 1977, and still aired during the Easter season.

Rosemary's Baby

Rosemary's Baby (1968), directed by Roman Polanski (1933–), is one of the scariest films of this period. Polanski hired the Polish composer Christopher Komeda (Krzysztof T. Komeda) (1937–1969) to score this chilling film. Komeda's promising career was cut short when he was killed from a brain injury he suffered when he accidentally fell.

The story is about a young married woman who gives birth to the Devil's son. Polanski had a terrifying childhood when growing up in Poland. He and his parents were taken to a Nazi concentration camp during World War II. His mother was killed there, but he somehow managed to escape. A group of German soldiers very sadistically used him as their target during target practice. He was able to survive this torture. Because of these early traumas, many of his movies center on a preoccupation with obsession and fear. This movie is no exception. The haunting vocal theme of Komeda and his effective underscore help to enrich the horrifying drama contained within this classic.

The Thomas Crown Affair

In 1999, the composer Bill Conti (1942–) scored a remake of the classic 1968 film *The Thomas Crown Affair*. He used several quotes from the haunting theme that was written for the original version of the film by French composer Michel Legrand (1932–). This theme called "The Windmills of Your Mind," became one of the hits of 1968 and won Legrand an Oscar for best song category. Paris-born Michel Legrand, like his popular musician father Raymond Legrand, studied in the United States with Paul Whiteman. Michel Legrand specialized in fusing popular French chanson with jazz. As a prolific composer, he is best known for his work on New Wave French films with filmmakers such as Jean-Luc Godard, Agnes Varda, and Jacques Demy. Legrand is seen in a cameo appearance composing a song in Varda's film *Cleo From 5 to 7*. He contributed much to the bittersweet image of Demy's films with his melancholy tunes. In addition to his successful international career as a composer and singer, Legrand has directed one film.

Planet of the Apes

The composer Jerry Goldsmith has always been recognized as an eclectic and versatile composer, even by his colleagues. He is not afraid to experiment and try new sounds in his scores. Studio musicians who regularly work with him have sometimes shown him unconventional instruments to be used in the percussion section or unorthodox sounds achieved on conventional instruments by using unconventional methods. One of the most amazing scores created for the cinema, and certainly one of the most innovative, has to be his score for the 1968 movie *Planet of the Apes*. Lovers of classical music can hear influences from composers such as Bela Bartók and Igor Stravinsky. The movie opens with the sound of a prepared piano. The **prepared piano** is a performance technique devised by the American composer John Cage in 1940. It is accomplished by placing screws, rubber erasers, blocks of wood, and other objects on or between the piano strings so that when played, the piano tones will be altered and dampened. We also hear a bass slide whistle and a tone row made up of three-note woodwind clusters. The film opens with a group of astronauts crash landing on some distant planet. Three astronauts survive the crash, led by Taylor. Later, as these three men are looking for forms of life on the planet, they encounter a group of scarecrows up on a hill. As they reach the top of the bluff, they discover a waterfall and signs of possible life. When Taylor says, "To hell with the scarecrows," Goldsmith employs the unusual sound of stainless steel mixing bowls (as found in a typical kitchen) being placed upside-down and struck with percussion mallets. In other parts of the film, we hear percussion instruments that appear to echo themselves. This is a technique known as echoplexed percussion. The **echoplex** was a technique that was popular in movie scores. It was created by using a tape delay system, whereby the player performs in a normal fashion that is instantly recorded on tape and then instantly played back. For *Planet of the Apes,* Goldsmith also achieved innovative sounds by using a ram's horn, water-drop bars, and a Brazilian culka (an instrument used to create the bizarre vocalization of the apes). A driving piano ostinato is heard during "the hunt" sequence, when the unseen attackers are

Charlton Heston stars in Planet of the Apes. *Courtesy of Archive Photos.*

finally revealed to be apes. It may be of interest to note that Goldsmith invited his old piano instructor, Jacob Gimpel, to provide the virtuoso piano playing. At the end of the film, Taylor discovers his destiny. At the final great revelation, Goldsmith lets this sequence play without music. Taylor and his colleagues had crashed on the earth in a world turned upside down, where apes rule and humans are their captives.

After the innovative score of *Planet of the Apes,* film composers continued to write scores that appealed more to the commercial side of filmmaking; that is, the composing of hit tunes or songs within the film that would help to sell the film.

At the close of the decade, Burt Bacharach (1929–) won two Oscars for best score and best song for his score to *Butch Cassidy and the Sundance Kid* (1969). He wrote a catchy song called "Raindrops Keep Fallin' on My Head," which accompanies a scene in the film. Although this song became enormously popular, helping to sell the film to the public, there were critics who claimed that the insertion of a song like this in a story at that point interrupts the flow of the story.

With the advent of pop, rock, jazz, and ethnic music in film scores, music for films would never be quite as it had been before this time. In the next chapter we will see a move from the conservative, traditional symphonic score to a more pop-oriented approach that has helped to shape the trends of today's film music.

16. What was the name of the last score that Herrmann would write for Hitchcock? ____.

17. From what famous classical composition did Al Newman quote for his score of *The Greatest Story Ever Told*? ____.

Define the following

1. Glissandos ________________________________.
2. Seventh chord ________________________________.
3. Ondioline ________________________________.
4. Quasi-baroque ________________________________.
5. Prepared piano ________________________________.
6. Echoplex ________________________________.

Chapter Nine

The Age of Versatility Continues (the 1970s, from *Patton* to *Star Wars*)

Patton

It is appropriate to start the survey of the 1970s with one of Jerry Goldsmith's most intellectual and ingenious scores—*Patton* (1970). According to Goldsmith, "It was probably the most intellectual exercise that I ever put forth on film."[1] This "exercise" almost did not reach fruition. Goldsmith was under contract to 20th Century Fox studios to do the music for the sequel to *Planet of the Apes*. Franklin J. Schaffner (1920–1989), the director of *Patton,* wanted Goldsmith for his film. Schaffner spoke to Richard Zanuck (1934–), head of the studio, and cleared the way for Goldsmith to do *Patton* instead.

This movie was made at a time in history when the American public was divided by an unpopular war in Vietnam. Because of this, one would think that to make a war film at this time would be ludicrous. Would the film even have any marketability? It certainly did: the film went on to win an impressive seven Oscars, including one for best picture.

Production of *Patton* ended in late May 1969, after thirteen weeks of shooting and exactly on schedule. Schaffner started working with Goldsmith in June 1969. The film runs 172 minutes, but contains only about thirty-two minutes worth of music. Goldsmith wanted to treat General Patton as a three-tiered personality because he was a very complex multilayered person. After a memorable speech by Patton to his troops, the film's main title sequence commences, complete with Goldsmith's musical description of Patton's character. *First* we hear a repeated **triplet figure** played by two

Triplet figure in trumpets

1. *Patton* CD liner notes, 1997, Kevin Mulhall, Varese Sarabande.

His style is quite eclectic. He continues to bring a wide variety of sounds to the world of film scoring. His music varies drastically among the many types of films he has scored.

Over the years, he has used Arthur Morton and Alexander Courage as his major orchestrators.

He has a large following of admirers both as fans and within his inner circle of colleagues.

He believes that a good film will carry a weak score, but a strong score won't save a mediocre picture.

He feels that music should be subordinate within a film. The less music there is in a film, the more emphasis it has when it enters.

In many of his films, his approach is essentially monothematic. Goldsmith feels that the film composer should be able to develop a principal theme that can "sum up what the film is about."

The piano is his most frequently used solo instrument.

He finds the scores of the 1930s and 1940s "cluttered and excessive" and therefore does not favor that idiom or approach to film scoring.

His final strength is his awareness of when to remain silent in his scoring of a film.

composer Francis Lai wrote a love theme that was easily accessible to the audience's ears. The theme was also crucial in helping Lai win the Best Score Oscar that year.

Lai introduced the theme as we see the young lovers in happier times. As we find out that the young girl has cancer, this builds us up to the big emotional torrent of tears when she dies. It is at this point that we hear the syrupy love theme once again, but now it helps to rip our emotions.

Earlier, we discussed how one movie executive had sent out a memo forbidding the use of minor keys in film music because he had thought that their use was the reason for his most recent film's doom. Actually, this very popular theme is in a minor key.

Love Story *main theme*

Summer of '42

One year later, another French composer, Michel Legrand, would make his presence known to American audiences by composing his Academy Award–winning score for *Summer of '42* (1971). This marked the first and only Academy Award for Legrand in the Best Score category and was the only time that two French composers won the Oscar in two successive years (Francis Lai in 1970 and Legrand in 1971).

The story involves the coming of age of three boys spending their summer together on an island off the coast of New England during World War II. They fantasize about a particular young woman (played by Jennifer O'Neill) who spends her time waiting for letters from her husband who is off fighting the war. Eventually she receives word of his death and she subsequently "initiates" one of the boys into adulthood.

The score contains a simple four-note theme that lends itself well to the melancholy recollections of this memorable summer back in the 1940s. Although neither Lai's *Love Story* score nor Legrand's score contained a great deal of substance, they were approachable and nonthreatening to the audience's emotions and sensibilities. That's why they worked and why they probably appealed to the Academy's members for the winning votes. This movie's theme is also in a minor key.

A Clockwork Orange

1971 was a landmark year for screen violence. In July, Ken Russell's *The Devils* opened to massive protests. Sam Peckinpah's contemporary Western, *Straw Dogs,* contained a controversial rape scene that disturbed people. Audiences were outraged and nervous as to what was happening.

In November of 1971, a very controversial film, *A Clockwork Orange,* premiered. The music of various classical composers such as Beethoven, Rossini, Elgar, and Rimsky-Korsakov was utilized. One of the key functions of the music in this film is to *play against the action* represented on screen. For instance, Rossini's *La Gazza Ladra (The Thieving Magpie)* opera overture is used in direct contrast to the attempted rape of a young woman by Billy Boy and his four sidekicks in a deserted theater. This could be looked on as a musical oxymoron, comparing two things that don't usually belong to one another, beautiful lyrical opera music with extreme violence. As in *Who's Afraid of Virginia Woolf?,* in which the music is used to tone down the brutal verbal action on screen, filmmaker Stanley Kubrick (1928–1999) used music in much the same way. The main character Alex (played by Malcolm McDowell) dances about chanting "Singin' in the Rain" in a somewhat syncopated manner as he rapes a woman and brutally beats her husband. It was said that director Stanley Kubrick and his cast spent days puzzling over possible ways of stylizing the violence to give it balletic distance.

Later in the film, Alex seduces two young girls back at his place to the musical accompaniment of Rossini's *William Tell Overture,* performed on the Moog synthesizer and then sped up as a bit of comic relief. The composer/performer Walter Carlos composed and realized the music for this score. (The electronic Moog synthesizer had been invented by Robert Moog in the late 1960s. Walter Carlos had used it for his phenomenally successful *Switched On Bach* record album.) He played some of the classical compositions on the Moog synthesizer.

Walter Carlos is now *Wendy* Carlos—*first film composer to have a sex change*. You might have seen two other films scored by Wendy Carlos—*The Shining* (1980) and *Tron* (1982).

A Clockwork Orange is a very disturbing film. It is a dark tale, based on a novel by Anthony Burgess, about the near-future world of decaying cities, murderous adolescents, and nightmarish technologies of punishment and crime. Although the film premiered in 1971, its theme is perhaps more pertinent to our society today than during the film's first release. Is this story prophetic of our seemingly more violent society? The question haunts us.

There is the question, does society affect cinema or does cinema affect society? Certainly in the case of this film, society and music have been affected. *A Clockwork Orange* became the blueprint for every designer violence youth-oriented movie ever since, from *The Warriors* to *Natural Born Killers, Quadrophenia* to *Trainspotting,* and *Romper Stomper* to *Fight Club.*

A Clockwork Orange was the first "punk" film. While "punk" erupted in London, a small clique of Sheffield bands took *A Clockwork Orange* as their inspiration for a robotic pop future. Caberet Voltaire and the Human League were the scene leaders, inspired as much by the film's electronic score as its plot. Thus was born the first wave of British technopop. The punk culture has been evident in society ever since.

Anthony Burgess was apparently appalled by the Walter Carlos score. This came as a surprise to Kubrick, because he knew that Burgess was a classical music connoisseur and sometime composer. Because the film's controversial content would likely be rated "X," severely limiting potential audiences, all parties involved in the making of this film agreed on a modest budget of $2 million. There would be no international stars and no specially commissioned score. Wendy Carlos later stated that Kubrick had temp-tracked the movie in places. True to his usual form, he refused to eliminate some of the "temps." Carlos was forced to give in to his whims. Also, Carlos later stated that time did not permit her to electronically realize the Rossini opera overture to *La Gazza Ladra* as she had wished, so for the film, we hear this work performed not on synthesizer but with live performers.

The way Carlos got the scoring assignment is rather interesting. She and her producer, Rachel Elkind, had both been fans of Stanley Kubrick's previous work. They saw a London newspaper clipping that Kubrick was planning on filming the book by Anthony Burgess, which Carlos had just finished reading and was thoroughly captivated by its vision of a future society filled with ultraviolence. As fate would have it, Carlos had been working on a modern piece called *Timesteps* that seemed to "capture the exact feeling of the opening scenes of the book." When the two read that Kubrick had just finished the movie, Carlos and Elkind were excited because Carlos's music also had just been completed. Rachel Elkind had a literary agent friend who contacted Kubrick's U.S. representative and made arrangements to have Kubrick listen to this new music by Carlos. Kubrick liked what he heard and sent word for Carlos to come to London for collaboration. Carlos had also sent Kubrick her synthesized arrangement of the fourth movement from Beethoven's *Ninth Symphony*. Kubrick was very happy to use her version of the famous Beethoven movement for the movie. For the main title music, Carlos electronically realized the Baroque period composer Henry Purcell's (1659–1695) music for the *Funeral of Queen Mary,* in a synthesizer version. This provides the viewer with an eerie-sounding anticipation as to what is to follow.

Shaft

The composer Isaac Hayes (1942–) provided a very jazz-oriented score for a hit movie about a black private investigator named John Shaft (played by Richard Roundtree). The title song became a popular hit tune and helped to publicize the movie.

The Godfather

The filmmaker Francis Ford Coppola (1939–), who had shared an Oscar for the script of *Patton* in 1970, was the director of one of the greatest American films of all time, *The Godfather* (1972). This is a masterful "operatic-scale epic" of the dark, hard-hitting lives of a Mafia family and its business dealings. The film became one of the biggest money-makers of all time and won the Best Picture of the Year Oscar at the Academy Award ceremonies.

Coppola selected the Italian composer Nino Rota (1911–1979) to lend an air of authenticity to the needed Italian flavor of the film. The score was widely acclaimed and became very popular, especially the main love theme, but suffered a rather unusual fate at the Academy Awards.

During the nominations for the individual categories, *The Godfather* received *eleven* when tallying up the first set of votes. However, when the members of the Academy learned that parts of Rota's score had been heard in one of his previous European movies (including the love theme for *The Godfather*), they withdrew the musical score for eligibility. The Italian movie that Rota had used this material in was a 1957 movie called *Fortunella*.

This score is composed of three basic themes that are played by solo instruments such as the trumpet, oboe, English horn, clarinet, mandolin, and guitar. The color of the mandolin is important in conveying the atmosphere of time and place, in this case the island of Sicily and the Italian Mafia in New York.[3]

Coppola realized the power of music in association with his film. In one example, he uses the same music to play over two contrasting sequences as he intercut the two together. At first we see a simple baptism of a baby. As this sequence continues, Coppola shows us a group of Mafia hitmen carrying out a strike on a rival gang. The sequence goes back and forth between the two; one a joyous moment, the other an extremely violent act of brutality. What "marries" these two contrasting scenes together is the nonstop continuous flow of music played on an organ. Some of this music is taken from Johann Sebastian Bach's *Passacaglia in C Minor*.

Sleuth

Two of the greatest English actors that lived in the twentieth century were Laurence Olivier (1907–1989) and Michael Caine (1933–). The director Joseph L. Mankiewicz (1909–1993) pitted these two dramatic geniuses together in a tour-de-force performance and film adaptation of Anthony Shaffer's play *Sleuth* (1972).

The English film composer John Addison (1920–1998), who won his one Oscar for his score for *Tom Jones* in 1963, wrote a brilliant score to enhance the goings-on of these two eccentric characters, who are forever trying to outsmart one another. One might say that the music plays the part of a third participant within the film. The music illustrates hidden commentary on these two characters and their wit. Because the story calls for certain sections to be dialogue only, Addison knows just when to interject his musical prowess. The score features the clever use of the harpsichord to represent Michael Caine's character, Milo Tindle. Although this score did not win, it was nominated for best score in 1972.

The Sting

To remind us how film scores had undergone a radical change in the course of one decade, it was in 1962 that Elmer Bernstein started a new trend of composing scores in a more *intimate* setting by using smaller ensembles of instruments for his masterpiece, *To Kill a Mockingbird*.

Now, in 1973, New York–born Marvin Hamlisch (1944–) won the Best Score Oscar *not* for his own original score, but for *adapting* a dead composer's music! The ragtime composer Scott Joplin (1868–1917), known as the "King of Ragtime," had written some music back at the beginning of the early twentieth century that lent itself very well to creating the atmosphere of time and place for the movie *The Sting* (1973). Although the movie supposedly took place a few years after the ragtime craze, Hamlisch's arrangements worked very well in setting the right atmosphere. It was the director of the movie, George Roy Hill, who had made the request for Joplin's music.

3. To show how ridiculous the edict mentioned earlier regarding the use of minor keys in film scores being detrimental to the success of a film, note that all *three* of the major musical themes in this score were in a minor key.

Hamlisch had made a recording of Joplin's very popular ragtime tune "The Entertainer," with Hamlisch playing the piano. This single recording became extremely successful in sales.

The Way We Were

1973 was a very good year for Marvin Hamlisch. In addition to his one Oscar for his *score adaptation* for *The Sting,* Hamlisch won two additional Oscars that year; one for best score for *The Way We Were,* the other for best song for the same film. As a matter of fact, *Hamlisch became the first person to ever win three Oscars in one night,* causing a sensation the night of the Oscars ceremony.

Barbra Streisand starred with Robert Redford in a story about a campus radical (Streisand) who hoped to marry a college athlete who also wanted to be a writer (Redford). Hamlisch wanted to make sure that the title song that he wrote would not give out too much information in advance, so he wrote a melody "that was sad, but also had a great deal of hope in it."[4] Hamlisch knew what he was doing. Not only did his song win at the Oscars, it went on to become the biggest hit of 1974.

The Exorcist

The Exorcist (1973) is a movie that underwent several stages of development before the final score was intact. Bernard Herrmann was strongly considered for the assignment but he turned it down. According to the producer and director of the film, William Friedkin, there is another side to the story. Herrmann wanted to record the score in London. This would have been unsatisfactory for Friedkin, who was racing against time to finish the film in Los Angeles. There simply was not enough time left for this. Herrmann had been living in England after he had been "stung" by his bad experiences working with Lew Wasserman. After viewing *The Exorcist,* Herrmann told Friedkin to "get rid of the first ten minutes of the film . . . all of that bullsh** in Iraq. It gets you nowhere. It's just f**king boring. Get rid of that sh** and a few other things and I think that my music can save your picture." Also, when Herrmann told Friedkin that he wanted to use an organ in his score, Friedkin supposedly shook Herrmann's hand and said, "Thank you for letting me meet an interesting person," after which time Friedkin walked away and thought no way was he going to use Herrmann. His approach to the score was not the same as Friedkin's.

A score was then written by Lalo Schifrin at the suggestion of executive producer Noel Marshall. Friedkin did not want any scary music and the music that he did want Schifrin to compose was to be used only in the montage sections. As the director said, "the music should be like a cold hand on the back of your neck." Because Schifrin, who was originally from Argentina, was known for writing in a Latin American style, Friedkin said, "I don't want a Samba score, Lalo." Schifrin then proceeded to write about twenty-three minutes of dramatic underscore and eight pieces of source music to be used during the party sequence. Schifrin's score called for forty-four string players, five percussionists, with the addition of keyboards and a harpist. Like Herrmann would do, Schifrin specially tailored this score for the needs of this movie, using no brass or woodwinds.

The score that Schifrin wrote was rejected by Friedkin. He hated it. It was very innovative for its day, containing very modern-sounding clusters in the strings that were both harsh and complex to the ear and utilizing bizarre percussion sounds that gave an out-of-this world effect. Schifrin was very proud

4. Quote from Gary Theroux and Bob Gilbert, *The Top Ten: 1956–Present* (New York: Simon and Schuster, 1982), p. 229.

of his work on this film, later claiming this to be one of his best works for any of his film assignments during his career. Schifrin was jolted by the sobering experience of being let go after only the second day of recording the score. The way it happened was when Friedkin stopped by the scoring sessions to see how things were going. Evidently Friedkin said to Schifrin, "OK, Lalo, let's hear it." Then the orchestra began to play the music as written by Schifrin. When the music cue ended, Friedkin got up out of his chair and said, "Well, Lalo, that music is *never* going to be in *my* movie."

What Friedkin finally did was to track in already existing music from various commercial recordings. The completed soundtrack includes contemporary music by avant-garde composers such as Krzysztof Penderecki (1933–), Anton Webern (1883–1945), Hans Werner Henze (1926–), and George Crumb (1929–). In addition to this, he used the "Tubular Bells" from Mike Oldfield's 1973 album and some newly composed atonal music written specifically by Jack Nitzsche to link together the pieces by the above-mentioned composers. Friedkin apparently liked Oldfield's "Tubular Bells" because it reminded him of an innocent nursery rhyme theme to represent Regan, the twelve-year-old girl who would become demon-possessed.

It was later stated that one of the reasons Schifrin's score was rejected by Friedkin was not because the music was bad, but because Friedkin wanted the viewer to be all alone in their journey through the film, to be free to interpret the events as they saw them. This would be without the intervention of an overpowering score that might sway the viewer in the wrong direction. Friedkin felt that Schifrin's approach was too overdomineering, that his score would overpower the rest of his film. Supposedly, one version of this story has Friedkin grabbing the audiotape from the Schifrin scoring sessions, going out the front of TODD-AO scoring stage, and throwing the tape across the parking lot. This is one film that could actually work *without* music. Friedkin even said that he never planned to put music in any of the "big moments" of the film, because the big moments carry themselves without music. The movie is very powerful and very disturbing. It still ranks as one of the most controversial films of its time and as one of the most frightening films ever made, it qualifies as being a cinematic landmark in its genre.

Sisters

Because Herrmann had left Hollywood in disgust, he had no plans on returning to score any other films. A group of young directors such as Martin Scorsese and Brian De Palma recognized the overabundance of talent still left in the master composer. As a result, these two men hired Herrmann to score some of their films. Bernard Herrmann's terrifying score for Brian De Palma's movie *Sisters* (1973) utilizes a Moog synthesizer for a horrific effect. The movie is about conjoined twins who are surgically separated. During the procedure, one of them dies, leaving the one surviving. She becomes a murderous lunatic who seeks revenge on several people in the film. Herrmann's music is perfect for this kind of story.

Papillon

Jerry Goldsmith's score for Franklin J. Schaffner's film *Papillon* (1973) contains one of his more hauntingly beautiful tunes. Goldsmith believes that the real problem of film music is blending art with commerce. Movie making is a big-business enterprise, not merely a group of artists coming together to make a work of art. Yet, somehow he manages to deliver a quality score time after time without fail.

Although this story about daily life in a French prison does not call for a wall-to-wall score, Goldsmith supplies this recurring theme to achieve impressive results.

American Graffiti: (The Compilation Score)

One of the best examples of a song compilation score (a film score composed of existing popular songs or tunes, instead of original material) was for young filmmaker George Lucas's (1944–) production of *American Graffiti* (1973). Instead of hiring a composer to score the film in the traditional sense, Lucas borrowed over forty hit songs of the 1950s and 1960s to provide atmosphere of time and place. Not only did this movie feature a cast of actors who would become some of today's leading stars, the hit tunes used in this song compilation score became a hit release at the record stores.

The Godfather Part II

To show how strange fate can be, Nino Rota's score for *The Godfather Part II* (1974) won as Best Score of the Year in 1974. The unexplainable thing is that much of the material that earned the praise of the Motion Picture Academy in order to win was actually the *same* material that was *disqualified* two years before, because it had been used in Rota's previous film score for the 1957 film *Fortunella*!

To set the record straight, this Oscar was shared with Carmine Coppola, who died in 1991 (the father of the director).

This score resurrected some of the same themes from the original film and introduced some new ones as well. Many critics felt that this sequel was actually better than the original *Godfather* of 1972.

Chinatown

Jerry Goldsmith scored *Chinatown* (1974) for four pianos and four harps, played by striking their strings or by plucking them to achieve unusual sounds. We also hear some modern "atonal" string passages and a haunting trumpet solo as the love theme that could have easily come out of an old film noir movie of the past. As it is, this Roman Polanski movie could be classified as a *color noir* film, because it was filmed in color and has all of the qualities of the *film noir* movies of the 1940s.

Goldsmith had only ten *days* to write and record his score for *Chinatown*!

Jaws

John Williams's (1932–) landmark score for *Jaws* (1975) was significant for Williams, Spielberg, and the advancement of film music before the public's eyes and ears. This film launched the careers of both John Williams and Steven Spielberg. Perhaps as important, it made moviegoers all over realize the power of film music. The simple two-note ostinato could be altered to fit the needs of the moment within the film.

Bilitis: Composer Francis Lai

Francis Lai (1932–) had won the Academy Award two times (for *A Man and a Woman* [1966] and *Love Story* [1970]) before he wrote a score that accompanies a rather obscure film, the French production of a coming-of-age film of a young girl named *Bilitis* (1976) who learns several things about life along her path to adulthood. This score has had a cult following among soundtrack collectors and contains a good representation of Francis Lai's unique style of music.

This score features a combination of instruments, electronics, and solo female voice that is as haunting as it is seductive. Francis Lai has written a score for this film, directed by the great erotic photographer David Hamilton, that is dripping with a seductive quality. Its broken chordal accompaniment is as beautiful as the lingering melody that it accompanies.

Taxi Driver

The score for *Taxi Driver* (1976) by the master film composer Bernard Herrmann is included here primarily because of its place in film music history. Martin Scorsese had admired the work of Herrmann and was glad to bring this genius of film music color back into the film scene in America.

The plot centered on a man who became a New York City cab driver in order to deal with his insomnia and pent-up rage and frustration. Scorsese wanted Herrmann to write a jazz-oriented score, something that was uncomfortable for Herrmann to do. He borrowed some of his own music from the past.

Herrmann wrote a lyrical saxophone solo for the main theme that is hauntingly memorable.

On December 23, 1975, some of the musicians who were present at the scoring sessions for *Taxi Driver* were concerned about Herrmann's health. There were many people who came by to see the great master of film composition at work in Hollywood once again, including a young Steven Spielberg. Spielberg came up to Herrmann and complimented him on his outstanding talent as a film composer. Herrmann looked back at Spielberg in anger, shouting out, "If you like my music so much, why do you keep hiring Johnny Williams to do your scores?" Those who were at the scoring session told Herrmann to go back to his hotel and wait to record the final cue after the Christmas holidays. Herrmann said no, that he wanted to finish everything so that he could get back to England.

Later, after finishing the last cue for the movie, Herrmann and his wife went to dinner at an Italian restaurant in Santa Monica with Larry Cohen and his wife. Cohen wanted Herrmann to score his just completed picture called *God Told Me To*. Herrmann remarked that he liked Cohen's new film and later returned to his room at the Universal Sheraton Hotel a little past midnight on Christmas Eve. Fellow film composer Fred Steiner was to meet Herrmann for breakfast the next morning. Herrmann was found dead the next morning in his bed wearing a look of complete contentment on his face. His cause of death was diagnosed as congestive heart failure.

Carrie

Herrmann had been scheduled to score Brian De Palma's (1940–) film *Carrie* (1976). Because of Herrmann's untimely death, De Palma hired the Italian composer Pino Donaggio (1941–) for the assignment. Donaggio was not a seasoned veteran at the time, having only scored a few films.

According to Donaggio, his career began as a singer and songwriter in Italy, and he became one of Italy's most popular singers. He was approached by the producer Ugo Mariotti to score a movie about a person with ESP called *Don't Look Now* in 1974. Brian De Palma got a copy of *Don't Look Now* and screened it several times in the privacy of his home. As he watched it, according to Donaggio, he closed his eyes so that he could concentrate better on the score. Donaggio said, "One day I got a call. It was Brian De Palma who said that he wanted me to score *Carrie*. He wanted either Johnny Williams or me and I won the assignment."

Donaggio's music captures the essence of Herrmann's style through his unusual instrumentation and experimentation of colors. The opening main title sequence is a haunting vocal. Donaggio *uses electronics for* sound design, particularly in the horrendous murderous rampage inside the gymnasium. We hear long sustained pedal points as scored for electronic synthesizer during this mayhem. The surprise ending with Amy Irving and her bouquet of flowers would inspire many future horror films. Donaggio's music helped to relax the viewer, making him or her vulnerable for the big surprise!

Donaggio has even been paid the ultimate compliment by being deemed "The Italian Herrmann," a title gladly accepted by Donaggio. Note his reference to the *Psycho* murder cue in the gymnasium sequence.

The Omen

In 1976, Jerry Goldsmith composed a score (*The Omen*) that would bring him his first (and *only*) Oscar. Many people thought that it was long overdue. He had already gained eight previous Oscar nominations without ever winning. He was one of the most sought-after composers in Hollywood.

The director Richard Donner (1939–) asked Goldsmith if he had any ideas for the music in his movie *The Omen*. Goldsmith replied, "I hear voices."

Although Goldsmith is known for normally needing two weeks to develop basic material for a score, he was able to come up with the main motif and the whole choral layout in one day. Goldsmith gives great credit to his pal and colleague Arthur Morton. According to Goldsmith, it was Morton who greatly improved at least 65 percent of the choral writing as Goldsmith's orchestrator on this film project.

The opening main title music, *Ave Satani* (somewhat similar to Carl Orff's scenic cantata *Carmina Burana* [1937]) is stunningly eerie and brilliantly sets the turn of events that will soon transpire in the film.

The story traces the lives of Robert Thorn (played by Gregory Peck) and his wife (Lee Remick). They adopt a child who, as they eventually realize, turns out to be the antichrist. Goldsmith's music is both inventive and effective. The music figures very prominently in the overall plot of the film. It is used sparingly, but when it is heard, it heightens the impact of each scene's emotions. About twenty-four minutes into the movie, the Thorns and their son, Damien, are on their way to a wedding. Damien had never been in a church before. As their car pulls up to the church, Goldsmith employs an effective use of an ostinato pattern. Damien goes crazy and so does the music. Goldsmith also wrote a short love theme. He was able to take portions of this theme and use them throughout the entire film.

Jerry Goldsmith had Lionel Newman (Alfred's brother) conduct the scoring sessions with the National Philharmonic Orchestra at the Music Centre in England.

Rocky

The American-born composer Bill Conti (1942–) provided the music for *Rocky* (1976) in the form of a fanfare; this music became the most recognizable film music of 1976 and helped to launch both Conti's career

Jerry Goldsmith scored the chilling movie The Omen *(1976). Courtesy of Archive Photos.*

as a film composer and the career of Sylvester Stallone. This "Rocky theme" is still among some of the most memorable music taken from the vast output of film music in the last several decades by all of the composers working during that time. As with other familiar themes, such as that from the James Bond films, all one needs to do is play just a few of the opening notes; there is almost universal recognition.[5]

Conti is a very successful composer and writes some of the very best *contrapuntal imitation*—different instruments and voices entering in imitation at different times—in the business.

Conti has composed around one hundred scores for movies and television. He is best known for his theme from the movie *Rocky* ("Gonna Fly Now"), his James Bond song "For Your Eyes Only," his work on the television miniseries *North and South,* and his work scoring the *Rocky* movie sequels and the *Karate Kid* movies.

Bill Conti

This was by no means Bill Conti's first film score. Born in Providence, Rhode Island, in 1942, he attended Louisiana State University on a bassoon scholarship, later switching to composition. He went from there to Juilliard School of Music in New York where he studied composition with Luciano Berio (1925–), Vincent Persichetti (1915–1987), and Roger Sessions (1896–1985).

Bill and his wife Shelby went to Italy, where he survived by playing jazz in a piano bar for a number of years. It was very difficult to feed a family of four (they had two daughters) on his small income. His father-in-law in Baton Rouge, Louisiana, was concerned about his daughter marrying one of those wild musicians who would probably never amount to anything. Several years passed. One day, Conti met a film editor from England who was working on a film in Madrid. Conti said, "I'm a film composer" (although at that time, he had not written a single note for a film). The Englishman believed him and Conti got the job of writing the score for this low-budget picture. Conti began to ghostwrite for a number of low-budget films released in Europe, and gained experience composing for films. It was when he saw how little he was making and how much the named film composers were making for music that *he* had written that he decided that things have got to change.

Bill Conti. From the author's collection.

When Paul Mazursky (1930–) came to Italy to direct *Blume in Love* in 1973, he met Bill Conti. Thinking that Conti was a native Italian, Mazursky spoke to him through an interpreter for some time. Conti went along with the misunderstanding to see how long it would take for Mazursky to realize that he was an American who spoke perfect English. He hired Conti to arrange some music that was played in the background as source music in *Blume in Love* when the two main stars are seen

5. This is why the majority of products that are advertised on radio or television use music in their commercials. People associate the musical logo with the product instantly.

sipping coffee at an outdoor café on their honeymoon. This led to Conti being hired for Mazursky's next film project, *Harry and Tonto* (1974).

Two years later, Conti decided to take a gamble on a movie that was written by an unknown actor by the name of Sylvester Stallone. Stallone insisted on playing the part of a boxer who wanted to go up against the heavyweight champion. This movie was called *Rocky*.

Conti got the job scoring *Rocky* after two other composers had turned it down. He was paid $25,000 for the task, but had to pay for the recording costs out of this. He did the entire score in one three-hour session and pocketed $15,000.

Much to everyone's surprise, it was a runaway hit and garnered ten nominations at the Academy Awards, including Bill Conti's theme song, "Gonna Fly Now." Although Conti's song did not win, the film won best picture. This was the needed catalyst to help his career take off. As Conti says, "If you're going to make it in this town, you need to be associated with a hit film."

As a footnote to his father-in-law's concern for his daughter: With Bill Conti's success, he would never again have to worry about his daughter's well-being. Conti told this author that his new house was so big that his entire former house could fit in his new living room.

Bill Conti finally won the coveted Oscar for his score to *The Right Stuff* (1983). It should be pointed out that he won his second Oscar nomination for his song "For Your Eyes Only," used in his James Bond score for the movie with the same title, *For Your Eyes Only,* in 1981.

Since 1977, Bill Conti has been a frequent conductor of the Academy Awards orchestra during their ceremonies.

Star Wars

When George Lucas decided to rerelease his *Star Wars* trilogy for its twentieth anniversary in 1997, he was shocked to find that his master print of the 1977 film had already started to decay! He set out to restore a new print, along with the enhanced sound technology of the late 1990s. Added to this was never-before-seen-footage and newly created scenes incorporating modern computer graphics. Audiences once again thrilled to this classic of science fiction cinema.

One of the most crucial elements of this classic film is its now-famous music by composer John Williams. As the director of *Star Wars* (1977), George Lucas had told Williams that he wanted a classical score "with a Korngold kind of feel." He went on to say that even though it is a futuristic science fiction drama, it's also "an old-fashioned kind of movie and I want that grand soundtrack that they used to have in movies."[6]

George Lucas, who also wrote the story, says that he writes while listening to music and in many cases the music he uses becomes the temp track material for his movie. Lucas had temp-tracked *Star Wars* with music from classical composers such as Gustav Holst (1874–1934), Antonin Dvorák (1841–1904), and William Walton (1902–1983), as well as a few others. Also borrowed was music from Miklos Rozsa's score to *Ben-Hur* (1959). Williams came up with his own original themes but with some of the same emotional thrust of the temp-track material. Those people familiar with Holst's *The Planets* (1916), will surely recognize those moments that inspired Williams's score. Lucas was very happy with the results.

John Williams was brought on the assignment as a recommendation from his friend Steven Spielberg. Spielberg had worked with Williams on two films, including *Jaws,* and couldn't praise him more highly to Lucas. Back in December 1975, Lucas and Williams began discussion on this film. Lucas gave Williams a copy of the script. Williams's usual method of operation for a film is to view a completed

6. Quote from interview on laser disc (*The Empire Strikes Back,* 1997).

A scene from the megahit Star Wars *(1977). Courtesy of John Springer/Corbis-Bettmann.*

movie from beginning to end, without any discussion. He prefers "to react to its rhythmic impulses and feel its kinetic thrusts." He states that "from a composer's point of view, scripts lack the dynamics of the film that corresponds to music."[7]

Most science fiction films that deal with the future would normally be scored with something other than traditional music from the classic films of the 1940s. Most films of this genre over the years have been scored with electronic music, dissonant layers of musical textures, or something in between.

In providing the music for *Star Wars*, Williams used a unique approach. The general feeling was that since this film dealt with unknown creatures, places, and sounds, it would be scored with music to which the viewer could more easily relate. Since the movie is a combination action adventure/love story, both Lucas and Williams decided to use music that could reach people on a more familiar emotional level. John Williams wrote several leitmotifs that would be used throughout the story to represent the various characters. He wrote a "fairy tale princess type melody" for the beautiful Princess Leia. For Luke Skywalker, Williams "composed a brassy, bold, masculine, and noble" theme that we hear right at the beginning of the film, as the *Star Wars* theme. For Darth Vader, Williams penned a theme in the lower voices of the orchestra (the bassoons and muted trombones).

The score contains about eighty-eight minutes of music for a film that is 121 minutes long. George Lucas hired the London Symphony Orchestra to perform the music. The eight scoring sessions were

7. *Star Wars* LP liner notes, 20th Century Fox, 1977.

John Williams. From the author's collection.

JOHN WILLIAMS

American-born composer
(Also known as Johnny Williams
or John T. Williams)

Born: February 8, 1932
(Long Island, New York)

He had aspirations to become a concert pianist early in his career.

He began as a studio pianist in the Hollywood movie industry working for many of the major composers. He was given the opportunity to arrange/orchestrate some music, which helped to launch his career as a composer. He started as a television composer for shows such as *Wagon Train, Gilligan's Island, Checkmate,* and *Lost in Space*. His first movie score was in 1959. Steven Spielberg brought Williams to prominence by using him to score *Jaws* in 1975. (They had worked together once before on *Sugarland Express* in 1974.)

Spielberg recommended Williams to George Lucas for the *Star Wars* scoring assignment in 1977.

John Williams's score for *Star Wars* helped to rejuvenate interest in the full symphonic type of score once again, which had gone somewhat out of fashion in favor of pop/rock/jazz-oriented scores of the 1960s and 1970s.

His scores for *Jaws* (1975), the *Star Wars* trilogy, *Close Encounters of the Third Kind* (1977), *Superman* (1978), *E.T. The Extra-Terrestrial* (1982), the *Indiana Jones* trilogy, *Hook* (1991), *Jurassic Park* (1993), *Schindler's List* (1993), and *The Lost World* (1997) are among some of his most popular scores.

(continued)

He is one of the most highly respected composers working in the world of film music.

His style of music for the big action films showcases big brassy marches, prominent woodwind runs, cymbal crashes, harp glissandos, lyrical sweeping themes, and pounding support rhythms. He is also very capable of scoring films of a more intimate nature. *Schindler's List, Accidental Tourist,* and *Home Alone* are a few examples.

He believes that a film composer needs to think of the dialogue as part of the score.

He relies heavily on the piano when scoring.

From 1980 through 1993, he was the conductor of the Boston Pops Orchestra.

Because of his great success (with over forty Academy Award nominations to his credit), John Williams is considered by many to be the preeminent film composer of the late twentieth century.

Of the living film composers, he has won more Academy Award nominations than any other *living* film composer.

held at Anvil Recording Studios in Denham, England, and ran from March 5 to March 16, 1977. The score was conducted by John Williams and called for an eighty-six-piece orchestra. Orchestrations on this famous score were done by Williams's friend and colleague, Herb Spencer.

Of course, as stated earlier in this book, the opening fanfare theme of *Star Wars* is reminiscent of the scores of Korngold. Perhaps more important than that, the score for *Star Wars* resurrected interest in the full symphonic score once again, at a time when it had gone out of fashion in favor of pop-oriented scores of the 1960s and 1970s. It paved the way for some of the exciting film music we continue to hear well into the twenty-first century.

In spite of the incredible success and talent of John Williams, his score for *Star Wars* is still *considered his best-known film scoring achievement.*

It is interesting to note that 1977 marked a double milestone in film music and its influence on the future. The music for *Star Wars* made popular the use of orchestral scores again and the music of the Bee Gees ushered in the disco fad for several years to come as heard in the film *Saturday Night Fever*. The soundtrack recordings for both films sold millions of copies worldwide.

Saturday Night Fever

The decade of the 1970s was a time when the symphonic score was pushed out of the limelight in favor of pop, rock, or jazz-oriented soundtracks. Even though the symphonic score for *Star Wars* would turn things around with an interest back to the use of the symphonic score in film scoring, another trend started in 1977, because of the extreme effect of one movie and its music. The movie was *Saturday Night Fever* (1977). The music contained within the movie had a driving disco beat that created a sensation that affected an entire generation of people. Disco was born. Not only were there countless other movies that followed using a disco-styled score, people all over took disco dance lessons, classical music was rearranged to be performed using the disco beat, and people copied the fashions used in this movie.

A pop group called the Bee Gees supplied some of the music in the film that became an overnight sensation.

Close Encounters of the Third Kind

John Williams was very busy in 1977. He not only brought the world his landmark score for *Star Wars,* but he also composed a memorable score for Steven Spielberg's classic *Close Encounters of the Third Kind,* which rivals some of his best work from any other year. Williams wrote a five-note leitmotif that is associated with the alien spacecraft and their attempt to "communicate" with people on Earth. It is heard as played by the tuba and the oboe, a rather peculiar combination of instruments.

Five-note "communication" theme:

Williams supposedly tried over 250 variations of five-note leitmotifs before arriving at the now-famous theme. He had wanted to use more than five notes in the motif but Spielberg made a wise observation. Anything with *more* than five notes could be interpreted as an actual *melody* instead of a short form of communication.

The score presents several layers of atonal underscoring, along with a rather effective quotation of the song "When You Wish Upon a Star" from Walt Disney's film *Pinocchio* (1940). This inclusion of the song originally written by film composer Leigh Harline (1907–1969) was Spielberg's idea.

Williams had a lot more input on this film than usual. He met Spielberg twice a week for dinner to discuss the unfinished script. This started two years before the film was finalized. Both men agreed that Williams should compose a short musical motif that would be the greeting code on which much of the film would eventually center. Williams actually wrote some of the music for the film first, then Spielberg would construct his scenes based on what Williams had written.

Spielberg later admitted that he used the talents of John Williams as a creative force during the mixing and editing phases of postproduction. This phase continued onward for fifteen weeks, with Williams being present every day!

Had John Williams scored this film in any other year, he probably would have won the Academy Award for best score. As luck would have it, he was up against some pretty tough competition that year, including his own score for *Star Wars,* which of course won the coveted prize for Williams.

Coma

As we have learned, music makes more of an emphasis or impact on the viewer if it is only used when it is absolutely necessary. The Michael Crichton thriller *Coma* (1978) is a wonderful example of a film composer showing incredible restraint. Jerry Goldsmith waits almost fifty minutes into the film to bring in the first hint of musical underscore. The music that he has written is composed of another innovative set of orchestrations. We hear strings that are accompanied by four pianos and one set of timpani.

Halloween

Once in a while a film will come along that will surprise everyone, and in some cases even the director of the film! *Halloween* (1978) was a good example. After several advanced showings that were unfavorable, the filmmaker and composer John Carpenter (1948–) composed a score that features an eerie recurring leitmotif in a Herrmann-like simplicity and with his minimalistic repetition that helped to save the film. This theme, the *Halloween* theme, is written in an unequal rhythmical meter, with *five* beats per measure of music instead of the more conventional two, three, or four beats per measure. The theme is played by the piano and was used as the leitmotif that helped to provide unity to the sequels that followed.

Superman

The filmmaker Richard Donner made a feature-length film production of the character *Superman* in 1978 starring Christopher Reeve. John Williams wrote a bold and exciting march to represent the "man of steel." This main title theme for *Superman* was actually written to sound out the word "Su-per-man!" This march theme could be added to a list of other film music marches by Williams that have come along over the years. Examples of these include the march from the movie *Midway* (1976), the march theme from the film *1941* (1979), the march from *Raiders of the Lost Ark* (1981), and the Imperial March from *The Empire Strikes Back* (1980).

The score also contains one of Williams's most touching love themes of his career. This song, "Can You Read My Mind" became a big hit.

Star Trek—The Motion Picture

Robert Wise (1914–) entered films in 1939. In the early 1940s, he worked as film editor on two masterpieces, *Citizen Kane* and *The Magnificent Ambersons*. He later became a director of films such as *The Day the Earth Stood Still* and won Academy Awards for his direction of *West Side Story* and *The Sound of Music*. He continued to direct and produce a wide variety of films, although his success has been less than stellar since the 1960s.

In 1979, Jerry Goldsmith was hired to score *Star Trek—The Motion Picture,* the first in a series of motion pictures based on the famed television series of the 1960s. Robert Wise directed this movie. Goldsmith managed to capture the necessary qualities of this futuristic drama by composing a heroic march for the spacecraft *Enterprise* as the main title theme. This musical theme was later used as the main title theme of the new television series called *Star Trek: The Next Generation,* when the original series was resurrected for television. Goldsmith's score was nominated for an Oscar for best score, but did not win.

Alien

Jerry Goldsmith composed yet another science fiction score in 1979 by scoring the terrifying outer space thriller *Alien*. This score contained some truly grizzly, innovative orchestral sounds by using some modern orchestration techniques of twentieth-century concert hall composers.

Goldsmith had planned to restate his main theme at the end of *Alien*. However, the director Ridley Scott (1937–) replaced Goldsmith's original music with that of the American composer Howard Hanson (1896–1981). Scott edited in a portion of Hanson's *Romantic Symphony* at the end of the movie for the theatrical release of the film. With the popularity of films being released on DVD, it is now possible to watch *Alien* in both versions: the way it appeared in theaters and the way it appeared with Goldsmith's complete score.

The Amityville Horror

In 1979, Lalo Schifrin was nominated for best score for his work on *The Amityville Horror*. Schifrin begins the movie with a main title theme that is suggestive of a deranged lullaby for children. We hear children's voices chanting a haunting two-note leitmotif composed of a descending half step. It is somewhat interesting to notice that the two notes used in this theme are the same notes that make up John Williams's famous shark theme from *Jaws* (1975). The difference is that they are the inversion of each other—the *Jaws* theme *goes up* from D sharp to E, and *The Amityville Horror* theme *goes down* from E to D sharp.

Jaws *theme: played by low strings*

Amityville Horror *theme: children singing*

The Amityville Horror is based on a book by Jay Anson about a family that is confronted by all kinds of poltergeist-like experiences in a house that they had moved into. The book is supposed to be based on events that really happened to a family in the state of New York. The eerie quality of the two-note leitmotif mentioned above is enhanced by the fact that *it is sung by a children's choir, using the repeated "la" as its text*. The thought of the house being controlled by innocent children's spirits is somewhat unnerving to the viewer of the film. Jerry Goldsmith would later use a similar approach in "Carol Anne's theme" from the 1982 movie *Poltergeist*, in which we hear a wordless children's choir used to haunt the viewer. Lalo Schifrin received his fourth Academy Award nomination for this score. It lost to a curious score by French composer Georges Delerue for the movie *A Little Romance*.

A Little Romance

Sometimes one must wonder about why things happen the way that they do. Georges Delerue (1925–1992) had written outstanding scores that were never recognized by the Motion Picture Academy and a few that were (*Anne of the Thousand Days* [1969], *The Day of the Dolphin* [1973], and *Julia* [1977]). Out of his massive output of over 230 film scores during his prolific career, his score for *A Little Romance* (1979) would be the only time he would win for best original score. To add to the mystery and frustration, the score for *A Little Romance* was not entirely original. It centered on the use of a baroque period *Concerto in D Major for Guitar and Two Violins* by the Italian composer Antonio Vivaldi (1678–1741). Although Delerue did write some *new* music for this score in the style of Vivaldi, one wonders why the Academy would find this score "more original" than the two scores by Goldsmith mentioned previously (*Star Trek—The Motion Picture* and *Alien*) or Schifrin's hauntingly effective score for *The Amityville Horror*.

The End of an Era

Film music underwent several radical changes in the 1970s. For the first time, the majority of the films would contain more than just a symphonic score. Filmmakers would intersperse their films with pop, rock, or jazz hits, and would concentrate less on the power that a gifted composer could bring to a film, with only original music as we had seen in the past.

Although Bernard Herrmann's death in 1975 was somewhat unexpected, other giants in the field of film composition passed away, including Alfred Newman in 1970, Max Steiner in 1971, and Dimitri Tiomkin in 1979. Herrmann was still active with several future film-scoring assignments lined up well into the next year. Newman had completed his last score for the film *Airport* (1970) just before his death, and Steiner had shown signs of slowing down—his last feature film score was for *Chuka* (1967). As for Tiomkin, after the death of his first wife, this seemed to signal to him a need to go into retirement. His last completed original score was for the film *Great Catherine* in 1968.

Review Questions

Discussion

1. How did Goldsmith approach *Patton,* the man, in his main title sequence?

2. Watch *Star Wars* and discuss John Williams's use of leitmotifs.

3. View *A Clockwork Orange* and discuss how the music plays against the action.

Short Answer

1. What is unique about the composer hired for *A Clockwork Orange*? ______________________

   ____.

2. What is significant about the score to *The Omen* for Jerry Goldsmith? ______________________

   ____.

3. How did John Williams approach his score to *Star Wars*? ______________________

   ____.

4. Why is this score significant? ____.

5. What orchestra performed and recorded the music for *Star Wars*? ______________________

   ____.

Chapter Ten

New Faces Enter the Ranks (the 1980s, from *Altered States* to *Batman*)

Altered States

The controversial movie director Ken Russell was out for an evening of relaxation in early 1979 to hear a performance of the Los Angeles Philharmonic at the L.A. Music Center (Dorothy Chandler Pavilion). Russell had been looking for someone to score his most recent film, *Altered States* (1980). He was listening to a concerto brilliantly performed by the clarinetist Michele Zukovsky, was composed by the avant-garde composer John Corigliano (1938–). The bizarre sounds from this concerto were fascinating to Russell. As Russell put it, "Here were sounds of magic and grandeur I had long since despaired of hearing from a modern musician. . . . I knew I was looking at an American composer of the stature of Ives and Copland. If only he could compose the music for *Altered States* instead of some commercial Hollywood hack we directors are usually saddled with."[1]

Well, as it turned out, Ken Russell got his wish. John Corigliano signed on to compose what would be his first film score. Corigliano's film score for *The Red Violin* (1998) gained him his first Oscar for best original score at the 2000 Academy Award ceremonies. To view *Altered States without* music is a mind-expanding experience. To see it *with* the music supplied by Corigliano is an *unforgettable* experience! The story centers on a research scientist, Dr. Eddie Jessup (played by William Hurt in his dazzling screen debut). He believes that other states of consciousness are as real as the everyday reality we all experience. He experiments by floating in an isolation think tank, using sensory deprivation equipment, finally adding powerful hallucinogenic drugs to explore these "altered states."

1. *Altered States* CD liner notes, 1981, BMG Classics.

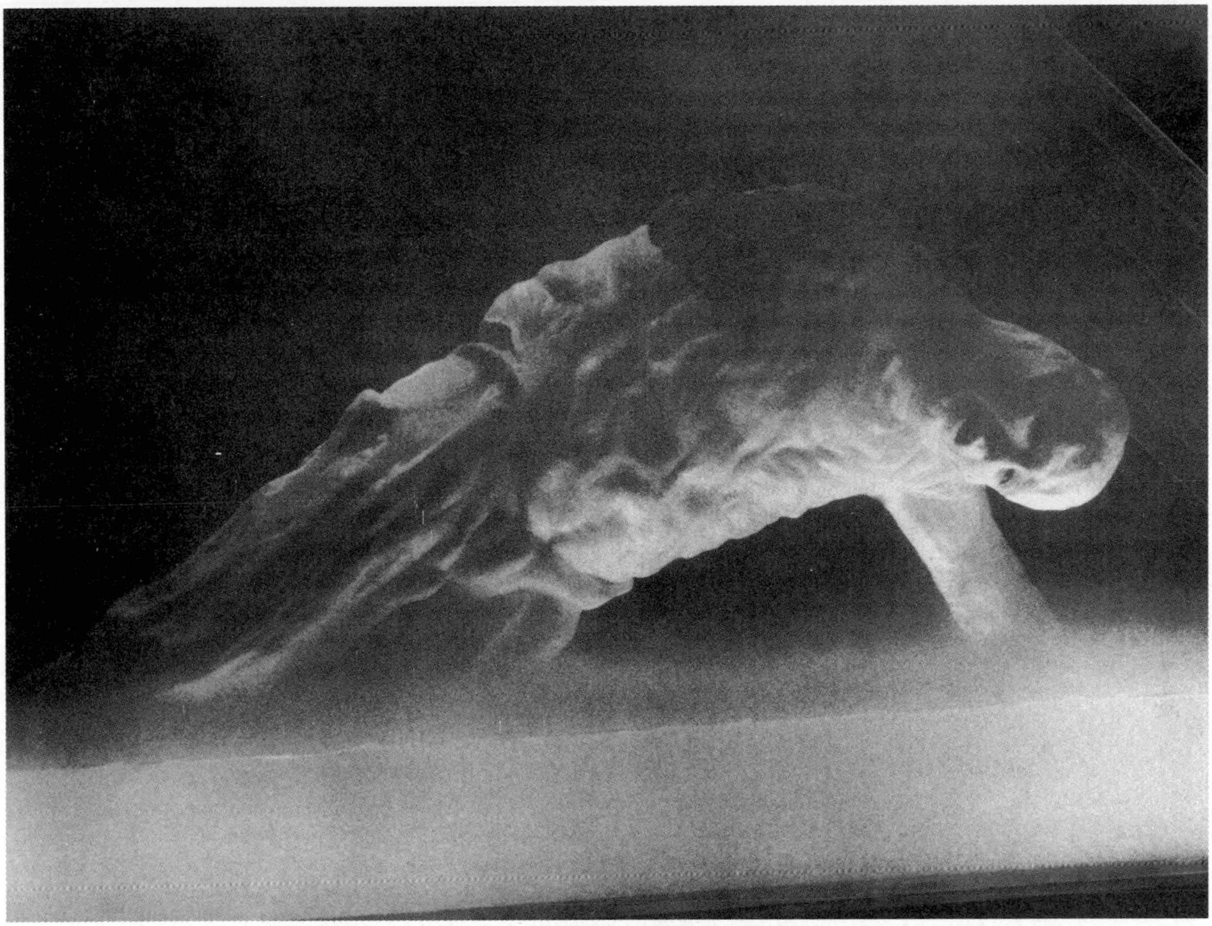

William Hurt being "transformed" in Altered States *(1980). Courtesy of Warner Bros./Archive Photos.*

Based on Paddy Chayefsky's novel, "*Altered States* defies every convention, breaks all the rules, it gyrates wildly through horror, fantasy, satire, farce and back to horror again."[2]

Corigliano's score also breaks rules. As a skilled concert hall composer, he came to the assignment with a wide palette of experimental know-how. Corigliano employs almost every modern convention known to twentieth-century composers. He uses dissonant-layered chord clusters, known as "**texture music**," as in the style of composers such as Gyorgy Ligeti (1923–) or Krzysztof Penderecki (1933–). He also uses **microtones** (a musical interval that is less than a half step), which are bent to change colors and pitch for fascinating effects. Individual instrumentalists employ flutter-tonguing and **multiphonics**, whereby instrumentalists are able to play more than one pitch at the same time by using unconventional fingerings and different lip pressure. Corigliano utilizes two pianos—one is tuned a quarter-step flatter than the other so that, when played together, they emit a haunting quality. The flutists are called on to create a jet whistle, buzz tone effect. Brass players blow through their horns without using their mouthpiece, under which we hear long sustained pedal points.

Despite all of the harsh effects in this score, there emerges one of the most haunting love themes from any movie in the last one hundred years. Corigliano wrote about forty minutes' worth of music

2. Quote from laser disc notes, 1980, Warner Bros.

for this 103-minute film. There are some very frightening sequences in which Dr. Jessup either hallucinates or is transformed into someone or something else. At one point in the film, Jessup experiments by eating some Hinchi mushrooms (known as the "first flower") prepared from an Indian tribe. The things he sees and experiences during this "head trip" are brought forth on the screen, both visually by Russell's brilliant direction and audibly by Corigliano's music.

In the final transformation of the movie, Jessup tells his girlfriend Emily, played by Blair Brown, that he was in that ultimate moment of terror that is the beginning of life. He goes on to tell her that that moment of terror is a real and living horror growing within him now. The only thing that keeps it from devouring him is her. Suddenly, he starts to turn into that hideous revelation. She says, "Defy it Eddie, if you love me, defy it." It's too late. He changes into a horrible-looking creature and as she touches him, so does she. The music is ghastly and frightening, like nothing ever heard in films before. Finally, as Jessup pounds his fist against the wall, willing this force to leave his body, both he and Emily return to normal-looking humans. As this happens, the music evolves back into the haunting love theme played first by the clarinet, then the flute, and finally the full string section of the orchestra.

Corigliano *introduced the moviegoing public to sounds never before heard on a film score*. This score was nominated for an Oscar, but lost to the movie *Fame*, scored by Michael Gore (1951–).

Tess

The French film composer Philippe Sarde (1945–) had his reputation enhanced in the United States and moved into the mainstream of composers from the French film industry by scoring the movie *Tess*. Although the release date was 1979 in Europe, it was eligible for the 1980 Academy Awards, for which it was nominated as best original score. The music provided by Sarde is reminiscent of English folk songs in minor keys such as the famous "Greensleeves," (also known as "What Child Is This?").

The Empire Strikes Back

With the great success of the first in a trilogy of stories in the *Star Wars* saga, John Williams once again added to the memorable powerhouse of this drama, making *The Empire Strikes Back* (1980) one of the favorites among *Star Wars* fans.

Continuing with his method of using a leitmotif, Williams wrote some material for some of the new characters, including the dark, ominous march theme for the Imperial force that is associated with Darth Vader, known as the "Imperial March."

This score was also nominated for best score in 1980.

Somewhere in Time

Although not well received during its initial theatrical run, *Somewhere in Time* (1980) has joined the ranks as a time-honored classic of celluloid romance. Much of the appeal of this movie is made possible because of the beautiful love theme written for this film by veteran composer John Barry.

This score was also nominated for an Academy Award.

Love theme from Somewhere in Time. *Notice the John Barry style of having a beautiful theme supported by broken chords in the bass voice.*

Fame

Michael Gore's (1951–) film composing career started on a high note when he won an Academy Award for his work on the teen musical *Fame* (1980). This film, about a group of talented kids at the New York High School for the Performing Arts, had a score that was primarily comprised of a group of vocal numbers that would be performed by members of the young cast as they trace their four years together all the way through to their graduation.

Unfortunately, Gore's work in film scoring did not continue at the same level of high expectations.

Gore was nominated for his score for *Terms of Endearment* in 1983 and composed the score for the popular film *Pretty in Pink* in 1986. Other than that, his output has been sparse.

The score to *Fame* does feature a variety of musical styles. Everything from rock, jazz, and even symphonic orchestrations are represented.

Raiders of the Lost Ark

One of the best films in the action category to come out of the 1980s was Steven Spielberg's *Raiders of the Lost Ark* (1981). Spielberg once again teamed up with his partner, the composer John Williams.

The plot involves the search for the Ark of the Covenant thought to be buried somewhere near the burial tombs of the Egyptian Pharaohs. What makes the film more hair-raising is the race against German Nazis who also are hoping to find the biblical treasure in order to dominate the world. You might say that this is a "James Bond" scenario. Indiana Jones (Harrison Ford) also pursues a girl (played by Karen Allen) along the way. This gave Williams a chance to write an additional leitmotif to represent her.

Williams's now well-known "Indiana Jones march" from this film became the main leitmotif that helps to unite the other films in this series. This score was nominated for best score, but lost to *Chariots of Fire*.

Chariots of Fire

The main theme from *Chariots of Fire* (1981) was phenomenally successful. The composer, Vangelis (real name is Evangelos Papathanassiou) (1943–), advanced the appreciation of a synthesized score one step further.

Although *Chariots of Fire* takes place during the Summer Olympics in Paris in 1924, somehow audiences did not seem to question the use of music that had not even come into existence yet for this movie. Now, in retrospect, the music does seem a bit out of place for this 1920s story. Nevertheless, the synthesized keyboard theme, used at both the opening and closing of the film, is forever locked into film music history. This score won for best score of 1981 at the Academy Awards ceremony.

Vangelis lives in London and continues to write an occasional score. He followed *Chariots of Fire* with scores for movies such as *Blade Runner* (1982), *Missing* (1982), *The Bounty* (1984), *Bitter Moon* (1992), and *1492: Conquest of Paradise* (1992). He continues to dabble in electronics.

Ghost Story

Philippe Sarde (1948–) is a composer who not only likes to *write* music for films but also *loves* to go to the cinema.

After an impressive film debut in America with his score for *Tess* (1979), Sarde's next assignment in America was the film *Ghost Story* (1981). That same year, Sarde would write the score for the Canadian production about Early Man's love affair with the eternal flame in *Quest for Fire* (1981). Sarde has done some of his finest work in the chiller *Ghost Story*.

Sarde has written a truly haunting waltz melody used in several parts of the film. At times it is played by orchestral instruments, on occasion, this theme is sung by a wordless choir. This score features some wonderful contrasting orchestral colors that are original-sounding, yet somewhat in the character of what Bernard Herrmann may have written had he lived into the 1980s. Sarde's music features woodwinds and strings with a heavy emphasis on bells and xylophone. This is suddenly jolted out of the comfort zone by loud brass chords. Sarde punctuates his musical statements with a screaming pipe organ to send eerie chills down any moviegoer's spine.

Body Heat

John Barry was hired in 1982 to score a modern film noir based on adultery, deception, and murder, as played out by Kathleen Turner and William Hurt. In order to capture the seductive quality of Turner's character and the heated chemistry of the two lead characters in *Body Heat,* Barry choose a sensual saxophone solo that greatly enhanced the simmering quality of the drama.

Conan the Barbarian

Basil Poledouris. Courtesy of the composer.

Although he has an exotic sounding name, the composer Basil Poledouris was born in Kansas City, Missouri, on August 21, 1945. His first score was for a rather racy film called *Extreme Closeup* in 1973, followed by *The Blue Lagoon* in 1980, before accepting an assignment that would become legendary for some of his fans. In 1982, his college buddy, the film director John Milius (1944–), asked Poledouris to score his next big project, *Conan the Barbarian.* This film helped to bolster Poledouris's career as a serious film composer.

What separates Poledouris from so many of his colleagues is his *background.* He is not only a composer, he is a capable *filmmaker.* He studied music at the University of Southern California. He had gone there hoping to study with Miklos Rozsa. Unfortunately, Rozsa left the summer before Poledouris started as a student in the fall. Fortunately, another master took his place—the great David Raksin. After one year, Poledouris changed his major to cinema to get a *film major* degree. He stayed at USC and earned a master's degree in cinema, but returned to college later to complete a degree in music at California State University in Long Beach. He felt more comfortable "in front of an orchestra than behind a camera." What helped Poledouris make up his mind was when George Lucas took Poledouris aside one day and said, "Basil, you're a much better *composer* than you are a director." This came as some relief, as his music-loving parents were quite upset that he wasn't going to make a living in music. Now, with his expanded knowledge of filmmaking from USC and his talent and love for music, he had the best of both worlds.

Dialogue was *not* a major factor to consider in this film, so Poledouris was given the green light to write some of the score in advance and some during the actual production of the film. This is an unusual luxury, not found in most scoring assignments.

Poledouris decided to use a large orchestra with unusual orchestrations, such as twenty-four French horns, as well as a violently pounding percussion section. He also used a chorus to give the score the well-known "Carmina Burana" vocal color that has become increasingly more popular in scores dealing with fantasy, the medieval period, Satanism, or the antichrist. The entire score was recorded in Italy, using members of the Chorus of Santa Cecilia in Rome.

The movie was temp-tracked with music by Prokofiev, Stravinsky, and Wagner. Poledouris had to compose about two hours' worth of music for this film that runs about 130 minutes. This was quite a task for any film composer.

Sophie's Choice

Marvin Hamlisch. Courtesy of the Tony Thomas Collection.

Of all the Marvin Hamlisch (1944–) scores written, his score for *Sophie's Choice* (1982) is arguably the most beautiful and perhaps the most effective. Although his work on *The Way We Were, The Sting,* the hit song from the James Bond thriller *The Spy Who Loved Me* ("Nobody Does It Better"), and the title song from *Ice Castles* is perhaps better known, Hamlisch rose to the occasion for this powerful tear-jerker. The great actress Meryl Streep put on another exquisite performance in a story about a refugee from Nazi persecution who now lives in New York. Alan J. Pakula (1928–), the director of the film, and Hamlisch decided not to underscore any of the scenes that took place in the concentration camps. The music is used only for the postwar scenes in America. Hamlisch wrote some extremely lyrical solos for solo oboe, English horn, and cello that haunt the listener long after the film is over once we learn what Sophie's choice was. This score was nominated for best score, but lost to John Williams's score for *E.T.*

Star Trek II: The Wrath of Khan

Star Trek II: The Wrath of Khan (1982) helped to establish the career of one of the hottest composers working in Hollywood today, James Horner (1953–). This score was written at a time when Horner was trying to establish himself in the industry, so he pulled no punches. This is ranked among the best scores written for the *Star Trek* movie series and, although other composers have scored the *Star Trek* films, only Jerry Goldsmith's work on the series is given such high ranks among trekkies.

Horner's score uses the *original television theme* fanfare by composer Alexander Courage (1919–) only sparingly for emotional impact. Otherwise, Horner wrote a new main title theme that is both heroic and lyrical. For the villainous Khan, we hear a powerful ominous theme that is pitted against the main theme during the exciting "Battle in the Mutara Nebula" sequence. In this movie, the beloved Mr. Spock dies. During the epilogue, as we hear Spock's voice, Horner cleverly underscores this with a hint of the original Alexander Courage theme. This helps to stir the emotions of anyone who has followed this series over the years. This glides boldly into the new main theme written by Horner for the end credit sequence. Horner's score illustrates a wide range of emotions, from high action drama to moments of great sadness. It is clear from examining this score that its young composer had great potential for success in the film music business.

E.T. The Extra-Terrestrial

E.T. The Extra-Terrestrial (1982) became the box-office earnings champ, a distinction it held until *Jurassic Park* was released in 1993.

Parts of the film were temp-tracked, with Howard Hanson's (1896–1981) *Romantic Symphony*. As might be expected, Spielberg hired his colleague John Williams to write the score.

This film concentrated more on human emotions and drama than many of the other films made by Spielberg during this phase of his career. Therefore, Williams chose to use the leitmotif concept. By writing musical motifs for each of the characters in the film, including E.T., the alien, the viewer builds strong associations. Williams is able to twist and vary a motif ever so slightly to convey or enhance an emotion. By using this time-honored technique, Williams was able to build the needed dramatic impact of emotions at the film's end when they all say goodbye, helping to give this film its tremendous appeal, and giving this scene its powerful punch.

John Williams continues to amaze us with his great talents as a film composer. His "flying theme" from *E.T.* is among the best-loved of any of his movie themes. It comes as no surprise that this score won as best original score for 1982 at the Academy Award ceremonies.

Poltergeist

Tobe Hooper (1943–) had made a name for himself as the director of the infamous *The Texas Chainsaw Massacre* (1974). This was a low-budget gorefest that was supposedly based on fact. Because of its cult following and huge success, Steven Spielberg decided to hire Hooper to direct his next project, *Poltergeist*, in 1982. Spielberg was a strong force in the decision making of the film but was busy directing *E.T.* and wanted to turn to someone else to direct *Poltergeist*. People who worked on the project said that even though Hooper had been named director, Spielberg remained in the background to make sure that things were going his way.

By now, many filmgoers had already associated the composer John Williams with Spielberg's films. Williams was not available for this Spielberg-produced film because he was busy at work on his score for Spielberg's *E.T. The Extra-Terrestrial*. As a result, Spielberg hired a man whose music he had greatly admired over the years, Jerry Goldsmith. Goldsmith later said that, "The problem with *Poltergeist* was to create warmth and emotion among all the suspense."[3] Spielberg had long admired Jerry Goldsmith from the moment he had heard Goldsmith's scores for *The Blue Max* (1966) and *A Patch of Blue* (1965). In this score, as Spielberg says, "The moments of greatest tension arise not from his brilliant off-rhythm ostinatos but more from a soothing tonal beauty."

The plot of the movie concentrates on an American family that purchases a tract home in the suburbs of a California town. This subdivision of homes was built on land that had once been an ancient burial ground. The developer of the neighborhood had failed to move the remains of the individuals buried underneath the homes, which led to strange visitations of angry spirits (poltergeists). (The word poltergeist comes from the German: *poltern* = to knock + *geist* = ghost. It is defined as a noisy, usually mischievous ghost held to be responsible for unexplained noises [such as rappings]. In Spielberg's story [he wrote the story and coauthored the screenplay], these poltergeists are more than just mischievous ghosts!)

Goldsmith composed this *very diverse score* from December 1981 to January 1982. The feature runs about one hour and fifty-four minutes. Goldsmith composed more than an hour of music. Arthur

3. *Soundtrack* magazine, September 1987.

Morton, his longtime orchestrator, transformed Goldsmith's nine-line sketches into full-page orchestrations for a seventy-six-piece orchestra, along with a few unusual instruments, plus a sixteen-voice choir. In all, there were four scoring sessions, January 25 and 26, and February 8 and 9, 1982. These sessions took place at MGM Studios, in the same room that so many great MGM movies were scored, located in Culver City, California.

A group of musicians from France who had performed at Royce Hall at UCLA used some long glass rods that they played while wearing gloves powdered with rosin. Emil Richards, a studio musician percussionist and colleague of Goldsmith, was fascinated by this, and had a man from San Diego make him several long rods, in strong aluminum instead of glass. When rubbed while wearing gloves, they gave off the most *ethereal, beautiful* sounds. These "**rub rods**," as they are called, are heard at the beginning of the movie, as little Carol Anne awakens from her bed and descends the stairway to investigate her new "visitors" inside the television set. As she answers unheard questions from someone or something inside the television, Goldsmith transitions into "Carol Anne's theme," one of cinema's most haunting yet beautiful themes to come from this genre of film. This "out-of-this-world sound" of the rub rods occurs in several other places throughout parts of the film.

Later in the movie, as Dr. Lesh is explaining to Carol Anne's brother, Robbie, about a "light" that people see when they die, we hear a lush neoimpressionistic accompaniment in the style of Impressionistic classical composers Maurice Ravel (1875–1937) or Claude Debussy (1862–1918), played by the string section. This music also has a quasi-religious quality to it.

Also included in the "swimming pool sequence" toward the end of the film, as Carol Anne's mother falls into the unfinished pool, is a grotesque sounding paraphrase (in the strings) of the ancient *Dies Irae* (Day of Wrath) theme. From the plainchant of the Middle Ages and used during Masses for the Dead, this *Dies Irae* theme has been a favorite among film composers over the years. This is one of the truly scary movies made in the 1980s, and it must be said that Goldsmith's score greatly contributed to making this a classic film in its own time.

The Right Stuff

The composer Bill Conti wrote a very patriotic-sounding score for this moving story about the U.S. space program from its beginnings in the 1950s to the early 1960s and the successes of the orbital flights of John Glenn and Gordon Cooper. The main theme for *The Right Stuff* (1983) is in the form of a gallant and dignified march in the style of the English composer Edward Elgar. There are hints of several other composers' styles present in his score, including the Russian composer Alexander Glazunov (1865–1936) and the English composer Gustav Holst (1874–1934). This is not meant to slight Bill Conti's talent—as Elmer Bernstein has stated, "We are all products of those who came before us." The Motion Picture Academy awarded Conti with the Best Original Score Oscar for 1983.

The Return of the Jedi

With his score for *The Return of the Jedi* (1983), John Williams would complete his monumental operatic-size trilogy for this portion of the George Lucas fantasy. Sixteen years would pass before John Williams would be asked to revive some of his thematic material from this series for the next installment of the ongoing *Star Wars* extravaganza for *Star Wars: Episode I—The Phantom Menace* in 1999. What is interesting to observe with the Jedi score is the apparent evolution of some of the leitmotifs, with their intricate musical fabrics.

The Natural

Randy Newman. Courtesy of Chasen & Company.

The composer/performer/songwriter Randy Newman (1943–) came from a rich dynasty of musical talent, perhaps the richest in Hollywood history. He is the nephew of Alfred Newman, Emil Newman, and Lionel Newman. His cousins include David Newman, Thomas Newman, and Maria Newman. This family has made a name in film music as no other family has in the history of cinema. Randy's father was one of eight brothers. His father was not a musician. Instead, Irving Newman chose medicine. He became the personal physician to many well-known Hollywood celebrities.

Randy Newman scored *Ragtime* in 1981 with some degree of success (considered his first legitimate film score), but it was his score for Milos Forman's (1932–) *The Natural* (1984) that met with critical praise from the Hollywood community and helped to establish Randy Newman as a film composer.

His score for *The Natural* is both original in concept and sound, yet it also imitates to a certain degree the music of the American composer Aaron Copland with its broad, all-American palette of expansive colors. The opening theme has become one of the most often used musical cues by film editors in making temp tracks and has been used countless times for background music of coming attractions. Randy Newman was nominated for his work on this score, but it lost to Maurice Jarre's score for *A Passage to India*.[4]

Indiana Jones and the Temple of Doom

The second installment in the Indiana Jones saga is like a nonstop rollercoaster ride. John Williams was also the composer of *Indiana Jones and the Temple of Doom* (1984). The film was criticized for its extreme gore, surprising parents who took younger members of their family. As a result, a new category had to be instituted in the ratings system, that of PG-13 (some material may be inappropriate for children under thirteen).

The score contains the usual Indiana Jones march theme to help tie the series together. Williams introduces some scary music for the temple of doom sequence and writes a memorable tune, which is cleverly used again in the end credits of the picture, called "Parade of the Slave Children." This score, along with another score written by Williams for a movie called *The River* (1984), were both nominated for the Best Score Oscar. They lost to Jarre's *A Passage to India*.

4. After sixteen nominations over the years, Newman finally won his first Oscar in the best song category for "If I Didn't Have You," from the film *Monsters, Inc.*, at the 2002 Academy Awards.

and was almost "too much music," as Broughton later said. However, in light of this, Broughton did say that "from a purely musical point of view, it was a great project to work on, especially recording it in London, but proved to me that music can never save a film that doesn't please or interest the overall moviegoer."

Witness

As we have already seen, film composers must be able to deliver any kind of music on demand. Their score must serve the film as well as please the wishes of the filmmakers. On occasion, a composer will encounter a rather unusual set of circumstances in the story of a film. For the 1985 film *Witness*, composer Maurice Jarre encountered such a challenge. *Witness* centers on the group of people known as the Amish. The Amish have a blueprint of expected behavior, known as the *Ordnung*, in which their private, public, and ceremonial life is regulated. The Amish do not allow music in their culture except as the music of ritual. When asked to score this film, Jarre did some research and discovered that, as he says, "Just any kind of instrument in this society [of Amish people] was considered to be more or less the weapon of the devil. Consequently, I thought if I was going to put any kind of acoustic instrument in the score, it would not be right, because the Amish society does not allow musical instruments, so I

Harrison Ford stars in Witness *(1985), featuring an all-electronic score by Maurice Jarre. Courtesy of Archive Photos.*

choose to use electronics." Also, Jarre goes on to state that he felt that the Amish have such a strict, clean way of life, it appears to express an empty coldness to many people. Jarre felt that symphonic (acoustic) instruments playing with the human warmth of vibrato, could not appropriately represent this "coldness." Jarre said, "I worked with the electronic musicians like a chamber music type of orchestra. So each player had five or ten different synthesizers and with six or seven instrumentalists you have an unbelievable choice of sound."[5] In *Witness,* it is interesting to note that electronic sounds do elude a kind of "icy" quality to the opening scenes, showing the Amish community's Pennsylvania settlement. Jarre's desired concept was perfectly realized. About thirteen minutes into the film, the young Amish boy witnesses the murder of an undercover narcotics agent. The score employs an effective use of a driving **ostinato pattern** to build nerve-wracking tension and suspense. The most memorable scene in the movie involving Jarre's electronic score has to be his "barn-raising" sequence. This sequence was originally temp-tracked with the **Pachelbel *Canon*.** Johann Pachelbel (1653–1706) was a baroque period German composer and organist. Peter Wier, the director of *Witness,* told Jarre that he could try and score this scene if he wanted, although he was planning on keeping in the Pachelbel *Canon*. On hearing what Jarre had written for this part of the movie, Wier was so excited that he never again mentioned using the *Canon. What Jarre wrote for the barn-raising sequence is basically a* ***passacaglia***. If you listen carefully to the bass line at the beginning of this music cue, you will notice it repeating beneath an ever more sophisticated series of upper voices. As the barn is being raised, the music becomes more complex and elaborate, complete with the addition of inner voices. This is symbolic of more lumber being added to the barn. Jarre's score for *Witness* was nominated for an Oscar, but lost to John Barry's score for *Out of Africa*.

Agnes of God

The French composer Georges Delerue (1925–1992) usually writes in a style that is prone to sounding like English folk songs written in a minor key, with a certain hint of sadness or tragedy. More often than not, the main thematic material for many of his scores is in a triple meter. The music that he wrote for *Agnes of God* (1985) is no exception to his trademark. Parts of the score are accompanied by a wordless choir to give the score its supernatural and religious quality.

This is the story of a young nun who had mysteriously given birth to a baby. To add to the drama, she was accused of murdering this child. The music helps to paint a tragic yet somehow spiritually uplifting quality to the picture. Some of the choral writing is very beautiful and could stand on its own merit. Delerue's use of flute and oboe solos—another part of his trademark style—depicts the emotions in this story. These solos are supported by a series of harp arpeggios, another part of his trademark style.

It is an interesting side story to know that Delerue was considered by many people in the film music business

Georges Delerue. Courtesy of the Tony Thomas Collection.

5. *Soundtrack* magazine, March 1993. All above Jarre quotes taken from this interview.

to have been the happiest and nicest man to have ever blessed the sound stages of Hollywood. One wonders how such a happy individual could compose such sad music. His unexpected death at age sixty-seven caught many of his friends, the studio players in Hollywood, off guard. As the record producer Robert Townson states, "Georges was the happiest and funniest man I have ever met. Remembering all the good times and not being able to be with him anymore is extremely sad, but the amount of wonderful, joyous and beautiful music he left us, together with all the dear memories of him, gives great cause to celebrate."[6]

Although Delerue loved the L.A.-based Hollywood musicians, he recorded the score for *Agnes of God* with members of the Toronto Symphony Orchestra and the famed Elmer Isler Singers supplying the gorgeous vocals for the wordless choir.

This score was also nominated for best score but lost to *Out of Africa*.

The Color Purple

The Color Purple (1985) was an unusual case in association with the Oscar nominations. Originally, the person or persons who compose the score should be considered for the coveted award—this means one or two composers, in most cases. For *The Color Purple,* there were originally nineteen people who had written various musical cues used within the film. Would it be fair to award the Oscar to someone for best original score who had written only a couple minutes' worth of music, when someone like Barry, Broughton, Delerue, and Jarre had put their entire energies into a major project? The members of the Academy met with Quincy Jones, the man who oversaw the music and was coproducer of the film. They were hoping that after looking at the various musical cues, Jones would be able to narrow the number of eligible composers down to two or three. To be fair to the composers who worked on the score, he was able to bring the number down to twelve, including *himself* as one of the eligible composers. This was not exactly what the members of the committee wanted to hear.

The Academy decided to give the nomination to Quincy Jones and the others who worked on the film. They lost, however, to John Barry's score for *Out of Africa*.

Flesh+Blood

This 1985 film is somewhat difficult to locate in video stores, yet it is a realistic telling of the adventure and at times gruesome lifestyle of several characters living in the Middle Ages. Jennifer Jason Leigh plays a virginal damsel who gets kidnapped and abused by a band of brawling outcasts. The director Paul Verhoeven hired Basil Poledouris to write the score. Poledouris provided the film with music that sounds dark and moody. He has written a beautiful love theme for the two main characters, Martin and Agnes. The main theme and its variations are heard throughout this 126-minute film. This is one of Poledouris's best efforts as a composer.

6. In May 1989, Townson and film music agent Richard Kraft were instrumental in producing a now-classic three-CD set of the best of Delerue's work in films. These legendary recordings are known as the "London Sessions," volumes 1, 2, and 3.

Out of Africa

John Barry has written for every kind of film genre except one—horror. His score for Sydney Pollack's (1934–) *Out of Africa* (1985) is among the most beautiful scores brought to the screen. His expansive main theme is perfect for illustrating his recognizable style to the layperson. Barry loves to write a lyrical theme that will be supported by a broken chordal accompaniment that is many times accompanied by a countermelody in the French horns. Other good examples of his style include *Walkabout* (1971), *Eleanor and Franklin* (TV movie 1976), *Hanover Street* (1979), *Somewhere in Time* (1980), *High Road to China* (1983), *Dances with Wolves* (1990), and *Chaplin* (1992).

Out of Africa Main Theme:

The long sustained chords lend themselves to the incredible vistas of the African landscape. *Out of Africa* was nominated for eleven Oscars and walked away with seven, including Best Picture, Best Director, and Best Original Score.

The Mission

Ennio Morricone, like Bernard Herrmann, felt that a film composer should always orchestrate his or her own film music as they composed. One particular score that stands out is from *The Mission* (1986). *The composer singled this score out as one of his favorites,* although when he first viewed the completed film without music he wasn't sure that he wanted the scoring assignment. He had said that the movie moved him so much that he had doubts about scoring music for it. The orchestration combinations are very interesting. The film is based on actual events that took place around 1750, when Jesuit missionaries attempted to convert natives in the jungles of Argentina, Paraguay, and Brazil. Therefore, the composer combined the sounds of native drums and flutes that are indigenous to the area, along with a choir singing—almost chanting—music from a Catholic mass. Superimposed over this was the beautiful, lyrical "Gabriel's oboe theme" played by a flute or recorder. The oboe line is reminiscent of baroque ornamentation around 1750. Morricone definitely did his homework. One of the missionaries, Father Gabriel (played by Jeremy Irons) plays the oboe. It was through his efforts of playing this tune for the members of the tribe that he eventually gains their trust. This opens them up for conversion to Christianity.

Gabriel's Oboe Theme from *The Mission:*

The Mission is considered one of Morricone's masterpieces. Although many Clint Eastwood fans knew the sounds of Morricone's scores from his Westerns, it took *The Mission* to bring Morricone's name before the American populace as an accomplished film composer. It did not hurt that this score was also nominated for best score of 1986. It lost to Herbie Hancock's score for *Round Midnight* (1986).

The Name of the Rose

James Horner's score for *The Name of the Rose* (1986) has a haunting quality that works beautifully for this murder mystery set in a monastery during the medieval period. The story of this movie was based on a novel by Umberto Eco and starred Sean Connery, F. Murray Abraham, and Christian Slater. Horner's score utilizes a combination of long, sustained vocal clusters, pedal points and dissonant clusters in the strings, and a solo voice that is distorted electronically. We also hear a rich and thick cello line, in a minor key, above which we hear a sad musical line played on an organ. There is a returning musical motif played on an instrument known as a **water gong**. The instrument is struck and then lowered into a tub of water, which lowers the pitch and creates an eerie, sagging quality. Horner gives the movie its authentic character of being in a monastery by using ancient chants such as the *Kyrie, Beata Viscera,* and *Veni Sancte Spiritus.*

Aliens

James Horner was very busy in 1985 and 1986, writing six scores in 1985 and five scores in 1986. Among his output for 1986 was a score for the sequel to *Alien,* a film called *Aliens* (1986). Horner was criticized for not being very original during this phase of his career. The score he wrote for *Aliens* was one of the scores that came under fire. One person said that Horner's "originality is questioned by many and simply dismissed by others, who regard him as only an imitator of classical and film predecessors." Horner got the last laugh. His score for *Aliens* was among the five chosen that year for Oscar consideration.

Platoon

If you were to talk to most people who saw the emotionally moving Vietnam War movie *Platoon* (1986) and asked them to describe the music, chances are they would recall the sad music at the end of the movie. That music—*Adagio for Strings*—was actually not written for this film or any other film for that matter. It was written by Samuel Barber (1910–1981) in 1936. The *Adagio* has been used in countless films over the years, from *The Elephant Man* (1980) to *The Scarlet Letter* (1995).

The director Oliver Stone (1946–) had worked with composer Georges Delerue on the film *Salvador* the same year as *Platoon.* They had a good working relationship on *Salvador.* For that reason, Delerue was looking forward to another film with Oliver Stone. However, for *Platoon,* most of Delerue's score was rejected in favor of the *Adagio.* Stone liked Barber's piece so much that he had Delerue write and record a cue in the same style as the *Adagio.* Stone felt that Delerue's musical cue did not have the warmth and pathos needed to bring the movie off.

Empire of the Sun

In 1987, Spielberg hired John Williams to score the fictional story of a young boy who spent his early years in China, four of which were in a Japanese prison camp during World War II. Spielberg was reportedly so moved by Morricone's score to *The Mission* that he asked Williams to pay tribute to that style in his score for *Empire of the Sun* (1987). As a result, Williams uses choral writing to achieve deeply moving and emotionally inspiring results. In fact, *this score contains more choral cues than any of John Williams's other scores.* The cue "Cadillac of the Skies," scored for chorus and orchestra, is breathtakingly beautiful. Williams uses a wordless choir to give the out-of-this-world quality to the overall sound.

The film was a milestone, because it would be the first major Hollywood film ever shot inside the People's Republic of China. As usual, Spielberg wanted authenticity for his shots. He got more than he expected on arriving in Shanghai on March 1, 1987, for principal photography inside the city. Amazingly, the city had not changed in the last forty years since the end of World War II, so the exterior shooting conditions were extremely favorable. The only things that needed changing were the signs and billboards, which had to be restored to their traditional Mandarin lettering.

Lionheart

There are times when a movie's score outshines the movie that it accompanies. A good example of that happening is with the film *Lionheart* (1987), in which the score by Jerry Goldsmith is one of his finest, most exciting, elegant, and beautiful efforts. This is a movie score that can stand on its own.

Goldsmith's usual philosophy is that the *less* music there is in a film, the *more* emphasis it has when it enters. Although this is generally true, this is one of the longest scores of his career, nearly ninety minutes long.

Goldsmith steps out of his usual monothematic approach in this score. Here, he very effectively utilizes the leitmotif approach, by composing a theme for each of the major characters. Goldsmith bases each of these musical cues on a single three-note motif that is heard throughout the film. The only exception to this is for the bittersweet love theme composed for Robert and Blanche. For this cue, Goldsmith has written a beautiful series of woodwind solos, with the oboe predominating. In some of the sections of this love theme, Goldsmith (who is forever looking for new sounds) uses the electronic synthesizer to realize the tone color of the oboe. For the menacing Dark Prince character, Goldsmith has composed a powerful low brass theme that is somewhat reminiscent of the famous *Dies Irae*.

Goldsmith combined electronic colors with the live instruments of the orchestra, giving this score a mysterious quality, especially in the cue written for the lake. Goldsmith continued to dub in synth sounds to his orchestral scores over the next decade of his career.

Lionheart was not released in a large number of theaters. It is available on video and Varese Sarabande has released a recording of the soundtrack. The story is a fictional account of events that supposedly took place during the Children's Crusade during the second decade of the thirteenth century.

The Untouchables

Ennio Morricone wrote a fine score for the Brian De Palma crime drama, *The Untouchables* (1987). The movie opens in the year 1930, during a time when ganglords such as Al Capone ruled over Chicago to compete for control of the city's billion-dollar illegal alcohol empire. The opening main title theme is brutal and hard-hitting, featuring a constant pulse in the snare drum over which we hear a syncopated piano and a haunting tune superimposed on this on the harmonica—the harmonica is one of Morricone's favorite solo instruments. The score that Morricone wrote for this period picture does not reflect the music of the 1930s. Instead, Morricone chose a more *contemporary sound,* complete with dissonant string clusters and pounding percussion. This score was nominated for an Oscar, but lost to the score for the movie *The Last Emperor* by Ryuichi Sakamoto, David Byrne, and Cong Su.

Willow

James Horner was more fully established in his career by the end of the 1980s. He composed a brilliant score for Ron Howard's film *Willow* (1988). Maurice Jarre was one of the first mainstream film composers to introduce exotic and ethnic instruments combined with orchestral instruments within his scores. Another key figure was James Horner. *Willow* was an excellent example of this approach. Right at the beginning of the main title sequence, a wordless choir helps set the dreamy, almost spiritual world of magic and sorcery that are a part of everyday life in this film. Eventually, we hear the breathy sound of the Japanese Shakuhachi flute. Horner's use of ethnic instruments provides a cultural diversity of styles of colors that works extremely well.

Horner wrote longer than normal musical cues for his films. Many of his cues are of five to seven minutes long, with some cues clocking in at over eleven minutes. We also hear him using the wordless choir in many of his scores. *Willow* is no exception.

James Horner conducted the sessions at Abbey Road Studio, using the *Star Wars* orchestra, the London Symphony Orchestra. Although Horner is known for doing many of his own orchestrations for his scores, he employed the late Greig McRitchie on *Willow*.

A Summer Story

Some of the films covered in this book are a little more difficult to locate than others. The 1988 film *A Summer Story*, scored by Georges Delerue, is one such film. This British film was released in limited engagements throughout the United States, yet appeared on cable television quite often and was released on videotape. This story was directed by Piers Haggard and stars the English actress Imogen Stubbs as a young lower-class girl who happens to fall in love with a young English chap (played by James Wilby) from a well-to-do background. This makes for a bittersweet romance. The melancholy main theme played on the solo cello is among Delerue's most haunting yet beautiful movie themes.

Main theme from A Summer Story

Field of Dreams

"If you build it, he will come" is an expression from the 1989 film *Field of Dreams*. Over the years, films start trends, change fashions, establish what is acceptable in society, and sometimes contain "catch phrases" that go down in history forever by becoming part of the everyday vocabulary.

Field of Dreams is the story of a man who hears a mysterious voice that tells him to turn part of his Iowa cornfield into a ballfield so that a group of ballplayers will come.

The score provided by James Horner is a combination of orchestral instruments and synthesizer. A beautiful French horn line, performed by the Hollywood studio musician Jim Thatcher, is heard in the main title sequence. When the main character recognizes that one of the ghost ballplayers who came to play ball at his makeshift ballfield is actually his own father as a young man, the theme is played once again on horn and strings. The score provides a perfect ambiance for the sequences in which the main character (played by Kevin Costner) either sees a vision or hears a mysterious voice. Horner's score was nominated for an Oscar, although it lost to Alan Menken's score for *The Little Mermaid*.

Glory

One of James Horner's finest scores was written for the civil war drama *Glory* (released in 1989). This is based on the life of Robert Gould Shaw (played by Matthew Broderick), a young white man who ends up commanding a regiment of black soldiers in the Union army during the American Civil War. What made this significant was the fact that this was the first black regiment to fight for the north during the American Civil War. This drama is brought to life by Horner's powerful score that combines a haunting theme, sung at the beginning of the film under the narration, with some dramatic orchestral writing. This same theme is heard at the very end of the film.

Throughout the course of the film we have come to know and respond to each major character within the black regiment. When the men decide to lead the battle in the front lines of the Union soldiers in attempt to take the Confederate Fort Wagner in South Carolina, we applaud their heroic efforts knowing that this gallant act would mean the loss of life for many of them. As they are charging the fort, Robert Shaw, their fearless leader, is shot and killed. Horner's music starts the moment that Shaw falls to the ground. Because there is no dialogue in the final moments of the film, it is Horner's powerful music that moves our emotions for the rest of the picture to the very end of the film. This section of the score (during the battle sequence) is somewhat reminiscent of Carl Orff's *Carmina Burana,* sung by the Boys Choir of Harlem. In the aftermath of the battle, when we see the survivors burying all of the casualties (including Robert Shaw), we hear the return of the opening hymn. This time it takes on the form of an elegy to haunt our emotions.

When the film played in theaters, audiences sat still, emotionally stunned and overwhelmed by the power of this story as the end credits rolled by. One of the key elements in making this film so effective was Horner's music. At the time, people wondered why Horner's score was not even mentioned at the Academy Awards. Irwin Kostal (1911–1994) was on the nominating board of the Academy at the time, and he stated that Horner's score was considered. Unfortunately for Horner, the score had to be withdrawn because the committee felt that parts of the score resembled the temp music that was used for the film. Not only is the film's battle music sequence similar to *Carmina Burana* but also the film's main theme is reminiscent of Sergey Prokofiev's (1891–1953) score to *Ivan the Terrible* (1945).

Henry V (1989 Version)

There have been many remakes of movies over the years, some good, some bad. The actor/director Kenneth Branaugh's screen adaptation of Shakespeare's drama about the Battle of Agincourt is an emotionally powerful retelling of the story.

The composer, Patrick Doyle (1953–), has written a masterful score for a film of this genre. Perhaps the most memorable contribution that the score made occurs at the end of the battle. We see Patrick Doyle, who also appears in the movie as an actor playing the character known as Court, standing in a driving rainstorm. Touched by the emotion of the moment, he begins to sing an old Latin song, "Non nobis, Domine," in memory of those who have just given their lives in battle. A moment later, the rest of the men join him in singing. To add to the drama, Doyle accompanies the voices with an orchestral entrance that tops off the musical climax.

The score for this updated version of this drama is rich in emotion. Steven Spielberg liked it so much that he used some of this score as a temp track when editing parts of *Jurassic Park*. Patrick Doyle is no amateur when it comes to film scoring. The late Henry Mancini said that, next to Jerry Goldsmith, Patrick Doyle was his other favorite film composer.

Casualties of War

Ennio Morricone wrote a powerful score for the powerful subject of rape and murder in the Vietnam war saga *Casualties of War* (1989). This is a sobering drama directed by Brian De Palma, in which an American soldier witnesses the brutal rape and murder of a young Vietnamese woman by members of his own squad of soldiers.

In order to give the score its exotic feel, Morricone composed a theme to be played on the pan flute. This esoteric instrument returns several times throughout the score, as does a wordless choir that provides the needed atmospheric shadings.

One of the musical highlights of Morricone's score is his powerful "Elegy for Brown." This is an emotional rendering of a somber ballad played by solo horn and strings. This score was recorded in Rome at the Forum Studio and is scored for orchestra, pan flutes, and chorus.

Batman

Danny Elfman. From the author's collection.

Danny Elfman (1953–) launched his career with a Tim Burton film, *Batman* (1989). This was not his first film score. His first score was written in 1978—*Forbidden Zone* (released in 1980), followed by *Pee Wee's Big Adventure* in 1985. In all, Elfman had written ten film scores before *Batman*. Elfman's score for *Batman* (1989) made people perk their ears and say, Who wrote the score? Elfman started his career as a music director of a musical theatrical troupe known as The Mystic Nights of the Oingo Boingo, which evolved into a rock group called Oingo Boingo. He was able to experiment with different musical styles while with the group. By the time he started working on film scores, he said to himself, "Forget everything you've done over the last eight years, go back to yourself as a teenager, watching and loving films. I just tried to approach everything almost as a thirteen year old, going through those wonderful movies that I loved . . . all those great Bernard Herrmann scores. I just went back to those sources which were and still are so much a part of me."[7] In the main title

7. *Soundtrack* magazine, September 1990.

sequence of *Batman,* the first thing that is quite obvious is the dark quality of the opening moments. Elfman's music helps to exude this darkness through the use of his main theme in a minor key. To prove how much of an effect that Herrmann's music really had on Elfman's score for *Batman,* listen carefully to the first five notes of the theme. Now go back in time to Herrmann's score of the 1959 film *Journey to the Center of the Earth,* and listen carefully to the first five notes of the cue for "Mountaintop—Sunrise." Look at the examples below:

Batman *theme*

"Mountaintop-Sunrise" cue from Journey to the Center of the Earth

There have been people in the business who are either jealous or upset with Elfman's apparent rise to superstardom without paying his dues by working for many years in more lowly assignments. These same people refuse to give Elfman credit for his obvious talent. It was not until the Seventieth Anniversary of the Academy Awards that Danny Elfman finally got his first nomination for an Oscar for Best Original Dramatic Score. He was nominated for his score for the film *Good Will Hunting* (1997), but lost to James Horner's score for the megahit movie *Titanic* (1997). Elfman also was nominated for his score to *Men in Black.* This lost to Anne Dudley's score for *The Full Monty* (1997). Elfman had the help of three orchestrators on his score for *Batman.* His main orchestrator was his friend and colleague from Oingo Boingo, Steve Bartek. The other orchestrators were Shirley Walker and Steven Scott Smalley. Shirley Walker conducted the Sinfonia of London Orchestra for the scoring sessions.

The Abyss

Alan Silvestri was hired by the director James Cameron to score a science fiction drama about a crew from an oil rig who try frantically to find survivors aboard a sunken nuclear submarine. They find more than they expected when they come across extraterrestrial life in a deep underwater gorge. These extraterrestrials eventually help to save the world from catastrophic consequences. In order to give his score that "out-of-this-world sound," Silvestri utilized a combination of full orchestra, electronics, and a wordless choir. Silvestri has stated that he only uses electronics as a last resort *to create colors and sounds that are not possible with the instruments of the orchestra.* James Cameron described the score that Silvestri composed for *The Abyss* as "mysterious, fiercely driving, tender, and ecclesiastical."

The original theatrical release of the film ran at 140 minutes. This was arrived at after some test screenings in Dallas, Texas, using a musical temp track and lacking some of the completed special effects. James Cameron had wanted a film that ran about thirty minutes longer (twenty-seven minutes of story, three additional minutes of credits—about one thousand extra names of people who worked on the film!). With this added footage, the story was more credible and made better sense. According to Cameron, "The original goal of the film was to tell a story of a kind of apocalypse in which we are all judged by a superior race, and found to be worthy of salvation because of a single average man, an Everyman, who somehow represents that which is good in us: the capacity for love measured by the willingness for self-sacrifice." The aliens see in the main character in the movie (played by Ed Harris) the capacity for love and the basis for a hope that somehow humans can overcome their limitations and aggressions for violent behavior. When the film was reduced to 140 minutes, some of this message was missing.

Several Notable Scores

Georges Delerue wrote a very beautiful main theme to represent the bond of several women in a small Louisiana town in the film *Steel Magnolias* (1989). Elmer Bernstein used the ondes martenot as the solo instrument that performed the main theme for the movie *My Left Foot*.

Review Questions

Discussion

1. Discuss how the scores of the 1980s differ from those of the 1930s and 1940s.

2. If John Corrigliano had been asked to score *Star Wars,* how might his style of music have changed peoples' perception of the film?

Short Answers

1. Name some of the innovative techniques used by Corrigliano in his *Altered States* score.

   ____

   ______________________________.

2. What are rub rods? ______________________________.

3. What is unique about the score for *Witness*? ______________________________.

4. What piece of music had been used on the temp track of the "barn raising" sequence from *Witness*? ______________________________.

5. Why was Horner's score for *Glory* not eligible for an Academy Award? ______________________________

   ______________________________.

Define the following

Rub rods ______________________________

Ordnung ______________________________

Passacaglia ______________________________

Chapter Eleven

Sailing into the Twenty-First Century (the 1990s, from *Jurassic Park* to *Titanic* and Beyond)

Dances with Wolves

True to John Barry's knack for writing pleasing melodies that appeal to the masses, his main theme for *Dances with Wolves,* called the "John Dunbar theme" is indicative of his homophonic approach. (A **homophonic texture** is one in which there is a predominant melody in the top voice supported by chords that move along with the melody in the lower voices.)[1] His theme for "*Two Socks* the wolf" is also in this style. *Two Socks* is the name that John Dunbar gave to a wolf who had white paws and kept hanging around Dunbar. When it first appears within the movie, the "wolf theme" is beautifully played by the flute in a gentle triple meter. The flute line is supported by a *harp arpeggio*—the notes of a musical chord are sounded in succession rather than at the same time. This is accompanied by sustained chords in the strings.

Barry had received an assembly cut of the film that contained about four hours of footage. For this, Barry composed some thematic material that he then recorded and sent to Kevin Costner, who starred as well as directed the movie. Costner requested a score that would have a romantic feel to it, yet contain some Indian themes, along with music that would have an adventuresome quality to its scope. What Barry came up with was a score that musically illustrates "the dignity and graciousness" of the Sioux Indians, a concept that Costner was hoping to show in this film.

Dances with Wolves would require the longest score in Barry's career. He used a ninety-one-piece orchestra and a twelve-voice choir to provide color to the vastness of the prairies.

This would be the fourth Oscar win for Barry.

1. Barry's style is *a single melodic line supported by broken chords in the bass and a countermelody in another voice.*

John Dunbar theme from Dances with Wolves *(note the broken chords moving in the bass voice)*

Quigley Down Under

For the 1990 Austalian–U.S. production *Quigley Down Under,* Basil Poledoris had no trouble giving the film its needed "Western sound." Poledoris had already earned an Emmy Award for his work on the popular major television production *Lonesome Dove.* This two-hour adventure starred Tom Selleck in one of his best roles as an American who defends the Australian Aborigines against an evil landowner, masterfully played by Alan Rickman.

Poledouris uses the banjo in several cues to give the score its Western flavor. One of the cues, called "Marston's Murderers," features an exciting French horn line (played by several horns in unison) that is supported by the banjo plucking away in true Western fashion. This score also features a good example of Poledouris's trademark: starting a cue in a minor key and evolving into rich major chords for a spectacular effect.

The score was recorded at the MGM Studios (now Sony) and was orchestrated by Greig McRitchie and Mark McKenzie. It was written for a large orchestra and features some of the usual "Western clichés" that were laid down by previous composers of the Western genre such as Moross, Bernstein, Broughton, and Morricone. Among these clichés are powerful French horn/trumpet lines supported by syncopated rhythmic accompaniments, hoedownlike string parts, banjo and guitar obbligatos (an Italian term meaning "necessary"), and tuneful solos in woodwind parts.

JOHN BARRY

English-born composer (John Barry Prendergast)

Born: November 3, 1933 (York, England)

His father managed and owned several cinemas and also put on several concerts. Young Barry worked as a projectionist at his father's movie theaters and realized at a young age that he wanted to write film music for a living. John Barry studied trumpet and musical arranging. He formed a jazz combo called the "John Barry Seven" in 1957 that gave a series of tours as well as successful TV appearances.

After several minor film assignments, John Barry was asked to arrange Monty Norman's James Bond theme for the movie *Dr. No* (1962).

Barry went on to compose music for ten James Bond movies, and has won the Best Score Oscar for *Born Free, The Lion in Winter, Out of Africa,* and *Dances with Wolves.*

John Barry. From the author's collection.

Some of his other films that he scored include: *Midnight Cowboy* (1969), *Walkabout* (1971), *Eleanor and Franklin* (TV film, 1976), *Robin and Marian* (1976), *Hanover Street* (1979), *Somewhere in Time* (1980), *Body Heat* (1981), *Frances* (1982), *Jagged Edge* (1985), *Chaplin* (1992), and *Swept from the Sea* (1998).

His style is easily recognized. It has a homophonic texture in which a beautiful long, lingering melody is accompanied by a broken chordal accompaniment. He sometimes adds a countermelody as played by the French horns.

Barry is considered to be one of the most admired of all film composers. His music is usually very beautiful, yet he has the ability to compose for the jazzy detective or secret agent scenario with ease.

Robin Hood: Prince of Thieves

In 1991, director Kevin Reynolds brought a remake of the classic Robin Hood tale to the screen. Michael Kamen was hired to write a score that was sure to be compared with Korngold's classic score of the 1940s.

On occasion, a film will undergo last minute editing changes after preview audiences have panned them. If this happens, which can be frequent, this can and usually does represent a major headache for the poor film composer. In the case of *Robin Hood: Prince of Thieves* (1991), the main star Kevin Costner and the director Kevin Reynolds did not see eye-to-eye on certain aspects of the final cut of the film. As a result, the film was drastically recut with only days to go before the scheduled general release. Reel number one became reel number two and so on, to the point that Michael Kamen had to call many of Hollywood's best orchestrators to rescore the film overnight. The list included Jack Hayes, William Ross, Don Davis, Bruce Babcock, Albert Olsen, Pat Russ, Brad Warnaar, Lolita Ritmanis, Mark Watters, Eliot Kaplin, Jonathan Sacks, Richard Davis, Harvey Cohen, Beth Lee, and Chris Boardman.

Michael Kamen's score abounds with the sound of Renaissance merriment with the feel of fabled Sherwood Forest and the elegance and beauty of Maid Marian. Kamen said that he had borrowed the beautiful love theme for this film from a ballet score that he had written some years before. Kamen, an accomplished oboist, sometimes performs on his own scores. For this film, he wrote the beautiful love theme to be played on the oboe. To date, this is Kamen's longest score.

Michael Kamen. Courtesy of Chasen & Company.

Beauty and the Beast

With the popularity of animated features over the last several decades, it is hard to believe that only one has been nominated for the Best Picture Oscar.[2] This is the case. *Beauty and the Beast* (1991), an eighty-four-minute animated feature, has musical numbers that are reminiscent of Busby Berkelely in his heyday. Walt Disney Studios produced a visually stunning and ambitious retelling of the legend of a young woman who falls under the spell of a monster. Alan Menken masterfully set the lyrics of the late Howard Ashman. This film also helped to start a trend in major studios investing in the genre of the animated feature once again, a style of movie making that had fallen by the wayside over the years.

The Prince of Tides

One of the most beautiful and lush scores to come from the early 1990s was written by James Newton Howard for *The Prince of Tides* (1991), a powerful drama that has some rather shocking scenes. Nick Nolte plays an out-of-work football coach/English teacher who grew up in the marshlands of South Carolina. He travels to New York to help his sister unravel a past that is causing her great heartache and in the process finds out that he has fallen in love with his sister's psychiatrist (played by Barbra Streisand).

Howard had his score recorded at Sony Studios Scoring Stage. It was orchestrated by Brad Dechter, Marty Paich (who also conducted the studio orchestra for the scoring sessions), and Hummie Mann. It is scored for a chamber-sized orchestra and features woodwind solos, particularly a solo oboe with string accompaniment.

2. At the 2002 Academy Awards, a new category was added for best animated feature. The movie *Shrek* won.

Howard had replaced John Barry, the composer originally hired to score this picture. Barry had written some music but decided to leave the project because of professional differences with the main star and director, Barbra Streisand. John Barry was able to use his beautiful main theme originally intended for *The Prince of Tides* as the main theme for another score done for the IMAX film *Across the Sea of Time* (1995).

Hook

Since many people knew the story of Peter Pan, the film version of *Hook* (1991) was met with excitement by the moviegoing public. Although panned by many of the leading movie critics, audiences were excited to see how the world's most famous movie director would bring the story of Peter Pan and Captain Hook to life on the big screen, using three top Hollywood stars. This film never equaled the box-office drawing power of Spielberg's other masterpieces.

The score that John Williams provided for this great adventure is built on the leitmotif approach with easily recognizable musical motifs for each of the main characters, including a snappy march for Captain Hook. We also hear a Korngoldian influence in several of the music cues, particularly when we see Peter Pan flying.

Prospero's Books

Michael Nyman (1944–) has been affiliated with almost a half dozen of the visionary filmmaker Peter Greenaway's most controversial films. Nyman has a recognizable style in that he is a **minimalist** (he uses repeated patterns of notes almost *ad nauseam*) and he likes to use his twenty-three-piece Michael Nyman Band, which is composed of a saxophone ensemble, a small string ensemble of ten players, a bass guitar, one clarinet, one trumpet, two horns, two bass trombones, and Michael Nyman on piano. For *Prospero's Books* (1991), Peter Greenaway provides a "nonstop, overly layered, and overlapping display of sights and sounds" in this astonishing interpretation of William Shakespeare's *The Tempest*. This story finds Prospero (brilliantly played by the late John Gielgud), a mirror image of the Bard, as he relates the story of his exile as he imagines it happened. Nyman decided not to use music that was remotely close to Shakespeare's period of history (except for one small snippet from a John Dowland [1563–1626] song for the citation-hunters). The cue called "Prospero's magic" is indicative of the **typical Nyman style.** It features the strings playing repeated sixteenth notes surrounded by a countermelody in slower moving notes by the rest of the ensemble along with the piano providing the various chord changes. Vocals also play a key role in this score. Sarah Leonard performs the songs heard in the movie as "the boy soprano voice." This 135-minute film is difficult to locate in video stores, and actually works best if seen on the big screen in order to receive the full-intended effect and intent of the director's vision. The score was recorded at PRT Studios and Abbey Road Studios in London.

Year of the Comet

There are some films that are released without much hoopla by the media that end up being better entertainment than some of the major mainstream releases. A good example of this is *Year of the Comet* (1992), with a score by a man who up until this film had made his reputation as a film music orchestrator.

Hummie Mann (1955–) had scored two previous film projects, but this was his first major film release. He was one of the orchestrators on *Prince of Tides*. In addition, he worked on films such as *The Addams Family, City Slickers, For the Boys, Dying Young,* and *Misery*. His more recent films include *Robin Hood: Men in Tights, Dracula: Dead and Loving It,* and a series of television movies.

Peter Yates brought to the screen the story of a romantic action adventure that involves a rare bottle of wine from the year 1811. It is a film score that paints a musical picture of the beautiful Scottish countryside by featuring a main theme that has a lilting $\frac{6}{8}$ giguelike buoyancy that is effective in creating atmosphere of time and place.

Basic Instinct

Over the years, there have been some wonderfully compatible working relationships between the director and the composer. When Paul Verhoeven contacted Jerry Goldsmith to compose a score for his steamy murder mystery *Basic Instinct* (1992), this would become one of Goldsmith's distinct pleasures during the span of his illustrious career. He stated that the collaboration between the two men was nearly perfect—they saw eye-to-eye on each part of the film. According to Verhoeven, the result of this labor of love "is a wonderful score that is original, evocative, and audacious in its very simplicity."[3] He goes on to say that Jerry Goldsmith is the best film composer with whom he has ever worked.

The film was a scandal on its release, because of the explicit nature of the sexual scenes. Sharon Stone plays a provocative role as a wealthy author of murder mysteries. She becomes the chief suspect in a grisly ice pick murder of a man who was killed during a romp in bed with his attacker.

Goldsmith's main theme is written in an impressionistic style, with the string accompaniment reminiscent of the string sounds of Claude Debussy. The main theme is played by pairs of clarinets, flutes, and oboes that are supported by harp arpeggios and a string countermelody. Goldsmith had his old buddy Alexander (Sandy) Courage provide the orchestrations for this score. Goldsmith had set up ten electric synthesizers that were linked to a computer and a television monitor. This enabled him to demonstrate the rich orchestrations that he was going to utilize in this score to Verhoeven before the scoring sessions. The final sessions were performed by the National Philharmonic Orchestra in England with Goldsmith conducting. The score is a combination of electronic sounds added to the orchestra for variations of color and character within the score.

Bram Stoker's Dracula

Certainly one of the scariest-sounding scores of the 1990s had to be the Polish composer Wojciech Kilar's dark score for Francis Ford Coppola's *Bram Stoker's Dracula* (1992). Bernard Herrmann would have been proud to have claimed parts of this score among his own output, particularly the "Vampire Hunter's theme." This score has a certain *Satanic* aura that leaves the listener with an uneasy eerie feeling almost as though we were dealing with the antichrist instead of a bloodsucking fiend. The extreme darkness of this score is created by its use of low instrumentation (á la Herrmann) and minor tonalities. As with other movie scores that have tried to be innovative, this score is no exception. For the sequence called "the ring of fire," there is the addition of muted voices, distant cries, chanting, and evil laughter all connected with

3. Quote from CD liner notes.

a driving pounding beat that is accompanied by various animal noises that cry out for some recognition. Kilar has written some beautifully inspirational choral writing for the uplifting cue "Love eternal."

Far and Away

Six years before James Horner penned the now legendary score for *Titanic* (1997), John Williams brought a score with an Irish flare to the screen in the director Ron Howard's screen production of *Far and Away* (1992). Williams included a deal of Irish flavor into this film about a young Irishman (played by Tom Cruise) who lands in Boston with a feisty young woman (played by Nichole Kidman). There are many opportunities for Williams to provide a variety of musical styles for this small-scale epic. Perhaps two of the most memorable musical moments in the film occur right at the beginning of the film and later during the Oklahoma Land Rush. For the film's opening sequence, Williams supplies a haunting theme played first by a pennywhistle, joined by the French horn. This eventually evolves into the film's main theme, which will be heard throughout other portions of the film. It was said that when the crew filmed this opening scene, the helicopter carrying the film crew crashed, wrecking the very expensive camera, so it had to be refilmed. Fortunately, there were no other casualties. The other memorable sequence that also features music in a big way is the Oklahoma land-rush sequence. Williams's music for the race features this main title theme as well as snippets from some of the film's other secondary musical themes.

The Piano

Michael Nyman supplied original music for the highly praised film by New Zealand–born director Jane Campion (1955–), *The Piano* (1993). This film shared the Palme d'Or at the Cannes Film Festival with the film *Farewell My Concubine*. It also won Campion an Oscar for best screenplay, plus a nomination for best picture and best director.

Nyman's piano music has an impromptu quality to it that was appealing to the critics, although it was perhaps a little too modern sounding to have actually been performed in the nineteenth century (the film was set in New Zealand in the 1850s). Also, Nyman's use of the saxophones in this score (part of his usual Michael Nyman Band sound for many of his scores) was perhaps a little out of character, considering the fact that Adolph Sax only invented the sax in 1840. (Of course, Alex North used an ensemble of saxophones in *Cleopatra,* a film that features events that took place over two thousand years ago.) This is Nyman's most easily accessible score to the casual listener perhaps because of the folklike simplicity of the solo piano lines. Nyman's research into Scottish folk songs for the main character's piano sourcebook was effective in its helping to color and shape the story, because of her Scottish origins.

The Good Son

Elmer Bernstein chose the piano to represent the innocence of the young boy in *The Good Son* (1993). The main title theme tends to throw the viewer off direction, to believing that the son (played by Macaulay Culkin) is perhaps innocent of the homicidal tendencies that we think we are observing. This theme is hauntingly beautiful because of the addition of the ondes martenot. The ondes is played by specialist Cynthia Miller, who has since become a film composer. Elmer Bernstein also had his daughter, Emilie Bernstein, do the orchestrations for this film. The score was recorded at Paramount Studios in August 1993.

Sommersby

Ever since Danny Elfman's exposure to the mainstream filmgoing public as a film composer, he continues to impress those who follow his career seriously. It's true that there are those critics out there who like to lambaste certain film composers as not being worthy of their fame or position within the echelon of composers. It is sometimes felt that they either didn't serve their dues to work their way up the ladder of success, or they got where they are by various unscrupulous tactics. Elfman is a composer with a vivid imagination who can handle a variety of film genres at a consistently high rate.

The 1993 movie *Sommersby* is no exception. This is a very moving story of love, intrigue, and sadness. As stated in Chapter 2, the main title music says to the audience what kind of film will follow. In the case of *Sommersby,* the main theme, pitched in a minor key, tends to tell the listener that the story that they are about to see will have a tragic ending. Elfman has written a lush and beautifully sweeping main theme in a triple meter. The score also features several ethnic instruments. Elfman used his colleague Steve Bartek to do most of the orchestrations. The score was recorded at Todd-AO Scoring Stage.

Tombstone

Filmmakers from time to time try to revive interest in the movie Western. As fate would have it, two different films about Wyatt Earp and his associates were released within a year of each other. The other film was called simply *Wyatt Earp* (1994) and was scored by James Newton Howard. In 1993, the movie *Tombstone* was released with a score by Bruce Broughton. Unlike most films, this story opens *without* a main title theme right at the onset of the film. The score develops with the development of the story. What may be called the main theme, according to Broughton, does not appear until the arrival in Tombstone when we hear "the family theme," which is then followed by the main theme. The interesting thing here is that this main theme of the picture does not reappear again in its entirety until the end credits *at the conclusion of the picture*. Before then, all we hear are fragments of this theme. Although Broughton made quite an impact with his splendid Western score for *Silverado,* this particular score does not always have that "Western" sound that one might expect. This is primarily because of some of the more unusual orchestrations that Broughton decided to utilize within this score. If you listen carefully, instead of hearing the guitar, banjo, or harmonica (some of the major staple instruments for a typical Western score), you will hear some rather exotic sounds coming from the Hungarian cimbalom (a box zither that is related to the English dulcimer), the Irish tin whistle and bodhran (a frame drum), and the French contrabass sarrusophone (an instrument invented in 1856 that was intended to replace the contrabassoon). For those fans of Broughton who loved his score for *Silverado,* there are definitely moments in this score that have that exciting sound that made *Silverado* so appealing to a wide range of film music enthusiasts. In fact, parts of *Tombstone* were actually temp-tracked with Broughton's music from *Silverado,* thus making him the logical choice of the filmmakers to score this Wyatt Earp epic. He still has the powerful brass fanfarelike lines that are accompanied by a hoedownlike violin line as in the finale of *Silverado*. To add extra power in the low brass, Broughton uses the massive contrabass trombone. This score was performed by The Sinfonia of London and recorded at the Whittfield Recording Studios.

Broughton is one of the most highly respected film composers working today and has held that respect for several decades. Although he was nominated for his score to *Silverado* as best score, he has not yet been associated with a super high-profile Academy Award–winning film. Until that time comes, he may have to enjoy the superlative reputation without the coveted golden Oscar.

Rudy

On occasion, a film comes along that can make you sit up and say Yes! to the outcome of the trials and tribulations of the main character. *Rudy* (1993) is such a film. It is based on a true story of a young fellow who tells his friends and relatives that someday he is going to play football on the famous Notre Dame football team. What makes this story more unbelievable is the fact that Daniel "Rudy" Ruettiger is very small in stature and not a very good student academically. By sheer determination, after many rejections, Rudy finally sees his big day. At the last game of the season, in his senior year, with only seconds to go on the clock, Notre Dame has the ball. His teammates began to chant his name "Rudy . . . Rudy . . . Rudy." Since Rudy, who has yet to play even one play that season during his entire time on the squad, is on the defensive side, the only way he could possibly play would be for his team to score. Against the coach's wishes, the team runs a play and throws the ball for a touchdown. Now the defense for Notre Dame can come out on the playing field. This means that Rudy could actually have his big fantasy come true if the coach will allow it to happen. Jerry Goldsmith's musical score has been gradually building for the last four minutes ever since Rudy's teammates and people in the stadium started chanting his name. Finally, the coach calls for him to go out on the playing field. He is able to make two plays, becoming the heroic tackler in the last play of the game. As his teammates raise him up on their shoulders after the game to carry him off the field, we hear the return of the Rudy theme. This theme had been heard earlier in the movie. Now, this theme acts as a catalyst to move our emotions to tears. As a matter of fact, during the scoring sessions, composer Jerry Goldsmith broke down and cried during the playback of this final scene, it was that good! Also, the studio musicians gave him a standing ovation.

Jurassic Park

Surely any person in any civilized country of the world who was alive during the early 1990s either saw or at least heard of Steven Spielberg's monstrous hit, *Jurassic Park* (1993). The music for this film, scored by John Williams, was recorded at Sony Scoring Stage (formerly MGM) in Culver City, California. Spielberg is usually very active in all phases of production and postproduction. During scoring sessions for his films, he usually walks around documenting everything by taking pictures, meeting with the musicians, and providing a wonderful spread of food for everyone. In *Jurassic Park,* he found himself in a logistical bind that initiated a rather unique set of circumstances. He had recently completed a locked cut version of the film, but was unable to be in California for the scoring of the music and approval of the special effects that were so groundbreaking. Where was he? He was in Poland filming *Schindler's List* (1993). According to Spielberg, "It was because I didn't want to miss winter in Poland. We got snow when we started shooting *Schindler's List,* and we don't finish till early June, so we get the changing of seasons. That meant doing postproduction work on *Jurassic Park* here, or waiting a year." About three times a week, Spielberg would come back to his small hotel from making *Schindler's List* to approve dinosaur shots and listen to John Williams's music. He had a big satellite

Jurassic Park, *Universal Studios Home Video. Courtesy of Photofest.*

dish set up in the front yard of this hotel that would bounce the satellite signal from Poland to Washington, D.C., to San Francisco (for the special effects being done at George Lucas's Industrial Light and Magic in San Rafael, just outside of San Francisco) or to Los Angeles for the recording of the music. As the signals were sent back and forth, the transmission was scrambled on both ends so that no one else could pick up the feed. John Williams would call and send Spielberg his scoring over the DAT (digital audio tape) dish. Spielberg had the music fitted on large speakers, so he had the sensation of being present at the scoring sessions. Actually, as it turned out, John Williams had hurt his back, so consequently some of the sessions were conducted by his friend Artie Kane. Spielberg also flew to Paris from Poland over three straight weekends to work on postproduction in a dubbing room, mixing the basic soundtracks into one composite soundtrack.[4] This is the first time in history that a film was completed via satellite technology in this manner. The actual score contains several recognizable leitmotifs. The island where Jurassic Park is located has an exciting trumpet fanfare associated with it and later becomes associated with the T-Rex at the climax of the film, when it comes to the rescue of the main characters who are being pursued by two raptors. Williams has written a majestic, haunting, and ennobling cue for the huge brachiosaurus in the style of British composer Edward Elgar (1857–1934). The cue for the raptor attack is somewhat reminiscent of Max Steiner's music heard in *King Kong* when

4. The above quotes and story were related in a *Los Angeles Times* article, 1993.

we first see Kong, complete with similar low walking (stalking) sounds coming from the low reeds. The hatching of the baby raptor sequence contains one of Williams's most haunting cues performed by a wordless choir, accompanied by a harp arpeggio and an eerie piano counter melody. The "remembering Petticoat Lane" scene is underscored by a nostalgic music-boxlike accompaniment that provides for interesting listening pleasure even without seeing the film projected on screen. Finally, the T-Rex rescue and finale are done in the style of Russian composer Igor Stravinsky (1882–1971), complete with pounding timpani and screaming brass. The mere fact that John Williams's music evokes the styles of previous composers is not meant as a cut to his genius as one of the premiere composers of film music. As Elmer Bernstein has said, "Composers have always been influenced by each other. We're all products of what's gone before."

Although Williams is probably best known for his symphonic approach to scoring, he does introduce the synthesizer into the score, most prominently during the scene when Dennis steals the embryo. The score was orchestrated by John Neufeld (a former clarinetist whose father had been the concertmaster of the Universal Studio Orchestra for about forty years).

Schindler's List

The year 1993 would not only be a good year for Steven Spielberg (for the first time in his career finally winning the Oscar for best director), but also a good year for John Williams as well. He won the coveted Best Score Award for his very powerful underscoring for Spielberg's *Schindler's List*. This is probably one of Williams's greatest contributions to the legacy of film music. The way in which this score is so masterfully interwoven into the fabric of this film qualifies this score to be in the upper echelon of textbook examples of how a dramatic score is supposed to work (like, for example, Elmer Bernstein's score for *To Kill a Mockingbird*). There are people who stayed away from this film because of its gloomy subject matter, but for those who saw it, they were moved by the story, which was enhanced greatly by the score. Amazingly enough, many people were not aware of the music in many scenes because it was written to work with each nuance of the drama. One of the best examples of this from the film is the emotional scene in which Oskar Schindler finally realizes that he could have saved more Jews from being killed, had he not squandered away so much of his money. In this memorable scene, eleven hundred people who were on his list were seen thanking him for what he had done for them by giving him a gold ring. As we watch the unfolding of this moment, Williams's music is always present, yet not overpowering. It is possible to get so engrossed in the drama that you don't even notice the music in some of the scenes. To give the score its Jewish flavor, Williams wrote in that particular idiom. The somewhat unique thing about this Williams score is that part of it was recorded with members of the Boston Symphony Orchestra, with Itzhak Perlman as violin soloist, at symphony hall in Boston. The remainder of the underscoring was done at Sony Scoring Stage (MGM) in Culver City, California.

By the way, if you were to visit this facility, you would immediately ask yourself why the room at Sony Pictures looks like it's undergoing a facelift, because cosmetically it does not look like the walls have been cared for since it was built many years ago. The reason for this would be the great acoustics of the room. This is where so many classic MGM scores have been recorded over the years and the general feeling is to leave the room as it is. This scoring stage is still many people's all-time favorite location for film scores.

This is the world famous MGM Scoring Stage as it looks today, now known as the Sony Scoring Stage. Courtesy of David Ewart, Recording Musicians Association.

Carlito's Way

The filmmaker Brian De Palma hired Patrick Doyle to provide his film *Carlito's Way* (1993) with a powerfully moving score. According to Doyle, De Palma had premapped out every detail of his use of music within the film, making this the fastest and easiest spotting session Doyle has ever attended in his career. He was very impressed with De Palma's efficiency and extreme talent.

The opening of the film was written in the form of an elegy at the suggestion of De Palma. This is written in a style similar to the famous *Adagio for Strings* by Samuel Barber and is an excellent example of film music that can hold a listener's attention without having to have the picture that accompanies it. This cue is very powerful emotionally. Doyle stated that De Palma gave him very helpful pacing suggestions for several cues. Both men agreed that some of the thematic musical material should represent the softness of the main female character Gail and reflect the inner turmoil of the streetwise main character Carlito.

Doyle was concerned by De Palma's exacting attention to every detail that his score would not rise to the high standard of De Palma's work. For Doyle, the toughest cue to score was the exciting chase sequence. Although this movie did not have a huge following, it does contain some of Patrick Doyle's best film cues, especially the elegy.

Gettysburg

Who would ever think that scoring a Civil War epic with synth overdubs (electronic synthesizer sounds added) to a conventional orchestra would make for an exciting score? This is what composer Randy Edelman determined when he scored the four-hour epic film *Gettysburg* (1993), about the bloody three days in July 1863 that comprised the Battle of Gettysburg. Edelman has written a powerful underscore for this moving war movie. Surprisingly, the addition of electronic synth color really does work quite well in spite of the uneasy feeling one gets when trying to imagine the use of electronic synthesizer sounds to accompany an 1860s drama. Particularly heartwarming and memorable is Edelman's arrangement for the great Civil War song "Dixie." This score naturally contains a lot of military overtones with occasional snare drums, cymbal crashes, and brass. In addition to this, Edelman has composed some beautiful thematic material that is developed in the woodwinds. This film contains an extremely effective score and may be Edelman's greatest score of his career. Perhaps two other scores of his would come in a close second. One would be the popular score that he cowrote with Trevor Jones for the movie *The Last of the Mohicans* (1992) and the other could be his exciting and effective score for *Dragonheart* (1996).

Speed

The year 1994 saw the rise of a new film composer on the horizon in a film that was the surprise hit of the summer of 1994. The composer was Mark Mancina (1957–); the film was *Speed*. This was a high adrenaline action picture that called for seventy-two minutes' worth of music to propel the 116-minute film. The story centers on a vindictive psychopath who transforms a busload of passengers into a high-velocity time bomb by placing a bomb on board a city bus. Once the bus has reached a certain speed, it must stay above that speed or the bomb will detonate. The trick is to keep the bus going at a high rate of speed (above 50 mph) through crowded Los Angeles streets and freeways and save the people from doom. Mancina had five and one-half weeks to write the score, which featured a sixty-three-piece orchestra along with a fusion of metal samples and synthesizer suspense. These metal samples were sounds that he recorded to be used in the score such as "a combination of metal scraping, wires being hit with hammers, having musicians play on cans and hubcaps, and all sorts of metal effects."[5] The orchestra itself was composed only of strings, French horns, and percussion, and recorded at Sony Scoring Stage conducted by Don Harper. The result was a very effective pulse-pounding score that

5. Lukas Kendall, *Film Score Monthly*, Vol. 2, No. 5, July 1997, article by Daniel Scheiger.

employed the leitmotif approach. There is a heroic theme and a love theme for Keanu Reeves and Sandra Bullock. In one unforgettable scene, the bus must make a leap over an unfinished portion of a freeway bridge. Notice how Mancina's music builds to the point where the bus leaves the ground at which time we have silence to heighten the impact of the scene.

One hidden factor confronting Mancina and his approach to scoring *Speed* was the constant engine sound coming from the bus. Mancina found it challenging to write the music because he could not get below the sound of the bus with his instrumentation. Mancina had gotten his break in the business thanks to Hans Zimmer, who recognized Mancina's talents. The two had worked together on *The Lion King* (Mancina produced three of the songs) and then again on a movie called *True Romance*. The director, Jan De Bont, was looking for an innovative new sound for his film *Speed,* so he decided to give Mancina a chance. 20th Century Fox did not want to use an "unknown" composer on their expensive action film, so they fought *against* Mancina. The studio had wanted Michael Kamen and had actually hired him to score the film. The director said, "Absolutely not, I want Mark Mancina." However, when *Speed* proved to be such a great hit, every filmmaker in Hollywood of high-action films wanted to hire Mancina. He went on to score *Twister* (1996) with a similar percussive approach as used in *Speed,* but with an Aaron Copland "Americana sound" for some of the expansive scenes. Although his career has taken off, he still fights frustrations. When scoring *Moll Flanders* (1996), MGM did not have enough faith in him to set aside enough money for a symphonic score, so he had to do it with synthesizers and four players (yet, the same studio had enough money for a movie like *Species,* which I might add, had a wonderful score by Christopher Young). Mancina also was puzzled over the approach the studio used in releasing his score for *Speed.* They released it long after the movie had faded from most theaters, thereby making its sales effectiveness negligible. The same thing happened with his score for *Twister,* coming out four and one-half months after the movie was released and in most cases, after the movie had disappeared from theaters.

Mark Mancina, a successful composer for films of Jan De Bont. Courtesy of Chasen & Company.

The summer that *Speed* opened in theaters across America was also the time of the passing of one of America's great film composers. Henry Mancini died on June 14, 1994, of complications from pancreatic cancer. It may be somewhat ironic that the Lord would take one composer so that another composer with a similar name could step to the forefront of the film scoring scene.

Stargate

David Arnold, a successful composer for films of Roland Emmerich. Courtesy of Vangelos Management.

Mark Mancina was not the only brilliant new face to surface in the world of film composers in 1994. The British composer David Arnold (1962–) saw his career skyrocket with his impressive score for the Roland Emmerich film *Stargate* (1994). Few composers can claim to have had such an impressive and spectacular film-scoring debut as Arnold. Most composers struggle for years scoring film after film and may never get that needed "big break." David Arnold made the big time with just one film, *Stargate*.

When Arnold was only seven years old, he was impressed with the James Bond movie *You Only Live Twice* (1967, scored by John Barry). He was also impressed with the music from *The Wizard of Oz* (1939) and *The Omen* (1976, scored by Jerry Goldsmith). David Arnold actually got his experience by scoring more than twenty National Film School student films in England in a little over two years. While there, he worked with the filmmaker Danny Cannon, whose first big film, *The Young Americans* (1993), was brought to the attention of executive producer Mario Kassar, who introduced him to Roland Emmerich. They were so impressed with Arnold that within two days he was signed to score *Stargate*. Prior to this lucky break, Arnold jostled several different jobs, such as selling fireworks, cleaning corn flake ovens, and working on a construction site, to make ends meet financially.

David Arnold believes in interaction with almost everyone on the production team as well as discussion with principal actors. He also did extensive research in the use of traditional Egyptian rhythms, scale patterns, and instruments for the exotic sound we hear in this score. The score was orchestrated and conducted by Nicholas Dodd. Combining the forces of the sixty-five-piece Sinfonia of London Orchestra with the Chameleon Arts Chorus, Arnold wrote a bold and sweeping epic-proportioned score in the symphonic style of John Williams's *Star Wars* and Maurice Jarre's *Lawrence of Arabia*. Because the film was originally three and one-half hours long, he had written two and one-half hours' worth of music. After various test preview screenings, the film was cut to a running time of 122 minutes. Arnold's score was constantly being revised because of the radical changes in the film's editing during the final days. According to Arnold, "We were rewriting on the last day of recording. . . . They changed 27 cues. The film went through four or five very radical structural changes."[6] By the time everything was completed, Arnold's score ran about ninety minutes. It is interesting to remember that Arnold's first exposure to film music was with James Bond films. He had said that if he would only have the opportunity to score a James Bond film, his ambitions would come full circle. Fortunately, he was able to realize that fantasy by scoring *Tomorrow Never Dies* in 1997, *The World Is Not Enough* in 1999, and, as of this writing, Arnold will be the composer of all of the future James Bond films. John Barry, the composer of twelve of the earlier James Bond films, has gladly "passed the torch" to Arnold with respect and admiration, feeling that this young man has what it takes to carry on the tradition.

6. John Williams, *Music from the Movies*, Vol. 1, No. 7, winter 1994/95, interview by Paul Place.

Arnold's career continues to grow with scores to big-budget films such as *Independence Day* in 1996 and *Godzilla* in 1998.

Legends of the Fall

James Horner had worked with Edward Zwick before on a film that had the power and drama to move the filmgoer to tears. That film was the Civil War epic *Glory* (1989). These two men teamed up once again for another successful union for *Legends of the Fall* (1994), the powerful drama of a Montana rancher and his three sons who all went after the same woman. This movie is based on a novella by Jim Harrison and although the story takes place in Montana, the movie was actually filmed in Alberta, Canada. The score needed to represent the "old" place from which the Ludlow family had come, as well as the "new" wildness of the Montana prairie with its panoramic beauty and breathtaking vistas. Horner was successful in portraying a supportive score that brought out the drama of love and loss in a "brooding and lush" fashion complete with recognizable leitmotifs. The theme for the Ludlow family is a beautiful music-boxlike theme played in a triple meter like a waltz. Ed Zwick states very poetically the function of Horner's music:

> At the heart of every story is a sound—something so deep that it resonates like a pressure in your chest. It is this feeling that the film composer seeks to make heard: not merely to underscore the chases, clinches, climaxes, or to smooth over the directorial inadequacies of soft cuts and shaky transitions, but to give voice to an inner life—its soul, if such a thing can be said of film.

Zwick later stated that he felt that Horner somehow managed to capture the details of the story as well as the inner nuances. In addition to the sweeping orchestral sound, Horner employed perhaps the world's foremost interpreter of the Japanese wood flute—the shakuhachi—Kazu Matsui.

Horner conducted at the sessions that were held at Air Studios, Lyndhurst Hall, and Metropolis Studios in London, England. He used the London Symphony Orchestra. The score was nominated for best original score.

Sirens

The British composer Rachel Portman composed two scores for films that were released in America in 1994. The first of these was an interesting film called *Sirens*. The story is based on a true incident that took place back in the 1930s. The movie is about a staid minister who is shocked by an Australian artist who is showing his scandalous works of art at public exhibitions. When the minister visits the artist to convince him of his wrongdoings, he finds that his life is turned around by the shocking circumstances that befall him. If you look carefully, you can see the writer-director of this movie playing the part of a pompous village minister.

Rachel Portman's score is a combination of her usual recognizable style of writing for solo flute or clarinet supported by a broken harp line and, for this score, she employs a soft impressionistic sound. Although Portman does her own orchestrations, she uses David Snell to conduct her scores at the scoring sessions. In this case, this score was recorded at CTS Studios in Wembley, England.

The Road to Wellville

The other score by Rachel Portman in 1994 was for the quirky film *The Road to Wellville.* This is the story of a married couple who visit John Harvey Kellogg's natural health sanitarium in search of his famous cure but only find frustration and embarrassment. The score that accompanies this movie is reminiscent of music for a Gilbert and Sullivan operetta. There are a few additional twists to this score not heard in many movies. Portman has one of the performers sing into a comb and wax paper, for a rather comical rendition of some of the songs within the film. There also is some humorous-sounding soprano sax work played by Nicholas Bucknall, Portman's usual clarinetist for her scores. Portman does her own orchestrating and continues to use David Snell as the person who conducts the scoring sessions.

Forrest Gump

Alan Silvestri (1950–) has scored many well-known films over the years, from *The Abyss* and the *Back to the Future* films to *Romancing the Stone* and *Who Framed Roger Rabbit?* So far, his biggest success has to be his emotionally charged score for *Forrest Gump* (1994). The film was phenomenally successful, and earned Silvestri his first Academy Award nomination for best score, although it lost to Hans Zimmer's

Tom Hanks as Forrest Gump. Courtesy of Photofest/Photo by Phillip Caruso.

confinement that these men felt while in prison. To represent this quality, Newman has written an eerie cue that is composed of sustained synthesizer clusters along with monotonous muted piano chords that are softly repeated to represent the hopelessness of prison confinement. By waiting until the final moments of the story for the uplifting musical climax, Newman has created a more powerful ending. We might say that the main theme in this film does not occur until the final ending of the film, yet it somehow manages to move us emotionally as though we know the theme. (Actually, this theme is heard once before earlier in the film.)

The score was orchestrated by Thomas Pasateri, Newman's usual orchestrator, and recorded at Todd-AO Scoring Stage and Village Recorders in Los Angeles. It was nominated for an Academy Award as best score.

Interview with a Vampire

The New York–based composer Elliot Goldenthal has written a texturally beautiful score full of lush orchestral colors for the movie *Interview with a Vampire* (1994). To add to the unusual timbres, Goldenthal has added the sound of a boy choir (the American Boychoir), complete with a young soloist, the unique quality of a glass harmonica, combined with a solo viola da gamba, harpsichord, electronics, and a very large full orchestra. The concertmaster of the New York Philharmonic, Glenn Dicterow, performs some of the wicked-sounding violin solos on the soundtrack. Goldenthal utilizes most of the compositional devices known to twentieth-century concert hall composers such as chord clusters, texture music, deep breathing noises by members of the ensemble, and the like.

Elliot Goldenthal. Courtesy of Chasen & Company.

The River Wild

Jerry Goldsmith was hired to replace *The River Wild* (1994) with a new score after a score by Maurice Jarre had been rejected. Goldsmith had only three weeks in which to write and record the score. The main theme in the movie is based on the old folk song *"The Water Is Wide."* Goldsmith arranged a beautiful rendition of this old English tune to be played by solo flute and solo trumpet and then the violin section. At the recording session, Goldsmith remarked that he wished he had written that tune. He did an admirable job of supplying variations on this theme.

Main theme from The River Wild

Meryl Streep plays the part of an experienced white water tour guide who plans a rafting trip with her ten-year-old son and her husband that is interrupted by two convicts who need her help getting down the river in order to escape. The tension and action increase as we get farther into the story. Goldsmith is amazing in how he can have a short time in which to compose a score and yet still write music that is quite pleasant to listen to even without the picture. Aside from the beautiful main theme and its various quotations throughout the score, Goldsmith has written some exciting music that gradually builds on a syncopated theme.

Goldsmith was able to use his two favorite orchestrators, Arthur Morton and Alexander Courage. The scoring sessions took place at Todd-AO Scoring Stage and were captured on video by the film composer and film music expert Fred Karlin for his documentary on Goldsmith called Film Music Masters series, a highly recommended purchase for anyone wishing to see Goldsmith at work "behind the scenes."

Wyatt Earp

James Newton Howard composed a large-scale orchestral score for Lawrence Kasden's film *Wyatt Earp* (1994). This score has a grand bravura to represent the expanse of the American West and an intimate quality to represent the inner thoughts of some of the main characters. Howard employs some of the usual instruments usually associated with a Western score such as a guitar, a solo violin, and an accordion, but he also adds the sound of recorders. One can hear some influence of Aaron Copland and several of the early masters of Western scores such as Moross and Bernstein, but, for the most part, Howard has given this score an original sound. This score was orchestrated by Brad Dechter

(Howard's main orchestrator for his film projects) and Chris Boardman and Howard himself. It was recorded at Sony Studios Scoring Stage.

Miklos Rozsa Dies: The Death of a Giant (1995)

With the passing of Miklos Rozsa on July 27, 1995, the film music world lost one of its great talents from the Golden Age of Hollywood. Although David Raksin outlived Rozsa, the remaining composers were of a new era. Rozsa had put down his writing pen and not composed a single note of film music during the last fourteen years of his life. With his death, one of the giants of the industry was lost.

Braveheart

James Horner wrote an epic-proportioned score to accompany *Braveheart* (1995), one of the better large-scale dramas of the 1990s. Mel Gibson not only starred in this epic, he produced and directed as well and it was reported that he put up $15 million of his own money in order to complete the film. This is a retelling of the story of the great Scottish hero of the thirteenth century, William Wallace, who led his clansmen in an outnumbered attempt to revolt against the onslaught of British oppression. Although the battle scenes are bloody and gruesome, one can't help but feel that they are a necessary ingredient in order to gain sympathy for Wallace's cause.

Horner has composed some wonderful themes of which Miklos Rozsa would have been proud. To give the score its wonderful Scottish flavor, Horner utilized the uilleann pipes (elbow pipes, a bellows-blown bagpipe of Ireland—also referred to as the Irish organ), Bodhran drums, and whistles (flutelike instruments). He also employed various shadings with synths (synthesizers). If the reader listens carefully to this score, they may hear some snippets of music that have a similar sound to parts of Horner's *Titanic* score that would be written two years later. The love theme called "For the Love of a Princess" has certain qualities that are reminiscent of something Rozsa could have written. The London Symphony Orchestra was conducted by James Horner and joined by the choristers of Westminster Abbey to round out a memorable score. Horner did all of his own orchestrations for this film. The score was nominated for an Oscar for best dramatic score.

First Knight

While James Horner was busy composing the music for *Braveheart,* Jerry Goldsmith was concentrating on an epic about the King Arthur legend for a film called *First Knight* (1995). By its beginning, the score sounds as though it is paying homage to the likes of Miklos Rozsa's scores that so often feature powerful fanfares played so brilliantly by members of the brass section. It has been stated that this score reminds the sophisticated moviegoer of epic scores such as *El Cid* by Rozsa or *Captain from Castille* by Alfred Newman.

Goldsmith composed a beautiful love theme for this film to represent the magnificent beauty of Guenevere. Goldsmith introduces the theme to the audience by scoring its entrance on the flute. He has written a strong, bold, and masculine main theme for King Arthur. During Arthur's farewell, we hear the addition of a large chorus, in this case singing in a Latin text. This is one of the techniques used often in film scores when the filmmaker wants the composer to bolster the amplitude of an emotional climax. Add a large chorus to the mix! Perhaps a large chorus of singers will round out a massive buildup of action on screen, just at the right moment, to send chills down your spine. This is the case at the end of *First Knight,* as Goldsmith adds a large chorus to the climatic ending in the final moments of the film.

The Scarlet Letter

The trend of replacing a composer's score with that of another's has gotten increasingly more common than ever before. For the modern film version of Nathaniel Hawthorne's *The Scarlet Letter* (1995), Elmer Bernstein had been the original composer on the project. Because of circumstances, the veteran composer John Barry replaced Bernstein. The film was criticized for two reasons: First, the passion of this 1850 American classic was updated to be explicit and the ending was changed to conform to a happy ending. The movie was deemed "the worst remake." These comments were unfortunate because they tended to condemn anyone or anything connected with the project.

John Barry came through with flying colors by composing another gorgeous theme in his inevitably recognizable "John Barry style." The solo line is played by the flute with a broken chord arpeggio in the harp, long sustained chords in the low strings and low brass, and a weaving counter melody in the violins. It was also decided to use a vocal arrangement of the often-used *Adagio for Strings* by Samuel Barber, sung by the Robert Shaw Festival Singers with Robert Shaw conducting. The use of Barber's music is an example of tracking an already existing commercial recording (by Telarc International Corporation) into the composite soundtrack of a motion picture. In this case, the music supervisor would have to check copyright clearance from Telarc (the recording company) and G. Schirmer, Inc. (the publisher of the music).

The Grass Harp

Occasionally a movie comes along that has an excellent cast, an excellent score, but is rather dull because of an overuse of sentimentalism. One could accuse *The Grass Harp* (1995) of such an offense. This film is based on a novella by Truman Capote and depicts life in a small Southern town during the 1930s and 1940s. It covers the bittersweet memories of a boy's experiences spent with his two maiden aunts. Although the supporting cast is outstanding, the story falls short of greatness. Patrick Williams (1932–), who has been scoring films since 1968, has written powerfully rich music featuring unbelievably gorgeous flute solo work by the Hollywood studio flutist Paul Fried. The movie derives its title from a field of grass where the wind blows, telling the story of all the people who once lived there. Patrick Williams was successful in helping to make this drama come to life. Of interest is the fact that this movie was directed and produced by Charles Matthau, son of the famous late actor, Walter, who also starred in this movie.

The year 1996 was a big year in film music, for *it was the first time in history a woman film composer won an Oscar*. It was also a year that would see some new talent come into the limelight as well as some established composers busy at work.

The English Patient

The score that won in 1996 for best dramatic score was by the Lebanese-born composer Gabriel Yared (1949–). The director/writer Anthony Minghella had certain musical cues in mind that were to be used in *The English Patient*. This gave Yared something to enable him to work around for the final score. The only thing was, the musical cues given to Yared were as different as night and day, posing a real challenge for any composer. One cue was a traditional Hungarian song "Szerelem, Szerelem" ("Love, Love") and the other cue was the "Aria" from *The Goldberg Variations* by Johann Sebastian Bach. Minghella later said that he felt that instead of being constraining on Yared's creative powers, these two cues actually *aided* Yared in creating a score that could introduce themes, allow them to develop, intertwine within the dialogue, and resolve. Yared was allowed to work closely with the director from the very beginning of the project, something not usually afforded most film composers. After reading the script, Yared attended the first days of shooting and continued to view the earliest assemblies of the film as it was taking shape.

As Derek Richardson states in the liner notes of the CD, "Gabriel Yared's absorbing score for *The English Patient* forges its own dreamlike realm in which such seemingly disparate strains as traditional Hungarian folk tunes, spare Baroque themes, and dense Romantic orchestrations play hide and seek with one another." Composing music in an impressionistic style that includes suspensions that resolve helped Yared to create this dreamlike realm. (A *suspension* is where a harsh sounding note, heard within a musical chord, usually resolves downward to the next note creating a feeling of rest or resolution.)

Twister

Twister (1996) was a challenging film to score due to its ultraloud sound effects for the main "star" of the film . . . *tornadoes*. Mark Mancina was given the scoring assignment. Parts of this score have the Aaron Copland "Americana sound," combined with Mancina's own orchestral/synthesizer approach, using driving rhythms from a drum machine to propel the action. In addition to this, we hear a wordless chorus of singers that Mancina added to render a feeling of the stupendous supernatural strength of Mother Nature. Mancina is a talented composer who seems to have a knack for capturing the most with his music for action-packed sequences. For most of his scores, he uses a drum machine to provide the basic ongoing rhythmical pulse. Then, Mancina will bring in live studio musicians to "sweeten" the sound by playing their instruments on the soundtrack. For the scene in which the tornado trackers are finally successful launching their invention known as "Dorothy," we hear the return of a theme first heard toward the beginning of the movie (called "Wheatfield" in the score). As the tornado changes its course and heads right for the two main characters, we hear Mancina's use of a wordless choir (in this case, the Los Angeles Master Choral was employed to sing on the score) to give the music its eerie supernatural quality. Mancina did most of his own orchestrating but did use the aid of five other individuals for additional orchestrations. This score was recorded at both Todd-AO and Sony Scoring stages.

Independence Day

David Arnold returns for another bombastic orchestral score for *Independence Day* (1996), a megahit for 20th Century Fox studios and the same team that brought us *Stargate* in 1994 and *Godzilla* in 1998. Arnold had to compose two hours' worth of music for this two hour and twenty-five minute film. This movie deals with the human aspect of what happens when aliens from outer space attack the world. Arnold decided to look at this as "a corny disaster movie and a World War II fighter-pilot adventure."[7] He wrote the score using several leitmotifs. There is a patriotic march theme for the president of the United States, the major hero of the movie. Arnold also decided that what the movie needed to convey was nobility, "because the film is about how people retain nobility while facing what might be the end of the world." He goes on to say, "My music needed to be warm, and go underneath the superfluousness of the action to reveal what people are thinking and feeling."[8] Where *Stargate* relied on the choir for color, *Independence Day* uses instruments associated with patriotism, such as brass and percussion. Arnold wanted to represent the aliens with a theme, but there were thousands of them with no distinct personality. He therefore decided to concentrate on the destruction that they were bringing to earth by composing a death march that spells out the word "DIE" in Morse Code. If you listen, you can hear the pounding of two African jum-jum drums and one Japanese daiko drum giving the code: "dash–dot–dot–dot–dash." Arnold also employs the now often-utilized wordless choir for moments to represent the awe-inspiring beauty and mystery of the alien motherships that hover over the world's capital cities.

Nicholas Dodd conducting David Arnold's score for Independence Day *at Todd AO Scoring Stage. Note: Jo Ann Kane (music librarian) on the left and the late Patti Zimmitti (orchestra contractor) on extreme right can be seen in the foreground, at the table in the right-hand bottom corner. Courtesy of David Ewart, Recording Musicians Association.*

7. *Film Score Monthly*, July 1996.
8. *Film Score Monthly*.

Nicholas Dodd, the integral person in Arnold's orchestral scores, has done another outstanding job orchestrating the music and conducting the scoring sessions, which were held at Sony Scoring Stage in Culver City, Todd AO in Studio City, and Signet Sound Studios in West Hollywood. When Arnold writes a score, he has a close working relationship with Nicholas Dodd. Instead of giving Dodd a detailed sketch, when the time pressure is on, Arnold can give him a very bare sketch. Dodd will know what to do with it to complete Arnold's wishes. Arnold stated that if he were working with a different orchestrator, he would have to be much more detailed in his sketches.

Dragonheart

Mention of the score from the medieval adventure *Dragonheart* (1996) by Randy Edelman is included here for two reasons: One, it is a fine score. Two, it has become one of the *more often-used themes for trailers of coming attractions in recent years.* Anyone who watches a lot of movies has heard the main theme from *Dragonheart* used in such a manner.

Women Enter the Ranks of the Industry
Emma: Rachel Portman

The film music industry had been dominated by men from its earliest years. For sixty-nine years, women had never gained recognition by being awarded the Oscar. In 1997, things changed when the *British composer Rachel Portman was awarded the Academy Award for best score in the original musical or comedy score category for her 1996 film score for the movie* Emma.

Rachel Portman, first woman to ever win the Oscar (for Emma*—1996) in the original musical or comedy score category. Courtesy of Blue Focus.*

Portman does not think of herself as a woman film composer, just a film composer. She has a distinctive style, and likes to employ a lot of solo clarinet, soprano saxophone, and strings in her scores. Because she insists on capturing every orchestral nuance in her scores and because orchestral color and texture fascinate her, she prefers to do her own orchestrations. Her scores are filled with enchanting and wistful melodies, at times somewhat bittersweet, never entirely happy or entirely sad. She loves to write music for a visual medium. Her abilities to capture the feelings and hidden thoughts of the characters on screen through her intimate, almost chamber music-like sounds, are one of her greatest talents. Her underscore for the proposal scene from *Emma* needs to be seen by anyone doubting the immense power of subtle nuance in her music.

Portman has a strict composing routine set up for herself, usually working from 7 in the morning to 5 in the afternoon. She composes at the piano, watching parts of the film over and over again, until ideas come to her. She says about communicating with directors, "Tell me what you want to feel over this piece of film, and I can do the rest. A big percentage of this job is the psychology of people, getting to know what they really want."[9]

Emma is based on the Jane Austen novel, and requires a delicate and subtle score for the "rare qualities of insight, wit, and gentle empathy" as well as the "unspoken interplay between characters, the misunderstandings, the jealousies and deceits."[10] The score was conducted by David Snell, with outstanding solo work on clarinet by Nick Bucknall, harp solos by Hugh Webb, and flute by Linda Coffin. The score was recorded at Air Lyndhurst Recording Studios in England.

Anne Dudley. Courtesy of the Tony Thomas Collection.

Anne Dudley: Second Woman to Win Oscar

On March 23, 1998, the Academy Award for best musical or comedy score went to Anne Dudley for her 1997 score for *The Full Monty. Anne Dudley was the second woman to win the Oscar for film music composing.*

Women Music Contractors

Women are starting to make their mark in a previously male dominated industry. The top music contractor working for Hollywood-scored motion pictures is Sandy De Crescent. Even the studio orchestras are about one-third women, and this figure continues to change in favor of women. It has been difficult for women until recently. Back when Sandy De Crescent started in the business, it was unheard of for a woman to be the contractor of a major studio. Her start in the business is comparable to a Hollywood script for a movie. After attending UCLA for two years, she applied for a job at the MCA Talent Agency in Beverly Hills without any real job skills. She knew that she had good people skills and good organizational skills. She was assigned to Bobby Helfer, music agent for people such as Johnny (John) Williams, Elmer Bernstein, Johnny Green, and Bernard Herrmann. He was looking for an older woman for the job, not a nineteen-year-old! She came into his office and at first he was rather rude. He thought that it was ridiculous to have such a young woman for the job. Sandy De Crescent was able to talk him into giving her one month. She had said, "Give me one month to handle this office and you'll wonder how you ever lived without me." She got the job and

Sandy De Crescent, one of Hollywood's busiest music contractors. From the author's collection.

9. *Music from the Movies*, summer 1994.
10. *Film Music Good CD Guide*, 2nd ed., 1997, p. 167.

eventually their offices were moved to Universal Studios. It was here that they joined forces with Stanley Wilson. Both Wilson and Helfer were coheads of the music department at Universal. "At that time, they had composers under contract who did all of the shows. Elmer Bernstein was doing *Riverboat,* John Williams was working on *Bachelor Father,* an anthology series was Jerry Goldsmith's assignment, and Henry Mancini was scoring *Peter Gunn*. There were also Morty Stevens and Jack Marshall. A little bit later came Lalo Schifrin and Dave Grusin. It was a wonderful, wonderful time. This was a proving ground that the young composers today don't have. It will never happen again," according to De Crescent.

After the untimely death of Helfer, De Crescent was asked to assume the position of contractor. No woman had ever been a contractor for a major studio before. This was totally unacceptable to the "old guard." She said it was very tough. With the moral support of her husband Ron, and sheer determination, she persevered. What she ended up with was being in charge of eighteen television shows every week! Not one of them was a half-hour show. They were either sixty or ninety minutes long.

Twelve years ago she decided to leave Universal and form her own company called Sabron. "I had no clients. It was frightening. Universal had been my home since I was a young girl." This happened during a writers' strike. Everything shut down for about six months. Then Dave Grusin called and said that he had heard that she had gone independent. He wanted her to contract the musicians for his next movie. It wasn't long before Jerry Goldsmith called for the same need. Next came John Williams, which was the turning point in her career. The film was *Born on the Fourth of July* (1989). Williams had recorded many of his previous scores in London and De Crescent saw an opportunity to show him the capabilities of the Los Angeles musicians at that time. He said, "Okay, Let's go for it!" She got off the phone and shook for ten minutes. She thought, "Lord, what have I gotten myself into?" She went through three days of agonizing. She hired Stuart Canin, former concertmaster of the San Francisco Symphony, to be John Williams's concertmaster.

Based on her expertise and word of mouth, she assembled about three hundred names of some of the finest musicians in the business. Today, this number has grown to about seven hundred. From that point, her business grew and now she has about forty film composers as her clients and she contracts anywhere from fifty-five to seventy films a year. Sandy De Crescent's biggest goal is to make the studio musician feel more appreciated. These are some of the finest musicians in the world and they were not always given the recognition that they deserved. *She has brought about change. Now John Williams prefers recording in Los Angeles*. Sandy De Crescent has also worked to keep other scoring jobs in Los Angeles since some producers prefer to record with nonunion orchestras in places such as Seattle or Utah, for economic reasons. De Crescent feels that with the massive sales of the *Titanic* soundtrack, the future for soundtracks looks very promising. *Titanic* has sold millions of copies, exposing many people to the sound of acoustic (symphonic) instruments for their first time. De Crescent said that she used to be involved in contracting for eight to ten soundtracks per year.

Other Women Composers

Anne Ronell

The *first woman to conduct a soundtrack scoring session was Ann Ronell* (born 1910). She was educated at Radcliffe and was a student of composers such as Walter Piston and George Gershwin. Her early career found her composing songs ("Willow Weep for Me," 1932) that gained her an invitation to Hollywood, where she wrote various musicals and shows. She was the *first woman to be nominated for the Academy*

Award for best Score for her work with Louis Applebaum on the movie *The Story of G.I. Joe*. They lost to Rozsa's *Spellbound* score in 1945.

Elisabeth Luytens

Elisabeth Luytens was born in London, England, on July 9, 1906, and died there on April 14, 1983. All of her film credits were for British productions, except her last film, which was for a Dutch company. Paramount Pictures and 20th Century Fox helped to distribute some of her works, the titles of which ranged from *The Earth Dies Screaming* to *Dr. Terror's House of Horrors*. Records show that she was active as a film composer from 1947 to 1975, although her output was limited to only fifteen film scores.

Angela Morley

Angela Morley (1924–) has received three Emmy Awards, two Oscar nominations, and has composed over seventy-five scores for television and film. Born in Leeds, England, she worked for several years in bands and studio orchestras in London. At the age of twenty-six, she gave up playing for a career as an arranger, composer, and conductor. She started composing for films at the age of twenty-nine and was appointed musical director of Philips Records (London) the same year. In addition to her own works, she has arranged or orchestrated for film composers such as John Williams, Johnny Mandel, David Raksin, Miklos Rozsa, Alex North, Bill Conti, and Andre Previn.

Debbie Wiseman

Debbie Wiseman (1963–) was also born in England and shows a promising career ahead of her, judging by her screen credits. With only a handful of movie scores to her credit, she has already been nominated for an Oscar with her first feature film score for *Tom and Viv* (1994). Her second film score for the movie *Haunted* (1995) is quite a showcase for her talents. Although she seems quite comfortable using a variety of styles in this score, it is her hauntingly beautiful piano themes for two of the movie's characters (Juliet and Christina) that provide us with a glimpse of her talent. Until her entry into film score writing, she worked exclusively in scoring for television. In 1993, Wiseman won the TV Theme Music of the Year Award for *The Good Guys*. Her score for the 1997 film *Wilde*, based on the life of Oscar Wilde, is another testimony of her abilities to give a sensitive musical portrayal of the characters within a movie. The score features a beautifully haunting main-title theme.

Most contemporary women film composers have had a formal education in music at the college level, although few have had actual training in composing music for films. For example, Nicky Holland (films include *The Great Outdoors* and *She's Having a Baby*) has a bachelor's degree in music, but no formal training in film music. The electronic music specialist Suzanne Ciani (films include *The Incredible Shrinking Woman* and *Mother Teresa* [film documentary]) has a master's degree in composition from the University of California at Berkeley and partly learned the craft of film music from teaching electronics to film composers. Nan Schwartz-Mishkin, a five-time Emmy nominee, began in college as a piano major, then switched to radio and television production, which eventually brought her back to music. When she was first starting her career as a composer, she met an agent who met with her to hear her demo tape. He not only talked through the entire tape, he told her that the tape was too long and that she should go home, get married, and raise babies! Later, as her career began to take off, her new agent sent her demo tape to a potential employer and got very positive responses about her music, but had received a note with the question, "Can't you send me a man?" *She became the first female to be a regular composer/ conductor for a weekly television series.* Anne Dudley was born on May 7, 1956, in Chatham, Kent, England. She won the Academy Award for her *The Full Monty* (1997) score in the best original musical or comedy score category at the 1998 Academy Awards. Dudley has both a bachelor's and master's degree in music and comments that "film music studies do not really exist in the U.K."[11] where she obtained her degrees.

Lesley Barber

Lesley Barber is a Canadian film composer. Her score for *Mansfield Park* (1999) made an effective contribution to this film. Her first scores were for the films *When Night Is Falling* (1995) and *Turning April* in 1996.

Shirley Walker

Shirley Walker (born on April 10, 1945, in Napa, California), who has worked on many feature films, is a pianist with no formal training. She basically "learned on-the-job." She feels that a formal education gives the future film composer only about one-quarter of what he or she might need to survive. The remaining factors include knowing the "politics" and the "unwritten rules of behavior" required in the business. She started her career in high school when she was a piano soloist with the San Francisco Symphony. Her first big break was working as a synthesist on the score for Francis Ford Coppola's classic film *Apocalyse Now* (1979). Walker "paid her dues" in the 1980s working as a conductor of other film composers' music as well as "ghost writing" for some composers. She stated that by working on low-budget films, she was able to build self-confidence in herself as a composer for the times it really counted later in her career, as the assignments became more big-time.

Most women composers have "broken into the business" the same way that most men do, by obtaining work through an acquaintance or a professional contact. It's not necessarily *what* you know, it's *who* you know that can be important for success. Many times an aspiring film composer might study or apprentice with an active composer. If they are lucky, they might get the possibility of either arranging or ghostwriting for the composer. If the timing is just right, there will usually be at least one occasion when the film composer will have too many projects going on at once, and will give the overload out to his or her students. This is how Nan Schwartz-Mishkin got into television composing. Shirley Walker got her start doing industrial films, but now enjoys a move into the mainstream film world. She composes, orchestrates for other composers, and conducts (her most famous conducting assignment to date was conducting Danny Elfman's music for the 1989 movie *Batman*).Walker won a Daytime Emmy Award as musical director on the acclaimed animated *Batman* series. Some of her nominations include a CableACE nod for the Blair Brown film *Majority Rule*, a Prime Time Emmy nomination for the Fox series *Space: Above and Beyond,* and two Annie nominations; one for the *Superman* main title theme and for her original score for HBO's *Spawn* series. Her advice is: "being a film composer has very little to do with writing music; being a film composer is getting yourself hired to do the job."[12] Preferred film-scoring assignments are ranked in the minds of the composers with small documentaries being the least esteemed and feature films the most prized. The women film composers of today seem to have as much drive, ambition, and talent as men. They all realize that they will have to work harder than their male counterparts to achieve the same ends.[13] Shirley Walker has maintained her

11. *The Musical Woman,* Vol. 3, 1986–1990, article by Leslie N. Anderson (New York: Greenwood Press, 1993).
12. *The Musical Woman.*
13. *The Musical Woman.*

status as one of today's most respected members of the composing community and is widely credited as a pioneer for women composers in the film industry.

Titanic

It's been called "The Gone with the Wind of our Generation." It's currently (as of 2003) the blockbuster movie of all time. The film is James Cameron's mighty epic, *Titanic* (1997). Before the success of *Titanic,* that word was synonymous with doom, disaster, or bad luck. Now we think of the huge size of the original ship and the unsinkable quality it originally boasted to the public. These two original descriptions can once again be applied, but this time to the huge, unsinkable movie, not the ship. The *Titanic* was the biggest, most luxurious ship of her day. Her size is legendary; as tall as an eleven-story building and four city blocks long. She set sail on her maiden voyage on April 10, 1912, carrying 1,316 passengers and 891 crewmembers. Roughly two hours and forty minutes after it had collided with an iceberg on its fifth night out, this giant "titan" of the sea, deemed unsinkable, was swallowed up by sea. April 14 would be the last full day that 1,502 passengers and crew would ever spend here on earth. That night, the ship sank before the light of day on April 15. The forty-three-year-old Canadian-born director James Cameron has

A scene from the megahit Titanic *(1997). Courtesy of Photofest.*

stated that "first and above all [*Titanic* is] a love story."[14] This is a movie that has something for everybody. It's a costume drama with action, special effects, a love story, with humor and tragedy thrown in. Cameron went on to state that "the passion, the intimacy and the heartbreak one feels in watching a love story on film are created by the actors . . . of course, the music is the most important addition to the actor's work for increasing the emotional impact of the film."[15] James Horner's score was everything that Cameron had hoped for. This music "deftly leaps from intimacy to grandeur, from joy to heart-wrenching sadness and across the full emotional spectrum of the film while maintaining a stylistic and thematic unity. James [Horner] has walked the tightrope by using synthesizer, vocals and full orchestra to create a timeless sound which tells us that these people were not so very different from us."[16] Horner's score bridges "the gap of time . . . making these people seem so alive, so vibrant, so real that the dreaded event, when it finally comes, is terrifying in its authenticity. And most importantly, he has made us one with Jack and Rose, feeling the beat of their hearts as they experience the kind of love we all dream about, bur seldom find."[17] The score was recorded at Todd-AO Scoring Stage in Studio City, California. Cameron brought James Horner on the assignment in February 1997, with about two more months of filming to go before completion. The opening date was originally planned to be July 4, but it was postponed to December 19 to coincide with the holiday season. Horner used a ninety-two-piece orchestra plus vocals, synth sounds, and a few ethnic instruments. The assembly cut for *Titanic* was thirty-six hours long. The theatrical version was cut down to about three and one-quarter hours. Horner tried to give the score a timeless quality, to create a romantic mood, but without making it a period piece. He used synthesizer and voice for almost 75 percent of the score, while the rest is full orchestra.

Horner's concept of "synth" sounds is that of "organic colors" that he can manipulate, not "synthetic sounds" as most people might expect from an electronic synthesizer. He would experiment with different colors and then would "paint" the given scene with these "synth colors," writing the orchestra parts on top after this. The haunting, wordless vocals heard in this score were sung by Norwegian singing star Sissel Kyrkjebo. Horner had heard a CD that she had made. Her "Enya-like" style was the color that he was searching for. Horner equated her voice as the "instrument" he needed to complete his concept of this score. We hear her wordless "oohs and ahhs" at the very beginning of the film singing what we later realize is the "Rose Theme." There are 138 minutes' worth of music in this score, excluding the source music of the White Star Line five-piece combo and Gaelic Storm, the "Irish" group that performed the dance music down in the third-class steerage. Horner wrote four basic themes (leitmotifs). There's one for the ship in happier times, separate themes for Jack and Rose, and finally a love theme to represent their love for one another. He designed these themes so that they can be played separately or played simultaneously and interwoven around each other.

To look briefly at the use of these themes in this very popular film, we can see how Horner's approach helps to captivate his audience. The haunting solo vocal that we hear right at the onset of the movie is the "Rose theme." Rose, as we later learn, is a young lady (played by Kate Winslet) who, although engaged to another man who was heir to a wealthy Pittsburgh steel fortune, falls head over heels for Jack (played by Leonardo DiCaprio). The problem here is that Jack and Rose come from two totally different social classes. Rose was a high socialite, Jack was a third-class passenger and a common laborer. It was considered taboo for them to associate. About twenty minutes into the film, Horner provides us with the "Titanic theme," as we see the "Ship of Dreams" docked in the harbor, waiting for its ill-fated passengers to board. This is the theme that we associate with the *Titanic* in happier times. Actually, if you listen carefully, Horner had already provided glimpses of this theme on two earlier occasions within the first twenty minutes of the film. This theme returns about ten minutes later when Jack utters the now-famous line "I'm the king of the world!" A hint of the love theme is heard when

14. *Titanic* CD liner notes, 1997, Sony Classics.
15. *Titanic* CD notes.
16. *Titanic* CD notes.
17. *Titanic* CD notes.

Jack first lays eyes on Rose about thirty-five minutes into the film. He seems almost paralyzed by her beauty as he sits mesmerized with one of his third-class buddies on the deck below Rose. We hear a portion of the "Rose theme" a minute later as Rose attempts suicide by climbing over the railing of the mighty vessel, hanging on to the ship's stern. About eighty minutes into the film, we finally hear the love theme after a short introduction composed of a fragment of the "Rose theme." This is sung without words. It has a timeless, haunting quality. This occurs when Rose meets Jack up on the deck and says, "Hello, Jack. I changed my mind." The instrument that we hear in this introduction is a **penny-whistle**, a Celtic instrument that is used to create the right ambience, along with this haunting emotionalism. As Jack sketches Rose, wearing only *Le coeur de la mer* (the Heart of the Ocean, giant diamond necklace), and nothing else, we hear a piano rendition of the love theme in its entirety. Horner provides the love theme for us several minutes later, this time when the two make love in a Renault automobile down in the hold of the ship. This time it is played on the synthesizer to continue its haunting quality, yet with a different color. About 137 minutes into the picture, as Rose is being lowered into a lifeboat as the mighty ship is sinking, we hear a reprise of the "Rose theme" that leads into the love theme. As Rose lunges forward to come back on board the ship to join Jack, Horner superimposes the two themes. Roughly 174 minutes into the film, as Jack lays frozen in the water clinging on to the debris ridden by Rose, we hear the haunting "Rose theme" return to tear us apart emotionally. In the final moments of the film, we hear the "Rose theme" and the love theme intertwined together one final time during Rose's dream sequence (or perhaps she died and saw this?—James Cameron says, "You decide."), as Rose is being reunited with Jack on the ship's grand staircase.

"Love theme" from Titanic

The "Rose theme" from Titanic

composer for whom he worked. He moved to Hollywood in 1955 and he worked in advertising, writing jingles for radio and television ads as well as orchestrating, arranging, and composing for movies and television. One of his best-known jingles for a product is for "Rice-a-Roni . . . the San Francisco Treat!" Here is a partial list of some of the films and television programs on which he worked as an orchestrator:

Television
Charlie's Angels
Dynasty
Falcon Crest
Starsky and Hutch
The Love Boat
Fantasy Island
McMillan and Wife
North and South miniseries
Lonesome Dove miniseries
Amerika miniseries

Films
How the West Was Won
Dances with Wolves
Conan the Barbarian
The Hunt for Red October
Free Willy
The Color Purple
The Last of the Mohicans
Kindergarten Cop
Beastmaster
Quigley Down Under
Ruby Cairo
Indecent Proposal
The Specialist
Aliens
Glory
Starship Troopers
Straw Dogs
The Wild Bunch
The Gambler
Krull
Willow
Ghostbusters 2
Dragon: The Bruce Lee Story

In an interesting human-interest story, McRitchie was a stutterer. To illustrate his sense of humor, his California license plate read: "G-G-G-Greig."

Meet Joe Black

The composer Thomas Newman continued to showcase his distinctive style in a very long remake (180 minutes) of the 1934 film *Death Takes a Holiday* for the 1998 movie *Meet Joe Black*. The story has a rather interesting premise. When "Death" (Joe Black, played by Brad Pitt) is making his rounds collecting people whose time on earth has come to an end, he makes a detour. He takes human form and falls in love with the daughter of his next victim. Anthony Hopkins (Bill) stars in this rather controversial remake.

Newman feels that film music is of secondary importance. "It's there to help, it's not there to be listened to, unfortunately." Newman has become a master of shadings and sound design for setting the correct mood or ambience of a given scene. His father Alfred died when Thomas was fourteen years old. A year or two later, Thomas began to take up composing. His recognizable style is slowly emerging through his film scores. As we saw in our discussion of his score for *The Shawshank Redemption*,

Newman's style is composed of long sustained chords or clusters of sounds, surrounded by occasional muted chords on the piano. In addition to this, he might feature a recurring theme that could go through several sets of variations.

The score for *Meet Joe Black* has a certain English flavor of Ralph Vaughan Williams (1872–1958) with its rich, dark modal sonorities for the strings. (The word modal refers to music being based on a mode rather than the conventional major or minor scale. This reference usually applies to music that used church modes of the Middle Ages or the Renaissance period.) In *Meet Joe Black,* Newman has written a beautiful love theme that fills the long sequence starting by the indoor swimming pool as Bill's daughter makes love to "Death" for the first time. The musical cue lasts nearly four minutes and is the only thing we hear. About two hours and forty-four minutes into the movie, when Bill's daughter asks him to go down to the river to watch the fireworks in honor of his sixty-fifth birthday, he says, "You go ahead honey. I'll soon catch my breath." At this point, a gradual buildup in the music starts that helps the movie reach its emotional climax when Bill realizes his time has come. He says, "It's hard to let go." Newman toys with our emotions with his powerful dramatic underscoring to the very end of the picture. Thomas Newman used his usual orchestrator, Thomas Pasatieri, to provide the necessary orchestrations for this score, which was recorded at both Todd-AO and Paramount Scoring stages.

Elizabeth

The Indian director Shekhar Kapur brought a splendid look at Queen Elizabeth I of England to the screen in 1998. The story traces the rise of this young Elizabeth Tudor to Queen of England in 1558 and her reign of intrigue and betrayal. David Hirschfielder made an impressive debut as a film composer of considerable breadth in writing this complex score. Hirschfielder captures the essence of the sixteenth century with idiomatic writing complete with a Renaissance feel. The Coronation scene is a particularly good example of this style of sonority. Also borrowed as source music are two pieces by sixteenth-century composer Tyman (also spelled "Tielman") Susato (c. 1500–c. 1561–4). We hear his *Rondes I* and *VII.* Hirschfielder's score turns dark and sinister to accompany the creepy shadowy cinematography of Remi Adefarasin. The composer and Ric Formosa were responsible for the orchestrations. The David Hobson Chorale and the Australian Boys Choir provided the vocals. The score was recorded in Melbourne, Australia, at Allan Eaton Studio and Deep Red Studios. The extremely emotional *Nimrod* movement from Edward Elgar's (1857–1934) *Enigma Variations* (1889) is used in the film for a dramatic impact during the conspirators sequence toward the film's end, as is the *Requiem Introitus* from Mozart's *Requiem.* Cate Blanchett won the Golden Globe Award for Best Actress for her portrayal as the famous "Virgin Queen." Queen Elizabeth's reign, the Elizabethan Period, was a time of notable triumphs in literature (William Shakespeare rose to prominence during her reign) and war (the defeat of the Spanish Armada). Elizabeth was the daughter of King Henry VIII and Anne Boleyn. The state of Virginia is named after Elizabeth, the "Virgin Queen."

The Mask of Zorro

Following the success of his *Titanic* score, James Horner wrote a smashingly exciting swashbuckling score in the styles of Korngold and Rozsa for *The Mask of Zorro* (1998). This is a score that contains an *El Cid*-like love theme, "a la Rozsa," and some action cues that are reminiscent of Korngold in his heyday. This score was performed by studio musicians in both England at Lyndhurst Hall (London) and at

Todd-AO Scoring Stage in Studio City, California. Horner used two of the world's leading studio musician contractors, Isobel Griffiths in London and Sandy De Crescent in Studio City. To add exotic color, Horner employs the Shakuhachi flute and the sounds of Flamenco dancers. The Zorro leitmotif is a perfectly rendered Spanish-styled flamenco dance form.

Mask of Zorro *theme*

Godzilla

Beginning in the 1990s, audiences became ever more moved by bigger and better special effects for each new release that came out in the theaters. With this came a certain amount of secrecy attached to the postproduction stage of the films. For *Jurassic Park,* Spielberg did not want anyone present at the scoring session in March of 1993 to see the spectacular groundbreaking computer graphics, so he had inserted blank leader in place of the actual footage. For the 1998 film *Godzilla,* the production company made all of the studio musicians sign an agreement not to discuss the film with anyone outside of the scoring sessions so as to keep the aura of mystery surrounding the new look of the Godzilla monster.

The music written for the film seems to work in light of the fact that David Arnold had only three or four weeks to compose one hundred minutes' worth of music. He had to compose at the rate of four or five minutes' worth of usable music per day in order to meet the deadline. The score was written for a large orchestra with chorus. Arnold employs the low brass and horns to provide an ominous descending four-note theme (leitmotif) for the giant monster. This score features some of Arnold's techniques that he used in *Independence Day,* such as a wordless choir, to give the score its jaw-dropping potential when seeing something bigger than life; shifting major and minor chords; large constant pounding drums; and a snappy march tune complete with snare drums, brass, and piccolo.

The Horse Whisperer

John Barry originally was meant to be the composer for Robert Redford's drama *The Horse Whisperer* (1998). Thomas Newman wrote the final score, instead. Newman captures the essence of the story of a teenaged girl injured in a riding accident by using his usual method of combining sustained chords (either in the strings or by electronics) with muted chords in the piano (*his identifiable trademark sound*). We also hear shades of Aaron Copland and a mysterious modal color to the score. Newman also features the prepared guitar (similar to prepared piano), guitar and mandolin, a bowed bass dulcimer, a birdsong, and wind machine. Newman used his usual orchestrator, Thomas Pasatieri.

Mansfield Park

The Canadian composer Lesley Barber was hired to provide a score for this 1999 film adaptation of the Jane Austin novel that "reflected the era but also gave it a contemporary accessibility."[19]This score shows an influence of the **minimalistic style** of composer Michael Nyman, whether intentionally or not. There are many repeated musical figures that have the uncanny ability of sounding both "of the period" and yet somehow of the late twentieth century as well. To give this score a more historical authenticity, Barber used the **glass harmonica** and a **Hurdy Gurdy**. The *glass harmonica* was invented by Benjamin Franklin in 1761. It works on the principle of taking a series of tuned glass bowls pierced in the center that are strung vertically in close position on a wire spindle and rotated by means of a treadle. The glasses were suspended above a trough partly filled with water. In 1784, attempts to attach this to a keyboard were finally successful. This instrument became known as a "keyed harmonica." Wolfgang Amadeus Mozart composed several works for the glass harmonica, as did many of his contemporaries. It finally went out of fashion in the nineteenth century. The *Hurdy Gurdy* is an instrument of medieval origin that looks like a large fiddle with a hand crank down at its bottom. The Hurdy Gurdy was held across the lap and had its crank on the left side. On top of this were a series of keys that when depressed with the right hand would make contact with the rotating interior wheel that set all of the strings in vibration. The Hurdy Gurdy is known today as a folk instrument from France to Hungary, although it was very popular for a time by the court over the years. Its popularity was cut short by the French Revolution, but revived again in the nineteenth century. Lesley Barber's film composing credits started in 1995 with the film *When Night Is Falling*. She is a very promising composer and should see a successful career as a film composer.

The Red Violin

The New York–based composer John Corigliano won his first Oscar (best original score) for his fine score for *The Red Violin* (1998). The film was not on the same high level as this interesting score. Corigliano knew that he was to compose some music before the shooting was to start so that the characters in the film would have something to play when on camera. He created a concert piece for solo violin and orchestra from a "singable" theme first heard by the violin master's wife, Anna. As she hums this theme ("Anna's theme"), it eventually mutates into the theme played by solo violin. Underneath this haunting violin melody is a seven-chord **chaconne**. (A chaconne is a variation form in which there is usually a repeated harmonic progression.) The score undergoes several variations of musical styles. From purely classical-sounding music to clashing dissonances of the late twentieth century, Corigliano masterfully journeys through a maze of intricate textures. In an interesting twist of plans, the filming of the movie kept being pushed back so that instead of Corigliano writing all of the underscoring *after* the film was shot, the film's underscore drew much of its inspiration from the already completed concert piece. *Corigliano did all of his own orchestrations on this score*. The majority of the score was recorded at the famous Abbey Road Studios in London, with the great violin virtuoso Joshua Bell providing the violin solos for the film. The plot of the film spans three hundred years in the life of a famous violin that derives its reddish color from the mixture of blood mixed into its finish. The viewer watches as the violin travels from Austria to England to China and Canada, leaving both good and evil in its wake.

19. Quote from *Film Score Monthly*, Vol. 5, No. 1.

Shakespeare in Love

Stephen Warbeck won an Academy Award (Best Original Musical/ Comedy Score) for his work on the hit film *Shakespeare in Love* (1998). This is the story of Shakespeare and his dilemma with "writer's block" and how he manages to handle it. The outcome is a clever telling of the origin of the first performance of his *Romeo and Juliet.* The movie has an excellent screenplay with outstanding actors. Warbeck's score contains a constant, driving broken bass line that acts to both propel the action and sound somewhat historically accurate in a distorted kind of way. The score does contain some period instruments, such as the recorder. The source music that we hear about twenty-eight minutes into the film when Will Shakespeare first lays his eyes on Lady Viola (played by Gwyneth Paltrow in her Academy Award–winning performance) features a lute, tambourine, and the recorder, all of which were used during the Renaissance period. The score was recorded in London at the famous CTS Studios, home of many of the James Bond scores.

The Cider House Rules

Rachel Portman wrote a beautiful main theme in her usual recognizable "music-boxlike style" complete with a singing melody accompanied by a broken bass line for the award-winning drama based on John Irving's bestselling American classic *The Cider House Rules* (1999).

This is a story about a young man named Homer who is groomed to take over for his mentor, Dr. Larch, when he leaves the post as head doctor at St. Cloud's Orphanage in rural Maine. Homer has other ideas, as he leaves the orphanage and explores the world on his own, finding love and the lessons of life. At the death of Dr. Larch, when Homer finally returns to the orphanage, we hear the main theme gush out over the speakers for a great feeling of emotional homecoming.

This score was nominated for best score but did not win. Portman did many of her own orchestrations with the aid of Jeff Atmajian. The score was recorded in London and conducted by David Snell, at the CTS Studios. Although Rachel Portman is capable of composing for different genres of films, it would appear that she specializes in the touching dramas that move people emotionally as opposed to horror movies or science fiction extravaganzas. Her more recent films, *The Legend of Bagger Vance* (2000) and *Chocolat* (2000), continue in this tradition and one would expect her future scoring assignments to follow a similar pattern.

The Mummy

Although *The Mummy* (1999) received mixed reviews, it had a very exciting score by Jerry Goldsmith, who is amazing in his ability to capture the complete essence of a film with one or sometimes two themes. The film opens with an exotic flute solo that eventually evolves into a powerful, bold French horn theme that paints the mysterious quality of the story that is about to unfold by hovering around the interval of an augmented second. During this opening, we can hear the addition of a wordless choir to help provide this mysterious atmosphere. The main theme of the film is then played by the English horn and handed to the strings. During the caravan in the desert, Goldsmith also adds the color of a wordless choir. The great composer takes the main theme through a very exciting set of variations during the camel race sequence. In this score, the French horn section represents the great fierceness of Imhotep by proclaiming a bold masculine quality. As we progress into the story we begin to realize that the main theme is also the love theme. Goldsmith's score uses a large percussion section, several ethnic instruments for ancient Egyptian ambience, a wordless choir, "synth" sounds and colors, and a large French horn section. For the attacking flesh-eating scarab beetles, he characterizes their frightfulness by utilizing atonal string passages that are composed of two "choirs" of instruments that move in *contrary* motion to one another, creating a chilling effect.

Stephen Sommers did a fine job of directing a dashing adventure loosely based on the 1932 Boris Karloff film of the same name. Brendan Fraser stars as an American adventurer who travels to the ancient ruined Egyptian city of the dead known as Hamunaptra. There, along with the beautiful but clumsy British librarian Evelyn (Rachel Weisz) and her Egyptologist brother Jonathan (John Hannah), the trio accidentally set off a series of events that unleashes the cursed mummified priest Imhotep (Arnold Vosloo). Imhotep wants to use Evelyn to resurrect his dead girlfriend (seen in the opening moments of the movie). It has been said by many who saw the film that they wish more films could be made like this, the way films used to be made back in Hollywood's heyday. Goldsmith's score for this film is a reminder of his consistently high level of artistry. It's no wonder that he is so highly revered by his colleagues. It is too bad that the Academy of Motion Picture Arts and Sciences hasn't seen fit to recognize his impressive output with more than just one Oscar (*The Omen* in 1976). With his distinguished career unquestionably secure in the history books about film composers, his great contributions to film scoring set a zenith that may be equaled by only a very few other mortals. The score was recorded in London, composed and conducted by Jerry Goldsmith, and orchestrated by his old friend Alexander Courage. The orchestral contractor was Isobel Griffiths.

The Matrix

The Wachowski brothers (Andy and Larry) wrote and directed *The Matrix,* one of the hit movies of 1999. This film is a clever twist on reality, in which it would appear that everything around our main character is just a computer-generated illusion, manufactured by machines that use humans as the electrical energy source. Because of its futuristic concepts, Don Davis provided a score that contains the combinations of all of the compositional techniques utilized by concert hall composers of the twentieth century. Because the audience is seeing things that it had never seen before in a movie, Davis thought that it would be novel and appropriate to compose in this postmodernistic style. In the twentieth century, film composers started by writing primarily for the symphony orchestra. As developments in electronic instruments and the discovery of new sounds from ethnic instruments and new "instruments" such as *rub rods* began to surface, film composers started cross-fertilizing all of these components for a richer source of sounds and effects. The layering of chord clusters, the use of electronics, computers, midi, and the like all comprise this **postmodern style**. Davis helps to accent certain parts of the story by building up to a certain revelation with music, to suddenly drop out to silence for that effective impact as studied in Chapter One of this book. We also hear dissonant clusters of texture music, repetitive minimalism, pounding percussion, **polytonality**, **polyrhythmic sections**, electronics, wordless choral passages, driving **techno music**, prepared piano, and numerous orchestral shadings provided by a ninety-piece orchestra. This score practically has it all!

As is more the norm with many of today's films and young film composers, Don Davis did his own **mockup temp track** for the test screenings. Davis had apparently turned down an orchestrating project to work with Elton John on the film *The Muse*. Davis got his start in the business as an orchestrator for some of the top film composers in the business.

Davis spoke to Larry and Andy Wachowski about two years before the film was completed and was given a script by the two writer/filmmakers. Because the film was shot in Australia, Davis was not able to keep in close touch in the daily and weekly progress of the film. Davis did not begin to conceptualize his score until after he received a rough cut of the film. This gave him time to formulate some ideas in his own mind before there would be any more communication from the Wachowski brothers. Davis had a couple weeks to think about the possible directions he might take to present the best possible score for this innovative film. On the brothers' return to the United States, there was a spotting session with Davis. Unfortunately, this version of the film had changed significantly from the rough cut sent to Davis. After several more meetings, Davis proceeded to write the temp score (which would evolve into the final score). The brothers had wanted a romantic underscore when Trinity kisses Neo and he comes back to life. Judging from comments made by audience members at the test screenings, Davis and the Wachowski brothers agreed that the music was too melodic and had to be reformulated to fit the modernistic approach used throughout the film. The biggest change made to the score after the test screenings was to make it sound less romantic toward the end of the film. In addition to this, about ten minutes' worth of film was trimmed from various scenes, although not cutting out any entire scene. All original scenes remained intact, except from the minute trimming. This, of course, meant that Davis had to redo his score to fit the new timings.

Davis had about ten weeks to work on this one hundred-minute score. He worked at the rate of about four minutes of usable music a day. After he had done the synthesizer version of the score, he had to orchestrate that music for the ninety-piece orchestra. He did three and one-half minutes of orchestrating per day. After the score was completed, Davis conducted the scoring sessions in Los Angeles at the Newman Scoring Stage (named after Alfred Newman) located at 20th Century Fox studios. This was over a seven-day timeframe spread out from February 8 to February 23, doing two sessions per day (six hours per day). Once this was completed, Davis went to Salt Lake City, Utah, and recorded the atmospheric wordless choir sounds with forty members of the Mormon Tabernacle Choir.

The electronics in the score were reserved for many of the percussive big slams, such as the pile driver sounds that help to accent certain scenes. Davis also used electronics for certain ambient texture colorings such as cymbal scrapes. These were essentially recorded samples of the real thing that he processed electronically. Davis does not like to double string lines with a synthesizer as many other film composers have a tendency to do. So what you hear are real violins, not a homogenization of the two.

The casual viewer of this rather complex and innovative film may not initially see all that is contained within all of the inner workings captured by Davis and his score. After all, films are usually made for entertainment purposes, not as intellectual exercises. What Davis brought to the film subliminally is clever and also functional to an end. As Davis states, "The theme of this film is about the discovery of what reality is all about, what it can be, or even might be. That's the reason why reflection is so important in this picture. This thing that we all consider to be real is really not real." It's like looking in a mirror. What you are looking at is a *reflection* of the real thing, *not* the thing itself. Davis wanted to illustrate this "reflective" quality or imagery by using orchestral echoes from one instrumental family to another. This **antiphonal effect** dates back to the medieval period, and is represented by different sections of the orchestra imitating one another at varying speeds in order to support the film's heavy use of reflective imagery. What we hear in the score are sections where the first violins play a musical motif that is "echoed" by the second violins a moment later. Davis also employed a **polytonal dialogue** (the simultaneous use of two or more different tonal centers, that is, sounding a C Major chord along with a D Major chord) between the trumpet section and the horn section. The trumpets play one chord loudly, then as they diminish in volume, the horns crescendo (get louder). This overlapping of tonalities symbolically pits one reality against another.

DON DAVIS

American-born composer (Anaheim, California) Born: 1958

Don Davis. Courtesy of Chasen & Company.

In high school, he took arranging and theory classes at Fullerton College in the evenings.

He tried writing for big bands in high school.

He studied composition at UCLA.

He met Joe Harnell and did some orchestrations for him for the television shows *The Incredible Hulk* and the miniseries "V."

Mark Snow allowed him to score several episodes of the television show *Hart to Hart*.

His formal training was with Henri Lazarof. He claims to have learned a lot through attending concerts, watching films, and listening to other composers' film scores.

He was an orchestrator for composers such as Bruce Broughton, Michael Kamen, James Horner, and Randy Newman.

He states that "nobody should hesitate to become an orchestrator for it's a good living."

He also states that "it's harder to make the transition from television composer to feature film composer than it is to make the transition from orchestrator to film composer."

He continues to do his own orchestrations.

His films include *Hyperspace* (1986), *Bound* (1996), and *The House on Haunted Hill* (1999).

His television credits include *Beauty and the Beast* and *Seaquest DSV, NBC's House of Frankenstein,* and *Star Trek*.

He has garnered eight Emmy Award nominations and two wins.

He was orchestrator on movies such as *Robin Hood: Prince of Thieves, Die Hard II, The Last Action Hero, Toy Story, The Pelican Brief, Clear and Present Danger, Legends of the Fall,* and the blockbuster *Titanic*.

The Sixth Sense

James Newton Howard's score for *The Sixth Sense* (1999) proved to be a great asset to this very popular film from 1999. It became one of the top ten grossing films of all time. This has been deemed by some of the people in the industry to be among Howard's best scores. The score is a combination of conventional orchestral sounds along with an eclectic peppering of texture music, solo piano, electronics, a wordless choir, and woodwind and brass solos. Some of the electronics give the illusion of Jerry Goldsmith's *Poltergeist* rub rods along with high **harmonics** in the upper strings. (On a stringed instrument such as a violin, a harmonic can be achieved by touching the string very lightly at a specific point that will produce a tone with a cold, silvery quality.) Parts of the score show an influence of Bernard Herrmann. M. Night Shyamalan, the director of the movie, wanted Howard to represent the sixth sense as a living entity that was "morphing" from room to room throughout the house. According to the director, the sound of people breathing into a microphone also played a key role in establishing an eerie background. This helped to create the feeling that even though a room is supposed to be empty, the sounds of these multiple "breaths" created a scary ambience. When Cole Sear, the little boy in the story who says that he sees dead people reveals this fact, Howard brought in a chorus of many people who would cry, groan, or scream very softly on the soundtrack to represent the scope of the many people who had died and gone before us. This was done so softly that it is impossible to discern any one voice that is actually saying anything. Producer Frank Marshall felt that the music and the sound effects in *The Sixth Sense* were also characters. These two important aspects of the film (music and sound effects) helped to create a more emotional and spiritual quality in this movie.

JAMES NEWTON HOWARD

American-born composer (Los Angeles, California) Born: June 9, 1951

James Newton Howard. Courtesy of Chasen & Company.

He started piano lessons at the age of four.

He studied piano at the Santa Barbara Music Academy and attended the University of Southern California School of Music as a piano major.

He studied orchestration with legendary arranger Marty Paich.

He worked extensively doing session work for two years with singers such as Carly Simon, Diana Ross, Ringo Starr, Leo Sayer, Harry Nilsson, and Melissa Manchester.

He joined the Elton John Band and toured with the group.

He became one of the most sought-after musicians in the industry. He worked with celebrities such as Barbra Streisand; Earth, Wind and Fire; Bob Seger; Rod Stewart; Toto; Glen Frey; Olivia Newton-John; Randy Newman; Rickie Lee Jones; Cher; and Chakha Khan.

His first film score was for the Tri-Star production of *Head Office* (1986). With over sixty-five films to his credit, he has been nominated for the Oscar five times, including three for best original score: *The Fugitive, The Prince of Tides,* and *My Best Friend's Wedding.*

He has composed scores for quite a few popular movies such as *Pretty Woman, Flatliners, Wyatt Earp, Waterworld, The Postman, Runaway Bride, Dinosaur, Atlantis,* and *Treasure Planet.*

His style is extremely versatile; no matter what genre film he scores, he always comes up with some original sounds and ideas.

End of Days

John Debney (1956–) made a name for himself scoring the episodes of *Seaquest* on television. His score for *Cutthroat Island* (1995) was one of the winning attributes of the film, although the film did not do well at the box office. Written in the swashbuckling style of Korngold, Debney's score for this pirate movie was among some of the best scoring in this part of the last decade of the twentieth century. (Actually, Debney replaced David Arnold, who was originally slated to compose the score for *Cutthroat Island*.)

Doomsayers predicted massive mayhem with the computer glitches of Y2K, the destruction of our world by earthquakes, meteor showers, collisions with comets, and planetary alignments that would create a world of all-out destruction. With this fear of the unknown in the minds of everyone, the creators of *End of Days* (1999) were able to capitalize on our vulnerabilities and our fears of impending doom. This is a film about our worst nightmares. The main character (played by Arnold Schwarzenegger) did not choose his circumstances, yet in the process, rediscovers his faith. Schwarzenegger plays the part of a New York City cop who is assigned a particular security detail where he ends up saving the life of a girl, the fate of the entire world, and his own soul as he comes face to face with his most powerful enemy ever.

This film is about seduction and faith. Will Satan be successful in luring the main character over to the evil side or will faith prevail? John Debney wanted to stress an element of loneliness of the main character, so he featured the haunting boy soprano (twelve-year-old Theo Lebow), who sings a distant "lone voice crying out in the darkness." What Debney wrote for the boy to sing is an eerie reminder of the opening four notes of the Demonic-sounding *Dies Irae* theme (meaning "Judgment Day" or "Day of Wrath") from the Roman Catholic Mass for the Dead. This lone voice "represents the main character who ultimately must face his own demons to save the world."

Debney has composed seventy-two minutes' worth of music that was recorded at Todd-AO Scoring Stage by an eighty-piece orchestra over the span of three days. As he states, "This score has many of the sounds that reflect life at the end of the twentieth century. I tried to encompass as many elements of world music which represent where we are at the end of the twentieth century as possible. The score is very diverse, containing many eclectic elements. I used backward vocals, murmurings, and whisperings, to give the score a pastiche of colors in order to avoid the typical scary movie sound. There are sound environments and textural diversity that come from instruments of ancient times to the futuristic colors of electronics and techno." The score contains such diverse sonorities as modern drum and noise loops, a Tibetan long horn, a ram's horn, Duduk, ethnic flutes, a Shofar (a ritual horn of ancient and modern Hebrews made of ram's horns), an eighty-piece orchestra, a chamber choir, electronic vocal samplings, the bizarre sound of Tuvan throat singing, a boy soprano, and numerous electronics. As much as he admires Jerry Goldsmith's score for *The Omen,* Debney felt that it was imperative to avoid copying that style for this movie. The whole intention was to create a score that utilized elements from world music, classical music, and contemporary styles such as techno. Debney, in his vocal writing, also decided not to give in to the "Carmina Burana school."

Debney has a novel idea about the interaction of film composers and music supervisors in the future. Regarding his work on this score, he states, "We have a number of songs from really great bands, and the idea is to make the songs and the underscore not seem like two separate elements, to somehow blend the songs with the score. To have them all integrated and flow into each other is a much more elegant way to do it." Debney sees a time in the future when more film composers will work with rock artists. He goes on to say, "In the past, film composers and music supervisors have lived in two separate worlds. It is so much better for film if we can all be on the same page and communicate and collaborate together." *What we have is an excellent example of a powerful score by a very talented composer that helps to sum up the state of film scores at the end of the twentieth century. That fate being the homogenization of several musical styles coming together to enhance the seductive power of cinema on the viewer.*

JOHN DEBNEY

American-born composer Born: August 18, 1956 (Burbank, California)

John Debney. Courtesy of Chasen & Company.

He started on guitar at age six. He took up the piano when he was eleven years old.

He studied acting and music at Loyola University.

He attended Cal Arts for a degree in musical composition.

He spent his summers working in the music library at Disney Studios.

His father had been a producer for Disney. Young Debney was once introduced to Walt Disney by his father. He said, "There was just a feeling from the man, a warmth. He seemed to exude power and strength." This meeting left a mark of determination on Debney. It bolstered his confidence and gave him a goal toward which to work.

His work at Disney led to a full-time job as a music copyist, orchestrator, and arranger for Disney Studios.

He gained experience scoring television shows such as *Cagney and Lacey, Fame,* and *The Young Riders* (for which he earned his first Emmy Award).

He won his second Emmy for his work on *Seaquest DSV.*

His score for *Cutthroat Island* was written for the 120-piece London Symphony Orchestra and a sixty-voice choir. This score paid homage to Korngold. Debney considers that for him the hardest part about scoring a film is coming up with a musical theme. He composed about ten main title themes for *Cutthroat Island* before coming up with the one used in the movie. He states that he likes to approach a picture in the sense of trying to discover what the tone should be for the major theme and work back from there.

For his score for *Liar, Liar* (originally to be scored by James Newton Howard; Howard had a conflict on another assignment and recommended Debney), Debney wrote some thematic material for the piano because, as he stated, "When you're dealing with Jim Carrey's relationship with his son, you want something childlike, poignant and innocent . . . hence the piano."

Debney prefers to write his scores at the piano. He started as an orchestrator for composers for television such as Mark Snow and Mike Post.

He has a fondness for John Barry's score for *Somewhere in Time.*

He won his third Emmy in 1997 for his work on the pilot of *The Cape.*

For the Claude Van Damme film *Sudden Death,* he wrote a driving, techno-style score.

Other well-known movies scored by Debney include *I Know What You Did Last Summer, Hocus Pocus, The Relic, Inspector Gadget,* and *Dick.*

Debney doesn't mind scoring a film that already has a temp track as long as the temp track is "well-crafted, because it will provide a jumping-off point for discussion with the director."

(continued)

He feels that John Williams is the ultimate blend of craftsman, artist, and musician.

He said that "comedies require a lot of stamina, while scoring dramas enable one to write melodies and explore the depths of emotional context.

When he composes a score, Debney puts in every note and orchestrational color in his sketches for orchestrator Brad Dechter. Some additional orchestrators who have worked with John Debney include Ira Hearshen, Frank Bennett, Don Nemitz, Jeff Atmajian, Chris Klatman, Don Davis, Walter Sheets, Bill Ross, and many other gifted musicians.

He sees film music trends going in the direction of techno and electronica, with the likelihood of returning to classical music roots once again.

John Williams has had a powerful influence on his career and musical style (particularly a score like *Star Wars*).

He feels that having stamina, knowledge of all styles of music and most importantly, possessing good communication skills are great attributes to staying active in the business.

His advice to up-and-coming young composers: Get a degree in classical composition, play jazz, orchestrate your own music to learn what works and what doesn't, and study conducting. Don't be afraid to pay your dues over and over again; stay humble and focused, be open to the study of music; study and condense scores; learn what electronics can and can't do; remember that human beings can emote better than machines, and finally, develop a very thick skin (with regards to rejection).

He has no definable "style." Rather, John Debney is a bit of a musical chameleon, jumping from style to style and genre to genre with great success.

American Beauty

Thomas Newman. Courtesy of Chasen & Company.

Thomas Newman helped to bring the last decade of the twentieth century to a close with his unique "trademark" approach of using "muted" chords that are seemingly repeated ad infinitum. Although bordering on the minimalistic sounds of composers like Philip Glass, Newman's repetitions are not as tedious to the listener's patience, because they are accompanied by interesting countermelodies. Toward the beginning of the film, the repetition of Newman's music illustrates the monotonous boredom of a forty-two-year-old man, Lester Burnham, who feels as though he is a loser and that his life is going nowhere. He wants to get back his once-youthful appeal. Later in the film, as Lester imagines that his teenaged daughter's cheerleader friend is coming on to him through a series of events, Newman's score uses a combination of exotic percussion and string instruments to exude the fantasy atmosphere. Some of the instruments Newman uses are the tablas (drums from India), kim-kim drums, bird calls, an appalachian dulcimer, a bass tin whistle, a processed bass flute, an arpeggiated violin, a detuned mandolin, a banjo, a ukulele, a sax, a flute, a piano, and the ewi (electronic wind instrument). Toward the end of the movie, after Lester realizes that the girl of his fantasies was just a kid, he picks up a photo of his wife, daughter, and himself. He realizes that he nearly lost his family to a stupid affair. But it is too late, he is shot dead. During these final minutes of the film, Newman captures the essence of the final message of the film with the return of his trademark "muted" piano chords.

The score was orchestrated by Thomas Newman's main orchestrator, Thomas Pasatieri, and was recorded at Signet Soundelux Studios and the Todd-AO Scoring Stage.

The Death of Arthur Morton: Grand Orchestrator

The film music world lost a great talent with the passing of Arthur Morton on April 15, 2000 (age ninety-one). He was born on August 8, 1908, in Duluth, Minnesota, and started working as an orchestrator/arranger on Hollywood films in mid-1930s. His list of films as orchestrator is mind-boggling. His huge list of credits included such hits as *Star Wars, Patton, Planet of the Apes, The Omen, Superman, Poltergeist, Hoosiers, The River Wild,* and *Star Trek: First Contact*. Morton was a close friend and collaborator with Jerry Goldsmith, orchestrating most of his film scores since the mid-1960s.

Gladiator

Russell Crowe in Gladiator. *Courtesy of Dreamworks LLC / Universal Pictures/Photofest.*

It may seem fit to end our survey of film music in this edition with a look at a massively bold epic film, *Gladiator* (2000). It was made in the grand spectacle style of films such as *Spartacus* and *Braveheart*. It is an impressive recreation of the golden age of the Roman Empire, complete with its grotesque brutality. *Gladiator* also happens to be the first epic-scale gladiator movie in roughly four decades, the last being *Spartacus* in 1960. The film, which has all the hallmarks of a heroic story for success, was released on May 5, 2000, and continued to play in theaters across the United States for many months after its initial release. *Gladiator* was several years in the making. The German-born composer Hans Zimmer (1957–) was brought in on the project in November 1997, and he ultimately spent six months composing more than two hours of music for this mighty epic. Zimmer shared the musical billing with singer/composer Lisa Gerrard, whose hauntingly beautiful voice can be heard throughout the film. Her voice has a unique quality that acts as a paintbrush that colors, accentuates, and highlights the ambience of certain powerfully emotional scenes. One scene in particular is when Maximus (Russell Crowe) finds his dead family. The day the two recorded this cue, the dramatic power of Gerrard's unique singing voice brought Zimmer to tears. He was embarrassed at first until he turned around and saw that Gerrard was also weeping from the powerful emotion of the scene. Zimmer credited her vocals with providing an "other-wordly" quality to the film score. According to Zimmer, he says that Lisa Gerrard "is the secret amazing element in this movie. The first time I heard her voice I didn't think that anybody could sing like that. I didn't know that anyone had a voice like that; her voice is absolutely amazing." Together, Gerrard's and Zimmer's music catches the ominous majesty of the cruel Roman Empire. The two worked together with the director Ridley Scott and the film editor Pietro Scalia at Zimmer's studio (called Media Ventures). Zimmer would sometimes just hold one note down or a chord on the keyboard and Gerrard would improvise. He stated that some of the best work that they did was around two o'clock in the morning, when her voice would practically be gone. To add to the agony of her fatigue, Scott had been smoking "thousands" of cigars in the studio, which caused a cloud of smoke to bellow in the room, making it difficult for her to breathe, much less sing.

The film opens with a grisly battle headed by General Maximus. As he gives the signal to his men to "unleash hell," thousands of spears and flaming arrows are sent flying into the air in a barrage of massive carnage. Zimmer accompanies this battle with a waltz-style theme. Zimmer states that he "wanted to take this rather beautiful form (the waltz) and make it completely savage." He wanted "to turn beauty on its head and pervert it." All of the action scenes in this movie are accompanied by waltzes . . . not exactly what you'd expect for a brutal massacre. Zimmer contributed to about 75 to 80 percent of the whole score. Amazingly, *there are nineteen distinct themes in this large score*! Each one is given a chance to develop within the story. Considering the amount of extra time that was given to both composers (Zimmer and Gerrard), it is no wonder that their collaboration for this monumental score rivals that of a complex opera. As a matter of fact, Zimmer was given the opportunity to view the film without dialogue or sound effects, only his music was heard. He stated that when the movie was over, he was happy to agree that his score tied in beautifully with the picture images on screen and was able to tell the whole story without the dialogue. This is a good test to see if a score works or not. Scott had wanted Zimmer to compose some music before the opening battle sequence was shot. As it turns out, Scalia actually edited the film of the battle sequences to fit the music. We also hear the exotic sound of the Armenian **duduk** (like an Armenian clarinet), and a distorted quotation of the *Dies Irae*. The duduk is that strange-sounding instrument heard when the story takes us to Zucchabar. (Listen for the duduk in Jerry Goldsmith's score for the 1990 movie *The Russia House* and in Peter Gabriel's score for the controversial Martin Scorsese film *The Last Temptation of Christ*.) Although Zimmer used a great deal of electronics and computer technology in this score, it does not sound like it. He states that "there are more electronics and computers in this movie than any movie" he has ever done before. The electronics are in the background. What the filmgoer hears is the sound of the symphony orchestra and Gerrard's vocalizations.

There are three interesting footnotes about this amazing score: (1) Zimmer used the words from the speeches of Roman Emperor Marcus Aurelius (who has been dead for more than eighteen hundred years) as the text to be sung by the chorus of singers on the soundtrack; (2) Zimmer was able to attract a female audience to this film by making the typically male-oriented gladiator theme toned down with powerful emotionalism in his score. His music drew women by its shear emotional quality into the story itself. His ambition was "to get every woman to not leave the theater once the film was underway." He wanted everyone involved in the emotional aspect of the story. "Even the battle sequences are very much a part of the emotional texture of the movie"; (3) Zimmer did all of this without *knowing how to read music*! He does everything with computers and synthesizers and is *one of the few major film composers in the business who doesn't yet know how to read music.*

The score was orchestrated by Bruce Fowler (who had been the trombonist in Frank Zappa's band over the years) and performed by the Lyndhurst (England) Orchestra. Zimmer likes to use Fowler because he is one of the people in the business who can "make sense out of his mess." Zimmer was not classically trained in music, so he needs Fowler there to make sure that the music is playable by each instrumentalist.

Review Questions

Discussion

1. Discuss the future of film scoring.

2. Discuss the *Jurassic Park* scoring session dilemma.

3. Discuss Alan Silvestri's leitmotifs in *Forrest Gump*.

4. Discuss the role of women in film scoring.

5. Compare the movie *Titanic* with *Gone with the Wind*.

Short Answer

1. Why is the score to *Schindler's List* so effective? ______________________________
____
____.

2. What did Mancina use in his *Speed* score that was so unusual? ____________________
____.

3. What made scoring for *Twister* more difficult? ____

____

____.

4. What had David Arnold been doing before his success as a film composer? ______________

____.

5. What secret "code" does Arnold employ in *Independence Day*? ________________________

____.

6. Why do you think that only a small handful of women go into film scoring? ____________

____.

7. What is Rachel Portman's philosophy of scoring? _____________________________________

____

____.

Select Bibliography

Ascher, Steven, and Edward Pincus, *The Filmmaker's Handbook* (completely revised and updated) (New York: Plume/Penguin Putnam Inc., 1999).

Atkins, Irene Kahn, *Source Music in Motion Pictures* (Rutherford, NJ: Fairleigh Dickinson University Press, 1983).

Bazelon, Irwin, *Knowing the Score: Notes on Film Music* (New York: Arco Publishers, 1975).

Bell, David *Getting the Best Score for Your Film: A Filmmaker's Guide to Music Scoring* (Los Angeles, CA: Silman-James Press, 1994).

Bernstein, Charles, *Film Music and Everything Else* (Beverly Hills, CA: Turnstyle Music Publishers, 2000).

Brown, Royal S., *Overtones and Undertones* (Berkeley and Los Angeles: University of California Press, 1994).

Brownlow, Kevin, *David Lean: A Biography* (New York: St. Martin's Press, 1996).

Brownlow, Kevin, *The Parade's Gone By* (Berkeley, Los Angeles, and London: University of California Press, 1968).

Bruce, Graham, *Bernard Herrmann: Film Music and Narrative* (Ann Arbor, MI: UMI Research Press, 1985).

Burlingame, Jon, *TV's Biggest Hits* (New York: Schirmer Books, 1996).

Burlingame, Jon, *For the Record* (Hollywood, CA: RMA, 1997).

Burlingame, Jon, *Sound and Vision: 60 Years of Motion Picture Soundtracks* (New York: Billboard Books, 2000).

Carlin, Dan, Sr., *Music in Film and Video Productions* (Stoneham, MA: Focal Press, 1991).

Carroll, Brendan G., *The Last Prodigy: A Biography of Erich Wolfgang Korngold* (Portland, OR: Amadeus Press, 1997).

Cook, David A., *A History of Narrative Film,* 2nd Edition (New York: W. W. Norton, 1990).

Darby, William, and Jack Du Bois, *American Film Music* (Jefferson, NC, and London; McFarland Co., 1990).

Davis, Richard, *Complete Guide to Film Scoring: The Art and Business of Writing Music for Movies and TV* (Boston: Berklee Press, 1999).

Dolan, Robert Emmett, *Music in Modern Media* (New York: G. Schirmer, Inc., 1967).

Duchen, Jessica, *Erich Wolfgang Korngold* (London: Phaidon Press Limited, 1996).

Eyman, Scott, *The Speed of Sound* (New York: Simon & Schuster, 1997).

Evans, Mark, *Soundtrack: The Music of the Movies* (New York: Da Capo Paperback, 1979).

Faulkner, Robert R., *Hollywood Studio Musicians: Their Work and Careers in the Recording Industry* (Chicago and New York: Aldine-Atherton, Inc., 1971).

Faulkner, Robert R., *Music on Demand: Composers and Careers in the Hollywood Film Industry* (London: Transaction Books, 1983).

Finler, Joel W., *Hitchcock in Hollywood* (New York: The Continuum Publishing Co., 1992).

Garnett, Tay, *Directing: Learn From the Masters* (Lanham, MD and London: The Scarecrow Press, 1996).

Goodell, Gregory, *Independent Feature Film Production* (fully revised and updated) (New York: St. Martin's Griffin, 1998).

Gorbman, Claudia, *Unheard Melodies: Narrative Film Music* (London: BFI Publishing, 1987).

Hagen, Earle, *Scoring for Films* (updated edition with CD) (Los Angeles, CA: Alfred Publishing Co., Inc, 1971).

Hagen, Earle, *Advanced Techniques for Film Scoring* (includes CD) (Los Angeles, CA: Alfred Publishing Co., Inc, 1990).

Hall, Ben M., *The Best Remaining Seats: The Golden Age of the Movie Palace* (New York: Da Capo Press, 1975).

Harris, Robert and Michael Lasky, *The Films of Alfred Hitchcock* (Secaucus, NJ: The Citadel Press, 1976).

Hemming, Roy, *The Melody Lingers On: The Great Songwriters and Their Movie Musicals* (New York: Newmarket Press, 1986).

Herman, Jan, *A Talent For Trouble* (New York: G. P. Putnam's Sons, 1995).

Hollyn, Norman, *The Film Editing Room Handbook* (3rd edition) (Los Angeles, CA: Lone Eagle Publishing Co., 1999).

Holman, Tomlinson, *Sound for Film and Television* (Newton, MA: Focal Press, 1997).

Honthaner, Eve Light, *The Complete Film Production Handbook* (revised with a CD) (Newton, MA, 1997).

Huntley, John, *British Film Music* (London: Skelton Robinson, 1947).

Kalinak, Kathryn, *Settling the Score: Music and the Classical Hollywood Film* (Madison: University of Wisconsin Press, 1992).

Karlin, Fred, *Listening to Movies* (New York: Schirmer Books, 1994).

Karlin, Fred, and Rayburn Wright, *On the Track: A Contemporary Guide to Film Scoring* (New York: Schirmer Books, 1990).
Karney, Robyn (editor in chief), *Chronicle of the Cinema* (London: Dorling Kindersley, 1995).
Kassabian, Anahid, *Hearing Film: Tracking Identifications in Contemporary Hollywood Film Music* (New York: Routledge, 2001).
Katz, Ephraim, *The Film Encyclopedia* (New York: Putnam Publishing, 1979).
Kendall, Lucas, *Film Score Monthly* (published by Vineyard Haven LLC, 8503 Washington Blvd., Culver City, CA, published monthly).
Konigsberg, Ira, *The Complete Film Dictionary* (2nd edition) (New York: Penguin Putnam, 1997).
LaLoggia, Nicole Shay, and Eden H. Wurmfeld, IPF/West *Independent Filmmaker's Manual* (Woburn, MA: Focal Press, 1999).
Laskin, Emily (editor), *The American Film Institute Getting Started in Film* (Englewood Cliffs, NJ: Prentice Hall, 1992).
Leonard, Geoff, Pete Walker, and Gareth Bramley, *John Barry: A Life in Pictures* (Bristol, England: Sansom & Company, 1998).
Limbacher, James L. (editor), *Film Music: From Violins to Video* (Metuchen, NJ: Scarecrow Press, 1974).
Lone Eagle Publishing staff, compilers and editors, *Film Composers Directory* (5th edition) (Los Angeles, CA: Lone Eagle Publishing Co., 2000).
MacDonald, Laurence E. *The Invisible Art of Film Music: A Comprehensive History* (New York: Ardsley House Publishers, Inc., 1998).
Mancini, Henry, with Gene Lees, *Did They Mention the Music?* (Chicago: Contemporary Books, 1989).
Manvell, Roger and John Huntley (revised and enlarged by Richard Arnell and Peter Day), *The Technique of Film Music*, (London: Focal Press Limited, 1975).
Marcuse, Sibyl, *Musical Instruments: A Comprehensive Dictionary* (New York: W.W. Norton & Company, Inc., 1975).
Marmorstein, Gary *Hollywood Rhapsody: Movie Music and Its Makers 1900 to 1975* (New York: Schirmer Books, 1997).
Mast, Gerald, and Bruce F. Kawin, *A Short History of the Movies, 7th edition* (Needham Heights, MA: Allyn and Bacon, 2000).
McCarrty, Clifford, *Film Composers in America* (New York: Da Capo Press, 1953).
Morgan, David, *Knowing the Score* (New York: HarperCollins Publishers, Inc., 2000).
Northam, Mark, and Lisa Anne Miller, *Film and Television Composer's Resource Guide* (Milwaukee, WI: Hal Leonard Corp., 1998).
Orrison, Katherine, *Written in Stone: Making Cecil B. DeMille's Epic The Ten Commandments* (Lanham, MD: Vestal Press, Inc., 1999).
Palmer, Christopher, *Dimitri Tiomkin: A Portrait* (London: T.E. Books, 1984).
Palmer, Christopher, *The Composer in Hollywood* (London and New York: Marion Boyers Publishers, 1990).
Parkinson, David, *History of Film* (New York: Thames and Hudson, 1996).
Prendergast, Roy M. *Film Music: A Neglected Art*, 2nd edition (New York: W. W. Norton, 1992).
Previn, Andre, *No Minor Chords: My Days in Hollywood* (New York: Doubleday, 1991)
Rebello, Stephen, *Alfred Hitchcock and the Making of Psycho* (New York: Dember Books, 1990).
Robinson, David, *From Peep Show to Palace: The Birth of American Film* (New York: Columbia University Press, 1996).
Rona, Jeff, *The Reel World: Scoring for Pictures* (San Francisco: Miller Freeman Books, 2000).
Rozsa, Miklos, *Double Life: The Autobiography of Miklos Rozsa* (New York: Hippocrene Books, Inc., 1982).
Russell, Mark, and James Young *Film Music Screencraft* (Oxford: Focal Press, 2000).
Sadie, Stanley (editor), *The Norton/Grove Concise Encyclopedia of Music* (New York: W. W. Norton, 1988).
Schelle, Michael, *The Score: Interviews with Film Composers* (Los Angeles, CA: Silman-James Press, 1999).
Smith, Geoffrey-Nowell (editor), *The Oxford History of World Cinema* (Oxford: Oxford University Press, 1996).
Smith, Jeff, *The Sounds of Commerce: Marketing Popular Film Music* (New York: Columbia University Press, 1998).
Smith, Steven C., *A Heart at Fire's Center: The Life and Music of Bernard Herrmann* (Berkeley, Los Angeles, and Oxford: University of California Press, 1991).
Sperling, Cass Warner, and Cork Millner, with Jack Warner, Jr., *Hollywood Be Thy Name: The Warner Brothers Story* (Rocklin, CA: Prima Publishing, 1994).
Spoto, Donald, *The Art of Alfred Hitchcock* (New York: Doubleday, 1992).
Spoto, Donald, *The Dark Side of Genius: The Life of Alfred Hitchcock* (Boston: Little, Brown & Co., 1993).
Thomas, Tony, *Film Score: The Art and Craft of Movie Music* (Burbank, CA: Riverwood Press, 1991).
Thomas, Tony, *Music for the Movies*, 2nd edition (Beverly Hills: Silman-James Press, 1997).
Walker, Mark (editor), *Film Music Good CD Guide* (London: Gramophone Publications, 1997).
Williams, John, *Music From the Movies* (1 Folly Square, Bridport, Dorset, Great Britain, published quarterly).
Withers, Robert S., *Introduction to Film: A Guide to the Art, Technology, Language, and Appreciation of Film* (New York: Barnes & Noble Books, 1983).
Zolotow, Maurice, *Billy Wilder in Hollywood* (New York: Limelight Editions, 1987).

Glossary

(Whenever a term appears in **bold,** see the corresponding definition within the Glossary)

Academy Award An award given in the form of a gold statuette known as an Oscar by the Academy of Motion Picture Arts and Sciences. This practice started in the year 1929 for the achievements of films made in 1927 and 1928. Since 1934, awards have been given for each calendar year.

Acoustics The study of the science of sound. Understanding how to record the various instruments (such as microphone placement and what type of mike to use) is crucial in reproducing the best playback. Also important is understanding how to record voices and sounds both indoors and outdoors for the most effective playback in the theaters or auditoriums.

ADR (Automatic or Automated Dialogue Replacement) Used during the **postproduction** phase of film making, ADR is when a performer will watch a playback of a certain scene, and will rerecord a better version of the original **production sound.** There are many times when the production sound (sound recorded live on the set when the scene is being shot) cannot be used as part of the finished soundtrack. Perhaps an actor's voice is distorted because of wind noise or maybe the microphone picked up unwanted extraneous noises. An actor will be called back into the studio for the recording of a cleaner rendition of the original production sound. In this case, the production sound will act as a guide. ADR is also known as **looping**.

ADR Editor The person responsible for recording and placement of the newly recorded dialogue track during **ADR**.

Antiphonal effect A term that describes when an ensemble is divided into two or more distinct groups, performing in alternation and together. Listen to the brass music of Giovanni Gabrieli for an example of this technique.

Arpeggios The sounding of the notes in a musical chord in succession rather than all at the same time; in keyboard music this is the breaking (known as a "broken chord") or spreading of a chord.

ASCAPT (American Society of Composers, Authors, and Publishers) This is a performing rights society that pays out royalties owed to its members on a quarterly basis. A blanket fee for use of the music in ASCAP's catalogue is paid by TV and radio stations, restaurants, nightclubs, and companies such as **Muzak** that provide "atmospheric background music" for shopping malls, grocery stores, and doctor and dentist offices (known as "elevator music" to some people). ASCAP collects these fees for its members and distributes them accordingly. There are two other performing rights groups that some composers belong to, known as BMI and SESAC. Note that a film composer can only belong to one of these organizations at a time.

Atonal music A term that applies to music that is not tonal, that is, not in a key. Most of the music that we listen to is *tonal* music . . . music with a tonal center . . . whether it be a pop song by one of today's recording artists or a symphony by one of the Classical masters. If music lacks a tonal center, it is said to be *atonal* . . . such as the sound you would hear if a cat ran across the keyboard of your piano.

Audion tube The vacuum tube invented by Lee De Forest in 1906, which greatly improved the amplification of sound. This led to the development of both radio and sound films.

Avant-garde Cinema and/or music that is considered "advanced" in that it denies the traditional structure and techniques as laid down by previous creators; perhaps "that which is not widely accepted by the masses due to its experimental qualities."

Bass voice or bass line Refers to the lowest voice or lowest line in music.

Blimp A soundproof housing that surrounds a movie camera to prevent the motor noise from being recorded on the soundtrack.

Booth person This is usually an **orchestrator** or music editor who will sit in the engineer's recording booth during scoring sessions who will aid the composer/conducter by following the score to check for wrong notes, out-of-tune passages, bad synchronizations, and the like.

Cameo appearance When a recognizable performer or person makes a brief "guest appearance" within a film. Film composers such as Jerry Goldsmith, Bernard Herrmann, Erich Wolfgang Korngold, and Marc Shaiman have all made such appearances.

CGI (Computer Generated Imagery) This has really changed movie making in the last few years. We have gone from recreating dinosaurs in *Jurassic Park* (1993) to creating "synthespians" (a cast of hyperrealistic, computer-generated human characters) for movies such as *Final Fantasy: The Spirits Within* (2001)

Chromatic tones Based on an **octave** of twelve semitones, a chromatic tone is one of these twelve tones within each octave. In layman's terms, a chromatic scale is when you go up or down the piano keyboard playing all of the white and black keys. The distance between a white key and the next black key is a semitone (also known as a half step).

Chronophone The earliest-known gramophone synchronizer, first exhibited in London in 1904.

Click track A recurring equidistant set of "click" sounds that are designed to aid in perfect synchronization of a music cue and its accompanying scene on film. If the studio musicians perform their music exactly in tempo with the clicks, the music and picture will be perfectly "lined up." This click track is made by the music editor using a digital metronome.

Closing credits The list of the personnel who worked in and/or on the film. This includes technical and production personnel and a list of any music and recordings that were used within the film. Sometimes referred to as **end titles** or **end credits**.

Director The person who brings the script to life by guiding the actors in their performance and by supervising the staging of the action and any other detail of the shooting of each scene. After the production of the film, the director will work with the film and sound editors to ensure the best possible results.

Director's cut The edited version of a film the way the director would like to see it released in theaters. The director gives it to the producer or studio with the understanding that the film could be altered without the director's approval.

Dolby noise reduction This is a process that diminishes the tape "hiss" by compressing the signal during recording, then expanding the signal or decoding it during playback.

Dubbing, postdubbing In **postproduction**, it is possible to have the performers rerecord (dub in) their own voices to give a clearer production under the ideal recording conditions of a recording studio. There are times when it is more convenient to shoot a scene without sound (i.e., when we see two characters walking down the beach) and then add their voices later. See **ADR**.

Dubbing room, dubbing stage A specially designed recording studio equiped with the necessary mechanics for **looping** or **dubbing** (**ADR**).

Editing The process of choosing the best shots from each scene photographed, of trimming those shots for pacing, and of assembling those shots for continuity to the story line. Also a process in **sound editing** wherein the editor adds the best or most appropriate or effective sounds to a given scene. The editor takes the best recordings of each musical cue and adds them into the final music track.

Electronic synthesizer An electronic instrument capable of generating and processing a wide variety of sounds. Although the earliest synthesizers in the mid-1950s were very limited in their capabilities, today's synths make possible many of the great colorations heard in film scores.

End titles, end credits This is the section right at the end of a movie when the credits scroll across the screen. This section is almost always accompanied by music. In many of today's films, the end credits will start off with some of the original score material by the film composer and will then transition into a pop tune or song by a singing artist.

EVI Electronic valve instrument

EWI Electronic wind instrument

Fanfare A flourish of trumpets or other brass instruments, often with percussion, usually used for ceremonial purposes such as coronations, Olympic games, or the like. Their tradition goes back to at least the Middle Ages.

Film music Music that accompanies a film. It can be played "live" (as in the case of films from the silent era), it can be an original score written specifically for the film itself, or it can be borrowed music from a prerecorded source.

Film noir A term meaning "black film" coined by French critics used to describe a style of film made during the 1940s and 1950s. These films were characterized by having an emphasis on "bleak settings, heavy shadows, and sharp contrasts of light and dark." In addition to this, these films usually featured characters who were neurotic, perhaps brutal, who may have dealt in crime or corruption. Examples of films in this category include: *Laura* (1944), *Spellbound* (1945), and *The Killers* (1946).

Final cut, fine cut The final version of a film with no intensions of further editing. Some directors are given the right to have their "director's cut" released without any changes. This is referred to as a final cut. See also **locked cut**.

Flutter-tonguing A type of tonguing in which the player rolls the letter "r" on the tip of his or her tongue when playing.

Foley artist, foley walker A specialist who creates sounds on the foley stage to match and enhance especially the body movements of actors, to make them more audible for playback on the soundtrack in the theater. Named after Jack Foley, the man who invented this technique.

Frame An individual picture area on a strip of movie film. Almost all sound films run through a movie projector at the rate of twenty-four frames per second. Prior to 1920, most films ran at the rate of sixteen frames per second. During the mid-1920s, films ran from eighteen to twenty-four frames per second.

Free timing The name given for two ways of lining up the music with the picture cues, either the **punch and streamer method** or the **stopwatch method**. It is called free timing because it allows some elasticity or "give and take" to the **tempo** during the performance and recording of the musical score, thus being "free."

Glockenspiel A percussion instrument consisting of a series of tuned steel bars arranged in two rows, as are the keys of a piano, and played with two knobbed beaters (similar to the military bell lyre).

Gregorian chant The original official music of the Roman Catholic church dating back to c. 800. Often used in motion picture music to represent mysterious "end of the world" scenarios (curiously enough), Satanic worship, or for the more obvious movies with a "Catholic theme."

HUAC (House Committee on Un-American Activities) A former committee of the U.S. House of Representatives that was formed to discover and investigate disloyal or subversive activities in America, specifically Communist activities. Ten members (known as the "Hollywood Ten") of the Screen Writers Guild were banned from future work in the industry because of their suspected membership in the Communist party. From 1947 until 1954, the HUAC had a major impact on Hollywood when over three hundred individuals in the film industry were blacklisted (known as the "Hollywood blacklist") as a result of the committee's investigations.

Inversion The playing of a melody upside down from the original version.

Kinetscope Edison's battery-operated peephole viewer, invented by W. K. L. Dickson.

Leitmotif A recurring musical theme or fragment of that theme that is associated with a character or a situation within a film. Originally formulated by the German opera composer Richard Wagner in the nineteenth century.

Locked cut The version of the film that is comprised of the **final cut** and synchronized soundtrack. The only changes to this version will be some refinements during **postproduction**, perhaps the addition of visual special effects, sound effects, and music.

Looping See **ADR**.

M & E track, M & E stem The soundtrack that contains only the music and sound effects but no dialogue. This track is made for releases in foreign countries, where the local dialogue can be mixed with the original music and sound effects.

Main title music The music heard toward the beginning of a film when the main title and the credits appear on the screen. Main title music is crucial to setting the tone and attitude of the film that follows. It helps the audience to get the feel for the drama that will follow.

March Music composed for marching. A march usually features an ornamentation of a regular and repeated drum rhythm over which we hear a snappy tune sometimes accompanied by a counter melody. There are many fine examples of marches heard in films. Several well-known marches include the Indiana Jones theme from any of the Indiana Jones films, "The Colonel Bogey March" from *Bridge on the River Kwai,* and the main title march from *Patton*.

"Mickey Mousing" When the music within a movie parallels the action so that the music seems to describe what is taking place on screen.

Microphone boom A long pole on which a microphone is mounted so that it can be placed over a scene for sound recording.

Microtones A musical interval smaller than a semitone. See **Chromatic tones**.

Minimalistic Music characterized by containing static harmony, patterned rhythms, and repetition. In films, we hear examples in the Herrmann score for *Psycho,* Barber's score for *Mansfield Park,* and most scores by Michael Nyman.

Multiphonics The sounding of two or more pitches simultaneously on an instrument that normally sounds only single notes.

Mockup A mock demo of a planned score by a film composer made to demonstrate that score for the director. See also **synth demo**.

Montage Taken from the French word *monter,* "to assemble." In European films, this term refers to assembling (editing) all of the shots in a motion picture. In American films, this term usually applies to the poetic overlapping of two different images, many times accompanied by music and used as a transitional device. The early filmmakers in Russia (Eisenstein) used this term to describe abrupt editing. Hitchcock used montage to describe the particular ways his films were assembled.

Movie trailer Another name for the "coming attractions" or previews of an upcoming movie.

MPAA (The Motion Picture Association of America) This organization views motion pictures released in the United States and provides ratings such as G, PG-13, R, or NC-17.

Muzak The name of a company that has provided "elevator music" (commercial background music) for shopping areas, restaurants, doctor and dentist offices, and the like.

Octave The interval (distance) on the keyboard between the first and eighth notes of a musical diatonic scale. Notes that are an octave apart have the same letter name (i.e., "e natural" up to the next "e natural").

Ondes Martenot (pronounced: "Ond Marr-ter-no") An electronic instrument invented by Maurice Martenot in 1928. It is a keyboard instrument that is monophonic (can play only one tone at a time). The player's right hand plays the notes on the keyboard (with a slight lateral movement the player can produce a vibrato) while the left hand controls the timbre (tone color) and dynamics (volume). It is also possible to alternate the pitch by using a sliding matellic ribbon. Although used by famous French twentieth-century composers such as Varèse, Messiaen, and Boulez, film composers such as Maurice Jarre and Elmer Bernstein have put the Ondes Martenot to effective use in their scores.

Organ chorale A hymnlike tune played on the organ.

Ostinato (pronounced "oss-tee-nah'-toh") A repeated figure in music.

Passacaglia (pronounced "pahss-sah-cahl'-yah") A musical composition that had a repeated melody, usually in the bass line, with a set of musical variations in the upper voices.

Pentatonic scale A musical scale consisting of only five notes per octave.

Phonofilm An early *sound-on-film* process invented by Lee De Forest.

Picture cueing A technique used in motion picture scoring wherein the musical conductor is looking at the moving images on screen for cueing purposes during the scoring sessions.

Polyrhythmic The simultaneous use of two or more rhythms that are not readily perceived as deriving from one another. Sometimes referred to as "cross rhythm." An example would be the coexistence of duple meter and a triple meter.

Polytonality The use of two or more tonal centers at the same time generally created by superimposing chords, **arpeggios**, or melodies, each of which defines a different tonality.

Postproduction The phase of filmmaking that occurs after the film has been shot.

Prerecording, prescoring, playback recording The recording of the music for a scene *before* the scene has been shot. Used for scenes that will require music in advance such as scenes involving dance numbers, and scenes showing actors playing an instrument or perhaps singing.

Producer The person in charge of the film production from beginning to end, from the conception of the screenplay through the shooting and editing stages to the end result in the movie theaters. The producer is in charge of the funding of the project and, in most cases, the hiring of the personnel associated with the film.

Production code This code was adopted in 1930 in response to public concern of the immorality of the film industry. It spelled out very carefully how certain subjects were to be treated in films made in the United States. Initially, the code was voluntary. By 1934, because of pressure from the Catholic Legion of Decency (which advocated boycotting any film deemed inappropriate by all Catholics), the production code was enforced. The code had considerable influence on the content of any American film and its treatment of sex, crime, violence, religion, and family life.

Production designer This is the person who oversees the visual elements in the movie. Formerly known as the *art director*, today's production designers work with the director in establishing the "look" of the sets, color design, costumes, adapting the locations outside of the studio, and designing the entire "vision" of the film.

Production sound The sound recorded live on the set as the film is being shot. Many times this sound recording will be inadequate to be used in the final film; therefore, actors will be called back to **loop** their scenes and **foley artists** and **sound designers** will "sweeten" the sound effects. In this case, the production sound is used as a guide when replacing it with the newly recorded dialogue and sound effects. Also called "live sound."

Public domain Any work that is not protected by a copyright and is therefore available for use without the payment of royality or the need for permission.

Punch and streamer A punch is a round hole that is punched in the actual film stock that, when projected, appears as a bright round flash of light. This flash acts as a signal for the conductor of the score during the scoring sessions. A streamer is created by using either a wax or grease pencil or a sharp stylus to draw a diagonal line (usually three feet long) on the actual film stock. When projected, the streamer will appear as a straight up and down vertical line and take two seconds to move across the screen from left to right. The streamer usually acts as a two-second warning for the conductor of the score to watch for the bright flash (the punch) that would follow. This bright flash could signal the start or end of a musical cue. If they are using a *video copy* of the film during the scoring sessions as opposed to *real film*, these markings (punches and streamers) will be supplied electronically by a computer.

RAM The letteres stand for "random access memory," the standard type of memory in a computer system. The advantage of RAM is that one can access any portion of the memory without having to proceed through the other data.

Room tone, room sound, room noise The overall *ambient sound* of a room, also known as *presence*. It is very important for the **postproduction** personnel to incorporate the room tone when the characters are not talking or there is no background music. Room tone will be recorded separately on the same day as the shoot or it may be created artificially by the sound designer.

Rough cut This is a version of the film that is usually within five to fifteen minutes of the film's ultimate length because of changes made by the studio or producers. Some people refer to this as the **director's cut**.

Score The original music composed or arranged for a motion picture.

Set recording When the dialogue or music is recorded "on the set" at the same time the picture is being shot. Also referred to as **Standard recording**.

Single-shot film In the early days of filmmaking, many films were made where the camera remained stationary on a tripod and utilized no additional camera setups or angles.

SMPTE Society of Motion Picture and Television Engineers.

Song compilation score A score that is comprised of different popular songs and may or may not contain any original music such as dramatic underscoring by a film composer.

Song driven score A score that has been inspired by a popular song.

Sound designer A person who designs needed sounds for a movie and/or lays in recordings of existing sounds from a prerecorded library of special sounds.

Sound editing The art of combining or mixing the best possible sounds when making the master soundtrack. The person in charge of this is known as a mixer, sound mixer, sound editor, rerecording mixer, or dubbing mixer.

Soundtrack The combination of all sounds (dialogue, sound effects, and music) heard in a film. For the study of **film music**, people refer to the soundtrack of a film as the musical score. In recent years, it has become common for there to be two separate recordings released for purchase; a film's **soundtrack recording** (which might contain pop songs heard within the film) and the film's **score** (the dramatic music written by the film composer).

Soundtrack recording This term has changed meaning over the years. It originally referred to the original music heard within a film along with the possible inclusion of several pop songs used in the film. Now, many studios are releasing a "soundtrack recording" from a movie and a "score" from the same movie. The *soundtrack* might contain pop tunes heard in the movie from various artists, whereas the *score* would be the original music written by the film composer.

Spotting session The meeting when the **director**, composer, film editor, music editor, and sometimes **producer** get together to watch the completed film to determine where the individual sections of a musical score should be placed within the motion picture.

Standard recording When the music is recorded live on the set when the scene is being shot. Also referred to as **set recording.**

Star system The method and manner of exploiting the on- and offscreen lives of movie personalities so as to create a mystique. Certain people were given labels (Mary Pickford was known as "America's Sweetheart," John Wayne as "The Duke," James Cagney and Humphrey Bogart became the antiheroes, etc.). When the studio system collapsed in the 1950s, the star system deflated.

Stopwatch method A method of free timing in which the conductor conducts the music for a **scoring session** by using an oversized stopwatch located on the podium or music stand.

String mute Usually a three-pronged clamp attached to the bridge of the stringed instrument that absorbs or dampens some of the vibration of the strings making the resultant sound rather veiled or slightly nasal. It "mutes" the sound.

String tremolo Tremolo is created by the rapid reiteration of a note by up-and-down movements of the bow on the string. The string tremolo in film music can be used to create agitation or suspense. In loud *tutti passages* (when the whole orchestra is playing), the tremolo can create fullness of sound from a string section.

Studio system This was the large-scale mass production line method of making films from the 1920s to the 1950s. The major studios had complete control over the financing of their movies, the distribution of the films in their studio-owned theaters, and they were able to force individual theater owners to block-book all of their films by putting pressure on them. 1948 spelled the beginning of the end of the studio system when the Supreme Court ordered that all major studios had to divest themselves of their theater holdings. This ended the studios' control of the market.

Synth demos In recent years, it has become commonplace for a director of a film to request synth demos of the score (see **mockup**) before final approval of each musical cue. A synth demo is simply a demonstration of the proposed musical cue done on synthesizer to check to see how the cue will sound and work within the film when fully orchestrated.

Tempo This is the pace or speed at which the music is to be performed.

Temp track Temporary music inserted during the rough cut phase of a movie to aid in the editing process, to help preview a new film before the original score is ready, and to help determine what musical concept might work best for a given scene and to demonstrate that concept to the film composer.

Texture music Music that creates different "textures" of sound and color by combining clusters of different tones. If one were to lay their arm across a portion of a piano and push down on the keyboard, this cluster of tones would give an example of various "textures."

Theremin This is an early electronic instrument invented in 1920 by the Russian Lev Termen. It operates on the principle of heterodyning two radio frequency oscillators. There are two antennae; one controls the pitch, the other controls the volume of the sound. The player of the theremin moves his or her hands to and fro near the antennae to change pitches and can create a vibrato by using a slight rocking of the wrist.

Timecode An electronic synchronizing system that was standardized by the Society of Motion Picture and Television Engineers (and also the European Broadcasting Union) that is used to edit and synchronize music, sound, and picture. There are a series of numbers that appear on screen that determine the exact location within a film for the starting or stopping points of a cue.

Triplet figure In music, this is a grouping of three notes that are played one after the other.

Twelve-Tone row A type of composition that evolved in the early 1920s generally associated with Arnold Schoenberg and his followers. It is based on the ordering of all twelve chromatic pitches known as a "tone row."

Variable click track A click track that is not steady in its constant beat. It will vary according to the pacing of the scene that it is being used to line up music with the picture.

Vibraphone This is an instrument in the percussion section that has tuned, graduated metal bars arranged in two rows in the manner of a piano keyboard, with tubular metal resonators suspended below them. These metal bars are played with padded beaters or mallets. These sustain the tone and also produce a characteristic vibrato by means of motor-driven propellers affixed to the top of each resonator. Both bars and resonators are suspended from a metal frame set on wheels.

Vibrato A slight fluctuation of the pitch used by performers to enrich or intensify the sound.

Vitaphone The *sound-on-disc* process used by Warner Bros. in the early days of sound film. It was eventually replaced by the *sound-on-film* process.

Wild recording Recording music for a movie without the benefit of seeing the picture. This is the cheapest method used, but it is least effective because the music and picture seldom line up accurately.

Window burn, window code This is the name given for the series of numbers that appears at the top or bottom of the screen when working with **timecode**.

Xylophone An instrument in the percussion section that consists of a series of graduated, tuned wooden slabs, laid parallel to one another. These slabs are struck with a pair of mallets or knobbed beaters.

Music Credits

Grateful acknowledgment is made to the following sources for permission to reprint material copyrighted or controlled by them:

King Kong: "Main Theme," RKO Pictures.
King Kong: "Ann Darrow Theme," RKO Pictures.
King Kong: "Variation of Ann Darrow Theme," RKO Pictures.
King Kong: "Courage Motive," RKO Pictures.
King Kong: "Aboriginal Sacrificial Dance," RKO Pictures.
Bride of Frankenstein: "Monster Theme," Universal Pictures.
Bride of Frankenstein: "Bride Theme," Universal Pictures.
Bride of Frankenstein: "Pretorius Theme," Universal Pictures.
Wuthering Heights: "Cathy's Theme," Goldwyn Studios.
Wuthering Heights: "Cathy's Death," Goldwyn Studios.
Gone with the Wind: "Tara Theme," Selznick Studios.
Suspicion: "Ecstasy Theme," RKO Pictures.
Suspicion: "Sea Cliff Theme," RKO Pictures.
Suspicion: "Variation on Main Title," RKO Pictures.
Suspicion: "Extension of Main Title," RKO Pictures.
Suspicion: "Repeated Ostinato," RKO Pictures.
Lost Weekend: "Obsession Theme," Paramount Pictures.
Spellbound: "Love Theme," United Artists.
Spellbound: "Paranoia Theme," United Artists.
The Sea Hawk: "Fanfare," Warner Brothers.
The Sea Hawk: "Dona Maria Theme," Warner Brothers.
The Sea Hawk: Love Theme," Warner Brothers.
The Sea Hawk: "Sea Hawks Theme," Warner Brothers.
King's Row: "Main Theme," Warner Brothers.
Superman: "Main Theme," Twentieth Century Fox.
Star Wars: "Main Theme," Twentieth Century Fox.
The Bishop's Wife: "Dudley's Theme," Goldwyn Studios.
The Bishop's Wife: "Professor Theme," Goldwyn Studios.
The Bishop's Wife: "Julia Theme," Goldwyn Studios.
The Bishop's Wife: "Religious Theme," Goldwyn Studios.
The Bishop's Wife: "Deeds of an Angel," Goldwyn Studios.
Citizen Kane: "Rosebud Theme," RKO Pictures.
Citizen Kane: Power Theme," RKO Pictures
The Trouble with Harry: "Harry's Body Theme," Paramount Pictures.
The Ten Commandments: "Red Sea March Theme," Paramount Pictures.
The Ten Commandments: "Deliverance Theme," Paramount Pictures.
The Spirit of St. Louis: "Main Theme," Warner Brothers.
The Big Country: "Main Title, Strings Ostinato Passage," United Pictures.
The Big Country: "Blanco Canyon Ostinato," United Pictures.
The Big Country: "Welcoming Theme Variation," United Pictures.
The Seventh Voyage of Sinbad: "Facsimile of Autograph Score," Columbia Pictures.
Journey to the Center of the Earth: "Facsimile of Autograph Score," Twentieth Century Fox Pictures.
The Nun's Story: "Chant Theme," Warner Brothers.
Psycho: "Facsimile of Autograph Score of the Murder cue," Ensign Music Corporation.
Vertigo: "Main Title Theme," Paramount Pictures.
Psycho: "Opening Music," Ensign Music Corporation.
Mysterious Island: "Facsimile of Original Autograph," Columbia Pictures.
Jason and the Argonauts: "Facsimile Autograph," Columbia Pictures, 20th Century Music Corp.
Marnie: "Facsimile Autograph," Universal-International Pictures, Hawaii Music.
Somewhere in Time: "Love Theme," Duchess Music Corp.
Out of Africa: "Main Theme," MCA Music Publishing & Music Corp. of America.
The Mission: "Gabriel's Oboe Theme," EMI Virgin Music Ltd.
Batman: "Main Theme," Twentieth Century Fox Pictures.
Journey to the Center of the Earth: "Mountaintop Sunrise Theme," Twentieth Century Fox Pictures.
Dances with Wolves: "John Dunbar Theme," EMI Virgin Songs, Inc., Affirmed Music, and Tig Music.
Forrest Gump: "Main Theme," Ensign Music Corp.
The River Wild: "Main Theme," MCA Music Publishing.
Titanic: "Love Theme," Famous Music Corp., Ensign Music Corp., and TCF Music Publishing, Inc.
Titanic: "Rose Theme," Famous Music Corp., Ensign Music Corp., and TCF Music Publishing, Inc.
Mask of Zorro: "Theme," TSP Music, Inc.

Index